QMW Library

23 1106480 1

BR 795 BOL

D1333420

079628
6·1·70

THE CAROLINE TRADITION
OF THE CHURCH OF IRELAND

WITHDRAWN
FROM STOCK
QMUL LIBRARY

THE CAROLINE TRADITION OF THE CHURCH OF IRELAND

WITH PARTICULAR REFERENCE TO BISHOP JEREMY TAYLOR

BY

F. R. BOLTON

Published for the Church Historical Society

LONDON
S·P·C·K
1958

First published in 1958 by
S.P.C.K.
Holy Trinity Church, Marylebone Road, London, N.W.1

Printed in Great Britain by
Butler & Tanner Ltd., Frome and London

© F. R. Bolton, 1958

CONTENTS

v

ILLUSTRATIONS

KEY TO MAP

1. Diocese of Mayo, united to Tuam 1572.

2.   ,,   ,,   ,,   Annaghdown, united to Tuam 1553.

3.   ,,   ,,   ,,   Clonmacnoise, united to Meath 1560.

4.   ,,   ,,   ,,   Inniscattery, incorporated with Limerick in 15th century.

5.   ,,   ,,   ,,   Ardmore, incorporated with Lismore in 12th century.

6. Part of the diocese of Tuam.

PRINCIPAL ABBREVIATIONS

B.L.	Bodleian Library, Oxford
B.M.	British Museum
C.L.E.	Coimisiun Láimhscríbhinnt nahÉireann
C.S.P. (Irel.)	*Calendar of State Papers (Ireland)*
C.U.L.	Cambridge University Library
Eccles.	*The Ecclesiologist*
H.M.C.	*Historical Manuscripts Commission*
L.A.C.T.	Library of Anglo-Catholic Theology
Legg, *Eng. Ch. Orders*	J. Wickham Legg, *English Church Orders for Consecrating Churches in the Seventeenth Century*
Legg, *Eng. Ch. Life*	J. Wickham Legg, *English Church Life from the Restoration to the Tractarian Movement*
Mant, I	Richard Mant, *History of the Church of Ireland from the Reformation to the Revolution*
Mant, II	Richard Mant, *History of the Church of Ireland from the Revolution to the Union of the Churches of England and Ireland*
M.L.	Archbishop Marsh's Library, Dublin
N.L.I.	National Library of Ireland
N.S.	New Series
P.R.O.	Public Record Office, England
P.R.O.N.I.	Public Record Office, Northern Ireland
R.C.B.L.	Library of the Representative Church Body, Dublin
[Taylor,] *Works*	*The Whole Works of ... Jeremy Taylor ...*, ed. Heber, revised and corrected C. P. Eden
T.C.D.	Trinity College, Dublin
V.R.	Visitation Returns
Watson's *Almanack*	*The Gentleman's and Citizen's Almanack*, compiled by successive members or connections of the Watson family

PROVINCES AND DIOCESES OF THE CHURCH OF IRELAND, 1152–1833
(Based on Beaufort's Ecclesiastical Map of 1792)

"Nostra Ecclesia in multis dissidet ab Ecclesia Romana, at nullibi sine firmamento aut rationis aut Scripturae Sacrae aut sanctorum Patrum."

ROGER BOYLE, Bishop of Clogher 1672–87: *Summa Theologie Christianae* (1681), Secunda Pars, Sect. XV, 3

PREFACE

THIS BOOK is a study of the Caroline Churchmanship of what the Preamble to her Victorian Constitution terms "this ancient Catholic and Apostolic Church of *Ireland*", or what to-day is said to be "the most Irish thing that there is in Ireland". With a history and development of her own the Church of Ireland was never an offshoot or extension on Irish soil of the Church of England. Her Caroline Churchmen insisted that she was "a free national Church", and not dependent upon or subordinate to "the Convocation of any other Church". Even when the Act of Union of 1800 made her for seventy years part of "the United Church of England and Ireland", she retained her own form of clerical subscription, her machinery of metropolitan visitation, her convocational additions to the Book of Common Prayer, and, now together with the English code, her own Caroline Canons of 1634 with additions of 1711. Sudden disestablishment and disendowment by the English government in 1870 left her free to revise the Prayer Book of 1662 and her own Canons. New regulations, rubrical and canonical, were designed to check innovation and to perpetuate what was then the normal ceremonial usage of both Churches. "Our somewhat Cistercian austerity in ritual matters" to-day often provides a stumbling block to those members of the Church of England who have been taught to attach theological significance to outward ceremonies and Ornaments, some of which have gradually become general in England since 1870. Differences in external matters of secondary or tertiary importance from the present Church of England, however, can remove neither from members of that excellent Church the privilege of attending Anglican worship when they are in Ireland, nor from us the classical Anglican tradition handed down to us from Caroline times. As Ussher maintained in 1634 there is no necessity for Churches which are independent of each other to have the same rites and ceremonies, for "Rome and Milan might have different Canons and modes and yet the same faith, and charity, and communion".

This book is written in the belief that the Church of Ireland has made a rich contribution to the common Anglican heritage. Its purpose is to introduce her Caroline Churchmen in relation to the Church they served, bringing to notice differences from the sister Church in development, organization, and formularies; to set forth the main trend of Caroline

teaching on Churchmanship, particularly where it stands apart from
Tridentine definitions; to reconstruct from contemporary sources the
Caroline way of worship; to give from very scattered evidence as comprehensive a picture as possible of what Irish churches were like and how
furnished in Caroline and subsequent times; and finally to draw attention
to what is at once a literary masterpiece and a fine expression of Caroline
Churchmanship, the Irish rite of 1666 by which new churches were consecrated, the text of which is given in Appendix 1.

It is difficult to appeal to the Caroline divines of either Church without
being told that they can have no relevance to "the contemporary situation" since we are living in the twentieth century, or that they were only
giving their own fallible opinions and what alone matters is "the Catholic
faith". Nowhere does this book advocate an exact reproduction of Caroline teaching, of Caroline vituperation in controversy, of Caroline liturgical usages, or of Caroline sanctuaries however much in harmony with
our present Canons. But it is written with the conviction that much may
be learnt even to-day from the Caroline method of seeking Catholic
truth in the mines of antiquity without the aid of Tridentine definitions;
from the critical attitude of Ussher and others to the Fathers, separating
the spurious from the genuine; from the rejection by Caroline divines of
Roman additions to the Catholic faith; from their interpretation of the
Prayer Book and other Anglican formularies; from their Moral Theology;
from their worship and its setting; from their piety and their charity.
This treasure house of faith, worship, and witness should enable us to
value more fully our Anglican heritage and to face "the contemporary
situation" with greater fortitude. Since it is possible to find Caroline
precedent for almost anything from albs to the amalgamation of parishes,
let it be said at once that Caroline Churchmanship stands altogether apart
from that curious species of Churchmanship sometimes found outside
Ireland which tends to take over "the whole current Roman system
except the Papal Infallibility and the Papal condemnation of Anglican
orders".

The chapter on Caroline teaching is selective and leaves many gaps, no
separate treatment being given, for example, to the doctrine of the Church
or to Moral Theology. These subjects have been admirably dealt with
in recent years by Dr H. F. Woodhouse in *The Doctrine of the Church in
Anglican Theology 1547–1603*, extending many times into the Caroline
period, by Dr H. R. McAdoo in *The Structure of Caroline Moral Theology*,
and by the Reverend T. Wood in *English Casuistical Divinity during the
Seventeenth Century*.

The claim of this book to have "particular reference to Bishop Jeremy Taylor" rests largely upon the case put forward in chapter 5. At the same time new material which was intended for a separate study of Jeremy Taylor in Ireland has been incorporated here in further support of this claim. It consists partly of a more extensive use of the very regular letters of Major George Rawdon of Lisburn to Lord Conway at Ragley or at Kensington ("Conway Papers" in the Public Record Office, London), with repeated references to Taylor from January 1657/8 to August 1667; partly of the letters of Bramhall and other Bishops to Ormonde or his secretary (MS. Carte in the Bodleian Library, Oxford); and partly in contemporary Irish ecclesiastical records. Taken together the new evidence in many ways changes the picture hitherto drawn of the Irish period of Taylor's life. Again, Taylor's altogether forgotten Latin letter of 1662 is reprinted for the first time in Appendix 2.

This book was written in two stages. Chapter 5 was first drafted in 1947 and intended as a separate study. It was very kindly read about that time by two liturgical experts, Canon J. Purser Shortt, of Dublin, and the late Dr J. H. Srawley, of Lincoln; by two historians, Mr J. C. Beckett, of Queen's University, Belfast, and the late Professor G. V. Jourdan, of Trinity College, Dublin. It was also read by Dr A. M. Ramsay, now Archbishop of York, at whose feet I had sat as a theological student, and by a reader for the Church Historical Society. I am extremely grateful for the constructive criticisms and encouragement they gave. Too technical to stand by itself, I decided to place the liturgical work discussed in its Caroline setting. This was no artificial arrangement; for I would never have met with the liturgical work in question if I had not from at least 1936 taken an interest in the works of Irish Caroline divines and in the development, organization, and formularies of the Church to which they and my forefathers belonged. For the earlier chapters I am deeply grateful among others to Dr J. Wyse Jackson, Dean of Cashel, Dr A. R. Vidler, the Reverend R. P. Symonds, the Reverend R. V. Larmour, and especially to the Reverend Alexander Morris, who most kindly translated certain passages I wanted to use from the sometimes very obscure Latin of Bishop Roger Boyle's *Summa Theologie Christianae*. I am most grateful for the kind hospitality of Canon E. W. and Mrs Greening at Swords, Co Dublin, of St Francis House, Cambridge, and of the Community of St John the Divine, Oxford, which enabled me to gather material in the Library of Trinity College, Dublin, in Cambridge University Library, and in the Bodleian Library, Oxford. I am also grateful for the facilities given me for reading in a number of Libraries and for kind permission to quote manuscripts; and to the County Librarian of Nottinghamshire, Mr W. B. Wray, for getting me the loan of many books from various Libraries when I had a parish in that county. Since moving to Ireland in 1955 I have become indebted to several Dublin Rectors who kindly let me examine the Vestry Books and other records in their keeping, to Miss G. FitzGerald, Librarian of the Church Representative Body, Dublin, for her never-failing help, and not least to my wife for the difficult task of correcting the proofs.

F. R. BOLTON

KILSCORAN RECTORY
TAGOAT
CO WEXFORD
28 August 1957

IRISH CAROLINE CHURCHMEN

I. THE FIRST CAROLINE PRIMATE

"Ussher", declared Dr Johnson, "was the great luminary of the Irish Church, and a greater no Church could boast of, at least in modern times." His life covers an important epoch of Irish history. One of the first students to enter his native university, when Trinity College, Dublin, was first opened to students in 1594,[1] James Ussher became Primate of All Ireland in 1625, the year Charles I ascended the throne. He had already from the age of 20 spent time, besides his main patristic studies, "in gathering together the scattered antiquities of our nation", and had recently published a work which enables us to see the Church of Ireland as this Caroline Churchman saw it.

To her first Caroline Primate the Church of Ireland was no new Church. She was the Church of St Patrick, St Columba, St Columbanus; the Church of Claudius, Sedulius, and Johannes Scotus; the Church which in her golden days of independence had taught primitive simplicity and sent missionaries and scholars as well to Northern Britain as to the continent of Europe. She was a Church with a history and development of her own, being from the sixth century to the twelfth independent of Rome and Britain, monastic in organization, and miscellaneous in liturgical practice. All this is shown in Ussher's *The Religion anciently professed by the Irish and British* (1622). Ten years later Ussher published *Veterum Epistolarum Hibernicarum Sylloge*, a valuable collection of documents, showing the steps by which the old monastic organization of the Irish Church gave place to the diocesan, first in the Norse settlements of Dublin, Waterford, and Limerick, and then in 1152 by the division of Ireland into the four provinces of Armagh, Dublin, Cashel, and Tuam, and into more dioceses perhaps than any other nation in northern Europe, and how Ireland was brought under the jurisdiction of Rome and by the Synod of Cashel (1172) into liturgical conformity with the Church of England. Ussher also had a great respect for his fourteenth-century predecessor in the see

---

[1] "Anno 1591. 13 Martii jacta sunt illius fundamenta. 9 Januarii anno 1593. literarum studiosos hospitio excepit". *The Whole Works of the Most Rev. James Ussher*, ed. C. R. Elrington, xv, 11, n.p.

of Armagh, Richard FitzRalph (d. 1360) "commonly called St Richard of Dundalk".

Ussher would certainly dissent from the view of a nineteenth-century historian that the Church of Ireland in the seventeenth was "the most absurd ecclesiastical establishment that the world has ever seen", constituting a grave injustice to the Roman Catholic majority, on the one hand, and to the Presbyterians of the north on the other,[1] and that her "vast hierarchy" of four Archbishops and many Bishops had been set up at the Reformation by the English government.[2] To Ussher the Church of Ireland was neither the creation of the English government nor the extension of the Church of England on Irish soil. She was much nearer the ancient Celtic Church in doctrine and practice than the Church of Rome: her Bishops were in direct Irish succession from the ancient Bishops through the vast hierarchy set up by the native Synod of Kells in the twelfth century. The Roman Catholic titular Bishops, who had begun to reside in Ireland for the first time in the reign of James I, were of foreign succession:[3] they were encouraging and consolidating the recusants, hitherto almost the only native dissenters from the Church of Ireland. The Presbyterians of the north, on the other hand, were not native dissenters from the national Church, but settlers from Scotland, who when Ulster was planted from 1609, brought with them hostile notions of the Anglican Church wherever it was established, of episcopacy in particular, and of any notion of toleration. They set up a formidable opposition to the Church of Ireland in the greater part of the province of Armagh for the rest of the century.

When Ussher was born in 1581 the Church of Ireland was passing through a critical phase. From the Reformation she had moved on parallel, though not identical, lines with the Church of England. The Reformation, moreover, in Ireland had taken a more transitional course, and when he was a boy there was still some hope that the Irish nation would conform to the national Church. There is evidence that the Irish nation was prepared in large measure to accept the Henrician reformation,[4] but made little response to the Edwardian. On Elizabeth's accession most of the Marian Bishops continued in their sees.[5] Many submitted to the Crown, two on their return from the Council of Trent. Some sat on government commissions and had the well-being of the nation at

---

[1] Macaulay, *The History of England* (1883 ed. in 2 Vols.), I, 392 seq.   [2] Ibid., 34.

[3] H. J. Lawlor, *The Reformation and the Irish Episcopate*, 26 seqq.; "Table of Episcopal Succession in Ireland", W. Alison Philips, *History of the Church of Ireland*, II, in pocket at end.   [4] W. Alison Philips, op. cit., II, 226 seq.

[5] Ibid., 307 seqq.; H. J. Lawlor, op. cit., 32 seqq.

heart. Some kept up the old ceremonial with the Elizabethan Prayer Book either in English or Latin. Some played a double game, and together with some of their Protestant brethren sent over from England, enriched their kindred by impoverishing their sees. In order to commend herself to the Irish nation, the Church of Ireland needed energetic clergy, carefully trained in a native university, able where necessary to perform Divine Service, preach, and catechize in the Irish tongue, with proper provision for parochial residence, and decently restored churches for their ministrations. Instead, the Elizabethan Act of Uniformity had directed the Book of Common Prayer to be used "in the Latin tongue" where the clergy "had not the use of the English tongue", and the use of the Irish tongue was officially discouraged. For the most part the clergy were left without provision of parochial residence, and the churches in ruins. The failure to provide a native university earlier in the reign meant that the Church of Ireland lost a great deal of native genius. Sons of Irish chieftains were sent either to foreign universities or educated by capable Roman Catholic teachers in Ireland. While Ussher was still a boy the Jesuit missionaries were with great energy and success setting the Irish nation at variance with the national Church; and the Papacy, once regarded as the promoter of Henry II's invasion and of the English occupation, was now regarded as the protector of the Irish nation and the Church of Ireland as part of the English occupation. Irish people were forsaking the Church of Ireland in their hundreds;[1] and Trinity College "at its untimely foundation regarded as a bulwark of English and Protestant influence".[2]

When the Irish Convocation met on 24 May 1613,[3] possibly for the first time on the English model, the Church of Ireland had not received the English Articles of 1562, but only from 1566 Archbishop Parker's "Eleven Articles" of 1559. A royal licence being granted for the purpose[4] in 1614, this Convocation drew up articles of religion under the care, it is said, of Ussher, now Chancellor of St Patrick's, Professor of Divinity, and Vice-Chancellor of the University. The Irish Articles of 1615 incorporate many existing articles of English origin including the Lambeth

---

[1] Bishop Lyon of Cork complained in 1596 that within two years "where I had a thousand or more in a church at sermon, I now have but five; and whereas I have seen 500 communicants or more, now there are not three", that many clergymen had "forsaken their benefices by the persuasion of those seminaries that come from beyond the seas", that the best name they can give to the Divine Service of the Church is "the Devil's Service, and the professors thereof, devils". (Quoted from W. Alison Philips, op. cit., II, 547.)

[2] J. P. Mahaffy, *A Epoch in Irish History, Trinity College Dublin 1591–1660*, 52 seq.

[3] W. Reeves, "Convocation and Diocesan Synods in England and Ireland", *Report of Church Congress, Dublin, 1868*, 252.　　　　[4] Ibid.

Articles[1] of 1595, which though reflecting the widespread influence of Calvin's teaching had never become authoritative in England. Brought up when Calvinist influences from Cambridge were ascendant at Trinity College, it is not remarkable that Ussher's Lectures of 1603 or his contribution to the Irish Articles should be Calvinist in tone. But Ussher was too great ever to be a narrow party Churchman, and the further he pursued his patristic studies the more he freed himself from the narrow opinions of his early teachers.[2]

The first year of the reign of Charles I saw the first-fruit of Ussher's main study. At the age of 20 he set himself the task of reading through all the Christian Fathers, "observing out of them the doctrine of the ancient Church", and seeking accurate information "touching the authors, what time they lived, and what works are truly, and what falsely attributed to them".[3] He had also taken pains to arrange the Canons of the ancient Church,[4] and to collect, and encourage others in the collection of, ancient liturgical texts. Although greater inroads were made on his time when he became Bishop of Meath in 1621, he found himself drawn into a work "by a challenge made by a Jesuit in this country concerning the Fathers' doctrine in the point of traditions, real presence, auricular confession, priest's power to forgive sins, purgatory, prayer for the dead, limbus patrum, prayer to saints, images, free will, and merits". He handled therein "only the positive doctrine of the fathers, and the original of the contrary error", leaving until further challenge "the vindication of the places of antiquity abused by the adversary".[5] Ussher's *Answer to a Jesuit in Ireland*, published in 1625, represents a landmark in Anglican apologetics. No Anglican before Ussher had set such a weight of patristic evidence against the new articles imposed by the Roman Church, or shown so clearly how they had crept in, or used liturgical texts so extensively as evidence for the doctrine of the ancient Church. Ussher's work paved the way, and often provided the arguments as well as the quotations for later Anglican apologists.[6]

---

[1] The nine Lambeth Articles are incorporated into Irish thus: I and II into 12; II into 14; IV into 15; V into 38; VI into 37; VII, VIII, and IX into 32.

[2] *Works*, I (Life), 289 seqq., where Elrington gives the testimony of Brian Walton, Gunning, Thorndike, and others, and shows that Ussher held universal redemption. For Ussher's emphasis on "final grace", see *Works*, XII, 44. On the testimony of Hammond and Gunning, Ussher said: "Bishop Overall was in the right, and I am of his mind" (ibid., I, 291, 294). Overall had strongly resisted the adoption of the Lambeth Articles at the Hampton Court Conference in 1604.

[3] Ibid., xv, 3.   [4] Ibid., 37.   [5] Ibid., 186.

[6] Jeremy Taylor, for example, in the *Real Presence* and sections of both parts of the *Dissuasive from Popery*.

As Primate of All Ireland Ussher had to face the English government's traditional policy of giving half-hearted support to the Church of Ireland, clearly seen in a scheme of granting Irish Romanists a large measure of toleration in order to secure their contributions to increased army costs. Whereupon Ussher invited all Prelates to his house and there was drawn up "The Judgement of divers Archbishops and Bishops of Ireland, concerning Toleration of Religion", signed by the Primate, the Archbishop of Cashel, and ten Bishops. It declared the faith and doctrine of the Romanists to be "erroneous and heretical; their Church, in respect of both, apostatical. To give them, therefore, a toleration, or to consent that they may freely exercise their religion, and profess their faith and doctrine, is a grievous sin". It besought "the God of truth to make them, who are in authority, jealous of God's glory and the advancement of true religion".[1] To Ussher this was a matter of principle. If the Anglican faith and doctrine were true in England, they were equally true in Ireland and should be as firmly upheld. Ussher was no narrow bigot. He was perfectly prepared to exchange correspondence and information with, and to encourage, Roman Catholic scholars; and he could be roused to indignation by cases of oppression of the Roman Catholic poor by Protestant or other landlords.

When in 1629 William Bedell, who had just become Bishop of Kilmore, wrote to him hinting that Irish ecclesiastical courts were even more corrupt than the English, and that the Primate's was worse than others,[2] Ussher sent a spirited reply. "Complaints", he knew, "will be made against my court, and your court, and every court where vice shall be punished, and that not by the delinquents alone, but also by their landlords, be they protestants or others, who in this country care not how their tenents live, so they pay them their rents."[3] Richard Parr testifies to Ussher's protection of the poor "whom he found oppressed or wronged by those above them", and gives Ussher's "Letter to a person of Quality in Ireland relating to a tenent":

I am ashamed to receive such Petitions against you. Have you ever read, that the unrighteous, and he that doth wrong, shall not inherit the Kingdom of God? Think there is a God who heareth the cry of the poor, and may bring a rot upon your flocks, and curse everything you put your hand to, and if you think not of him because you see him not (although he sees you through and through) yet believe your own eyes, and consider that he hath appointed his deputies upon earth, the higher Powers, which will not suffer the Poor to be oppressed by you or those

---

[1] *The Tanner Letters*, ed. C. McNeill (C.L.E.), 387; cf. *Works*, xv, 366.
[2] *Works*, xv, 468.   [3] Ibid., 474.

that are greater than you: for shame, therefore, give content to this Petitioner, that you hear not of this in a place, where you must blush, and your ears tingle at the hearing of it. J.A.[1]

Bedell also strongly objected to the machinery by which the four Irish Archbishops visited each diocese of their provinces every third year, during the greater part of which the jurisdiction of the diocesan Bishop was suspended. His biographer, Alexander Clogie, thought it "a great honour to the bishops of England, and happiness to their clergy, that they are exempt from these sad visitations".[2] He recalled how Bedell first received from Ussher's metropolitan-apparitor-general the Primate's "Bull of Prohibition",[3] "that for that year he should exercise no episcopal jurisdiction &c.; that when he read these words, *ad quos omnis et omnimoda iurisdictio de iure devolvitur*, &c., and those other words, *propter imminens animarum periculum* &c., that he threw it out of his hand, as if he had said unto it, *Get thee hence*, and stamp't with his foot, &c. For that year he must act nothing as a bishop."[4] After this triennial Visitation of his dioceses of Kilmore and Ardagh, Bedell protested to the Primate that in his late visitation they saw "no profit, but taking of money".[5] Ussher reminds Bedell that in visiting the diocese of Ardagh he found the Clergy facing starvation. "I stood then in the gap", he claims, "and opposed myself for them against the whole country, and stayed that plague."[6] He also found the clergy of Kilmore oppressed by "that knave" whom Bedell was said to have absolved. "I took the pains myself to make up the table of all their tithes and duties; and at this very instant am working in England to have it firmly established unto them by his Majesty's authority. And yet the sums of money they paid me, were not so great, but I could make a shift to spend it in defraying the charges of the very journey."[7] In the same metropolitical Visitation of 1629 Ussher had found all things out of order in the diocese of Raphoe, where Bishop Andrew Knox refused to have a Chancellor, and "in which for the present there is not so much as a face seen of the government of the Church of England".[8] In Caroline and later times metropolitical Visitations were a powerful instrument for good.

"Your table of the tithes of Ulster and the business concerning the impropriations, are both past", William Laud, Bishop of London informs

---

[1] *Life of James Ussher*, 92.
[2] E. S. Shuckbrough, *Two Biographies of William Bedell*, 116.
[3] Ibid., 475.   [4] Ibid., 476.
[5] *Works*, xv, 468.   [6] Ibid., 475.   [7] Ibid., 476.
[8] Ibid., xvi, 510 seq. For John Livingston's account of his irregular ordination at Raphoe, see Mant, 1, 456 seq.

Ussher on 23 February 1629/30.[1] The correspondence with Laud began in 1628, and Ussher was always grateful for the former's efforts to restore the lost partrimony of the Church of Ireland. "You strike such a terror into the hearts of those who would despoil the Church," he wrote to Laud on 11 July 1631, "that if I merely mention your name at the Council Table it is like the Gorgon's head to some of them."[2]

Ussher had just sent Laud a copy of his lately published *Gotteshaulus* with a letter illustrating his scholarly attitude to "the questions now afoot touching predestination, faith, and goodwill". His book, he claimed, showed that they had of old been discussed by the Church and indifferently maintained by its doctors. The moderation of Remegius was much needed in the present disputes. "And although my special drift in setting forth this historical declaration", he adds, "was to bring either side to some better temper; yet I thought it fitter to publish it in the Latin tongue than in the vulgar, because I hold it not convenient that the common people should be troubled with questions of this nature."[3] Later in the year Ussher was called upon to suppress a work by Bishop George Downham of Derry, which had come out six months before his own *Gotteshaulus*, which "handled the controversy of perseverance and the certainty of salvation".[4] Ussher, who had taken an interest in the preparation of Downham's work, keenly felt this high-handed interference from the East, and affirmed that in his own *Gotteshaulus* Laud's own observation was fully verified, "that after Prelates had written against Prelates, and Synods against Synods, these things could have no end, until both sides became weary of contending".[5]

Downham in his early days had been famous for his skill in the new logic, and Cambridge had been known as "the university where Downham taught". He had been a stout advocate of episcopacy in the previous reign, and as Bishop of Derry (1616–33) had encouraged the use of the Irish language in worship and preaching. He belonged to a circle of Irish Bishops who were now dying out or becoming very old and infirm. William Daniel, Archbishop of Tuam (1609–29), Thomas Ram, Bishop of Ferns and Leighlin (1605–34), John Rider, Bishop of Killaloe (1613–33), and Jonas Wheeler, Bishop of Ossory (1613–40), had all encouraged the use of Irish long before Bedell came to Ireland, and like Bedell, had encouraged friendly discussion with Roman Catholic clergy and people. Archbishop Daniel had also revealed the same veneration as Ussher for

---

[1] *Works*, XV, 477.   [2] *C.S.P. (Irel.) 1625–32*, 622.   [3] Ibid., 618.
[4] *Works*, I, 129 seqq. The substance of this work had been given at St Paul's when Bancroft was Bishop of London.   [5] Ibid., 130.

the ancient Irish Church. In the letter to the Lord Deputy before his edition of the Book of Common Prayer, which he had translated into Irish, he wrote: "For as there came many swarms hither from foreign countries to be trained in learning and religion, so this Beehive sent many swarms of learned Philosophers and religious Monks (much differing from the Monks of these days) into foreign kingdoms, as divers Monasteries and Schools of good learning, in Britany, Burgandy, Helvetia, Franconia, and even in Italy must confess, being at the first founded by the religious Monks and Philosophers of Ireland."

In 1622 and 1632, as we have seen, Ussher's own contribution to the history of the ancient Church of Ireland appeared. From 1633 Ussher had to contend, almost single-handed, for the independence of "this ancient Catholic and Apostolic Church of Ireland", for in that year Laud was translated from London to Canterbury and immediately began to carry out a vigorous policy for the Anglican Church throughout the English dominion.

II. "A FREE NATIONAL CHURCH"

Members of the Church of England at different times have found that the Church of Ireland has continued modes of thought or practices which their own Church has laid aside. In the days of St Augustine of Canterbury they were shocked to find the continuance of the Celtic tonsure and date of Easter; when John Bale landed at Waterford early in 1553 he was horrified to find that the English Prayer Book of 1552 had not been received in Ireland and that the 1549 Communion Rite was used "altogether like a popish mass" with "bowings and beckings, kneelings and knockings";[1] in Elizabeth's reign English officials viewed with suspicion the survival of medieval ceremonial; in our own day English visitors are sometimes unduly disturbed by the canonical perpetuation of ceremonial which was normal in both Churches in the 1870s. So it was in 1633, when two energetic and capable Yorkshiremen came over to Ireland for the first time: one Lord Thomas Wentworth, as Lord Deputy; the other, his Chaplain, John Bramhall, as a Commissioner, and soon to follow Downham in the see of Derry.

They found the English Canons and Articles unadopted; and the Irish Articles of 1615, incorporating the Lambeth Articles, were regarded by Caroline Churchmen at home as unorthodox. They also found "the Church very ill used in her patrimony", her revenues often in the hands

[1] R. W. Dixon, *History of the Church of England*, III, 498.

of laymen or alienated by time-serving Elizabethan Bishops; most of the churches, in spite of extensive restoration by Jacobean Bishops, "open, uncovered, and ruined"; non-residence, pluralism, recusant wives and families of the clergy; the Second Service separated from the First after the earlier English manner;[1] puritan innovations dating from the time of Archbishop Adam Loftus. In Dublin, Bramhall informs Laud, "we find our parochial Church converted to the Lord Deputy's stable, a second to a nobleman's house, the quire of a third to a tennis court, and the Vicar acts as keeper"; the vaults under Christ Church Cathedral "are made into tippling rooms, for beer, wine, and tobacco, demised all to Popish recusants, and by them and others so much frequented in time of Divine Service, that though there is no danger of blowing up the assembly above their heads, yet there is of poisoning them with fumes."[2]

Bramhall further gives Laud rather an unfair picture of "the glorious tomb in the other Cathedral Church of St Patrick in the proper place of the Altar, just opposite his Majesty's seat, having his father's name superscribed upon it as if it were contrived on purpose to gain the worship which the Chapter and whole Church are bound by special statute to give to the East."[3] The Earl of Cork had certainly erected a large monument, filling and towering high above the eastern arch of the choir, to himself, his wife, her father, Sir Geoffrey Fenton, and grandfather, Chancellor Weston, who had been Dean of the Cathedral. He had also, the Archbishop of Dublin explained to Laud, raised the east end of the choir three steps higher than it was, paving it with "fair hewn stones", being formerly "a floor of earth, many times upon afresh drowned with water, where now the Communion Table is placed with more decency than in former times".[4] The Earl had also given order for a "fair screen", on which the Decalogue was to be "fairly painted", to be erected immediately behind the altar and westward of the monument, taking in some other tombs on either side. The Archbishop saw precedent in the choir of Westminster Abbey, "where there is a screen enclosing some monuments, and a way on each hand to the Chapel adjoining".[5] With Ussher the Archbishop shared the mistaken view that the tomb did not occupy the ancient site of the High Altar, but an arch, hitherto closed up, but formerly serving for a passage into the Lady Chapel beyond, "at the east end whereof the High Altar stood".[6] Ussher told Laud that he had consented to the screen, and thought its erection should remove all

---

[1] *Tanner Papers* (ed. C. McNeill), 8.   [2] *Works* (L.A.C.T.), I, lxxix.
[3] Ibid., lxxx.   [4] Quoted from W. Prynne, *Canterburie's Doome*, 86.
[5] Ibid.   [6] Ibid.

objection to the monument, "which otherwise cannot be denied to be a very great ornament to the Church".[1] Unfortunately, the screen had not been erected when the two Yorkshiremen arrived in Dublin; but in all fairness Bramhall should have mentioned the raised floor where the altar stood instead of giving the impression that there was no altar at all. Dean Leslie of Down further offended the Earl, who was Treasurer of the Realm, by selecting for his text of a funeral sermon in the Cathedral at which the Earl was present: "Go get thee unto this Treasurer and say, what hast thou here, and whom hast thou here, that thou hast hewed thee out a sepulchre, as he that hath hewed him out a sepulchre on high, and that graveth an habitation for himself in a rock."[2] The Dean, when reproved, persisted that no personalities were intended, and "the King laughed heartily at the comment which Dr Lesley made upon that tomb in Esay".[3] Early in 1634 Laud tells Wentworth that the explanations given by the two Archbishops do not fully satisfy him, and leaves the tomb to be viewed by the Lord Deputy and the Archbishops, and the Earl to the Grace of God.[4] Accordingly Wentworth met the two Arch-bishops, the Earl, with four Bishops and the Deans and Chapters of both Cathedrals in the choir of St Patrick's, "and made them so ashamed that the Earl desires leave to pull it down, without reporting further to England". "And there is the end of the Tomb before it come to be intombed indeed."[5]

Laud wanted Wentworth and Bramhall to bring the Church of Ireland into close conformity with the Church of England without, however, offending the Irish Primate. Ussher, for his part, wanted the Church of Ireland to regain her lost patrimony, but not at the price of losing her independence. He had great admiration for "the extraordinary zeal of our noble Lord Deputy". "I may justly term him", he writes to Laud, "a new Zerubbabel raised by God, for making up of the ruins of this decayed Church; who upon an occasion, openly declared himself an opposite to the greatest of those that have devoured our holy things, and made the patrimony of the Church the inheritance of their sons and daughters."[6] Although Ussher and Wentworth did not always agree,

---

[1] *Works*, XV, 572 seq. [2] Isa. 22. 15.
[3] Laud, *Works* (L.A.C.T.), VII, 70. [4] Ibid., I, 22 seq.
[5] Ibid., 343. Wentworth later reported that the tomb was "quite removed" and up "in Boxes, as if it were March panes and Banqueting stuffs, going down to the Christening of my young Master in the Country". Ibid., 397. In 1635 Sir William Brereton was told of its proposed re-erection "in the side of the same Choir". It was further moved in 1865 to the west of the nave.
[6] *Works*, XV, 574.

and these differences were magnified when both were dead, Bramhall could testify "what mutual and cordial respects passed daily between those two great persons, from the first day of their acquaintance to the last". On the one side, "witness all those constant and continual offices, which my Lord Primate did perform with cheerfulness to the State of Ireland during the Earl of Strafford's government, and to the Earl himself in order to the King's service, in the pulpit, in the Parliament, in the Convocation, at the Council-Table, in the Star-Chamber, in the High commission". And on the other side, among many services which Wentworth performed to the Primate, Bramhall mentions

the procuring of the King's warrant for him and his successors, Archbishops of Armagh, to take place of the Lord Chancellor of Ireland for the time being, in conformity to the custom of England;[1] and lastly, which weigheth more with me than all the rest, the choosing him to be his ghostly father and spiritual adviser at his death, and his receiving Absolution and the Holy Sacrament of the Body and Blood of Christ from his hands, when he had chaplains of his own in the city, doth convince me, and all ingenious persons that there was no dissatisfaction of either party against the other.[2]

When the first Caroline Convocation met in 1634, it was the intention of Wentworth, with the approbation of Laud and King Charles, to have the English Articles received *ipsissimus verbis*, and to leave the Irish Articles, to which the Irish Primate was affected, "as no way concerned, neither affirmed nor denied".[3] Unfortunately, the records, still extant a century later, have disappeared.[4] Moreover, the Convocation being bound to secrecy, Bramhall was unable to give Laud a detailed account of the proceedings.[5] Meanwhile Wentworth, irritated by Ussher's silence, pounced on the proceedings of a subcommittee of the Lower House, which had examined and prepared a report on the English Canons of 1603, proposing also an article for confirming the Irish Articles under pain of excommunication. He severely rebuked the chairman, Dean Andrewes of Limerick, and summoning the members of the committee in the presence of the Primate, four Bishops, and the Prolocutor of the Lower House, told them "how unlike clergymen, that owed canonical obedience to their superiors, they had proceeded in their committee", and "what

---

[1] He also for ever settled the question of the Primacy of All Ireland in favour of the Archbishop of Armagh and his successors.

[2] *Works*, 83 seq.   [3] Mant, I, 485.

[4] Bishop Nicholson noticed them among Lord Clarendon's Irish MSS. in the old Chandos Library (*Irish Historical Library*, 28). They were lost after the sale of that library.

[5] *H.M.C.*, Hastings, IV, 62.

a spirit of Brownism and contradiction he observed in their *deliber-andums*".[1] Wentworth then took a high-handed course with the President of the Synod. He rejected the Canon Ussher had prepared for adopting the English Articles, replaced it with one of his own making, and directed the Primate to "vote this canon first in the upper house of convocation; and so voted, then to pass the question beneath." [2] But Ussher was the President of a national Synod, and while avoiding the discussion of theological issues, appears to have allowed "a very full and free discussion" not regarding "the truth or untruth" of the English and Irish Articles but "the authority".[3] Wentworth's Canon was introduced not by Ussher, but by Bramhall.

As Bishop of Derry, Bramhall had a delicate task to perform. He was Ussher's suffragan, and not Laud's. "I am tied by promise", he informs Laud on 21 August 1634, "not to acquaint you with the passages in the Convocation House. The Irish articles had like to be confirmed the very last day of the session, so far as in the House, within two hours after they were proposed and received, together with the English, without consulting his Majesty or his Deputy; nay, I dare say before most that were present had read them, notwithstanding the canon of the Council of Cashell[4] that the Irish Church should be in all points conformed to the English." [5] "But we are so contented" to let the Irish Articles "slumber", and "to set up the English without any noise or show of retracting the former".[6] Bramhall encloses "the rough draft of sundry acts and the heads of some canons necessary for the Church, which have been seen and allowed by the Primate and sundry bishops", the necessity and use of them being "most evident to those that know the state of this Church".[7] From this letter it appears that the English Articles were confirmed, and the Irish Articles nearly confirmed together with them, but in the end passed by,[8] and that the English Canons were not adopted and Irish Canons were being prepared. Writing seventeen years later, Bramhall makes it clear that the opposition to the passing by of the Irish Articles came from Primate Ussher and Bishop Martin

---

[1] Mant, 1, 486 seq. "Dean Andrewes his Deliberations about the Canons of England and Ireland examined", with Wentworth's caustic comments are extant. T.C.D. MS. N. 2. 3.

[2] Mant, 1, 488.   [3] Bramhall, *Works*, v, 81 seq.

[4] Bramhall claims far too much for the Synod of Cashel (1172), which required liturgical conformity, which was already met by the use of the English Book of Common Prayer.

[5] *H.M.C., Hastings*, iv, 61.   [6] Ibid.   [7] Ibid.

[8] Ussher claimed that the Convocation let the Irish Articles "stand as they did before" (op. cit., xvi, 9), and Wentworth that the Convocation had "silenced" them.

of Meath, who were the only Irishmen in the Upper House. They were reluctant "rather out of a tender resentment of the honour of their Church, lest another Church should seem to give laws to them, than out of an opinion of the necessity of their Articles".[1] When the majority of the Upper House voted for the English Articles, Ussher sent for the Prolocutor and members of the Lower House, declared to them the votes of the Bishops, and moved them "to assent thereunto, which they did accordingly, all which the Acts and Records of that Convocation do sufficiently testify".[2]

For fuller information of the debates we depend upon the account given in 1676 by Bramhall's biographer, Bishop Vesey, who had been Archdeacon to Bramhall, the only surviving member of the Upper House of 1634, who may have given him an account of what took place. He also got information from his metropolitan, Archbishop Price of Cashel, who, though only a member of the Lower House in 1634, would get accurate information from Bishop Bedell with whom he was intimately associated. In addition to other oral tradition Vesey would have access to the now missing records of the Convocation of 1634, which may have been fuller than the very meagre records of the Restoration Convocation. The speeches of Bramhall for the English Articles and of Ussher against the English Canons bear every mark of being genuine, and they reveal much of the character of these two leading Caroline Churchmen.

The Bishop of Derry, Vesey relates,

discoursed with great moderation and sobriety of the convenience of having the Articles of peace and communion in every national Church worded in that latitude, that dissenting persons in those things, that concerned not the Christian faith, might subscribe, and the Church not lose the benefit of their labours for an opinion, which, it may be they could not help; that it were to be wished that such Articles might be contrived for the whole Christian world, but especially the Protestant Churches under his majesty's dominion might "all speak the same language": and particularly that those of England and Ireland, being reformed by the same principle and rule of scripture, expounded by universal tradition, councils, fathers, and other ways of conveyance, might confess their faith in the same form. For, if they were of the same opinion, why did they not express themselves in the same words?[3]

But because their sense was the same, he was answered, it was not material

---

[1] *Works*, v, 80 seq. In his *Answer to a Jesuit* (1625) Ussher undertook to defend the doctrine professed in the English Articles of 1562, which he claimed to be consistent with the teaching of "the Saints and fathers of the primitive Church". (*Works*, III, xii.) [2] Ibid., 82.

[3] "Life of Primate Bramhall" in 1676 ed. of his *Whole Works*, no pagination.

if the words differed, and therefore it was fitter to confirm the Irish Articles of 1615. To this Bramhall replied, "that though the sense might be the same, yet our adversaries clamoured much that they were dissonant confessions". To confirm the Irish Articles as well as the English would seem to question the value of the Synod of 1615, and consequently of the present: "for this had no more power than that, and therefore could add no moments to it, but by so doing might help to enervate both." [1] Bramhall then introduced the Canon, drawn up by the Lord Deputy, "and proposing it, it passed accordingly". It confirmed under pain of excommunication the English Articles of 1562, "for the manifestation of our agreement with the Church of England in the confession of the same Christian faith, and doctrine of the Sacraments" and "for avoiding diversity of opinions, and for the establishing of consent touching true religion".[2]

The Bishop of Derry, Vesey continues, "thought he had but yet done half his work, and therefore again moved, that as they had received the Articles, so they would the Canons of the Church of *England*, that there might be the same Rule of government as well as of belief". To this proposition "the Primate opposed himself with great earnestness".

For though we give the right hand of fellowship and all due honour, yet we must not make resignation of our right to that excellent Church: and if this which was proposed, were allowed, we might fear in time to have a Canon obtained in the Church, like *Poynings Act* (as it is called) in the State, giving the Church of England such a superintendence over us, that nothing shall be law here that were not first allowed there, and afterward, that we must refuse nothing here, that there had obtained a confirmation; that it was convenient some discrepancy should appear, if it were but to declare our ἀντεξία, and to express our sense of rites and ceremonies, that there is no necessity of the same in all Churches that are independent, as these are, one of another; that Rome and Milan might have different Canons and modes and yet the same faith, and charity, and communion.[3]

"The Bishop of Derry, not easily moved from what he had undertaken, said, they would no more resign their privilege and authority in receiving their Canons, than their faith in the Articles." But it soon became clear that both Houses were against the adoption of the English Canons, and finally it was resolved

that such Canons as were fit to be transplanted and agreeable to the soil, shall be removed hither, and others passed *de novo* and added to them; that so we might have a complete Rule peculiarly calculated for the Meridian of this Church. This

---

[1] "Life of Primate Bramhall" in 1676 ed. of his *Whole Works*, no pagination.
[2] Ibid.   [3] Ibid.

being voted, the business was chiefly committed to the Bishop of Derry, to be drawn up in form, his hand being generally employed in drawing up everything, wherein any knot or difficulty gave opposition.[1]

"I am clear of your Lordship's opinion," the Lord Deputy wrote to Laud,

it were fit the Canons of England were received here as well as the Articles: but the Primate is hugely against it; the business is merely point of honour...lest Ireland might become subject to the Church of England, as the province of York is to Canterbury. Needs forsooth we must be a Church of ourselves, which is utterly lost unless the Canons here differ, albeit not in substance, yet in some form, from yours in England; and this crotchet put the good man into such an agony, as you cannot believe so learned a man should be troubled withal.[2]

"God bless your free Church of Ireland," wrote Laud to Bramhall in May 1635,

though for my part I do not think the Canons of the Church of England would have shot any freedom of it. And, moreover, it is better having them materially and in substance with peace than formally with heart burning among yourselves. And little hurt can come by this alteration, and with it there will be some good. For though the canon of subscription lie a little too much under covert yet there it is; and some other canons have in some things mended the English, as well as in some other fallen short. But particularly I thank my Lord Primate and you for that about confession, for it may do a great deal of good, and an act of state may remedy the business of pluralities and commendams well enough.[3]

Laud should also have been particularly grateful for the Canon fixing the altar "at the East end of the Church or Chancel",[4] thus committing the four Irish provinces to the Laudian position at a time when Bishop Williams of Lincoln, later Archbishop of York, was appealing to the English Canon 82 in support of the movable Communion table. There are other ways in which the Irish Caroline Canons are more Laudian than the English Jacobean Canons. Archbishop Parker's *Advertisements*, which had frightened Dean Andrewes' committee with their ordering of copes in cathedrals, were not incorporated; and Bramhall no doubt smiled as he canonically committed the Church of Ireland to the *Ornaments* "prescribed in the Book of Common Prayer and in the Act of Uniformity printed therewith".[5] In line with Caroline ideals Marriages could be solemnized "neither in the time of Lent, nor of any public fast, nor of the solemn Festivities of the Nativity, Resurrection, and Ascension of our

---

[1] Ibid. [2] *Strafford's Letters*, I, 381.
[3] H.M.C., *Hastings*, IV, 67 seq. [4] Irish Canon 94. [5] Canons 7 and 13.

Lord, or of the Descension of the Holy Ghost".[1] The consecration of new churches was ordered at a time when the practice, not prescribed in the English code, was meeting with great opposition in England.[2] The Canons directing parts of Divine Service to be performed in Irish in Irish-speaking districts[3] were certainly "calculated for the Meridian of this Church". But Laud was particularly grateful to Ussher and Bramhall for Canon 19.

Canon 19 not only directed ministers to give due warning of "the administration of the holy Sacrament", but added:

And the Minister of every Parish, and in Cathedral and Collegiate Churches, some principal Minister of the Church shall the afternoon before the said administration, give warning by the tolling of the Bell, or otherwise, to the intent, that if any have any scruple of conscience, or desire the special Ministry of Reconciliation, he may afford it to those that need it. And to this end the people are often to be exhorted to enter into a special examination of the state of their own souls: and finding themselves either extreme dull, or much troubled in mind, they do resort unto God's Ministers, to receive from them as well advice and counsel for the quickening of their dead hearts, and the subduing of those corruptions whereunto they have been subject, as the benefit of absolution likewise, for the quieting of their conscience, by the power of the Keys which Christ hath committed to his Ministers for that purpose.

Four years later Laud, in considerable alarm, forwarded to Strafford a letter from James Croxton claiming he had in some measure done, in his parish of Gowran, County Kilkenny, that "which able men have sufficiently spoken of elsewhere". He had "sacramentally heard the confessions" of his parishioners "in the Chancel" before Easter, "they kneeling before the Altar".[4] Laud had not the Irish Canons by him at Croydon, but he doubted "Croxton hath born himself too boldly upon it". He did not send the letter to Primate Ussher who "hath a stitch against Croxton already", and he loved not to make things worse, "as very little trifles in Church pretensions make much noise, and are hardly laid down", as in the case of the Scottish Prayer Book of 1637, "which is grown very ill".[5] Strafford replied that he had heard neither objections to Croxton nor to the hearing of confessions; for although compulsory "auricular confession" was not allowed, yet did he "never hear any but commend the free and voluntary use of it".[6] "For though the *Irish* Canon in that particular", Laud answered, "be much better than ours, and that

---

[1] Canons 49.   [2] Ibid., 43.   [3] Ibid., 8, 86, 94.
[4] John Rushworth, *Historical Collections*, II, 184 seq.
[5] Ibid., 195.   [6] Ibid., 195.

which he hath done, for ought I know, according to it; yet I doubt, if it should come in question, he will be remembered for the difference which happened in Convocation." [1] Croxton had in 1634 introduced a theological controversy into the Lower House, which Ussher had taken care to avoid in the Upper, regarding the English and Irish Articles. [2]

Although the Irish Canons, when published, provoked controversy and were thought by some to be Popish and Arminian, they were regarded in the next decade as symbolizing a moral victory for the free national Church. In 1647 a group of Caroline Churchmen, some of them Englishmen, drew up a declaration to the Parliamentary Commissioners showing why they could not give up the use of the Prayer Book. "The reformed Church of Ireland", they explained, "is, and ever was, reputed a free national Church, and not subordinate unto, or depending upon, the Convocation of any other Church: and hence it was, that till the Convocation" of 1634,

the Articles of the Church of England were not held, or reputed the Articles of the Church of Ireland, and when they were received, they were not received with any acknowledged subordination to the Church of England, but for the manifestation of our agreement with the Church of England in the same Christian faith, and the doctrine of the Sacraments, as is expressed in the first Canon. Hence it is, besides our Canons were not imposed by the Church of England, nay, when somewhat highly the Clergy were invited to submit to the book of English Canons, the Convocation utterly refused the same, and framed a new book of Canons for the Church of Ireland. [3]

Meanwhile Ussher had returned to his studies. "I have been almost tired", he wrote to Dr Ward on 15 September 1635, "with continual attendance on our continued parliament and convocation; which being done, they would needs impose upon me also the moderating of the divinity act; and the creating of the doctors at our last commencement. I am now at last retired from Dublin to my old place, where I begin at length, *redire in gratiam cum veteribus amicis*." [4] Two months before Sir William Brereton had visited Ussher in Dublin and observed:

He doth most industriously apply his study, which he hath placed at a good

[1] Ibid., 212.
[2] Strafford had already told Laud that Croxton had scandalized the Primate by preaching up Arminianism, and himself found his discourses "so cabalistical, so deep in the controversies as I could never yet conjecture what it was he would persuade me, or what it was he would be at himself." Quoted from Lady Burghclere, *Strafford*, I, 309.
[3] *A Declaration of the Protestant Clergie of the City of Dublin* . . . *Printed in the Yeere 1647.*   [4] *Works*, XVI, 9.

C

distance from his house, to prevent distraction and diversion by access of any company to visit him, who are not admitted to disturb his studies. This course and order is so public, so that few come to him at any time of the day, save at the hours of relaxation, which is from eleven to one, and so about supper time; the rest of the day, from five in the morning until six in the evening, is spent ordinarily in his study.[1]

Ussher had already planned his greatest contribution to Anglican apology. The Anglican case for episcopacy, for example, had been weakened by the use made by her leading apologists of the twelve Ignatian letters of the long recension. Ussher's wide reading over a long period had led him to notice "that the quotations from S. Ignatius in three English writers, Robert [Grosseteste] of Lincoln (c. 1250), John Tyssington (c. 1381), and William Wodeford (c. 1396), while they differed considerably from the text of this father as hitherto known (the Greek and Latin of the Long recension), agreed exactly with the quotations in Eusebius and Theodoret. He therefore concluded that the libraries of England must somewhere contain MSS. of a version corresponding to the earlier text of Ignatius, and searched accordingly." [2] In 1629 he was waiting for "a transcript of the Latin Ignatius" in the Library of Caius College, Cambridge, and had already written "a large censure upon the Epistles of Ignatius".[3] In 1637 he intended to bring out an edition of Ignatius, as it was so important for a writer of his standing "to be freed (as much as may be) from those interpolations of later times".[4] Ussher's work did not appear until 1644, no doubt because he went on trying in vain to get a transcript of a manuscript of the original Greek of the middle recension in the Medicean Library at Florence. "To the critical genius of Ussher", declared Bishop Lightfoot, "belongs the honour of restoring the true Ignatius." [5] Altogether his book "showed not only marvellous erudition, but also the highest critical genius".[6] "By Ussher's labours the question between the Long and the Middle Recension was—or ought to have been—set at rest for ever." [7] Ussher's critical genius is also revealed in *De Romanae ecclesiae Symbolo apostolico vetere aliisque fidei forulis...diatribia*[8] (1647). At this time Ussher was also working on the history of Celtic Christianity, and his *Britannicarum*

---

[1] *Travels* (Chetham Society), 143.
[2] Bishop J. B. Lightfoot, *The Apostolic Fathers*, Part II, I, 76.
[3] *Works*, xv, 482.   [4] Ibid., xvi, 34.
[5] Op. cit., 231.   [6] Ibid., 232.   [7] Ibid., 233.
[8] See J. N. D. Kelly, *Early Christian Creeds*, 102 seqq., where "Ussher's brilliant surmise" is praised. Ibid. 104. Ussher also disentangled the history of the Athanasian Creed, *Works*, vii, 328 seqq., and ascribed the *Te Deum* to Nicetus, ibid., 300.

Ecclesiarium Antiquitates (1639), of immediate use to Caroline apologists, has proved to be of abiding value to historians.

Meanwhile Strafford and Bramhall, with remarkable energy, were instrumental in recovering much of the lost patrimony of the Church, which by June 1636, Strafford claimed, was already "bettered by 30,000 p.a." [1] Ussher, of too gentle a nature to be an effective reformer of abuses, was content to leave this work to others, while he served the Church by his scholarship. He knew that Trinity College needed greater discipline, and to this end had recommended Laud for the office of Chancellor, hinting to him that the Statutes, composed by Bishop Bedell when Provost, "conformable to those of Emmanuel College in Cambridge", were inadequate and gave "so little power to the Provost for redressing the things that are amiss, without the consent of the greater part of the senior fellows." [2] When, however, the Laudian Statutes of 1637 were framed, Ussher was dragged from his studies into fresh disputes. [3]

Bishop Bedell made history in 1638 by holding a diocesan Synod at Kilmore, at which twenty-two Canons were agreed upon, the Canons of ancient Councils being quoted in each case as precedent. There was much noise, and it was thought that this exemplary Bishop, by enacting Canons, had exposed himself to a *Praemunire*. Ussher advised that he should be let alone, "lest he should be thereby provoked to say more for himself, than any of his accusers could say against him". [4] Ussher would know that the Irish clergy had never made the same submission as the English clergy to Henry VIII, and that the English Act (25 Hen. VIII, c. 19) never extended to Ireland.

Of Ussher's later Irish contemporaries, George Webb, Bishop of Limerick (1634–42) was the author of *The Practice of Quietness*; Richard Sherlock, who had migrated from Oxford to Trinity College, and exercised his ministry in Ireland until 1641, later published *The Practical Christian* and other devotional works; John Maxwell, a pronounced High Churchman and an enthusiastic promoter of the ill-fated Scottish Prayer Book of 1637, was translated in 1640 from Ross in Scotland to Killala, [5] where he replaced Bishop Adair, who had apparently been deprived for expressing dangerous Scottish nationalist sentiments; [6] Henry Leslie, Bishop

[1] *Tanner Papers*, 8; W. Alison Philips, op. cit., III, 426 seq.
[2] *Works*, xv, 274.
[3] Ibid., 191 seqq.   [4] Ibid., 204.   [5] Translated to Tuam in 1645.
[6] For an account of this extraordinary case see Mant, I, 542 seq. In 1641, however, Adair was appointed to Waterford in place of Bishop Atherton, who had been hanged for alleged immorality.

of Down and Connor (1635–60), another High Churchman of Scottish origin, whose *Treatise of the Authority of the Church* (1637) reveals him to be a forceful and fluent writer of wit; Griffiths Williams, Bishop of Ossory (1641–72), like Lancelot Bulkeley, Archbishop of Dublin (1619–50), rather a turbulent Welshman,[1] had already published *The Best Religion wherein is largely Explained the Summe and principall Heads of the Gospel* (1636).

Like all Caroline Bishops of Down and Connor, Bishop Leslie found it a painful duty to enforce the discipline of the Church. In 1634 Bramhall had complained to Laud of the irregularities of even the conformist clergy of Down and Connor. "It would trouble a man to find twelve common prayer-books in all their Churches, and these only not cast behind the altar, because they have none, but instead of it a table ten yards long, where they sit and receive the sacrament like good fellows." [2] In August 1636 Bishop Leslie held a conference with the leading Scots ministers, by whom a manuscript report was circulated, which the Bishop regarded as a "libel" and "as falsely traducing all his proceedings".[3] Thus it was reported that Bishop Bramhall entered the church where a disputation between the diocesan Bishop and Mr Hamilton was proceeding, and having rebuked the Bishop for allowing such a conference, punctuated the continued discussion with such interjections as these: "It were more reason and more fit this fellow were whipped than reasoned with"; "That fellow talks clear nonsense"; "Get him helebere to purge his brain from madness"; "Give him Scripture for a peck of oats to his horse!"; and finally: "I will leave you, my Lord of Down; and I will assure you, ye cannot answer it that you have given them such liberty to-day." When the Bishop said he would attend the Bishop of Derry and gave order for the Court to be adjourned,

> *Bishop of Derry.* Sentence them first.
> *Bishop.* I must do it, and am sorry for it.[4]

"For the conference between my Lord of Down and his Nonconformists", Laud answered Bramhall on 5 April 1637, "I cannot discommend his good intention nor commend his discretion to suffer that which was settled by public authority in the Church to be disputed by refractory spirits. But I do not wonder that those men should make a false and

---

[1] Bulkeley had led a raid on a Roman Catholic Chapel in 1629 just before the celebration of mass, and himself had demolished the pulpit. *H.M.C., Franciscan*, 17. Williams gave uncommon trouble to the Convocation at the Restoration.
[2] *C.S.P. (Irel.) 1633–47*, 87 seq.   [3] Mant, I, 521.
[4] Reid, *History of the Presbyterian Church in Ireland*, I, 523 seqq.

unworthy repetition of the day's work. For never yet did I know any conference held with them, private or public, that was not afterwards set down by them according to truth." [1] Laud thought it fit that the Deputy or his Archbishop should persuade the Bishop not to hold further conferences. [2]

Although in this transaction and in other ways Bramhall appears to have acted as suffragan to Laud, and not to Ussher, he afterwards declared that under Ussher's "pious and moderate government" he lived sundry years a Bishop in the province of Armagh, "whilst the political care of that part of the Church did lie heavy upon my shoulders". "I praise God, we were like the candles in the Levitical Temple, looking towards one another, and all towards the stem. We had no contentions among us, but who should hate contention most, and pursue the peace of the Church with swiftest paces." [3]

But the peace of the Church, already threatened by Presbyterian agitation, was soon to be overwhelmed by the politico-religious devices of the Romanists, encouraged from the Continent and not least by the example of the English Parliament,[4] which suddenly broke out in the Rebellion of 1641. Many members of the Church of Ireland were massacred, benefices occupied by Roman Catholics, and churches reconsecrated to foreign rites.[5] Eight years later the Church of Ireland was to be driven further underground by the Cromwellian occupation of Ireland from 1649.

In the meanwhile, the Duke of Ormonde, who had succeeded Strafford as Lord-Lieutenant, consistently fought for the interests of the Church in all his negotiations with the King, on the one hand, and the Confederates on the other. When in 1647 he decided as the lesser of two evils to surrender Dublin to the English Parliamentarians, the Archbishops of Dublin and Tuam, nine Bishops, and sixty-six clergymen presented an address, thanking Ormonde for the wisdom and care with which he had preserved, not only in Dublin but "also in all the out garrisons, the free and full exercise of the true reformed religion according to the Liturgy and Canons". They also prayed Ormonde to continue his care to preserve the Prayer Book and "the true apostolical government of the

---

[1] H.M.C., Hastings, IV, 71.　　　　[2] Ibid., 71 seq.

[3] Works, V, 74.

[4] Swift claimed that the Rebellion of 1641 "was wholly owing to the wicked English Parliament", whose "rebellious spirit" gave encouragement, and which "held the King's hands, while the Irish Papists here cut our grandfathers' throats" (Sermon on Martyrdom of King Charles I).

[5] W. Alison Philips, op. cit., III, 59 seqq.; Mant, I, 554 seqq.

Church now exercised among us".[1] No Irish Act of Parliament had proscribed episcopacy or the Prayer Book, both of which had been set aside in England and Scotland. While the citizens of London were clamouring for the abolition of episcopacy, the citizens of Dublin for the most part had been frequenting "the daily accustomed service of God in the two Cathedrals and Parish Churches of this city". In England no Bishop was consecrated between 1644 and the Restoration: in Ireland a Bishop of Clogher was consecrated in 1645 and a Bishop of Killaloe in 1647, two days before the Parliamentary forces entered Dublin. When called upon to discontinue the Prayer Book and use the Directory, the leading Dublin clergy, together with the newly-consecrated Bishop of Killaloe, presented the dignified Declaration to the Parliamentary Commissioners, part of which we have already noticed,[2] giving their reasons for not complying with the request. The Book of Common Prayer had been received by the free national Church. "Shall we, therefore, receive or admit any other form, without the authority of the Church, we shall be held and esteemed before God and the world, guilty of conscionably betraying the liberty of the free national Church of Ireland." [3]

III. CAROLINE CHURCHMEN DURING THE COMMONWEALTH

(a) Irish Divines Abroad

Ussher was already in England when the Rebellion of 1641 broke out, and was never able to return to his native land. Earlier in that year, while Bramhall was imprisoned in Dublin Castle[4] on a charge of High Treason, Ussher visited Strafford in the Tower of London, received his confession, administered to him the Holy Sacrament, and carried last messages between him and Laud, another prisoner in the Tower. Ussher told Laud "that he never knew any layman in all his life, that so well and fully understood matters of divinity as the Earl did".[5] Ussher also told Laud of an offer made to Strafford through his brother-in-law, Denzill Hollis. "It was this, that if he would employ his power and credit with the King for the taking of Episcopacy out of the Church, he should yet have his life. His Christian answer was very heroical; namely, that

[1] Wilkin's *Concilia*, IV, 554 seq.
[2] See p. 17.   [3] *Declaration* of 1647.
[4] Together with Sir Richard Bolton, Lord Chancellor, Lord Chief Justice Lowther, and Sir George Radcliffe.
[5] Laud, *Works* (L.A.C.T.), III, 441.

'he would not buy his life at so dear a rate'." [1] The Earl's end was so patient, pious, and courageous, "that some doubted whether his death had more of the Roman or the Christian in it: it was so full of both." "Thus ended", added Laud in his diary, "the wisest, the stoutest, and every way the ablest subject that this nation hath bred these many years. The only imperfections which he had, that were known to me, were his want of bodily health and a carelessness, or rather roughness, not to oblige any; and his mishaps in this last action were, that he groaned under the public envy of the nobles, and served a mild and gracious prince, who knew not how to be or be made great." [2] Irish Caroline Churchmen at the Restoration held Strafford's memory in great veneration; for he was an outstanding benefactor of the Church of Ireland. The weight of evidence is wholly against the contemporary calumny that Ussher advised the King to allow Strafford's execution. [3] As Bramhall observed, in defending Ussher from the censures of Dr Heylin, "God had given him more of the innocence of the dove, than of the prudence of the serpent." [4]

At the earnest request of Bishop Hall Ussher undertook a tract on episcopacy, *Of the Original of Metropolitans and Bishops* (1641), confining his quotations from Ignatius to those Epistles his book of 1644 was to demonstrate to be genuine. At the same time he put forward a scheme of Synodical Church government to meet a desperate situation, and which should only be examined in the light of his case for episcopal government. In 1642 he was allowed to hold the see of Carlisle *in commendam* with the now impoverished see of Armagh. For the next fourteen years he went on with his studies until blindness nearly overtook him. We may well regret that he exhausted his energy on Biblical chronology and did not apply his critical genius to Biblical sources; but Biblical criticism as we now know it did not occur to Caroline Divines. Ussher was a constant preacher either in Oxford or London, as he had been at Drogheda and Dublin. And just as he was ever ready to protect the Irish clergy from oppression, so he used all his influence with Cromwell to allow the sequestered English clergy to continue the use of the Prayer Book, and was extremely pained when the Protector went back on his earlier promise. [5] In 1656 the great Primate died, whom Bramhall declared to be "an honour to his native country, an ornament to the Reformed Church, a conscionable preacher, and an exemplary pattern of piety". [6]

---

[1] Ibid., 442.   [2] Ibid., 443.
[3] *Works*, I, 210 seqq., where Elrington gives the accumulated evidence against this charge. For a more recent view, see S. R. Gardiner, *History of England from the Accession of James I to the Outbreak of the Civil War*, IX, 366.
[4] *Works*, v, 85.   [5] Life, *Works*, I, 271 seqq.   [6] *Works*, v, 85.

Most of the Irish Bishops and many of the clergy left Ireland. Thomas Fulwar, Bishop of Ardfert, and Henry Tilson, Bishop of Elphin, appear to have held a number of ordinations in England during the Commonwealth, the latter also publicly consecrating a new chapel and chapel-yard at Meltham in Yorkshire on St Bartholomew's Day 1651.[1] But the greatest service of all to the Anglican Communion was performed by the Bishop of Derry on the Continent. Most of his works were written during this period, when he was far from libraries, living in poverty, and forced for a time to auction fishing-boats at Flushing. *A Fair Warning to take heed of the Scottish Discipline* was published in 1649, *An Answer to M. de la Militiere* in 1653, *A Just Vindication of the Church of England* in 1654, *Replication to the Bishop of Chalcedon* in 1656, *Schism Guarded* in 1658, and his works against Hobbes began to appear in 1657.[2] Of his controversial works T. S. Eliot has written: "But for ordonnance, logical arrangement, for the mastery of every fact relevant to a thesis, Bramhall is surpassed only by Hooker; and I am not sure that in the structure of the *Just Vindication of the English Church* he does not surpass even Hooker." [3] T. S. Eliot also defends Bramhall's style; for although he is not an easy writer "his phrases are lucid and direct and occasionally have real beauty and rhythm".[4]

(b) The Coming Over of Jeremy Taylor to Ireland

Meanwhile three sequestered English Divines, who later became Bishops in Ireland, George Wilde, Robert Mossom, and Jeremy Taylor, were ministering to private congregations of Royalists in London. Taylor had left Wales early in 1657. "And going to London", Dean Rust said at his funeral, "he there met my Lord Conway, a person of great honour and generosity; who making him a kind proffer, the good man embraced it, and that brought him over into Ireland, and settled him at Portmore, a place made for study and contemplation, which therefore he dearly loved." [5] Portmore, bordering on Portmore Lough[6] in the parish of Ballinderry, was in Killultagh, Lord Conway's estate in northern Ireland, which was managed by his brother-in-law, Major George Rawdon, who lived in part of the Conway mansion at Lisnegarvey. While at Carrickfergus for the Epiphany Quarter Sessions Rawdon

---

[1] Legg, *Eng. Ch. Orders*, 204 seqq.
[2] *The Serpent Salve* (1643) was published before he went to the continent: *Protestants' Ordination Defended*, though written before 1654, does not appear to have been published until after the Restoration.
[3] *Theology*, July 1927.   [4] Ibid.
[5] Taylor, *Works*, I, cccxxiii.   [6] Commonly called L. Beg.

received a letter from Conway, now missing,[1] about his purpose to accommodate Taylor in a farm at Ballinderry held by Captain Roma. Rawdon, after some delay, answered from Lisnegarvey on 23 January 1657/8.

And as to yr Lordship's purpose to Doctor Tailor your sister and I are exceedingly joyed therewith and by the hope we have of much comfort and benefit by such a neighbourhood. I received your letter concerning it at Carrickfergus, and doubting the certainty of Capt Roma's removal from Ballinderry I writt to him (but not anything of yr Lordship's intention to dispose it thus), and he met me here (but after the last post)

Rawdon could not bring Roma, who had set his new farm near Coleraine to tenants, to a resolution to leave Ballinderry before May 1659. "Perhaps if the Doctor's family be not great the house may accommodate them both for a time, which I shall propound or the best expedient otherwise I can, that he come over sooner." [2] Rawdon, who had just returned from the Quarter Sessions and assessments of counties Antrim and Down,[3] would have replied a week[4] sooner had he been able to see Roma before the last post. Thus Conway's letter was forwarded and received before 16 January at Carrickfergus, "where we stuck three days on a riot";[5] and judging from the normal time letters took in winter to pass from Ragley or Kensington to Lisnegarvey,[6] it was almost certainly sent within two weeks at the most of Christmas 1657. In this case it is extremely probable that Taylor was considering Conway's offer when on 19 December 1657 he wrote to Dr Sheldon: "I have some thoughts of retiring from noise and company, and going to my studies in a far distant solitude, but not to Wales." [7] Taylor was feeling the strain of his ministry in London. "We are every day threatened, we are fiercely petitioned against by the presbyterians, we are agitated at the Council Table; only we yet go on, and shall still go on till we can go on no longer. If we are

---

[1] There is a gap in extant letters of Conway to Rawdon between July 1655 and 15 June 1658.

[2] P.R.O., S.P., 63–289–96a. Mrs Rawdon also thanked her brother for his "intentions to Dr Taylor". (Ibid., 97.)

[3] Ibid., 96a.

[4] Rawdon wrote to Conway nearly every Saturday. On 23 Jan. 1657/8 he promises to send Mr King's letter "next week": on 30 Jan. he has "little to add to my last long letter by the last post, only I send Mr King's letter." (Ibid., 96a, 98.)

[5] Ibid., 96a. Cf. Rawdon's letter of 13 Jan. 1665/6: "I am just back from the sessions at Carrickfergus and have received yr Lrp's of 12 and 26 December."

[6] Thus Rawdon wrote on 5 Feb.: "I have received both yr Lordship's letters of 19 and 26 January together yesterday"; on 13 Feb.: "I have newly received yours of the 2 of Feb:". (Ibid., 99, 100.) See also note 5.

[7] Op. cit., I, lxxii.

permitted (which is still *sub judice*) the common prayer book is certainly voted to be suppressed." [1] Further agitation at the Council Table on 22 December against the joint ministry of "Mr Gunning and Dr Taylor" [2] and the Christmas Day raid while Mr Gunning was administering the Holy Communion[3] may have hastened Taylor's decision to embrace Conway's offer.

Accommodation had first to be found in this "far distant solitude", for Conway's smaller house at Portmore was not begun until 1664.[4] Under repeated pressure from Conway Rawdon importunes Roma to leave Ballinderry before the coming midsummer, and by 13 February gets him to promise to look for "an accommodation elsewhere".[5] On 2 April Rawdon fears that Conway and Taylor may be mistaken in their expectations; for Mr King, recently returned from England, has told Rawdon that he understood Conway "had assured to Doctor Tailor 200l a year for his own life and his children's, and that a near friend of the doctor's had told him". But the sources of income Conway has written of to Rawdon—Roma's "parts of Ballinderry and Portmore" [6] and the tithes at Conway's disposal[7]—cannot together realize more than £116.[8] By the end of May Rawdon has "caused the ill way to be paved from the mill at Ballinderry to the house that Doctor Tailor may pass in winter".[9]

Meanwhile an assembly of thirty representative ministers, at Henry Cromwell's invitation, met in Dublin on 23 April and sat for five weeks.[10] On 26 May a delegate came to Rawdon in great haste having heard "strange news in the convention to-day" that Conway was "sending over Doctor Tailor to Lisnegarvey". Rawdon "satisfied him that it was otherwise" and "that the Doctor will meddle with nobody, but live retiredly at his studies".[11] Although the ministers had confused Taylor with Philip Tandy, formerly Anglican incumbent of Glenavy, who for some time had been designated Commonwealth minister of Lisnegarvey[12]

[1] Ibid.
[2] The Council resolved "to advise his Highness to send for Mr Gunning and Dr Taylor, and require an account of the frequent meetings of multidudes of people held with them, and to cause the Ordinance for taking away the Book of Common Prayer to be enforced." *C.S.P. Dom., 1657-8*, 226.
[3] Evelyn's *Diary*, under 25 Dec. 1657.
[4] S. Lewis, *A Topographical Dictionary of Ireland*, 112; M. Beckett, *Sir George Rawdon*, 57, 163.
[5] Letters of 5 and 13 Feb. (S.P. 63-287-99, 100).
[6] 180 Irish acres would not yield more than 36l if "set as the rest as 4s an acre".
[7] The tithes "will not come yet above 80l a year".   [8] S.P. 63-287-113.
[9] Ibid., 116.   [10] St John D. Seymour, *The Puritans in Ireland*, 152.
[11] Postscript to letter of 26 May (S.P. 63-287-116).
[12] Andrew Wyke, an Anabaptist, had been intruded at Lisnegarvey before Conway

and was now expected over from England, the rumour that Conway had presented Taylor provided the occasion for strong objections to be voiced. "They took it for granted that he was destined for Lisnegarvey Church", Rawdon reports on 2 June, "and resolved that he should not be admitted." Though divided in almost everything else, the ministers were unanimous in this; "and Dr Worth,[1] esteemed a very moderate man—and some call him an Old Protestant—spoke much against it." Therefore, if Taylor still come he should be provided by the Lord Protector's pass, "that he may not be subject to the trouble of petulant spirits".[2]

To Rawdon's discouraging letter Conway replied on 15 June, reporting that he had provided Taylor with the Lord Protector's pass and letters of introduction from Lord Petty and others to people of influence in Ireland, and adding, "Dr Loftus is his friend".[3] On 21 June Taylor was at Annesley in Nottinghamshire[4] showing little haste to continue his journey through Wales. "The mighty inconveniences of removing a family" would take time; and he would stay on the way in Dublin sufficiently long to use his letters of introduction "to Dr Harrison and several others", to the Lord Chief Baron, and the other introductions Conway had provided him with,[5] to renew his friendship with Dr Dudley Loftus,[6] and to become acquainted with Dr John Stearne and that circle at Trinity College with

became 3rd Viscount. The decision to replace him by Tandy had been taken before 5 Jan. 1657/8 (S.P. 63–287–94). During January Wyke revoked his promise to withdraw quietly, and Rawdon withdrew the tithes from him (ibid., 98; cf. 116).

[1] Formerly Dean of Cork.

[2] S.P. 63–287–117. The convention included the Presbyterians, Gregg and Hall, who later opposed Taylor's appointment as Bishop.

[3] Taylor, *Works*, I, cclxxxvi. This was the first letter about Taylor in the Conway-Rawdon correspondence known to Bishop Heber, who connected it with Taylor's letter to Sir John Evelyn of 12 May, turning down the offer made through a friend of an alternate lectureship with a presbyterian "vicar" and with a stipend "so inconsiderable". (Ibid., I, lxxxviii.) Heber conjectured that Taylor was expressing his first reluctance to Conway's offer made through Evelyn, and therefore transferred the conditions of the lectureship Taylor disliked to Lisnegarvey being the nearest town church to Portmore. These conditions, however, cannot apply to Lisnegarvey, where the lawful incumbent, Thomas Ives, was alive but sequestered; where the designated Commonwealth minister had been incumbent of Mageragall (1637) and Glenavy (1638); and where there is no evidence of any lecturer or lectureship at the time. (H. B. Leslie, MS. Succession List of Connor Diocese [R.C.B.].) Moreover, before April Conway had assured Taylor a considerable income, and long before that directed plans for his accommodation.

[4] *H.M.C., Rutland*, II, 5.　　　　　　　　[5] Letter of 15 June.

[6] Dr Dudley Loftus, Deputy Judge-Advocate in the province of Leinster, a collector and translator of ancient oriental texts, is probably that "learned person beyond sea", who had sent Taylor "extracts of the Easterne and Southerne Antiquities" to confirm Taylor's "opinion and doctrine" which he approved (Letter, Taylor to Evelyn, 15 Nov. 1656, op. cit., I, lv).

whom he later corresponded. He can hardly have reached Portmore before the end of July.

The first notice of Taylor's arrival in northern Ireland is given by Rawdon in a letter to Conway of 15 October from Hilsborough Castle, where the Taylors are guests and "Dr Tailor preached excellently this [Friday] morning". Mrs Hill promises to obey Conway's "command in her civilities to the Doctor and his lady". Tandy, still awaiting his admission to Lisnegarvey, "is now satisfied in all his scruples and very free to the Ordinances". "The Doctor and he sorte very well, and I think Dr Tailor has done him much good." [1] In the neighbourhood, as in other parts of Ireland, there were some Anglican priests serving as Commonwealth ministers; and no doubt the Rawdons expected those in Killultagh[2] to be "very free to the Ordinances", particularly regarding the Prayer Book. Another near neighbour, Digory Holman, Precentor of Dromore, continued to use the Prayer Book in his parish of Magheralin,[3] as did Prebendary Edward Synge in his Donegal parishes.[4] A frequent guest of the Rawdons and Hills was Dr Alexander Colvill, Precentor of Connor, who being driven from his parish lived privately in his castle at Galgorm.[5] He came over to Lisnegarvey, for example, for the wedding of Nan Whitby to Mr Bryars on 5 February 1657/8[6]—whose child Taylor baptized "with the sign of the cross" in the summer of 1659.[7] This freedom with the Ordinances was reported to the authorities either by Tandy[8] or by a "presbyterian and a madman".[9] By this time Tandy had become jealous of Taylor, thinking him "more welcome at Hilsborough than himself".[10] Taylor was certainly drawn to Hilsborough Castle, where during the Commonwealth the Prayer Book was "greatly valued and diligently used",[11] and where in 1659 Henry Leslie, "maugre all Anti Christian opposition, Bishop of Down and Connor", preached his sermons on *Praying with the Spirit*,[12] and probably where he held ordinations from January 1659/60.[13] Taylor may have ministered some-

---

[1] S.P. 63-287-113.

[2] Joseph Dunbar of Agohill and John Wallwood of Glenavy, for example.

[3] St John D. Seymour, op. cit., 172.   [4] Mant, I, 592; Leslie, *Derry*, 63.

[5] The Presbyterians regarded him as a formidable foe and as "an eager and intolerant prelatist" (J. S. Reid, *History of the Presbyterian Church in Ireland*, 1867).

[6] S.P. 63-287-99.

[7] Taylor, *Works*, I, cclxxxvii.   [8] So Conway (ibid.).

[9] So Taylor (ibid., I, lxxxiv). Possibly a picturesque reference to Tandy: more probably two or three distinct persons consorting in mischief.

[10] Q, v., n. 2.   [11] Taylor (ibid.), v, 255.   [12] Ibid.

[13] On 3 Jan. and 21 Feb. 1659/60 and 21 June 1660. Like John Leslie, Bishop of Raphoe (Mant, I, 593), Bishop Henry Leslie appears to have exercised episcopal functions in Ireland during the Commonwealth.

times to the private congregation here after the departure of Mr Bernham West, the Anglican chaplain,[1] in the early summer of 1659. It was with Will Hill, the son of Colonel Hill, that Taylor crossed over to England just before 28 March 1659/60;[2] and on his return as Bishop he took up residence in "a little house", too small for servants, "close to Hilsborough Castle".[3] As a guest Taylor may also have preached or ministered privately at Lisnegarvey Castle.[4] The local tradition, however, that he preached in Lisnegarvey and neighbouring churches cannot reach back beyond the autumn of 1660; for there is no evidence that Taylor exercised any public ministry in Ireland before his appointment as Bishop of Down and Connor. Conway regarded his provision as "an act of piety" towards Taylor and "all such as are truly disposed to virtue in those parts";[5] but, as Rawdon makes clear, he was to live "privately"[6] and "retiredly at his studies".[7] Indeed, Taylor was troubled that things in Killultagh were so that he could neither serve Conway, nor his sister, "but must be like a cistern under a conduit pipe ever receiving fresh water and returning nothing back". Yet he was grateful for his quiet, his peace, "his opportunities of study and devotion", and "freedom from distracting cares".[8]

At Portmore, "a place made for study and contemplation", Taylor completed his *Ductor Dubitantium*,[9] wrote the *Worthy Communicant*, and directed the reading of Mr Graham and Mr Sheridan, of Trinity College, who desired "to be wise and learned in the christian religion, as it is taught and professed in the church of England".[10] *Ex amoenissimo recessu in Portmore* Taylor also wrote a short Latin letter prefixed to Dr John Stearne's THANATOLOGIA *seu, De Morte Dissertatio.*[11] And probably before

---

[1] Sizar of Christ's, Cambridge; ordained at Peterborough 1641; "came near to being elected a fellow in 1646."   [2] S.P. 63-303-24, 25.   [3] B.L., MSS. Carte 31.

[4] The Rawdons had a succession of resident chaplains sent over by Conway, though on Sundays they attended, in Wyke's time, Kilwarlin where Mr Bernham West officiated (S.P. 63-286-151). Mr Wallwood of Glenavy preached at the Castle on a Saturday in Nov. 1657 (ibid., 287-8).

[5] Taylor, *Works*, I, cclxxxvi.   [6] S.P. 63-287-100.   [7] Ibid., 116.

[8] Letter, Taylor to Conway, 10 Mar. 1658/9 ("Copies of Original Letters" in the keeping of Sir John Murray).

[9] For an estimate of this work see *The Structure of Caroline Moral Theology*, by Dean H. R. McAdoo.

[10] *Works*, I, lxxxviii seqq. He sends a list of works essential for any "that would improve in the understanding of the doctrine of the church of England, so as to be able to teach others".

[11] The first edition appeared in 1656. On the verso of Taylor's letter are verses by Bishop Maxwell of Kilmore. In Stearne's *Animi Medela* (1658) are verses again by Bishop Maxwell, a letter by Bishop John Leslie of Raphoe, and a certificate of orthodoxy by Bishop Williams of Ossory, showing that these Bishops were not only available, but held in esteem by this learned layman.

leaving Portmore for England in March 1659/60 Taylor wrote his letter
on prayer for Bishop Henry Leslie's *Praying with the Spirit and with the
Understanding*, which was published early in 1660.[1] *A Collection of Offices
. . . Together with a Large Preface*[2] *in Vindication of the Liturgy of the Church
of England* appeared in 1658, that is, from 25 March, and therefore after
Taylor had accepted Conway's offer. He may have intended it partly for
use in Irish congregations and brought over copies with him.[3]

IV. RESTORATION CAROLINE CHURCHMEN

At the Restoration of the monarchy Dr Dudley Loftus wrote to the Duke
of Ormonde on 1 June 1660, reminding him of the legal position of "our
national Church". Episcopal government was still upheld by our laws;
and it was most improbable that any Irish Parliament, which alone could
repeal them, would assent to any alteration, both Houses delighting "in
nothing more than in the ancient government by Bishops". He therefore
begged Ormonde's watchfulness over the orthodox Irish clergy "for the
preservation of the sacred Order of Bishops and the use of the liturgy".[4]
Loftus enclosed a list of "Ecclesiastical Preferments voide in Ireland"
together with the names of persons fit to be preferred.[5] Of these "Deane
Margetson" was appointed Archbishop of Dublin, "Deane Pullen" Archbishop of Tuam, "Deane Boyle" Bishop of Cork, "Mr Singe" Bishop of
Limerick, and "Mr Seele" Provost of Trinity. Of the eight surviving
Bishops Bramhall was translated to Armagh, Fulwar to Cashel, and Henry
Leslie to Meath. These and other appointments[6] were made from July,
though the want of legal confirmation held up the consecration of the
new Archbishops and Bishops until the following January. On 27

---

[1] Before Leslie's translation to Meath and Taylor's appointment as his successor.

[2] As the *Offices* were only intended for use as long as the Ordinance against the
Prayer Book was enforced, the "large Preface", without the last three sections
(*Works*, VIII, 573 seq.), became after the Restoration the Preface to *An Apology for
Authorized and Set Forms of Liturgy* (ibid., v, 231 seqq.). The Preface implies that the
Prayer Book has been suppressed even in private congregations in England (ibid.,
232).

[3] He assumes that his *Collection of Officers* is available to students at Trinity. *Works*,
I, lxxxviii.

[4] B.L., MSS. Carte 30, 685.

[5] Ibid., 689. The sixth name is "Mr Domvill".

[6] Mostly of clergy who had suffered in the Royalist cause: Robert Price, driven
from Carrickfergus "houseless and homeless" (Ferns and Leighlin); Baker, agent for
the Irish Bishops and clergy in 1640 (Waterford); Hall, who with Margetson and
Synge had signed the Dublin Declaration of 1647 (Killala); Wilde (Derry), and
Mossom (Dean of Christ Church, Dublin).

October, Jeremy Taylor, destined for Down and Connor, complained to Lord Montgomery of the Ards that the delay of the consecration made the Presbyterian ministers "fancy that the King intends no Bishops in Ireland, and that keeps them off from complying". "From divers of the ministers" he had "received private notice that they will turn Nicodemus's and come to me in secret; and shortly they will be public." He had hopes of reducing his diocese "to good temper and a quiet and uniform religion according to the laws".[1] The pessimistic tone of Taylor's letters to Ormonde and Sir George Lane of 19 December[2] may be accounted for by the serious report of 3 December he had received from Robert Maxwell of a Presbyterian gathering at Newtown, which not only designed articles against him but resolved all of them to preach against episcopacy and the Prayer Book.[3] The Presbyterian clamour for Taylor's removal grew so loud that Bramhall had to intervene on his behalf.[4] Bramhall had also to deal with Anglican objections to Henry Jones, Bishop of Clogher from 1645, who had collaborated with the Cromwellian régime, and to the appointment as Bishop of Killaloe of Edward Worth, who had taken a leading part as a Cromwellian Minister. Bramhall ended these exceptions with a general consent, and "in the presence of all the Bishops absolved the Bishop of Clogher from his irregularity".[5]

The long delayed consecration of the Archbishops of Dublin and Tuam and the ten new Bishops took place with great solemnity on 27 January 1660/1 in St Patrick's Cathedral. The procession assembled at Christ Church at 7 in the morning and was led by the Mayor and Aldermen in scarlet, with the Sheriffs and City Council; then by the General Convention of Ireland led by the Speaker, having the mace carried before him. These came voluntarily "to show their respect to the Bishops".[6] The rest of the procession followed Bramhall's detailed directions:

That the pursuivant of the court of prerogative, and the apparitor general bare headed; the vergers of the said two Cathedrals; the choristers two and two, and the rest of the procedents also in order, two and two as followeth; Vicars Chorals, Petit-canons; Prebendaries; Dignitaries; the said two deans; the bishops elect in their albs; the Lord Primate's gent. usher, and secretary bare headed; the Lord Primate; the other Bishops consecrators two and two; the beadle of the university, the Vice-chancellor, or pro-vice chancellor and Provost; Deans and doctors two

[1] MS. Carte 31, 36.   [2] *Works*, I, ci seqq.
[3] C.S.P. (Irel.) *1660–2*, 128; *Conway Papers* (ed. M. H. Nicholson), 167 seq. The date "10 ber 3d" refers to the tenth month from March, and not January.
[4] MSS. Carte 221, 79, 150.   [5] Ibid., 221, 138.
[6] Dudley Loftus, *The Proceedings Observed ... in the Consecration of the Twelve Bishops*, 4, 8.

and two: that the above said order may proceed with a silent, solemn, and slow paced gravity, until the time of entrance into the west-gate of St Patrick's Church, where the vicars and choristers are to proceed singing into the Choir, and there continue singing the *Te Deum*, accompanied by the organ, until the Archbishops, Bishops, and the rest of the principal procedents shall be placed and seated in their respective stalls.[1]

We are told that the multitude in the street on that cold January morning "seemed to be so great as to deny Rome for a regular and solemn proceeding", yet they behaved with great reverence, "nor was any noise heard in the streets, save that of eulogies and Benediction from the people of all sorts to the Lord Primate all the way".[2]

Jeremy Taylor's sermon, observed Dr Dudley Loftus, "was such as gave great and general satisfaction, being elegantly, religiously, and prudently composed, and so convincingly satisfying the judgements of those who have opposed the order and jurisdiction of episcopacy as that the Lord Justices, the Lord Primate, and the General Convention have all of them severally ordered and desired the speedy impression thereof." [3] The anthem, sung immediately after the consecration "to that purpose composed by the Dean of St Patrick's", expressed the spirit of the restored Anglicans.

> *Treble.* Now, that the Lord hath re-advanced the crown,
> Which thirste of spoyle and frantick zeal threw down.
> *Tenor.* Now, that the Lord the miter hath restor'd,
> Which with the crown lay in dust abhor'd.
> *Treble.* Praise him ye Kings. *Tenor.* Praise him ye Priests.
> *Chorus.* Glory to Christ our high Priest, highest King.
> *Treble.* May Judah's royal sceptre still shine clear.
> *Tenor.* May Aaron's holy rod still blossoms bear;
> *Treble and Tenor.* Sceptre and rod rule still and guide our land!
> And those whom God anoints feel no rude hand!
> May love, peace, plenty, wait on crown and chair
> And may both share in blessings as in care.
> *Chorus.* Angels, look down, and joy to see,
> Like that above, a monarchie.
> Angels, look down, and joy to see,
> Like that above, an hierarchie.[4]

[1] "The Manner of Consecration of the Bishops in Dublin", *The Pillars of Priestcraft and Orthodoxy Shaken* (ed. Rich. Baron), II, 338 seqq.
[2] Dudley Loftus, op. cit., 8.
[3] Op. cit., Taylor, *Works*, VIII, 309 seqq.
[4] W. Monk Mason, *History of St Patrick's*, 194.

This was followed by Te Deum, sung for the third time, a "Solemn Offertory" and the rest of the Communion Service; and in the return from the Cathedral the procession was so altered that "the new consecrated archbishops and bishops" were "disposed with the other bishops consecrators, according to the respective dignities of their sees, quality, and seniority of consecration".[1] Bramhall informed Ormonde that the consecration "was done so nobly that it will be an hard task to find out another equal to it in Europe, where twelve Bishops were consecrated at one time. And all the orders of the kingdom, Justices, Council, Convention, Army, City, graced it with their presence." [2]

The restored Church of Ireland immediately faced the difficult task of dealing with the Commonwealth ministers of varying denominations who held church benefices, including some seventy Presbyterian ministers, half of them in Down and Connor, who were organized on a territorial basis extending into Armagh, Clogher, Raphoe, Derry, and Dromore. No Irish Act of Parliament had proscribed episcopacy or the Prayer Book, and no Irish Convocation had set aside the English Articles of 1562[3] or the Irish Canons of 1634. The Irish Canon 84 required every parson, vicar, and curate "at the Archbishops or Bishops first Visitation, or at the next Visitation after his admission" to "shew and exhibit unto them, his letters of Orders, Institution, and Induction". When several of his clergy could only exhibit such titles as they had received from the late powers, and not their Letters of Orders as the Canon required, Bramhall told them that he disputed not the value of their ordination, but administered the laws of the "National Church", and could not see how they could continue in their benefices without episcopal ordination. Where he persuaded them to receive ordination, he made it clear in their Letters of Orders, but not as has been supposed in the formula of ordination,

that he did not annul the minister's former orders, if he had any, nor determine their validity or invalidity: much less did he condemn all the sacred orders of foreign churches, whom he left to their own judge; but he only supplied, whatever was before wanting, as required by the Canons of the Anglican Church; and that he provided for the peace of the Church, that occasions of schism might be

---

[1] "The Manner of Consecration . . .".

[2] MSS. Carte 221, 156. In this letter Bramhall regrets the words of the oath of Supremacy. "Could not we have meddled with the pope's usurpations which are all condemned by the ancient laws of England long before the reformation, but we must meddle with papal power and authority? In the former . . . all Christian Kings would have joined with us. The latter widens and perpetuates the differences without necessity." (Ibid.)

[3] Received by Convocation in 1634. For the irrelevance of the Irish Articles of 1615 to the situation in 1661 see p. 63.

D

removed, and the consciences of the faithful satisfied, and that they might have no manner of doubt of his ordination, nor decline his presbyterial acts as being invalid.[1]

"I have led them all the dance in the first visitation, successfully enough", Bramhall wrote to Ormonde's secretary, Sir George Lane, on 16 March 1660/1. "Yet have I as many hereticks in my diocese as any man. But the surest way to take a populacy is by the ear. So God bless us." [2]

Bramhall's policy was extended to the whole province of Armagh. Dr Dudley Loftus, who as Vicar-General accompanied the Primate on his metropolitical Visitation of August 1661, testified that in every diocese of his province he concluded all things "ad norman propriae suae Dioceseos, prout ratio postulabat, et jubebat aequitas".[3] Yet biographers have too often represented Bishop Taylor as being less conciliatory than Bramhall in his treatment of Presbyterian ministers, whose replacement throughout the province of Armagh nevertheless took place during the year (1661) of Bramhall's triennial Visitation, for the greater part of which the jurisdiction of Taylor and other suffragan Bishops was suspended.[4] Transactions at their ordinary Visitations[5] earlier in the year and admissions to benefices would be subject to metropolitical approbation and confirmation. The Irish Canon moreover, required Letters of Orders to be exhibited not only at the "first Visitation" of both the diocesan Bishop and of the Metropolitan, but by all seeking admission to a benefice.[6] Bramhall's policy for the province was uniform: those Presbyterians who would not qualify for their benefices by episcopal ordination were replaced by the episcopally ordained. Attention has been focused upon Taylor simply because Bramhall's policy involved more replacements in Down and

---

[1] Mant, I, 624 seq.   [2] MSS. Carte 221, 162.

[3] *Oratio Funebris . . . Johannis Arciepiscopi Armachani*, 28.

[4] See p. 62. The prohibited period began six months before, and ended three months after, the triennial Visitation. The Bishop of Raphoe prayed for the restitution of his jurisdiction on 22 Nov. (*H.M.C., Hastings*, IV, 199).

[5] Writing at a later date Patrick Adair (*True Narative*, 247 seqq.) may have confused the outcome of the Bishop's Visitation with the Archbishop's. He makes it clear that the Presbyterians were unwilling to qualify for their benefices by episcopal ordination.

[6] Canons 84, 23. Having visited Meath, Kilmore, Clogher, Raphoe, and Derry, Bramhall began his Visitation of Connor on 27 Aug., assisted by Dr Colvill, Chancellor of that diocese. Letters of Orders were exhibited, and Bramhall pronounced those absent without excuse contumacious and reserved judgement. Next day Dr Loftus, the Vicar-General, began the Visitation of Down and Dromore, assisted by Dr Games as Chancellor. The Visitation being adjourned to the Hall of Hilsborough Castle was on 29 Aug. adjourned to Armagh Cathedral. In Down and Connor above thirty benefices were confirmed as being vacant. (Dr Reeves' Transcript of triennial Visitations by Primates, Diocesan Library, Belfast.)

Connor than in the other dioceses put together,[1] although Taylor himself ordained more Presbyterian ministers than the other Bishops.[2] The vacant benefices were filled partly by surviving Anglicans who had been driven out of them, partly by those Commonwealth ministers who qualified by ordination,[3] and partly by new appointments.[4] Bramhall's firm policy regarding the Presbyterians was called for by their exclusive territorial claim to the greater part of the ancient province of Armagh; and by withstanding ecclesiastical partition he secured the future of the Church of Ireland in those parts where to-day it is strong and vigorous. At the time there was no question of a peaceful co-existence.

Bramhall had a vigorous policy not only for his province but for the whole Church of Ireland. If as Bishop of Derry he had promoted the influence of the Church of England, as Primate he sought to preserve the freedom of the national Church. "The same judgement I made always of this Church", he now claimed, "I hold that we shall overcome all impediments quickly if we have no impediment out of the East". Meanwhile Bramhall became Speaker of the Irish House of Lords when the Irish Parliament opened on 8 May 1661. One of the first acts of the House of Lords was to draw up a Declaration "requiring all subjects of this Kingdom to conform to Church Government by Episcopacy and to the Liturgy". "I am exceeding glad", wrote Bishop Wilde from London to Bramhall a year later, "our Irish Declaration was out before the English Act of Uniformity." [5] We may notice here a remarkable protestation on the part of the Lords Spiritual against being taxed with the Lords Temporal—"The joint Protestation of all the Archbishops and Bishops, in Parliament assembled at Dublin, September the 10th, 1662". First, by the authority of Magna Carta the Church of England, and so likewise the Church of Ireland, should enjoy the immunity of not being taxed nor assessed but by herself in Convocation.

2dy. We affirm that the Church was never taxed or assessed, except only in case

[1] 3 Presbyterian ministers were replaced in Armagh, 3 in Clogher, 6 in Raphoe, 10 in Derry, 18 in Connor, 13 in Down, and 3 (not by Taylor, but by Bishop Leslie before his translation to Raphoe on 24 June) in Dromore.

[2] Taylor ordained at least 5 Presbyterian ministers, Bramhall 1, the Bishop of Derry 2, and the Bishop of Raphoe (at a later date) 1.

[3] Bramhall ordained several non-Presbyterian ministers including Edward Parkinson, whose Letters of Orders were cited by Bishop Vesey. Taylor also ordained several including Dr Games, Chancellor of Down and Dromore.

[4] Adair is wrong in ascribing to Taylor greater haste than other Bishops in filling up benefices vacated by Presbyterians (op. cit., 251). Apart from those of Adair and four others, Taylor made all his admissions to vacant benefices after the triennial Visitation: the other Bishops before.   [5] H.M.C., Hastings, IV, 133.

of invincible necessity, that ever we heard or read of, but by themselves in Con-vocation. 3dy. All just gifts are grounded upon the owners' own consent, and no man can give anything in a parliament but he that hath a represental in parliament to give it for him: but the whole body of the Inferior Clergy have not one repre-sentative in parliament, and therefore they cannot be taxed to any gifts, but by themselves in Convocation...[1]

The Irish Convocation met on 10 May 1661, provincial writs having been issued to the four Archbishops on 26 March, and the Holy Com-munion with the stated sermon celebrated on 9 May. The members of the Lower House walked in solemn procession from Christ Church to St Patrick's "two and two", while the Bishops followed on horseback. Primate Bramhall presided; and Dean Mossom was chosen Prolocutor of the Lower House, Dr Dudley Loftus Registrar of the Upper House and Dr Edward Cooke of the Lower. A little later the Upper House chose the Bishops of Cork and Elphin, and the Lower Dean Fuller of St Patrick's, to be their agents in placing the affairs of the Church of Ireland before the King. Their letters to the Primate are most revealing, and sometimes express impatience at the non-arrival of directions and documents from Bramhall at a time when he was busily engaged on his metropolitical Visitation of his province.[2] "The Bishops here", wrote Dean Fuller on 12 July 1662, "think the Church of Ireland under your care at this time, and my Lord Lieutenant's more than ordinary favour, to be more happy than this of England, where the rich Presbyterian lay party and the violent, cunning Presbyterian church party flatter themselves with the great hopes that a war will bring upon his Majesty a necessity of indulging their consciences to obtain the assistance of their purses." [3] This Convoca-tion gave full synodical sanction on 11 November 1662 to the revised Book of Common Prayer "lately published in London", four years before it received the temporal sanction of the Irish Act of Uniformity. It also ordered the publication of Bishop Taylor's *Discourse of Confirmation* (1663). This had been commissioned by the Upper House, as had his *Dissuasive from Popery*, though published in 1664[4] during the long proro-gation of Parliament and Convocation from the spring of 1663 to the autumn of 1665, which greatly hindered the work of the Church.

Parliament was prorogued as a precautionary measure in view of the discovery of a plot against Dublin Castle planned for 22 May. For some

---

[1] *Journals of the House of Lords* (Dublin, 1779), 1 (1634–98), 448 seq.
[2] H.M.C., *Hastings*, IV, 104–35 *passim*.   [3] Ibid., 125.
[4] Before 24 May 1664, when Dr Henry More wrote of its very good reception in Cambridge (*Conway Papers*, 223).

time meetings of displaced Presbyterian and other ministers had been officially suspected; and by Proclamation of 12 November 1662[1] all Bishops, Justices of the Peace, and others had to prohibit and report all such meetings within their several jurisdictions. Taylor's letter to Ormonde of 11 June 1663 about "the late meetings of pretended ministers" suggesting that they were "all more than consenting to the late design",[2] has been taken in isolation by biographers.[3] It was sent under cover with a joint letter from Lord Conway and Major Rawdon, who were "fully persuaded that all of them that were silenced are guilty".[4] Likewise Lord Orrery, from Co. Down, expressed the view on 23 May that it would be impossible to prevent rebellion in the north and found "all sorts of sectaries engaged in the plot".[5]

Bramhall was actively engaged in trying to recover more of the lost patrimony of the Church when death overtook him in June 1663. Taylor, in his Funeral Sermon, testified to the Primate's great services to the national Church as a wise Bishop, a learned doctor, "a zealous asserter of his religion against popery on the one side, and fanaticism on the other". The single perfections which make many men eminent "were united in this Primate and made him illustrious". For in him was visible "the great lines of Hooker's judiciousness, of Jewel's learning, of the acuteness of bishop Andrewes".[6] It was indeed providential that Bramhall had become Primate at the Restoration, for none knew better than he the needs of the national Church, and he was able to consolidate within three years the work he had begun before the civil war. As Bishop of Derry he had recovered much of the Church's lost patrimony; during the Commonwealth he had been the Athanasius of the Anglican Communion in exile; as Primate he left the national Church well set on the road to recovery. Yet no monument appears to mark the resting-place of this great Caroline Primate.

The third Caroline Primate, James Margetson, at first showed signs of

---

[1] *C.S.P.* (*Irel.*) *1660–2*, 615. There had been a plot against Dublin Castle on the eve of the Rebellion of 1641 then within living memory.

[2] *Works*, I, ciii.

[3] Gosse, *Jeremy Taylor*, 196 seq.; Stranks, op. cit., 260 seq.

[4] MSS. Carte 32, 556 seq.

[5] *C.S.P.* (*Irel.*) *1663–5*, 100. On 24 Feb. Conway sent Ormonde "the copy of the Intelligence" reporting Presbyterian movements in Antrim and Down, and recommending that if these men be apprehended "let it be upon account of nonconformity, or giving no obedience to the law upon the Bishop's account, so he may inquire greater matters of them afterwards" (*H.M.C.*, *Hastings*, II, 365 seq.). For important document on Presbyterian complicity see *Tanner Letters* (C.L.E.), 401 seqq. See also MSS. Carte 32, 469, 551, 651, 657, 664, 697; 45, 145.

[6] *Works*, VIII, 422.

being more favourable to displaced Presbyterian ministers, and suspended proceedings against them before his triennial Visitations.[1] When he visited Down early in June 1664 he found that the Romanist clergy had held a synod two days before with such secrecy that all he could learn was that "most of them were drunk all night". He found the Scotch clergy of Conner so ignorant in liturgical matters that "upon trial they knew not how to read in order the prayers of the Church". Unwilling to deal too severely with these professors of conformity, he left them "after an open and sharp admonition" to the discipline of Bishop Taylor. At Derry[2] he found "the clergy good and orthodox and most of the people conformable; and the rest tractable, except some women whom I rather persuaded than punished". "Yet a full conformity of that people cannot be expected, so long as the Presbyterian silenced ministers are permitted to live amongst them; one whereof now in the prison of Derry poisoneth the women with false and dangerous opinions; and they pervert their families".[3] In his Visitation of 1670 Margetson again found Romanists exercising a foreign jurisdiction, and at Lifford four Presbyterian ministers whom the Bishop of Raphoe had imprisoned, but "having maintenance, ease, and freedom of living in their own houses, under notion of prisoners", who would not at the Primate's entreaty take the oath of supremacy. Elsewhere in the province he found Presbyterian ministers actively engaged in politico-religious propaganda.[4]

For reasons which will become apparent Taylor's services to the Church of Ireland are considered separately.[5] So far little light, apart from uncertain tradition, has been thrown upon Taylor's later years; and his despondent letter to Archbishop Sheldon of 25 May 1664[6] has led to the view that they were altogether unhappy. This letter was written ten days before the metropolitical Visitation of Down, Connor, and Dromore, while Taylor's jurisdiction was suspended and Primate Margetson's policy still uncertain. Moreover, Taylor had just learnt that Lord and Lady

---

[1] Adair, op. cit., 298; cf. 282. Roger Boyle, Taylor's successor in Down and Connor, protested against the suspension of his jurisdiction before the triennial Visitation of 1670 (ibid., 300 seq.).

[2] The Bishop of Derry, George Wilde, was a vigorous promoter of Bramhall's policy. For example, he wrote to Bramhall on 8 Oct. 1661: "I gave your Grace some account last week how I had disturbed and in some measure routed the conventicles about Ballykelly and Newtown. And now I am told their trumpets of sedition are removed further off into the woods and towards the mountains. But I hope to reach them there". (H.M.C., Hastings, IV, 114; cf., 110, 128, and vigorous letters in the MSS. Carte.)

[3] MSS. Carte 33, 475.   [4] S.P. Ireland, 328, 147.

[5] See p. 269 seqq.

[6] Taylor begs for translation to an English bishopric. Works, I, cxix.

Conway, who had resided at Lisnegarvey Castle from 1661, were return-
ing to England in July.[1] Rawdon's regular letters to Conway, which
begin again in August 1664, throw some light upon Taylor's closing years.
In August Taylor objected to a clause in the proposed Act for Lisnegarvey
Cathedral,[2] by which "the Viccars Choralls were to be nominated after
the first by the Dean";[3] in September he chose a site for a new church at
Ballinderry, but the loss of £100 "hinders his getting a coach this year".[4]
Early in 1665 Taylor took a house in Lisnegarvey[5] and was "full of
thoughts (if it alter not) to go to England this summer and winter, and I
hear he is preparing court-sermons already".[6] In May, however, Taylor
began a lawsuit with Moses Hill,[7] and in July "was so close at his studies
replying to the Answer to his book against popery that he is hardly got
out of his closet".[8] Taylor held Visitations[9] in 1665 and 1666, and frequent
Courts besides. At Christmas 1666 Taylor entertained his neighbours,[10]
and in January organized civil defence[11] and spoke of building "a dining
room next spring".[12] On 1 August 1667 Taylor set out for Galgorm
Castle, the seat of Dr Alexander Colvill, Chancellor of the diocese of
Connor, to meet the Primate, who was making his triennial progress
from[13] Derry. When Margetson left Lisnegarvey for Drogheda on
9 August Taylor was dying.[14]

Attention at this point may be drawn to a Latin letter of considerable length which Taylor wrote for Dr John Stearne's *De Electione &*

[1] *Conway Papers*, 224.

[2] Created by Charter of Charles II with provision for "the choir and other officers
and ministers" (Erck's *Ecclesiastical Register*, 30).

[3] Taylor thought his successor would be wronged. Rawdon told him "if he did
hinder the Act upon that point, his successor would have more wrong by wanting a
Cathedral than the nomination of those Viccars Choralls" (S.P. 63–317–81). The
Act was indefinitely held up, and the Primate merely said, "this is not an age to build
Cathedrals" (*C.S.P. (Irel.) 1663–5*, 458).

[4] S.P., ibid., 82.   [5] *C.S.P.*, ibid., 533.   [6] S.P., 319–43.

[7] Moses was a son of Col. Hill by a former marriage and kept aloof from Hilsborough. Will Hill took Taylor's side in the dispute. (Ibid., 85.)

[8] Ibid., 107. The fact that Taylor unashamedly refers to *The Liberty of Prophesying*
in Part II of the *Dissuasive* (*Works*, VI, 319) makes it improbable that he burnt copies
of it.

[9] S.P., ibid., 80; 321–2. An Irish Bishop visited every year. *Rules and Advises to the
Clergy* ..., designed for distribution and not a Charge, being published in 1661
(Dublin and London) cannot have been "Given at the Visitation at Lisnegarvey"
before 25 Mar. 1661, but at the next Visitation early in 1662.

[10] Ibid., 321–3.   [11] Ibid., 322–19.   [12] Ibid., 28.

[13] Ibid., 323–43. Galgorm (near Ballymena) is *c.* 35 miles from Lisburn.

[14] Ibid., 56. On 10 Aug. Rawdon said Taylor had been "very ill these three or
four days past" (ibid.). Margetson had stayed with the Rawdons 3 to 9 Aug;
Taylor died on the 13th about 3. (Ibid., 62.)

Reprobatione AD Vitam Probam, which was published in Dublin 1662.[1] His shorter Latin letter before Dr Stearne's *Thanatalogia* of 1659 has hitherto been regarded as the only specimen of Taylor's latinity to survive apart from "the interminable epitaph on Lady Carbery".[2] Taylor had already testified to Ormonde of Dr Stearne's "great learning and skill in college affairs",[3] and when on 31 May 1661 the Petition of Dr Stearne was read in the House of Lords, "desiring that a College of Physicians may be created in this city", Taylor was one of the Lords to whom the Petition was referred for consideration.[4] In the longer Latin letter of 1662 Taylor returns, though in rather a subtle way, to a dangerous subject, of which his previous treatment had provoked severe criticism as well from Anglicans in England as Presbyterians in Ireland.[5] But he could not resist the temptation to deal with it; and even in one of his episcopal Charges he makes reference to "the intangled links of the fanatic chain of pre-destination".[6]

Of other Restoration Irish Divines Thomas Price, Archbishop of Cashel (1667–84), put into practice many of the ideals of Bishop Bedell, whose Archdeacon he had been before the Commonwealth. He held nine diocesan Synods at Cashel,[7] encouraged the use of Irish in worship and preaching, and by his friendship and arguments from the Fathers and Councils won over to the Church of Ireland the Jesuit, Andrew Sall, a former Rector of the Irish College at Salamanca. Roger Boyle, Bishop of Down and Connor (1667–72) and Clogher (1672–87), had as Dean of Cork published *Inquisitio in Fidem Chrisanorum* (1664). A more important work, *Summa Theologiae Christianae*, appeared in 1681. His purpose may be compared with that of Jeremy Taylor's *Ductor Dubitantium*. "It was a pity", he wrote in the Preface, "not to have a corpus of Theology which would be agreeable to the Anglican Church in every part, but we were forced to summon the help of Masters from outside: consequently we were not so well disposed towards Mother Church. For some have borrowed from these, others from those: thus we have become daggers

---

[1] Taylor's letter is given in Appendix II. There were also letters by Bishop John Leslie and Will Hill of Hilsborough Castle, and verses by Bishop Maxwell.

[2] Heber, op. cit., I, lxxxv seq.; C. J. Stranks, op. cit., 197.

[3] *Works*, I, xcv.   [4] *Journals of the House of Lords*, I, 222.

[5] Bishop Duppa, Bishop Warner, Dr Sanderson, and others in England, who regarded Taylor's views on original sin as being inconsistent with the Thirty-nine Articles. The Irish Presbyterians, in 1660, drew up articles charging Taylor with being a Socinian, a denier of original sin, an Arminian, "and so a heretic in grain". (*C.S.P.* (*Irel.*) *1660–2*, 115 seq.; cf. Adair, op. cit., 245.)

[6] *Works*, VIII, 532.

[7] Synods were held in 1667, 1670, 1671, 1674, 1676, 1677, 1679, 1680, 1682.

drawn with each other." [1] Boyle represents the Caroline spirit at its best when he writes: "Our Church differs from the Church of Rome in many things, but nowhere without the warranty either of Reason, or of Sacred Scripture, or of the Holy Fathers." [2] George Rust, Taylor's successor in the see of Dromore, was an interesting link between the Church of Ireland and the Cambridge Platonists. Edward Wolley, Bishop of Clonfert (1665–84), was the author of devotional works, including Ο᾽ΤΥΠΟΣ, or the Pattern of Grace and Glory in our Lord and Saviour Jesus Christ (Dublin, 1669), a book of meditations "collected out of the Holy Scriptures, Illustrated by the Ancient Fathers and Expositors". Ezekiel Hopkins, Bishop of Raphoe (1671–81) and Derry (1681–90), published learned expositions on the Catechism, but with a theological emphasis belonging rather to the days of Downham and Bedell. Josiah Pratt, the evangelical editor of Hopkins' works in 1809, claimed him as "one of the last of that race of sound Divines to which the Reformation gave birth; and who, in uninterrupted succession, had maintained in the Episcopal Chair, the genuine doctrine of Scripture and the English Church." [3] There was great opposition to his translation to Derry on the ground that he was "a sermon reader", who read "every line", so that "tradesmen despise him".[4] Edward Wetenhall, whom Henry Dodwell numbered with Hooker, Hamond, and Stillingfleet among "the great worthies of our Church", came to Ireland as Master of King Charles' Hospital in Dublin, and became in turn Precentor of Christ Church, Bishop of Cork in 1679, and Bishop of Kilmore in 1699. According to James Bonnell he excelled in "extempore preaching and practical casuisticalness", and was "besides a good master of critical learning and a scholar beyond most." [5] He had an open mind on the authorship of the Epistle to the Hebrews,[6] and he was a devotional and liturgical writer of merit. Towards the close of the reign of Charles II Thomas Wilson, a native of Cheshire and a medical student of Trinity College, was being drawn to the ministry of the Church through the influence of Michael Hewetson, a Prebendary of St Patrick's. No doubt Wilson, when made deacon at Kildare in 1686, would have continued his ministry in Ireland but for the threatened undermining of the national Church by James II. Instead he became curate to his uncle, Richard Sherlock, himself a graduate of Trinity, who had spent the first eight years of his ministry in Ireland. So the early influences on "the

[1] H. Cotton, Fasti, I, 15.   [2] Op cit., 58.   [3] Works, I, lvii.
[4] Tanner Letters, 453.   [5] Quoted from C. A. Webster, Diocese of Cork, 293 seq.
[6] He thus began his sermon at Bonnell's funeral in 1699, from Heb. 2. 23: "The eloquent and learned author of the Epistle ... St Paul, or St Luke, or St Barnabas, or whoever...".

Apostolic Bishop of Man" were directly and indirectly those of the Church of Ireland.

The Church of Ireland suffered far more severely than the Church of England under James II. Vacant bishoprics were filled by Roman Catholic titulars; churches restored at great cost since 1660 were in many cases badly damaged, if not demolished, or alienated to foreign rites; and at the darkest hour assemblies of Anglicans altogether forbidden. Loyalty to the Church made it extremely difficult for Irish Churchmen not to regard William III as a great deliverer and benefactor. Consequently the Irish Caroline tradition of Churchmanship was little shaken by any non-juring schism, though the Church of Ireland provided that movement in England with two of its ablest writers, Henry Dodwell and Charles Leslie. Dodwell, a disciple of Jeremy Taylor, had published before leaving Ireland *Two Letters of Advice. I. For the Susception of Holy Orders. II. For Studies Theological, especially such as are Rational* (1672), which were strongly recommended by Primate Margetson to Divinity students at Trinity, and *An Introduction to a Devout Life* by Francis de Sales "Fitted for the use of Protestants". In 1683 Bishop Anthony Dopping recommended him for the Provostship of Trinity as "a person of most excellent and profound learning in divinity and other sciences, and of a most grave, pious, and apostolical life".[1] Leslie, declared Dr Johnson, "was a reasoner, and a reasoner who was not to be reasoned against". His *Case stated between the Church of Rome and the Church of England* and his *Answer to the Bishop of Meaux* were included in the course for Divinity examinations at Trinity in the early nineteenth century, his works were praised by pre-Tractarian Churchmen, and the publication of his whole works in 1832 was regarded as a prelude to the Tractarian Movement. Opposed to doctrinal and liturgical innovation, Charles Leslie as a controversial writer represents the Irish Caroline tradition at its best.

V. LATER CAROLINE CHURCHMEN

Our picture of Caroline Churchmen would be incomplete without William King and some of his contemporaries, who were brought up in Caroline times and witnessed to Caroline ideals in the early eighteenth century. King had entered Trinity College the year of Jeremy Taylor's death, had suffered imprisonment under James II, and on becoming Bishop of Derry in 1691 had found his diocese ravished by the recent wars and its churches damaged or demolished. His controversial works against

---

[1] *H.M.C., Ormonde* (N.S.), VI, 544.

Peter Manby, the Dean of Derry who turned Romanist, and in defence of Anglican Worship, are a valuable guide to late Caroline Churchmanship, though he is better known as the author of *De Origine Mali* (1692), and for his sermon, *Divine Predestination and Fore-knowledge, consistent with the Freedom of Mans Will* (1709). King was a keen advocate of the daily offices, of weekly Communion, of catechizing, of open churches, and of the Church's public discipline. "I visited twenty-one Churches", he informed Archbishop Narcissus Marsh in July 1701, "and confirmed in nine; it held me employed twenty-three days. I carried my consistory with me, and prescribed penance to near an hundred people, for one thing and another, and ended several causes. I have yet another circuit containing about thirteen Churches, and had one before." [1] He had great crowds of dissenters everywhere and discoursed to them "generally showing the non-necessity of a separation on their own principles".[2] Since 1 June he had been "every day more or less on horse back, excepting two or three days";[3] and early in August he went on to Armagh to hold a metropolitical Visitation for Primate Boyle,[4] who had become increasingly infirm.

On his translation to Dublin in 1703 King showed great energy in restoring ruined churches and providing new ones, particularly in the growing parts of the city of Dublin. In addition to the annual Visitation of his diocese and the triennial Visitation of his province, King held diocesan and provincial synods. "Let me observe further to your Grace", he wrote to Archbishop Wake in 1717, the year in which the English Convocation was silenced,

that the Clergy of Ireland never made such a submission as the Clergy of England did to Henry the VIII, nor have we, that I know of, any law making it penal to us to make Provincial Constitutions. We have several of these Provincial Constitutions remaining, and an account of the synods that enacted them, and particularly in Queen Mary's reign. The Diocesan Synods are kept up in many dioceses, and I believe rules and orders may be made in them as is allowed by our 26th Canon for the Bishops to make them in their Visitations, as Bishop Bedell did in a synod of his diocese before the year 1641.[5]

The provincial Synod

has been dropt in the other three provinces, but has all along been kept up in that of Dublin, and is so still, according to ancient custom; and at it appear all the

[1] Mant, II, 105.   [2] Ibid.   [3] Ibid.

[4] Ibid., 106. King appears to have visited for Primate Boyle the diocese of Armagh four times and the whole province at least once.

[5] Quoted from William Reeves, "Convocation and Diocesan Synods in England and Ireland", *Report of the Church Congress held at Dublin 1868*, 249.

Bishops of the province, the Deans, Archdeacons, and Proctors of the Chapters, and other Clergy.[1]

A diocesan Synod, held in St Patrick's Cathedral in 1719, agreed to Offices King had drawn up for the "Consecration and Restauration of Churches" in the diocese of Dublin. In the *Discourse*, appended to the consecration form, King strongly advocates the provision of, and attendance at, the daily offices in the new Church, the making of obeisance on entering it, and the exercise in it of "Ecclesiastical Discipline". The new church, moreover, should stand open all day, for King knew from his own observation "that thousands have omitted their prayers, for the want of a place where they could conveniently offer them". Rich men had their closets for private prayer, but the poor had no privacy. "To these the Church is a retirement; there they can be free from the cries of their children, from the noise of their fellow-servants, from the importunity of people that have business with them, and from the sight of everything, that may divert, vex, or any way interrupt them; and hence it was, that the Church formerly stood open all day." [2] Into the framework of the older Irish consecration form of 1666 King inserted prayers of his own composition. One of them assumes the exercise of public discipline in the new Church.

O Merciful God, who hast founded thy Church, and, for the Preservation of Order and Discipline, hast committed the Keys of the Kingdom of Heaven to the Ministers thereof, charging them to reprove, rebuke, and admonish thy People with all Authority, and to cut off from the Communion of the Faithful, such as continue obstinate and disobedient: Grant, we beseech thee, that they who shall exercise this Power in the Assemblies of thy Saints, which are to be held in this Place, may always faithfully discharge that most sacred Trust, and so use the Severity of Discipline, that it may tend to the Good of the Whole, reform the Wicked, and encourage the Obedient, and even bring those, who are cut off thereby from the Society of Christians, to a Sense of their Guilt, that their Souls may be saved in the Day of the Lord. All which we beg for the Sake of thy Son Jesus Christ our Lord. *Amen.*[3]

In 1724 King wrote to Bishop Wilson of Man, who had been im-

[1] Quoted from William Reeves, "Convocation and Diocesan Synods in England and Ireland", *Report of the Church Congress held at Dublin 1868*, 250.
[2] *Offices to be used For the Consecration of a Church new built... 1719*, 34 seq. Likewise Archbishop Narcissus Marsh, in his Charge to the clergy of the provinces of Cashel (1692) and Dublin (1694) thought it "very unbeseeming (to say no worse)" that some Churches "stand shut all the week long". He required them to be kept open for the future.
[3] Ibid., 16.

prisoned for excommunicating the Governor's wife, urging him to continue steadfast in the exercise of ecclesiastical discipline, and complaining that the Bishops in England had almost laid all thoughts of it aside, in spite of the obligations that Christ, and the Laws ecclesiastical and civil, laid Bishops under. Wilson should not despond, but go on with new resolution and more caution. "We have Christ's promise to be with us to the end of the world, and if we do not fail in our endeavours, he will not fail of his word, and, therefore, I think no pains or costs ought to deter us from exerting ourselves in the cause of the Church." [1] No less apostolical than Bishop Wilson, King within a year of his death declared to Bishop Maule of Cloyne: "There is no stopping in this course, till God call us from it by death. I would have you propose no other example, but St Paul himself, and compare the progress you make to his. I am ashamed, every time I think of the course he ran, when I compare it with my own. I was consecrated on the day we celebrate for his conversion, and proposed him to myself for a pattern. But God knows how short the copy comes of the original." [2]

The greatest of King's contemporaries of English birth was Narcissus Marsh, who came over from Oxford to be Provost of Trinity in 1678, and who became Bishop of Ferns (1683), Archbishop of Cashel (1691), of Dublin (1694), and of Armagh (1703-14). His Charge to the clergy of the province of Cashel in 1692, repeated to the province of Dublin in 1694, is a mine of pastoral information and deserves to be better known. It deals with method in preaching,[3] funeral sermons,[4] the visitation of the sick,[5] the frequency and performance of Divine Service and Holy Communion, and with open churches. Other Bishops of English birth included Robert Huntington of Raphoe, who before becoming Provost of Trinity had spent many years as Chaplain at Aleppo, making interesting researches, procuring the translation of the Book of Common Prayer into Arabic, and establishing contacts with representatives of Eastern Churches; Thomas Milles, Bishop of Waterford (1708-40), "a learned Churchman of the Laudian and Caroline School", who "came from Oxford to Waterford introducing altar-pieces, separation of sexes in Church, and

---

[1] T.C.D., Transcript of King's Letters, III, 218 seq.

[2] Mant, II, 495.

[3] Scholastic terms, Latin and Greek quotations, etc. should be avoided. Sermons should be related one to another so that the people "in a little time may be well acquainted with the whole body of divinity".

[4] These should not be over lavish in praises of the dead, "lest others may thereby think themselves secure in following their examples".

[5] Caution not to "send some to Hell with false hopes, and let others go to Heaven without any", and not to "give Absolution upon slight repentance".

other customs of the kind, now regarded as modern ritualistic innovations";[1] and Charles Lindsay, Archbishop of Armagh (1714–24), who
like Bishop Milles had Jacobite sympathies. Of the older generation of
King's Irish contemporaries Richard Tenison, Bishop of Meath (1697–
1705)[2] and Thomas Smith, Bishop of Limerick (1695–1725) were exemplary; while John Vesey, Archbishop of Tuam (1679–1716), the sole
survivor of the Convocation of 1661–6, the biographer of Bramhall and
editor of his works, rebuilt Hollymount Church and had it dedicated
in 1714 in honour of "St Charles Late King of England and Martyr",[3]
and in May 1715 served with Archbishop King as one of the three Lords
Justices during the absence of the Lord-Lieutenant.

King, however, put his greatest trust in the younger generation of
Bishops of Irish birth, who had been members of the Lower House of
Convocation (1703–11) and shared his high sense of pastoral duty and his
anti-Erastian view of Church policy. The Lower House had insisted on
its status as part of a spiritual synod, and complained that they had only
been called in a civil capacity "as attendents and counsellors to the parliament" by the royal writ in the clause *praemunientes*. In their ecclesiastical
capacity they regarded it as absolutely essential to be summoned by
provincial writ. Accordingly the Upper House appealed for provincial
writs to the four Archbishops, after the precedent of 1661, and so the
clergy of the kingdom were able later to meet "in a perfect and entire
Convocation".[4] King thought the Lower House showed far more zeal
for the welfare of the Church than the Upper, which he feared was more
interested in the secular than the spiritual profit of the Church.[5] The
Lower House, he told Archbishop Vesey, had "sent up messages with
ample matter for canons", yet nothing was done.[6] It had petitioned,
inter alia, for a stricter observance of certain rubrics and Canons,[7] for
frequent Confirmations at convenient centres, for monthly Communions
in all churches; for stricter inquiry into the ordination of Romanist
priests received into the Church, and for their employment in the conversion and instruction of the Irish; for further use to be made by Bishops
of the counsel and assistance of Deans and Chapters in important matters,
particularly in the examination of ordinands; for the pastoral care of

---

[1] G. T. Stokes, Introduction to *Pococke's Tour in Ireland in 1752*, 6.
[2] Bishop of Killala (1682–91), of Clogher (1691–7).
[3] "... et in futurum a nomen Sancti Caroli nuper Anglice Regni et Marteris ..."
Instrument of Consecration in Tuam Diocesan Registry.
[4] Mant, II, 164.   [5] Ibid., 177.   [6] Ibid.
[7] Canons relating to excommunication, ordination, the life and conversation of
ministers.

every parish however few the Church members; and the holding of consistory courts at centres more convenient to the people summoned.[1] The Lower House also passed Resolutions on two works "of great Piety and Charity". (1) The bringing of French Protestant refugees into the communion of the Church of Ireland, by an affectionate Exhortation in French and in the name of the Synod, and by a published collection "out of the most eminent foreign divines of those passages wherein they approve of Episcopacy and the doctrine and Liturgy of our Church, and wherein they recommend conformity with us to those of their own Churches who come into these kingdoms". (2) The bringing of Irish Romanists into the Church by a concentrated mission in every diocese by Irish-speaking preachers.[2]

King, however, was disappointed in the work of the Convocation. In 1711 he complained bitterly to Swift, who was in London promoting the temporal interests of the Church of Ireland and helping Mr Richardson to get the Bible, Prayer Book, and Catechism printed in Irish, that the conversion of the natives was by no means desired by everybody, although the Irish Canons required Divine Service to be performed in Irish in Irish-speaking districts.[3] On 10 November 1711 King told Swift that the Convocation had at last drawn up a Representation[4] on the state of religion, to which he took exception.[5] "We have agreed likewise on some canons, of no great moment,[6] and some forms of prayer, and forms of receiving Papists, and sectaries, which, I think, are too straight. I brought in a paper about residence; but there was no time to consider it, nor that which related to the means of converting Papists. I did not perceive any zeal that way."[7] The four first Irish Canons of 1711 deal with ecclesiastical discipline and the imposition of penances, and the fifth with clandestine marriages. One of the forms of Prayer agreed upon was certainly *A Form of Prayer for the Visitation of Prisoners Treated upon...and agreed upon...in the Year* 1711, which became an integral part of the

---

[1] Also for the report of the proceedings of the last annual Visitation and Synod, and for more frequent parochial Visitations. The items are given fully in T.D.C., MS. F. 3. 24.

[2] Ibid.

[3] Mant, II, 224.

[4] *A Representation of the Present State of Religion, with Regard to Infidelity, Heresy, Impiety, and Popery: Drawn up and Agreed to by Both Houses of Convocation in Ireland,* "Printed by Order of the Upper House...", 1711.

[5] Mant, II, 228.

[6] *Constitutions and Canons Ecclesiastical Treated upon by the Archbishops and Bishops and the Rest of the Clergy of Ireland in their Synod Holden at Dublin Anno Domini 1711.*

[7] Mant, II, 228.

Book of Common Prayer as Printed in Ireland from 1721.[1] This office, Caroline in tone, contains prayers of great beauty and reveals deep pastoral insight.[2] The "forms for receiving Papists and sectaries", which King says this Convocation agreed to in 1711, are not so easy to identify. *A Form for Receiving Lapsed Protestants, and Reconciling Converted Papists to our Church* appeared in larger Prayer Books in Ireland from 1721 to 1757, but the identical office had already appeared in the edition of 1700.[3] Possibly the Convocation in 1711 gave their sanction to this existing form; but no order of the Lord-Lieutenant in Council appears to have been given for annexing this or any similar form to the Book of Common Prayer.

Of the members of the Lower House who became Bishops during King's lifetime Peter Browne, Bishop of Cork and Ross (1710–35), a former Provost of Trinity, was a philosopher and controversialist, a promoter of Caroline ideals, who celebrated the Communion with such reverence that those who heard him thought it "a heavenly composition", and who left behind a manuscript book of prayers steeped in the language of Jeremy Taylor. John Stearne,[4] the author of *Tractatus de Visitatione Infirmorum* (1697) and a munificent benefactor, examined his ordination candidates for a week exclusively in Latin.[5] Edward Synge, Archbishop of Tuam (1716–42), was the author of *The Gentleman's Religion in Three Parts, Catholic Christianity, Honesty the Best Policy*, and many popular tracts on prayer, the Catechism, Confirmation, Holy Communion, self-examination, and other subjects, and it was said that "his life was as exemplary as his writings were instructive". Theophilus Bolton, Archbishop of Cashel (1732–44), strongly recommended by King for Ferns in 1722, being "owned by all to be the best civilian and canonist in the Kingdom",[6] founded a diocesan library, furnishing it with a complete set of the Greek and Latin Fathers, where sixty years later John Jebb, the future Bishop of Limerick, pursued his patristic studies. Henry Maule,[7] another Caroline Churchman, was a promoter of Charter Schools; and

---

[1] With slight amendment in the General Synod in 1875 this office remained part of the Irish Prayer Book until the revision of 1926.

[2] In a contemporary number of *Pietus Londiniensis* we read under Ludgate Prison Chapel; "The most prudent layman reads, if no clergyman is in prison."

[3] This office is not to be confused with Bishop Dopping's similar office of 1691, though it may be Caroline in origin like the 1666 consecration form with which it was printed from 1700 to 1757.

[4] Bishop of Dromore (1713–17), Clogher (1717–45).

[5] S. Burdy, *Life of Philip Skelton*, in *Works*, I, xxii seq.

[6] Mant, II, 374. Bolton became Bishop of Clonfert in 1722, and of Elphin in 1724.

[7] Bishop of Cloyne (1726–32), Dromore (1732–44), Meath (1744–58).

as Rector of St Mary's, Shandon, had taken an active part in the foundation of the Green-Coat School at Cork, with its rule of attendance at the daily Offices and catechizing three times a week, and its library furnished with works by Jewel, Bramhall, Taylor, Wetenhall, and Robert Nelson. Nicholas Forster, Bishop of Raphoe (1716-44), had a high percentage of resident clergy, and took care of the religious instruction of the young people and the fabric and ornaments of the churches, in his diocese.

This high standard of pastoral care might have been extended and longer continued had Archbishop King been promoted to the Primacy on the death of Primate Marsh in 1714 or of Primate Lindsay in 1724, or had more Irishmen of worth recommended by him been appointed Bishops. From 1724, however, the Church of Ireland tended to become paralysed by what Bramhall would certainly have regarded as a serious "impediment out of the East". In 1724 Hugh Boulter, a fanatical Whig, was translated from Bristol to Armagh, and immediately he declared war on Archbishop King and the Bishops of Irish birth, requesting that none but Englishmen be put into great places in Ireland. "If I be not allowed to form proper dependences here", he wrote to the Duke of Newcastle, "to break the Dublin faction on the bench, it will be impossible for me to serve His Majesty further than in my single capacity." [1] He demanded that the next Archbishop of Dublin, although King was to live another four years, the Lord Chancellor, and the Master of the Rolls should all be Englishmen.[2] He distrusted Archbishop Synge, who had supported King in carrying "the words *great wisdom* to be added to his Majesty's *goodness* and *condescension* for which we were to thank his Majesty, for putting an end to *Wood's* patent".[3] He feared the appointment of Theophilus Bolton, then Bishop of Elphin, to Dublin, for he was "an enterprising man" and "would soon set himself, if he had that station, at the head of the Irish interest here".[4] Nor should he be translated to Cashel, since he was "as dangerous an Irishman as any on the bench".[5] In 1725 he asked Newcastle to have Swift, a "fomenter" of "disturbances" in Ireland, watched during his visit to England,[6] and in 1737 on the occasion of lowering of gold in Ireland complained that the Dean had

---

[1] *Letters* (Dublin, 1770), I, 12.
[2] Ibid., II, 17 seq.
[3] Ibid., I, 34 seq.; but the words *great wisdom* were thrown out after a long debate. (Ibid., 35.)
[4] Ibid., 115 seq. Bolton had made a speech in the Irish Lords "with very false reasonings, and some inflaming passages against England". Ibid., 191.
[5] Ibid., 134.   [6] Ibid., 51.

E

"raised some ferment" [1] and insulted the government.[2] He frustrated the appointment of George Berkeley to the deanery of Down in 1731 "by a villainous letter" representing him as "a madman and disaffected to the government".[3] He distrusted Trinity College as a nursery of the Irish faction and a potential "seminary of Jacobitism".[4] He entirely lacked that sense of humour which enabled Laud and Strafford a century before to fall in with Ussher's conception of a free national Church. On the other hand, he welcomed the promotion in 1727 of John Hoadly to Ferns, partly because he had "a great value and friendship" for his brother, Benjamin Hoadly, then Bishop of Salisbury, and partly because "he has spirit to help to keep up the English interest here".[5] Shortly before King's death Boulter recommended Hoadly for Dublin, for he had already proved "very hearty for the English interest".[6] Hoadly not only succeeded King at Dublin in 1729, but Boulter in the Primacy from 1742 to 1747, when George Stone, like Boulter and Hoadly a promoter of the English interest and of Whiggish Latitudinarianism, became Primate. The promotion of Englishmen to Irish Bishoprics not only represented a growing ascendency of the English interest over the Irish, but the impact of the growing Erastianism of the Church of England upon the free national Church of Ireland, whose Caroline tradition had been little disturbed by any non-juring schism, and which had to some extent retained diocesan, and in Dublin provincial, Synods, public ecclesiastical discipline, and a non-Erastian view of Church policy. And yet the Caroline tradition survived.

The survival of Caroline Churchmanship is largely owing to the remarkable part played by Trinity College in the life of the Church of Ireland. Restored to conformity with the Church of Ireland and its Caroline Statutes in 1660, Trinity College has been the spiritual training-ground of many of the clergymen and laymen of the Church of Ireland. In 1676 Andrew Sall witnessed to the devout behaviour of the students at the three daily statutory services, which were kept up all through the eighteenth century; in 1724 Swift claimed that the students were "trained with a much greater discipline than either in Oxford or Cambridge"; and in 1756 John Wesley never saw such decency in any chapel in Oxford as he saw at the Holy Communion in Trinity Chapel on 3 April.[7] Con-

---

[1] *Letters* (Dublin, 1770), II, 162.
[2] Ibid., 192. By setting a black flag on the tower of St Patrick, and causing a "dumb peal" to be rung "with the clappers of the bells muffled". Ibid., n.
[3] *H.M.C., Egmont*, 224.   [4] *Letters*, I, 145, 226.   [5] Ibid., 138.   [6] Ibid., 219.
[7] "Scarce any person stirred or coughed or spit from the beginning to the end of of the Service." *Journal*, under 3 April 1756.

servative in character, Trinity College has handed down to modern times a sound tradition in the teaching of philosophy and theology.

Nor must we overlook the important part taken in the life of the Church of Ireland by her lay members: the citizens of Dublin who attended and loved the daily offices while the citizens of London were clamouring for the abolition of episcopacy; the Rawdons at Lisburn and the Hills at Hilsborough, who kept up Anglican worship in their homes during the Commonwealth; James, Duke of Ormonde, who protected the Church of Ireland until 1647 and promoted her interests at the Restoration, a man of exemplary piety, whose integrity shone out in the notoriously corrupt Court of Charles II; John Stearne, the first President of the College of Physicians, who sought the approbation of proscribed Irish Bishops for works he published during the Commonwealth; Henry Dodwell; Dr Dudley Loftus, whom Ussher encouraged in the collection of liturgical and Oriental texts, who found an Armenian copy of St Mark's Gospel ending at the eighth verse of the last chapter, and who went on publishing works of antiquity which he believed to be "mighty confirmations of our tenets against Papists and Sectaries";[1] the members of the Religious Society of St Catherine's in Dublin, who in the middle of the eighteenth century made it their business "to reinforce upon one another the principles of Christianity, to live up to the doctrines of our Church, and to frequent the Holy Sacrament every Lord's Day, and the public prayers every day"; Edmund Burke, who wrote on the devout observance of Good Friday in *The Reformer* of 7 April 1746; Richard Houghton, a Dublin physician, who in 1771 published *Part of the Spiritual Works of the Celebrated Francis Fenelon, Archbishop of Cambray*, to which five Bishops, four Deans, and three Archdeacons of the Church of Ireland subscribed; Alexander Knox, a promoter of the older Anglican theology, who had an enormous influence upon clergy and laity alike; the laity who subscribed so generously when their Church was suddenly disendowed; the laity of to-day, who, though they in some ways worship with greater simplicity than their Caroline ancestors, yet exhibit the same strong sense of membership of, and loyalty to, their ancient Church.

Perhaps the most interesting Caroline layman was James Bonnell, whose early years were spent at the diocesan school at Trim, and who returned to Dublin as Accomptant-General in 1684. He was a weekly communicant, constant at the public daily Morning and Evening Prayer, and a strict observer of the Feasts and Fasts of the Church. His biographer, Archdeacon Hamilton, has happily given selections from Bonnell's

[1] *Tanner Letters*, 454.

meditations, and shortly after his death in 1699 published his *Harmony of the Gospels...with Meditations*. Hamilton found among his papers "some parts of the Greek Fathers, particularly Synesius, translated by him into English", together with "a correct translation of *The Introduction to a Devout Life* by St Francis de Sales". A man of wide reading and culture, he read many of the Fathers and Anglican Divines, of whom Hooker was a favourite. Hamilton holds Bonnell up as an exemplary member of the Church, "who has all the accomplishments she can give him; who has fully imbibed of her doctrine; gives himself up to the conduct of her laws; who joins daily in her devotions, and receives the Holy Sacrament from her hands; who partakes of her extensive charity, and is actuated by her primitive spirit." The Church of Ireland "he honoured and loved; and her misfortunes he bewailed; he saw her constitution primitive and apostolical; her doctrine pure; her Services rational and heavenly." [1]

It is difficult to find a *terminus ad quem* for our study of Caroline Churchmanship in Ireland where the Caroline tradition and spirit have survived in so many ways into modern times. For we can see it in the continued use of patristic evidence against Romanist additions to the Creeds; in the continued emphasis upon the apostolic ministry and succession against Romanist claims; in the teaching of Bishop Berkeley (d. 1753), whose sermons[2] H. G. Rose believed "to form a very precious monument of his truly Christian and Catholick spirit", and most of whose letter to Sir John James (1741) could have been written a century before; in the Discourses of Philip Skelton (d. 1787) which convey in simple and forceful language the main trends of Caroline doctrine, and early in the next century in the writings of Alexander Knox, Bishop Jebb, C. R. Elrington, and William Palmer, one of Jebb's first ordinands, whom Newman thought to be "the most thoroughly learned of the Tractarians". We can see it in the high pastoral standards of many of the clergy in town and country, Henry Echlin,[3] Philip Skelton,[4] John Fitzgibbon,[5] and others;

---

[1] *The Exemplary Life and Character of James Bonnell Esq., Late Accomptant General of Ireland* (1829 ed.), 212.

[2] H. G. Rose collected twelve of the notes of Berkeley's sermons preached at Long Island, and these together with a few entire sermons and other ecclesiastical remains were published in A. C. Fraser's edition of Berkeley's works. Other sermons were published by A. A. Luce in *Hermathena* (1932) and by J. Wild in his *George Berkeley* (1936). The fullest and richest collection of Berkeley's sermons etc. is given in Vol. VII of Dr A. A. Luce's *Works of George Berkeley*.

[3] Vicar of St Catherine's, Dublin (1716–52); see p. 182.

[4] Skelton's vigorous pastoral methods in three country parishes of the diocese of Clogher are fully described in his *Life* by Samuel Burdy.

[5] Vicar of St John's, Limerick (1820–32); see pp. 147, 159.

in the same care for the poor which we found in Ussher and his Caroline contemporaries shown by King, Swift, Berkeley, and Skelton; in the weekly collection for the poor continued from Caroline times into the nineteenth century; in the careful preparation of children for Confirmation;[1] and in the greater frequency than in England of celebrations of the Holy Communion. The Caroline tradition, little disturbed by the non-juring movement, was overwhelmed neither by the Whiggish Latitudin-arianism of Primates Boulter, Hoadly, and Stone, nor by the Act of Union of 1800, by which the Church of Ireland in great measure lost her identity as "a free national Church", nor by the Church Temporalities Act of 1833, which suppressed the archbishoprics of Cashel and Tuam together with ten bishoprics, nor by the Irish Church Act of 1869, by which the ancient endowments of the Church of Ireland were confiscated by the State, nor by the subsequent revision of the Prayer Book and Canons. "Disendowment", declared Archbishop Gregg in 1932, "has taken from us nothing that was spiritually ours. The Church of Jeremy Taylor, James Bonnell, George Berkeley, Richard Mant, Alexander Knox, John Jebb is for us the living home of grace that it was for them." [2]

[1] Palmer testifies to the care with which he was prepared in Ireland for Confirmation, and after Confirmation for the Holy Communion. *A Narrative of Events connected with the Publication of the Tracts for the Times*, 13.
[2] Report on *Church and State*, II, 220.

IRISH CAROLINE TEACHING

I. CAROLINE PRINCIPLES

IRISH Caroline Divines wrote in defence of those common Anglican principles which the Church of Ireland shared with the Church of England. While regarding their Church as "a free national Church", they thought of her as being part of what we would call to-day the Anglican Communion. No Irish writer before Edmund Burke, however, appears to have used the term "Anglican".[1] Ussher, with his strong loyalty to his ancient national Church, uses the terms "Church of Ireland" and "Church of England" interchangeably; Bramhall and Taylor often speak of the Church or Churches "of England and Ireland"; but almost invariably Irish Divines apply the term "Church of England" to the Anglican Church as a whole, not, as Bramhall explains, "of the English nation alone, but the British dominion, including the British, and Scottish or Irish, Christians".[2] Thus Bishop Berkeley, who was born, educated, and ordained in Ireland, where also he held all his ecclesiastical preferments, declared: "As Plato thanked the gods that he was born an Athenian, so I think it a peculiar blessing to have been educated in the Church of England." [3] In other words, Berkeley was thankful that he had been brought up not only as a member of the Church of Ireland but of the Anglican Communion. Irish Caroline and later writers used the term "Protestant" unashamedly, never in a party sense, but of the Anglican Church as a whole, to distinguish it not only from the Church of Rome but also from Dissent. In the same way they use the term "Catholic" of the Church as a whole,[4] and they would certainly regard its exclusive use by

---

[1] Letter to R. Burke (1797). In the next decades "Anglican" is frequently used by Alexander Knox, Jebb, Mant, and Whately, in Ireland, and also by some English writers, no doubt as a convenient alternative to "the United Church of England and Ireland" (1801–70). In England "Anglican" had occasionally been used by Caroline writers.

[2] *Works* (L.A.C.T.), I, 113.   [3] *Works* (ed. A. C. Fraser, 1901), IV, 532.

[4] In Bishop Dopping's office for admitting "Romanists to the Communion of the Church of Ireland", the penitent, standing without the Church door, is told that "the Arms of the Catholic Church are always open to embrace" the penitent (1691). For an interesting definition of "Catholic" see *A Familiar Exposition of the Church-Catechism* by Isaac Mann, Bishop of Cork (1772–99).

the High Church Party as being objectionable and illogical as its exclusive use by members of the Church of Rome. From Ussher to Palmer Roman Catholics are called "Romanists".

"We bring in no new faith, no new Church", declared Ussher. "That which in the time of the ancient Fathers was accounted to be truly Catholic, namely, that which was believed *everywhere*, *always*, and *by all*, that in the succeeding ages hath evermore been preserved, and at this day professed in our Church." [1] To the question, "Where was your Church before Luther?", Ussher replied that "our Church was even where it now is: in all places of the world, where the ancient foundations were retained, and those common principles of faith, upon the profession whereof men have ever wont to be admitted, by Baptism, into the Church of Christ." [2]

With Ussher Irish Divines took their stand upon "the ancient foundations", and by "those common principles of faith", which the third General Council of the Church, held at Ephesus in 431, had safeguarded under severe penalties. For this Council had decreed it unlawful for any man to publish another faith or Creed than that which had been delivered at the Nicene Council; and "that whosoever should dare to compose or offer any such to any persons willing to be converted from paganism, Judaism, or heresy, if they were Bishops, or Clerks, should be deposed— if laymen, anathematized." [3]

The Court of Rome had violated this Canon, declared Bramhall, and "obtruded a new Creed upon Christendom".[4] "The Court of Rome would have obtruded upon us new articles of faith; we have rejected them: they introduced unlawful rites into the Liturgies of the Church and use of the Sacraments; we have reformed them for ourselves: they went about to violate the just liberties and privileges of our Church; we have vindicated them." [5] "We do not challenge a new Church, a new religion, or new holy orders: we obtrude no innovation upon others, nor desire to have any obtruded upon ourselves; we pluck up the weeds, but retain all the plants of saving truth." [6] Bramhall had not the least doubt "but that the Church of England before the Reformation and the Church of England after the Reformation are as much the same Church, as a garden, before and after it is weeded, is the same garden." [7] "The Churches of England and Ireland", he affirmed in the Irish Convocation of 1634, had been reformed "by the same principle and rule of scripture, expounded by universal tradition, councils, fathers, and other ways of

---

[1] *Works* (ed. C. R. Elrington), II, 493.   [2] Ibid.
[3] Concil. Ephes. Part Secund. Art. 6. c. 7. Quoted from Bramhall, *Works*, I, 25.
[4] *Works*, I, 25.   [5] Ibid., 101.   [6] Ibid., II, 313.   [7] Ibid., I, 113.

conveyance".[1] They had been reformed, he affirmed at Christ Church, Dublin, on Charles II's Coronation Day, not tumultuously, "but soberly according to the rule of God's Word, as it hath been evermore and everywhere interpreted by the Catholic Church., and according to the purest fathers of the primitive times".[2] Our Church was "as careful to retain old articles of faith, as it is averse from new articles; the essence of all things do consist *in indivisibli*; faith is adulterated, as well by the addition of new articles, as by the substraction of old." [3]

In the *Dissuasive from Popery*, written at the request of the Irish Bishops, Taylor takes his stand by the Canon of the Council of Ephesus,[4] and sets out to show that the Roman Church, by making additions to the Creeds, "is neither Catholic, Apostolic, nor Primitive".[5] The first four General Councils, Taylor maintains, "are so entirely admitted by us, that they, together with the plain words of scripture, are made the rule and measure of finding heresies among us;[6] and in pursuance of these it is commanded by our Church that the clergy shall never teach any thing as matter of faith religiously to be observed, but that which is agreeable to the Old and New Testament, and collected out of the same doctrine of the ancient fathers and catholic bishops of the Church." [7] It was easier for Anglicans than for Romanists to show their religion before Luther. "And although they can shew too much practice of their religion in the degenerate ages of the church, yet we can and do clearly shew ours in the purest and first ages: and can and do draw lines pointing to the times and places where the several rooms and stories of their Babel was builded, and where polished, and where furnished." [8]

Bishop Roger Boyle in 1681 held that our Church differed from the Church of Rome only by the warranty of reason, Scripture, and the holy Fathers.[9] "Sure", claimed Bishop William King in 1687, "if Scripture, Tradition, and Council of Nice were sufficient authority to warrant Athanasius to oppose himself to the whole world, Scripture, Tradition, and Councils were sufficient authority for the Reformers to oppose themselves to a general and prevailing corruption that had no Scripture, Tradition, nor Council nor any thing but prevailing custom to support it, till the Council of Trent afterwards made it an Article of Faith." [10] King

---

[1] See above, p. 13.   [2] *Works*, v, 123.
[3] Ibid.   [4] *Works* (ed. Eden), vi, 1827.   [5] Ibid., 180 seqq.
[6] 2 Eliz. I, c. 1. 36. The Irish Act does not mention the assent of Convocation.
[7] Ibid., 182. This appeal to an English Canon of 1571 was legitimate since Taylor was a member of a Convocational committee for revising Canons on the basis of all English and Irish canons up to 1641.   [8] Ibid., 225.   [9] See above, p. 41.
[10] *A Vindication of the Christian Religion and Reformation...*, 24.

had already claimed that the old question, Where was your Church before Luther? had often been answered by showing that we made "no new Church at the Reformation, and we kept all the essentials of faith and worship received by our ancestors, and the same Creeds, the same God, Christ, Baptism, and Eucharist; and lastly, were governed by the same Bishops and Governors before and after the Reformation." [1]

In *A Form for Receiving Lapsed Protestants, or Receiving Converted Papists to our Church*, bound together with larger Irish Prayer Books from 1700 to 1757, there is a Form of Abjuration "answering in every point the new Articles of Pius the Fourth his Creed". Priests and likely teachers are further required to renounce "all other doctrines and decrees of the Council of Trent as far as they contradict the Thirty-nine Articles, or the Liturgy and Canons of the Church of England and Ireland", and to promise, by reading and study of the Scriptures, "together with the writings of the purer and more uncorrupt Fathers, especially of the three first centuries, to endeavour the perfect knowledge of the whole Body of Christian truth", and never to hold, teach, or maintain what is not agreeable to Scripture "interpreted by the joint consent of the said Fathers".

"The sincere Christians of our Communion", affirmed Bishop Berkeley in 1741, "are governed, or led, by the inward light of God's grace, by the outward light of His written word, by the ancient and Catholic traditions of Christ's Church, by the ordinances of our national Church which we take to consist all and hang together." [2] Berkeley disowned those who "without regard to the Holy Spirit, or the Word of God, or the writings of the primitive Fathers, or the universal uninterrupted traditions of the Church, will pretend to canvass every mystery, every step of Providence, and reduce it to the private standard of their own fancy; for reason reacheth not those things." [3]

In an ordination sermon of 1810 John Jebb, later Bishop of Limerick, shows that the Anglican Reformers were guided by the principle, "to innovate, is not to reform". They refused to cast away "the gold of Christian antiquity" because it had been mixed with "the adscititious dross" of later times. "They were not prepared, to desert the adamantine foundation, which was laid by the Apostles and Prophets; or the super-structure of gold, silver, and precious stones, which was raised by the Catholic Bishops and Fathers, merely because some wood, hay, and

---

[1] *Answer to...Peter Manby*, 9. For Andrew Sall's answer to the same question, see *True Catholic Faith...*, 330.
[2] *Works*, (ed. Dr A. A. Luce), VII, 146.   [3] Ibid.

stubble, had been added by workmen of inferior note." They felt that "the unanimous concurrence of councils, churches, bishops, and fathers, ought to be received as the voice of the Gospel".[1] In the Appendix to his *Sermons* of 1815 Jebb, like Taylor, appeals to the clause in 2 Eliz. I, c. 1. 26 and to the English Canon of 1571. He also appeals to the Preface *Concerning the Service of the Church* which makes "the godly and decent order of the ancient Fathers" the standard of our worship. "The standard of our worship is, in truth, the standard of our faith." [2]

Thus Caroline Divines and their successors took their stand by Scripture and antiquity. They further emphasized, on the one hand, their agreement with Christians of other traditions in these fundamental principles, and on the other the room for latitude in matters which concerned not these fundamental principles. Ussher readily acknowledges that the Greek Church follows antiquity in its prayers for the dead and in its form of absolution. Bramhall holds that the Greek Church agrees with the Anglican Church, and differs from the Roman, in fundamental principles. In the rule of discipline, "the Grecians and we have the same government of Bishops under Patriarchs and Primates". In the rule of faith,

the Grecians and we have both the same canonical Books of Scripture, both reject their Apocryphal additions from the genuine canon; they and we have both the same Apostolical Creed, both reject the new additions of Pius the Fourth; in sum, they and we do both deny their Transubstantiation, their Purgatory, their Justification by works "*in sensu forensi*", their doctrine of Merits and Superogation, their septenary number of Sacraments, their Image-worship, their Pardons, their private Masses, their Half-communion; and, to be brief, the Grecians do renounce and reject all those branches of Papal power, which we have cast out of the Church of England.[3]

Caroline Divines also regarded themselves as having internal communion, as we shall see, with other Christian bodies in so far as they adhered to, but not where they departed from, those common fundamental principles of faith.

Within the limits of the Anglican *via media*, paved by Scripture, Councils, and Fathers, there was room for diversity of emphasis on matters of secondary importance. Ussher, in early days, shared the prevailing Augustinian views of the age, which were promoted by Archbishop Whitgift of Canterbury and by Florence Conry, the Roman Catholic Titular Archbishop of Tuam (1609-29), whose published works on

[1] *Practical Theology*, I, 135 seq.
[2] *Sermons on Subjects chiefly Practical* (2nd ed.), Appendix, 360 seqq.
[3] *Works*, II, 634.

St Augustine had a profound influence on Jansen. Ussher found that the doctrines of Predestination, Grace, Freewill, Works, Justification, and Satisfaction were held by Sedulius and Claudius, "two of our most famous divines", while the contrary doctrines had been brought into the Church by Pelagius and Celestine, "the greatest depressors of God's grace and the advancers of man's abilities".[1] While breaking away from his early Calvinist influences Ussher held that these questions had been of old discussed by the Church and indifferently maintained by the doctors. He thought that the moderation of Remigius in the case of Gotteshaulus was much needed in the present controversies and that the Arminian High Churchmen were being immoderate.[2]

Bramhall, on the other hand, thought that Ussher's Irish Articles of 1615 were immoderate, whereas the English Articles left sufficient latitude for diversity of opinion in matters that concern not the Christian faith.[3] Dean Rust of Connor, a minor Cambridge Platonist, in 1663 claimed that in matters of opinion the Anglican Church allowed "so fair a latitude, that a sober, and ingenious spirit can hardly desire a greater" and "will no where else find there so much".[4] Jebb in 1810 claimed that the English Articles were "less rigid; more liberal, and less relaxed; more orthodox, and less dogmatic, than those of any other society, at present in existence." Those who framed them were "not desirous either literally to coincide with, or unlimitedly to dissent from, any particular communion, whether that of Geneva, Augsburgh, or of Rome. For it can be established, by a cloud of witnesses, that the Sacred Scripture was their text; and the harmony of all churches in all ages their great expositor."[5]

Among Irish Divines there long remained a variety of emphasis regarding the nature of the Church. The Augustinian view of the Church had come in with the Augustinian conception of grace; and the Irish Articles had distinguished between the one Catholic Church, identical with the Communion of Saints and designated the "Invisible Church",[6] and the "Visible Church", in which "the evil be ever mingled with the good".[7] In the post-Restoration period Bishop Ezekiel Hopkins likewise distinguished between the Visible Church, "the Kingdom of God's grace", and the Invisible Church.[8] In Taylor's Baptism Office of 1658 the child is admitted "into the bosom of the visible Church, the kingdom of grace", and prayer made that he may be God's "servant in the kingdom of grace",

---

[1] *Works*, IV, 259. [2] See above, p. 7. [3] See above, p. 13.
[4] *A Sermon Preached at New-Town The 29 of October 1663 at the Funeral of ... Lord Viscount Montgomery of Ards*, 38.
[5] *Practical Theology*, I, 138. [6] Article 68.
[7] *Ibid.*, 70. [8] *Works*, I, 82 seqq.

and God's "son in the kingdom of glory".[1] But in the *Dissuasive from Popery* (Part II) Taylor makes it clear that the Invisible and the Visible Church are not two Churches in separation from each other, "or that one can be seen of men and the other cannot; for then we must either run after the church, whom we ought not to imitate; or be blind in pursuit of the other church that can never be found." Though the members be visible, yet "that quality and excellency by which they are constituted Christ's members and distinguished from mere professors and outsides of Christians" is invisible.[2] Charles Leslie, who was no Calvinist, maintains that the article in the Creed about "the holy Catholic Church" is qualified in the next by "the Communion of Saints", that is, "only the elect, who are not visible upon earth, and therefore must be referred to heaven, where only is the true communion of saints, without mixture of the reprobates, who are not members of Christ, and are but in appearance of the Church" with whom we have no unity of spirit and are not one body (2 Cor. 6. 14, 15). "Therefore the archetypal and truly Catholic Church in heaven is that which is chiefly and principally meant by the holy Catholic Church, and the Communion of Saints in the Creed: and there only is perfect unity." [3] As we shall see, Bishop Berkeley used the Augustinian view of the Invisible Church as a useful mode of expressing internal communion with the good members of the Roman Catholic Church with whom there could be little hope of external communion.[4] William Palmer held that "the sanctified and elect are principally the Church of Christ", and "invisible" in the sense that they are not discernible as "essentially members of the Church" from hypocrites and false brethren, yet they are also visible members of the Church.[5] Although the Church of Ireland was comparatively free from Calvinism from the Restoration to about the third decade of the nineteenth century,[6] the Augustinian view of the Invisible Church appears to have had its influence on Divines who by no means held the Augustinian view of grace.

At this point we may usefully notice an estimate of the Caroline Divines by one who was very much in their tradition. While Jebb had a deep respect for their ability and erudition, he believed that "they excelled, rather in detail, than in comprehensiveness; rather in elucidating detached

---

[1] See below, p. 86.
[2] *Works*, VI, 340.   [3] *Works*, III, 73 seq.   [4] See below, p. 78.
[5] *Treatise of the Church*, I, 30 seq.
[6] Professor G. T. Stokes maintained that up to 1830 "Evanglical Theology, instead of being dominant, was struggling for bare existence in Ireland." Letter to *Guardian* (14 Sept. 1887).

portions of Christianity, than in exhibiting the Christian scheme, as a complete and well-regulated whole." They had raised "from the mines of antiquity, gold, silver, and precious stones, for the service of the sanctuary; but other workmen, more fully acquainted with the plan of the great Architect, will be necessary, to carry the edifice upward, to its full perfection." In the meanwhile, "new fields have been opened, in metaphysical divinity, in sound criticism, and in the philosophical study of Christianity, as a progressive scheme. Both the Greek and Hebrew Scriptures, have been diligently collated with the best MSS., and ably edited, both at home and abroad." The German divines "have afforded critical aids to the advanced student in theology, which, if used with caution, may be used with advantage".[1] The Caroline Divines were indeed limited by the philosophical outlook of their age and by rather an obscurantist attitude to Scripture; and we may well regret that Ussher exhausted his energy on Biblical chronology, and did not apply his critical genius to Biblical sources. Yet they "chalked out the path" in fundamental principles for the Anglican Communion; and the Church of Ireland, more certainly than any other branch, has from Caroline times followed the Anglican *via media*, "treading in the same hallowed steps with Vicentius, and the Catholic Bishops, and the ancient Fathers: proceeding as far as they proceeded, and stopping where they stopped."[2]

II. THE MINISTRY

(a) *The Irish Hierarchy and Formularies*

Although the Church of Ireland from earliest times has retained the three Orders of Bishops, Priests, and Deacons in her Ministry, the Order of Bishops has often suffered diminution. From the sixth century to the

---

[1] *Practical Theology*, I, 141 seq.

[2] John Jebb, *Sermons on Subjects chiefly Practical* (1816 ed.), Appendix, 360. The claim put forward by Dean R. G. S. King at the Church of Ireland Conference in 1932 is firmly in the tradition of Ussher, Taylor, Bramhall, King, Berkeley, and Jebb. The Church of Rome, he held, had ignored the warnings of Ephesus and added new professions of belief. "We hold the ancient faith declared by the Church at Nicea, and Constantinople, at Ephesus, and Chalcedon. They do not. If the Fathers of Ephesus were with us to-day they would join in the Creed with us. They would not join in the Creed of the Roman Church, that of Pope Pius put forth in 1564. For they would have no other Creed but the Nicene, and so it was in the Old Church. They were Catholic, Pius was Roman. We stand with them being Catholic, we refuse to stand against them as the Romans do." "The Reformation Period" in *The Church of Ireland A.D. 432–1932*, 135.

twelfth the Church of Ireland became isolated, her organization monastic, and her Bishops, without diocesan jurisdiction, subject to the coarb, whether abbot or abbess, of the monastery to which they belonged. In the twelfth century the diocesan system, already set up in the Norse settlements of Dublin, Waterford, and Limerick, was extended by the Synod of Kells in 1152 to the whole of Ireland, which was divided into four provinces and many dioceses. The four Archbishops, receiving their palls from the Pope, tended to become agents of centralization whereby the Bishop's pastoral office was continually invaded. In Elizabeth's reign most of the existing Marian Bishops continued in their sees and gave to the Church of Ireland an unbroken episcopal succession. "Ireland", claimed Bramhall, "never wanted a store of ordainers, nor ever yet did any man object want of a competent number of consecrators to an Irish Protestant Bishop." [1] Overruling the wish of Ebor Ellis, appointed to Kildare, to be consecrated in England, Archbishop King explained to the Primate in 1705: "Our succession in Ireland is more clear and unexceptionable than our neighbours, and therefore 'tis better to stick to it." [2]

With an unbroken episcopal succession the Church of Ireland, unlike the sister Church, retained until her disestablishment the medieval machinery of metropolitan Visitation, which some of her Caroline Divines regarded as an almost papal invasion of the diocesan Bishop's pastoral office by the Archbishop. We have seen how Bishop Bedell objected to Primate Ussher's "Bull of Prohibition", stating that in the year of the Metropolitan's Visitation, "the whole and entire jurisdiction of the diocese belonged to him... because of the great danger of souls of the people". Bedell felt that a greater danger of souls lay in the suspension of the Bishop's jurisdiction. Likewise at the Restoration, Griffiths Williams, Bishop of Ossory, complained that every third year the Irish Bishop stood in the same relation to his Archbishop as the *Legatos a latere* to the Pope, and only had "a Jurisdiction *ad placitum*, and so little better than a Cypher".[3] Williams complained that the Archbishop swallowed up almost all the jurisdiction of the Bishop in the year of triennial Visitation: for two or three months before he visited, then at the Visitation, and for another six months, or more at the Archbishop's pleasure.[4] The period of inhibition of the Bishop's jurisdiction gradually grew shorter until in Bishop Mant's time it was "at least in practice, limited to a few weeks, instead of being extended

---

[1] *Works*, III, 52.   [2] Mant, II, 175.
[3] *The Sad Condition of the Church and Clergy in the Diocese of Ossory, and I fear not much better in all Ireland*, 47.
[4] Ibid. This book was censured severely by the Irish Upper House in 1665.

throughout the year, as was the case when it encountered Bishop Bedell's reprobation".[1]

It has been suggested that the Church of Ireland was less explicit in her formularies than the Church of England regarding episcopal government. The Irish Articles of 1615 took over the English Article 23 ("Of Ministers in the Congregation") but not 36 ("Of Consecration of Bishops and Ministers"), which by its reference to the book of Ordering of Bishops, Priests, and Deacons, makes clear what Article 23 means by the words, "lawfully sent". The mind of this earlier Convocation (1613–15) on episcopacy, however, is revealed in the unpublished Canons drawn up at its request in 1614 under the care of Ussher, when Chancellor of St Patrick's. The second of these, which Nicholas Bernard found in Ussher's own hand, prohibits the use of any other form of ordination in this nation, "but which is contained in the book of Ordering of Bishops, Priests, and Deacons, allowed by Authority, and hitherto practised in the Churches of England and Ireland".[2] The Irish Articles, moreover, were laid aside in 1634, when the English Articles were adopted, and cannot justly be said to have any bearing on the displacement of Presbyterian ministers in the province of Armagh at the Restoration.[3] The Irish Canon 32 of 1634 also fixed the form of clerical subscription in Ireland as a declaration of "consent to the first four Canons of the present Synod, and everything containing therein". The fourth Canon, subscribed by all Irish clergy until the Disestablishment, leaves no doubt whatever about the mind of the Church of Ireland concerning episcopacy. It begins by repeating the substance of Ussher's draft Canon 2 of 1614, but adds: "And if any shall affirm that they who are consecrated or ordered according to these Rites are not lawfully made, nor ought to be accounted either Bishops, Priests, or Deacons; or shall deny that the Churches with this Government are true Churches, or refuse to join with them in Christian profession, let him be excommunicated, and not restored until he repent, and publicly revoke his error." The Church of Ireland thus required of her clergy a more particular assent to episcopal government than was required by the more general terms of the English form of clerical subscription for 1603 to 1865.

(b) The Ground of Episcopacy

The Church of Ireland had taken over an unbroken episcopal succession at a time when there was no settled theory of episcopacy in the west, and

---

[1] Mant, I, 443. [2] N. Bernard, Clavi Trabalis, 62.

[3] Alexander Gordon, in Articles on Bramhall and Taylor in D.N.B., and some of Taylor's biographers, imply that the Irish Articles were still in force in 1661.

when its primitive character was being further obscured and threatened with even greater diminution at the Council of Trent. The authority and order of Bishops in the Church of Ireland, Taylor maintained in 1664, "is preserved against the usurpation of the pope and the invasion of schismatics and Arians new and old".[1] Caroline and later writers sought a middle course between what Dean Graves in 1806 termed "the despotism of papal usurpation" and "the anarchy of indiscriminate equality". They appealed to Scripture and antiquity to establish, on the one hand, the equality of the apostolic mission and commission, and, on the other, the disparity from the beginning of the three Orders of Bishops, Priests, and Deacons. Sometimes they defended episcopacy from the attacks of Presbyterians, who tended to regard episcopacy as papacy in another form, sometimes from papal claims. In the one case they had to demonstrate episcopacy to be a scriptural and primitive institution ever to be continued in the Church: in the other that this scriptural and primitive institution had been undermined by papal centralization and invasion.

Anglicans, however, were not alone in their appeal to antiquity, and their case for episcopacy had been weakened by leading apologists, Whitgift, Hooker, Andrewes, and Jeremy Taylor, who quoted indiscriminately from the twelve epistles attributed to Ignatius. Ussher himself had done the same in his *Answer to a Jesuit* of 1625, but from 1628 he laboured to restore the true Ignatius, and by establishing the text of the epistles he believed to be genuine did the greatest possible service to the Anglican defence of episcopacy.

Three years before his work on Ignatius was brought to light, Ussher published in 1641 a tract on *The Original of Bishops and Metropolitans*, in which he confined his quotations from Ignatius to what his work of 1644 was to establish as the genuine text. "The ground of episcopacy", Ussher maintained, "is derived partly from the pattern prescribed by God in the Old Testament, and partly from the imitation thereof brought in by the Apostles and confirmed by Christ Himself in the New."[2] The Angels of the Seven Churches, to whom Christ indited letters, were "such as in the next age after the apostles were by the fathers termed bishops".[3] They were Bishops in name and authority, whose Churches were not barely parochial, but diocesan, and whose jurisdiction was metropolitical.[4] Patristic evidence is effectively produced for the episcopal succession at Ephesus,[5] Smyrna,[6] Rome,[7] Corinth,[8] and Jerusalem,[9] and the witness

[1] *Works*, VI, 284.   [2] Ibid., VII, 43.   [3] Ibid., 59 seq.
[4] Ibid., 61.   [5] Ibid., 47 seq.   [6] Ibid., 50 seq.
[7] Ibid., 52 seq.   [8] Ibid., 53.   [9] Ibid., 54 seq.

of Irenaeus cited to "the succession of bishops, unto whom the apostles committed the charge of the Church in every place".[1] Likewise evidence is given for the early metropolitical status of Ephesus and Rome.[2] Ussher thought it well worth observing, "that the fathers of the great Council of Nice, afterwards confirming this kind of primacy, in the bishops of Alexandria, Rome, and Antioch, in the metropolitans of other provinces, do make their entrance into that Canon with "τα ἀρχαιᾶ ἔθη κρατ εττω, Let the Ancient customs continue".[3]

In the same year Ussher drew up a scheme of Synodical Church government to meet a desperate situation in England. From the Fathers and ancient Canons Ussher, in the Preface, shows that Presbyters often joined with Bishops in the government of the Church, just as they were charged in the Anglican Ordinal to administer "the discipline of Christ". Of the four propositions the second is the most interesting. The number of suffragan Bishops being "conformed unto the several Rural Deaneries into which every Diocese is subdivided", the Deanery Synod would meet every month, and at it impenitent persons presented from the weekly Parish Meeting (I), if impenitent still, would be excommunicated. The Diocesan Synod (III), consisting of all suffragan Bishops and of representative, if not all beneficed, clergy from every Deanery, would meet once or twice a year; and (IV) provincial Synods, or a national Synod, might be held every third year.[4] The scheme was thought to entrench too far upon the Bishop's authority. Ussher knew that the Rural Deaneries of his former diocese of Meath had in the twelfth century been for the most part tiny dioceses which were not altogether absorbed into the larger diocese of Meath until the thirteenth. He had also himself, like other Irish Archbishops, entrenched upon the jurisdiction of the Bishops of his province every third year. This scheme deals exclusively with Church organization and government, and should be examined only in the light of Ussher's positive affirmation in episcopacy as an apostolical institution "confirmed by Christ Himself".

With Ussher, Bramhall and Taylor believed that episcopacy was confirmed by Christ himself in the letters indited to the Seven Angels in the Revelation.[5] Daniel Burston, in a book strongly commended by the Irish Convocation in 1663, held that the testimonies of Scripture and antiquity revealed Christ to be the sole legislator of the Church and "the

---

[1] Ibid., 52.   [2] Ibid., 62 seq.   [3] Ibid., 63 seq.
[4] Ibid., XII, 527 seqq. The scheme is also given in Collier, *Ecclesiastical History* (1840 ed.), VIII, 387 seqq.; *Synodalia* (Feb. 1855), 160 seqq.; *Theology* (Jan. 1947).
[5] Bramhall, op. cit., I, 271; Taylor, op. cit., V, 35.

F

Fountain head of all purely ecclesiastical authority and power"; and that Christ "ordained and confirmed the apostolic office, at, and after, his Ascension, as a standing office to be continued with his Church".[1] In 1732 Swift asked, "Whether episcopacy which is held by the Church to be a divine and apostolical institution, be not a fundamental point of religion, particularly in that effectual one of conferring holy orders." [2] In 1767 Philip Skelton cited John 20. 21 to show that the authority of the Bishop was "the authority of God". " 'As my Father hath sent me', said Christ to his apostles, 'so send I you'; and so sent they their successors; so sent Paul his Timothy to Ephesus, and his Titus to Crete, to ordain and govern the two lower orders of the Church, and to preside over the whole laity, no less than clergy..." [3] In 1810 Jebb held that Christ's promise in Matthew 28. 18–20, was "not occasional or temporary, like that of miraculous powers: but conveying an assurance, that Christ himself, will, in spirit and in power, be continually present with his Catholic and Apostolic Church; with the Bishops of that Church, who derive from the Apostles, by uninterrupted succession; and with those inferior, but essential orders of the Church, which are constituted by the same authority, and dedicated to the same service." [4] "The power to institute Sacraments as means of grace and salvation", C. R. Elrington believed, "can rest in Christ alone; and in Him alone must also rest the power of sending those who can minister them. That authority then of serving in Christ's Church can only be had by an uninterrupted succession of persons empowered by Christ to qualify others." [5] Likewise Bishop Mant repeatedly dwells on the apostolical succession, and his "Hymn Commemorative of the Ministerial Commission" represents episcopacy to be of Divine institution.

> Lord, by whose care thy Church arose
> A goodly frame, Thy Church defend:
> And bless her Pastors, sent by those
> Whom Thou hast given power to send.[6]

Another view was sometimes expressed that although episcopacy was not directly of Divine institution, it had been established by the apostles under the direction of the Holy Ghost or in obedience to the Will of

[1] *The Evangelist yet Evangelizing, submitted to the Judgement and Censure of the Churches of England and Ireland*, 107.
[2] *Works*, (ed. J. Hawkesworth, 1767), III, 290.
[3] *Works*, III, 395; cf. 360 seqq.   [4] *Practical Theology*, I, 117.
[5] *Apostolical Succession* (Dublin, 1839), 12.
[6] *Hymns from the Roman Breviary, to which Original Hymns are Appended* (1836).

Christ. Thus Bishop Downham (d. 1633) held that what the apostles did in the execution of their apostolical function they did by the direction of the Holy Ghost (Acts 15. 28; 20. 28); and in the ordination of Timothy, Paul was certainly the instrument, but the Holy Ghost the author and director, "for he was made Bishop by Prophesy".[1] In 1722 Edward Synge, later Bishop of Elphin, affirmed that episcopacy was agreeable to the Will of Christ "because settled by the apostles, who fully knew his will, were entrusted with the execution of it, and had the assistance of the Holy Spirit to guide and conduct them in all important actions relating to the settlement of the Christian Church".[2] The usages observed by the Bishop in ordination, claimed Bishop O'Beirne of Ossory in 1796 "have been derived, through the apostles, from the Lord himself".[3]

Other Divines appealed to tradition. Bishop Berkeley, for example, maintained that the advantages of Church membership "are conveyed unto us in a regular dispensation by the hands of a Hierarchy constituted by the Apostles, and from them continued down to us in a perpetual succession". This if it may "not be demonstrated from Scripture, is nevertheless sufficiently evident from tradition, a tradition so ancient, so universal, so uninterrupted that the Canon of holy Scripture itself is not received on better grounds. And surely what comes thus recommended to us has an equal claim to our zeal, with the other positive institutions of Christianity, [and] is to be treated with no more coldness and indifference than if it had been expressly contained in the written word of God."[4] Archbishop Synge of Tuam thought that those who maintained that the government of the primitive Church had undergone a change after the death of the apostles must have credulity enough "to receive all the fables of the Legend for true history".[5]

Or again, we find at the opening of the nineteenth century the same careful investigation into the early history of episcopacy which Ussher made in 1641. Thus Dean Graves in a consecration sermon of 1806, claimed that it was possible to trace back

catalogues of the succession of bishops presiding over every church, from the latest period of the Roman empire, even to their original appointment by the apostles—at Jerusalem and Rome, at Antioch and Smyrna, at Alexandria, Ephesus

[1] *Two Sermons, the One commending the Ministrie in Generall: The Other Defending the Office of Bishops*, 91 seq., 94.
[2] *The Constitution of our Established Church, as founded on Law Divine and Human, consider'd*, 10.
[3] *Sermons ... Charges* (London, 1799), 275.
[4] Op. cit., VII, 20.
[5] *The Divine Authority of Church-Government and Episcopacy*, 1 seq.

and Crete. We find the order recognized, and obedience to its jurisdiction enjoined, in the most forcible and earnest manner, by the truly apostolic Clement, in his epistle to the Corinthians: and by the pious and venerable Ignatius, in his epistles to the Churches of Magnesia and Philadelphia, Smyrna, Trallia, and Ephesus—without any, the remotest hint, that amongst the bishops of those Churches, or of Rome, (to which he also addressed an epistle), any one possessed universal supremacy, much less infallible authority.[1]

(c) Apostolic Succession and Regiment

Just as Ussher set the historical investigation of primitive episcopacy on the soundest basis, so Bramhall (d. 1663) provided the most powerful defence of primitive episcopacy against its invasion by papal centralization. The Roman Church, Bramhall held, was neither Apostolical, orthodox, nor Catholic, because it had changed the Apostolical Creed, succession, regiment, and communion. It had changed the Apostolical succession "by engrossing the whole succession to Rome, and making all other Bishops to be but the Pope's Vicars and substitutes, as to their jurisdiction".[2] Without abolishing episcopacy in the abstract the Popes limited the power of Bishops in the concrete at their pleasure by exemptions and reservations, "making all episcopal jurisdiction to flow from them, and to be founded in the Pope's laws", on the ground that "it was but delegated to the rest of the Apostles for term of life, but resided solely in St Peter as an ordinary, to descend from him to his successors, Bishops of Rome, and to be imparted by them to other Bishops as their vicars or coadjutors, assumed by them into some part of their charge".[3] "By this account", Bramhall maintained, "the Pope must be the universal or only Bishop of the world; the keys must be his gift, not Christ's; and all the Apostles except St Peter must want their successors in Episcopal jurisdiction."[4] In this way episcopacy was trampled upon, and the line of Apostolical succession taken away.[5] Later Irish Divines made the same point. The papacy, Charles Leslie contended, "would engross the whole episcopal power into the single see of Rome, by making all other Bishops dependent upon that which only they call the apostolical chair".[6] The Bishop of Rome, Philip Skelton believed, "had made himself the only Bishop, and reduced all the rest to cyphers".[7]

---

[1] *Works* (ed. R. H. Graves), III, 602.
[2] *Works*, I, 72.   [3] Ibid., 252.   [4] Ibid.
[5] Ibid. Taylor also held "the pope's universal bishopric" to mean that the Pope only is a Bishop "by immediate divine dispensation, and others receive from him whatsoever they have: for to this height many of them are come at last." *Works*, VI, 218.
[6] *Works*, (Oxford, 1842), VII, 125.   [7] *Works*, III, 360.

The Roman Church had also changed the Apostolical regiment, Bram-hall believed, "by creating a visible and universal monarchy in the Church".[1] The twelve apostles were "equal in mission, equal in commission, equal in power, equal in honour, equal in all things". "No single Apostle has jurisdiction over the rest." [2] The Fathers held "all Bishops to be Vicars and ambassadors of Christ (not of the Pope)".[3] "The sovereignty of episcopal power was in the Apostolical College, to which a general Council now succeedeth." [4] The Christian world for the first six centuries never knew of this "universality of jurisdiction, and sovereignty of power above general Councils".[5] The Popes had violated the decree of the Council of Ephesus by invading and occupying provinces which "formerly and from the beginning" were not under their own or their predecessors' power.[6] "They *quitted* their pretended Patriarchal right, when they assumed and usurped to themselves the name and the thing of Universal Bishops, Spiritual Governors, and sole Monarchs of the Church and Masters of Christendom." [7]

Jeremy Taylor also held that "the apostles governed all" and "exercised a common jurisdiction", and that in the whole New Testament there is "no act or sign of superiority, or that one apostle exercised power over another; but to them that Christ sent He in common entrusted the Church of God." [8] "This unity and identity of power without question and interruption did continue and descend to bishops in the primitive Church, in which it was a known doctrine that the bishops were successors of the apostles; and what was not in the beginning could not be in the descent, unless it were innovated and introduced by a new authority." Not only St Peter, "but every apostle, and therefore every one who succeeds them in their ordinary power, may and must remember the words of St Paul, 'We are ambassadors' or legates 'for Christ': Christ's Vicars, not the pope's delegates: and so all the apostles are called in the preface of the mass, *quos operis tui vicarios eidem contulisti prae esse pastores*; they are 'pastors of the flock of Christ'; and so also they are in the express terms of S. Ambrose, and therefore it is a strange usurpation that the pope arrogates that to himself by impropriation which is common to him with all the bishops of Christendom." [9]

---

[1] *Works*, I, 72.   [2] Ibid., 152.   [3] Ibid., 153.   [4] Ibid., II, 288.   [5] Ibid.
[6] Ibid. The same objection could be raised to the Church Temporalities Act of 1833, by which the Archbishop of Armagh was compelled to occupy the province of Tuam, and the Archbishop of Dublin the province of Cashel. Ussher had cited this Canon of Ephesus to show the antiquity of ecclesiastical provinces. *Works*, VII, 67 seq.   [7] Ibid., I, 260; cf. II, 34, 175, 305, 333, 547, 641 seqq.
[8] *Works*, VI, 219.   [9] Ibid., 219 seq.

Irish Divines also believed that the Church of Rome had prepared the way for Protestant Dissent. "We may further ascribe the reviving of the Arian heresy in these latter days," Bramhall affirmed, "to the dispensation of the Court of Rome, who licenced ordinary priests to ordain, and confirm, and do the most essential offices of a Bishop. So their Schools do teach us;—'a Priest may be the extraordinary minister of Priesthood and inferior orders by the delegation of the Pope';[1]—again,—'the Pope may confer the power of confirmation upon a simple priest.' By such exorbitant practices as these, they chalked out the way to innovators. And yet they were not able to produce one precedent of such dispensation throughout the primitive times." [2] Taylor complained that for six centuries the Papacy had "invaded the rights of bishops, and delegated matters of order and jurisdiction to monks and friars".[3] Charles Leslie declared that when the Pope at the Council of Trent failed to have episcopacy, except that of the Bishop of Rome, accounted not to be *jure divino*, he took another method. He set up "a vast number of presbyterian priests, that is, Regulars, whom he exempted from the jurisdiction of their respective bishops, and framed them into a method and discipline of their own, accountable only to superiors of his and their own contriving, which is exactly the presbyterian model".[4] According to Leslie the Jesuits and others who disputed on the Pope's part at Trent "used the same arguments against the divine right of episcopacy, which from them, and the popish canonists and schoolmen, have been licked up by the Presbyterians and other of our dissenters: they are the same arguments which are used by pope and presbyters against episcopacy." [5] "Whosoever would write the true history of presbyterianism must begin at Rome, and not at Geneva." [6]

Bishop Roger Boyle, on the other hand, maintained against the Presbyterians the disparity from apostolic times of the three Orders of Bishops, Priests, and Deacons. The Presbyterians held that although these names were in use in apostolic times, it was not perhaps in the same sense of the words which now they have acquired.

Why are you so suspicious? I will show you why I have no suspicion. These powers existed in the Church in the time of the apostles, for they baptized, preached, celebrated the Eucharist, ordained priests and deacons, etc. 'Yes', say they, 'but surely these duties were not the prerogative of separate orders as they

---

[1] The marginal reference to "Thom Aquin, Summ., P. iii, Qu. lxx. art. 11 ad primum" is given by the nineteenth-century editor, and not by Bramhall.
[2] *Works*, v, 262; cf. ii, 71.   [3] *Works*, vi, 220.
[4] *Works*, vii, 125 seqq.   [5] Ibid.   [6] Ibid., 127.

are now?' All the Churches of the present day (speaking as contemporaries of Calvin) think that they were, and, as nothing is found to the contrary either in Sacred Scripture or in the commentaries of the Holy Fathers, most assuredly they were so. There is much supporting evidence, but nothing to the contrary except turbulent fanaticism. Our Church differs from the Church of Rome in many things, but nowhere without the warranty either of Reason, or of Sacred Scripture, or of the Holy Fathers. The Presbyterians set against the practice of the Universal Church none of these things, but they prefer one man, Calvin, even without argument, to them all. But without proof that these things are different now from what they were in the time of the Apostles, all men of sound judgment will resolve that no change ought to be made, lest happily we oppose the Apostolic Constitution, and so God.[1]

Nor did Boyle understand the Scholastic view that the order of the ordained is transmitted from the order of the ordainer as like to like. He could not see in ordination "any 'physical' action of the ordainer upon the soul of him who is ordained, but only a 'political' one".

A bishop does not therefore join with priests in conferring the order of priesthood because they are all priests, but because a bishop with priests has the power of communicating the order of priesthood; just as the King does not make a baron because he is a baron, but because he is the King i.e. the source of every honour. You will say, "Bishops confer the order of episcopacy, why not priests that of priesthood?" I reply: A bishop belongs to the highest order in the Church and so has authority over all orders.[2]

Early in the decade preceding the Tractarian Movement in England, Divines in Ireland were boldly proclaiming what historians of that movement too often have claimed as a long-forgotten doctrine. "In our own day it has happened", complained Archbishop Laurence in a Charge to the clergy of Cashel in September 1822, "that the sacerdotal functions of our clergy, derived in regular succession from the apostles themselves have been singularly magnified." [3] In the following month Archbishop Magee, in his Primary Charge at Dublin, made a "singularly magnified" pronouncement on the subject. He urged his clergy to contend for "the apostolical origin and succession of the Christian ministry" as "the only ground, on which the just rights of the Church can be maintained, and on which the duty of strict communion can be legitimately enforced". The Church of Ireland was "hemmed in by two opposite descriptions of professing Christians: the one, possessing a church, without what we can properly call a religion: the other, possessing a religion, without what we

---

[1] *Summa Theologie Christianae* (1681), 58 seq.
[2] Ibid., 59.   [3] Op. cit., 19 seq.

can properly call a church: the one so blindly enslaved to a supposed infallible ecclesiastical authority, as not to seek in the word of God a reason for the faith they possess; the other, so confident in the infallibility of their individual judgement as to the reason of their faith, that they deem it their duty to resist all authority in matters of religion." [1]

(d) Non-Episcopal Orders

Notice must now be taken of the attitude of Irish Divines to non-episcopal orders. Ussher could not excuse from being schismatical "the ordination made by such Presbyters as have severed themselves from those Bishops unto whom they had sworn canonical obedience", and although he regarded the Church which had no Bishops as being "very defective in their government, and that the Churches in France, who living under a Popish power, cannot do what they would, are more excusable in this defect than the Low Countries that live under a free State"; yet for testifying his communion with these Churches he was prepared to receive the Blessed Sacrament at the hands of Dutch ministers if in Holland, as he would at the hands of French ministers if in Charentone. For he loved and honoured these foreign reformed Churches "as true members of the Church Universal".[2]

Two Irish Bishops cited Richard FitzRalph, Primate of All Ireland (d. 1360), who said: *Videtur quod si omnes Episcopi simul essent defuncti, Sacerdotes minores possent ordinare Episcopos.* They held that the same situation existed where the order of Bishops was "morally extinct" and the only Bishops to be had were heretical and would demand subscription from orthodox ministers to heretical tenets. Thus Bishop Downham, while condemning ordinations by Presbyters where orthodox Bishops were established, thought Presbyters were wisely brought in "where orthodoxal Bishops could not be had".[3] Bishop Wetenhall in 1678 took FitzRalph to mean that if "all the order of Bishops were extinct (or, which is much the same, were heretical, enemies to the true doctrine of the Gospel, and would ordain none but first sworn to maintain that enmity), who shall say but the power of Ordination justly enough devolves to such Catholic and orthodox Presbyters?"[4] "It is one thing for Presbyters thus deserted and abandoned by heretical Bishops, to assemble and ordain, where there can be, or will be suffered, no ordination by orthodox and truly Catholic Bishops; and another thing for them to

---

[1] *Works*, II, 444.
[2] Quoted from N. Bernard, *Judgment of the Late Archbishop of Armagh*, 125 seqq.
[3] Op. cit., 97.   [4] *Of Gifts and Offices in the Publick Worship of God*, 715 seq.

thrust out such Bishops, usurp their office, and refuse ordination from them." [1]

Bramhall distinguished between those whose strong desire for episcopacy was sufficient to excuse their want of it; those who approved it, "and wanted it only out of invincible necessity"; and those who have "neither the same desires, nor the same esteem, of Episcopacy, but condemn it as an Antichristian innovation and a rag of Popery".[2] The Romanists were no fit persons to object, "whose opiniastrety did hinder an uniform reformation of the Western Church". Their avaricious commissions and delegations, in giving Presbyters episcopal jurisdiction and the power to ordain and confirm, were "the source of these present controversies about Episcopacy and ecclesiastical discipline, which do now so much disturb the peace of the Church".[3] Bramhall dare not "limit the extraordinary operation of God's Spirit, where ordinary means are wanting, without the default of persons".[4] Anglican Divines did not unchurch foreign Protestant Churches.[5] They distinguished between "the true nature and essence of a Church, which we do readily grant them, and the integrity and perfection of a Church which we cannot grant them, without swerving from the judgement of the Catholic Church".[6]

Other Divines were less ready to excuse reformed Churches whose ordinations had always been without Bishops. While leaving them to stand or fall to their own Master, Jeremy Taylor thought "those good men might have had order from the bishops of England or the Lutheran Churches".[7] Charles Leslie thought their excuse a poor one. "They might have had bishops from other places, though there were none among themselves, but those who were popish: and they might as well have had bishops as presbyters without the countenance of the civil magistrate. It might have raised a greater persecution against them; but that is nothing to the truth of the thing: and if they thought it the truth, they ought to have suffered for it." [8] No doubt Jeremy Taylor and Charles Leslie would have approved of the desire of the Spanish Reformed Church for episcopacy, and of the consecration of Señor J. B. Cabrera in 1894 by the Archbishop of Dublin and the Bishops of Clogher and Down[9] on Spanish territory, but not of the telegram of condolence sent by the English Church Union to the Roman Catholic Archbishop of Toledo.

[1] Ibid. [2] *Works*, II, 70. [3] *Ibid.*, 71.
[4] Ibid., III, 475. [5] Ibid., 517.
[6] Ibid., 578. For Bramhall's letters of Orders, see p. 33 seq.
[7] *Works*, V, 121. [8] *Works*, VII, 179 seq.
[9] Or of another consecration for the same Church in 1956 by the Bishop of Meath and two Bishops of the American Episcopal Church.

We find the same refusal to unchurch members of foreign reformed Churches in William King,[1] Philip Skelton,[2] and William Palmer, all powerful asserters of episcopacy. In his *Treatise on the Church* Palmer excuses the first foreign reformers on the ground that they wished to appeal to a General Council, expected reunion with a reformed western Church, and therefore had no desire to set up a rival hierarchy.[3] Palmer claims that his view of the position of the foreign Reformation was the view of the majority of Anglican theologians and Bishops "from the period of the Reformation to the present day".[4]

This traditional view found practical expression in the dual attitude, often misrepresented, of the Church of Ireland to Presbyterians, on the one hand, and to French Protestant refugees on the other. The Presbyterians were concentrated in the province of Armagh, and the general Synod of Ulster exercised a jurisdiction on a territorial basis. From time to time plans were considered for extending the Presbyterian system to other parts of Ireland. At the Restoration, and again at the Revolution, Presbyterians agitated for the abolition of episcopacy.[5] Their "avowed principle", Bishop King of Derry declared in 1696, "is to tolerate nobody when they are in power". "They bring along with them from Scotland", Swift complained in 1708, "a most formidable notion of our Church, which they look upon at least three degrees worse than popery; and it is natural it should be so, since they came over full frought with that spirit, which taught them to abolish episcopacy at home".[6] Swift had read above fifty pamphlets by as many Presbyterian Divines, "loudly disclaiming this idol *toleration*, some of them calling it (I know not how properly) a rag of *popery*, and all agreeing it was to *establish iniquity by a law*". There was no evidence that their successors had renounced this doctrine.[7] "We are fully convinced in our consciences, that *we* shall always *tolerate them*; but not quite so fully that *they* will always *tolerate us*, when it comes to their turn; and *we* are the majority, and *we* are in possession."[8] In Scotland they were in possession and persecuting Episcopalians. In 1693 Alexander Cairncross, formerly Archbishop of Glasgow, in turn persecuted by Presbyterians and deprived by James II, was promoted to Raphoe, partly in compensation for his sufferings and partly to "open an inlet and shelter in his diocese to the Scottish episcopal clergy, who were forced to flee from Scotland".[9] The Sacramental Test, im-

---

[1] *Answer to ... Peter Manby*, 29 seq.   [2] *Works*, III, 367.
[3] Op. cit. (1842 ed.), II, 310.   [4] Ibid., I, 301.
[5] Mant, II, 3 seqq.   [6] *Works* (ed. Hawkesworth), III, 238.
[7] Ibid., 242 seq.   [8] Ibid., 246.   [9] Mant, II, 34 seq.

posed in 1704, seemed to Irish Churchmen a necessary safeguard against a genuine fear of Presbyterian usurpation and persecution of their national Church.[1] Even so, compared with Episcopalians in Scotland, Presbyterians in Ireland had practical toleration, the *Regium Donum*, and really little to complain of.

Although the non-conforming French Protestants might appear to be little removed from Irish Presbyterians in doctrine and discipline, the Church of Ireland regarded their status as being quite distinct. Their forefathers had become separated in France from unorthodox Bishops and from an unreformed Church. The Presbyterians, on the other hand, had rebelled against their lawful and orthodox Bishop both in Scotland and Ireland and had gone out from a pure and reformed Church. At the same time the Church of Ireland, in spite of the Act of 1692 giving them complete freedom of worship, regarded French Protestants as potential members of the Church. In 1702 Bishop Moreton of Kildare wrote a letter to the French congregation at Portarlington, giving notice that he would consecrate their new church and sending a copy of the Irish consecration form of 1666, which he intended to use, translated into French, that they might become "thoroughly acquainted with all our proceedings". Notwithstanding the privileges of the late Act of Parliament they were within his diocese, and consequently within his "pastoral cares". As it was his hearty desire and prayer to God, that they should be "conformable to this innocent and harmless, as well as orthodox Church of ours", so he would make it his constant endeavours, by all gentle and easy means, to bring them all to that conformity. He was "with all sincerity and affection" their "faithful servant in our Lord and Saviour".[2] His accurate translation into French of a markedly High Church liturgical form suggests that this Bishop did not swerve from Anglican principles in his excellent purpose of bringing French Protestants in his diocese to conformity. The Lower House of Convocation (1703–11) had proposed

---

[1] As late as 1780 there was great alarm when a Bill was sent over from England for the repeal of the Sacramental Test. The four Archbishops and Bishops met, sought the help of the English Primate, and strongly recommended a Declaration by office-holders that they did not believe Church of Ireland worship to be sinful and idolatrous etc., without which they feared the Church would soon be overthrown, "and if they adhere to their ancient tenets will not even be tolerated". *H.M.C., Sackville*, 267.

[2] "Letter de My Lord Eveque de Kildare . . . En Anglois & en Francois", prefixed to *Formulaire de la Consecration & Dedicase des Englises & Chapelles Selon l'Usage de l'Eglise D'Irelande. Traduit de l'Anglois par l'Ordre de My Lord Eveque de Kildare & en faveur des Protestans Francois Refugies habitans a Portarlington, Comte de la Reine.* (Copy in N.L.I., L.O.; given in *Hierurgia Anglicana*, III, 189 seq.)

friendly measures for encouraging French Protestants to conformity; but the *Representation*, published by authority of both Houses in 1711, was less friendly in tone. It regretted that these refugees had broken out into nonconforming congregations "in contradiction to the known principles as well of other Reformed Churches and Divines, as of those of *France*; who, since the Reformation, have kept in strict communion with our Church, and on all occasions give ample approbation of our Doctrine and Worship." [1] In *The Case of Protestant Refugees from France considered* Philip Skelton points out that they cannot immediately conform on coming to Ireland being "wholly unacquainted with our language". Afterwards "they seldom or never communicate with our native dissenters", but either keep up their own French congregations, "or come over to the established Church by hundreds every year, and by their unfeigned piety and virtue, rank themselves with the very best members she can boast of".[2] The Book of Common Prayer, translated into French, was published in Dublin, abridged in 1666, and entire from 1715 to 1817.

(e) Internal Communion

Bramhall distinguished between the internal and external communion of "the Christian Catholic Church". The internal communion consisted principally in holding the apostles' doctrine, judging charitably one of another; excluding "none from the Catholic communion and hope of salvation, either eastern, or western, or southern, or northern Christians, which profess the ancient Faith of the Apostles and primitive Fathers, established in the first general Councils, and comprehended in the Apostolic, Nicene, and Athanasian Creeds: to rejoice at their well doing; to sorrow for their sins; to condole with them in their sufferings; to pray for their constant perseverance in the true Christian Faith, for their reduction from all their respective errors, and their re-union to the Church in case they be divided from it", and "to hold an actual external communion with them '*in votis*'—in our desires, and to endeavour it by all those means which are in our power".[3] External communion, on the other hand,

---

[1] Op. cit., 8.

[2] *Works*, III, 380. Among the papers of Dean Letablere of Tuam (1759–75) was found a list of persons of Huguenot extraction living in Ireland. Among those serving in the Church of Ireland at that time were Bishop Chevenix, three Deans, and thirty-three clergymen, besides nineteen ministers of French Churches in various parts of Ireland. Samuel Smiles, *The Hugonots . . . in England and Ireland*, 316. At Portarlington there had been six non-conforming pastors between 1694 and the consecration of the new Church in 1702. From 1702 to 1817 there were five pastors all in episcopal orders. Ibid., 314 n.

[3] *Works*, I, 103 seq.

consists in the same Creeds, Sacraments, Liturgical forms, rites, and ceremonies, communicatory letters between Churches, and the same discipline
and episcopal government.[1] External communion may sometimes be
suspended; but "internal communion is due always from all Christians
to all Christians".[2]

"The Churches of England and Ireland", William King affirms in
1688, "receive the Sacraments and Liturgy of the Grecians and Eastern
Churches, as to the substantials of them. We do indeed disapprove their
novel opinions and late additions to their Services; but yet we do not
think them to be such as to exclude these Churches from being members of
Christ's mystical Body. Hence we do not exclude them from our Communion." [3] "Our Church doth actually communicate in Sacraments
and Liturgy with the foreign reformed Churches." The differences "between her and them are neither in Sacraments nor Liturgy, nor are they
of such consequence as to hinder our members to communicate with them
when they chance to be amongst them, or theirs from communicating
with us." [4] "We communicate likewise with all the knowing and honest
parts of the Churches of France, Spain, and Italy, who were left to their
free choice and not circumvented by fraud, or forced by compulsion."
The Anglican Church also communicated "with all Christian Churches in
those things that they retain of our common Christianity: if they add to,
or diminish from, those necessary truths or practices, we are not obliged
to communicate in their errors." [5]

In commending the needs of non-conforming French Protestant
refugees to members of his own Church, Philip Skelton claimed: "They
are your fellow-Christians, united to you in the same body of Christ...
you feel their distresses through Christ your Saviour, who suffers in their
afflictions." [6] Skelton showed the same attitude to the Roman Catholic
poor when he twice sold all his books to relieve them in time and famine;
and the weekly collection kept up in all Irish Churches throughout the
eighteenth century, chiefly for the relief of the Roman Catholic poor,
suggests that the Church of Ireland regarded them as members of the body
of Christ. Thus we find the Augustinian view of the Invisible Church
sometimes held by Irish Churchmen who by no means held the Augustinian view of grace. It provided a useful mode of expressing internal
communion with the majority of the population with whom there could
be little hope of external communion. "There is an invisible Church,

---

[1] Ibid., 104.   [2] Ibid.
[3] *A Vindication of the Christian Religion and Reformation...*, 29.
[4] Ibid., 30.   [5] Ibid., 32.   [6] *Works*, III, 367.

whereof Christ is the head", writes Bishop Berkeley to Sir John James, who is tempted to join the Church of Rome, in 1741, "the members of which are linked together by faith, hope, and charity." [1]

There is no reckoning the elect by the number of visible members. There must be the invisible grace, as well as the outward sign; the spiritual life and holy unction to make a real member of Christ's invisible Church. The particular Churches of Jerusalem, Antioch, Alexandria, Rome, &c have all fallen into error, (Art. XIX). And yet, in their corrupt and erroneous state, I believe they have included some true members of that body whereof "Christ is the head"; of that building whereof He is "the corner stone".

On the foundation

there may be superstructures of "hay, stubble", and much contemptible trash, without absolutely annihilating the Church. This I take to have been evidently the case. Christ's religion is spiritual and supernatural; and there is an unseen cement of the faithful, who draw grace from the same source, are enlightened by the same "Father of lights", and sanctified by the same Spirit. And this, although they may be members of different political and visible congregations, may be estranged, or suspected, or even excommunicated to each other. They may be loyal to Christ, however divided among themselves. This is the charitable belief of the true sons of our Church, however contrary to the damning temper of Rome, and the sour severity of Dissenters. [2]

III. THE SACRAMENTS

(a) Introductory

The teaching of Irish Caroline and later Divines on the Sacraments stands altogether apart from the Tridentine definitions. "If anyone shall say", decreed the Council of Trent in 1547, "that the sacraments of the new law were not all instituted by Jesus Christ our Lord; or that they were more or less than seven, viz.: Baptism, Confirmation, the Eucharist, Penance, Extreme Unction, Orders, and Matrimony; or that any one of these seven is not truly and properly a sacrament, let him be anathema." [3] Bramhall found the septenary number of Sacraments "never so much mentioned in any Scripture, or Creed, or Father, or ancient author; first devised by Peter Lombard; first decreed by Eugenius the Fourth; first confirmed in the provincial Council of Sens, and again in the Council of Trent." [4] If the word "Sacrament" be taken largely, "then there are

---

[1] *Works* (ed. Luce), VII, 145.   [2] Ibid., 147 seq.
[3] Concil. Trident. Sess. vii. can. 1.   [4] *Works*, I, 55.

God knows how many Sacraments more than seven".[1] If it be taken "strictly for a visible sign, instituted by Christ, to convey and confirm grace to all such partakers thereof, as do not set a bar against themselves, according to the analogy between the sign and the thing signified; and in this sense the proper and certain Sacraments of the Christian Church, common to all, or (in the words of our Church) 'generally necessary to salvation', are but two, Baptism and the Supper of our Lord." [2]

The rest [Bramhall affirms] we retain more purely than yourselves, though not under the notion of such proper and general Sacraments. As Confirmation, Ordination, Matrimony, Penitence (though we neither approve of your preposterous manner of Absolution before satisfaction, nor of your ordinary Penitentiary tax); and lastly, the Visitation of, and Prayer for, the Sick; which only is of perpetual necessity, the unction prescribed by St James being appropriable to the miraculous gifts of healing or recovering men out of sickness then in use, whereas your custom is clean contrary, never or rarely to enoil any man, until he be past all hope of recovery.[3]

It is none of the Anglican doctrine, Jeremy Taylor declared in 1664, "that there are two Sacraments only, but that of those rituals commanded in Scripture which the ecclesiastical use calls Sacraments (by a word of art) 'two only are generally necessary for salvation' ".[4] In 1663 Taylor speaks of Confirmation as a "Sacramental",[5] and observes that the imposition of hands signifies "all the Sacramentals of the Church: it signifies confirmation, ordination, absolution, visitation of the sick, blessing of single persons (as Christ did the children brought to Him), and blessing marriages".[6] This list includes the "other five", but adds the blessing of single persons. Although *Sacramenta et sacramentalia* are often mentioned in English Acts of Consecration of Churches drawn up by clerks of Bishops' chancellors in the seventeenth century, the Irish consecration form of 1666 alone gives liturgical expression to this distinction: "Be present with thy grace in all our ministeries of Sacraments and Sacramentals." [7]

Although Bramhall's definition of a Sacrament appears to agree with the Tridentine statement that Sacraments "confer grace on those who

---

[1] Jeremy Taylor: "The fathers and schoolmen differ greatly in the definition of them, and consequently in the number of them: S. Cyprian and S. Bernard reckon 'the washing of the disciples' feet' to be a sacrament; and S. Austin called *omnem ritum culti divini*, a sacrament, and otherwhile he says there are but two; and the schoolmen dispute whether or no a sacrament can be defined." *Works*, VI, 379.

[2] Ibid. [3] Ibid., 56. [4] *Works*, VI, 422.

[5] Ibid., V, 661. [6] Ibid., 631. [7] Appendix, lines 204 seq.

do not place a bar",[1] he nowhere suggests that "Sacraments confer grace, *ex opere operato*".[2] Roger Boyle, on the other hand, pointed out in 1681 the danger of the Tridentine statement that the Sacraments of the new dispensation confer the grace of which they are the sign.[3] "Thus in Baptism is signified the cleansing of the soul; and when we are baptized we are cleansed. In the Eucharist the body and blood of Christ are signified as being received by the soul, and they are received. If, however, they wish the real and natural body to be signified by the bread, this would not be conceded except by the 'Transubstantiators' or the 'Consubstantiators'."[4] In other words the Tridentine statement could easily be interpreted by the Scholastic theory of the *opus operatum* which Trent upheld. Lest the reception of a Sacrament might be held to be a substitute for grace, Boyle thought it better "to say that sacraments increase grace rather than that they confer it", and that they are "means of obtaining grace from God, than that they are the instruments of God for conferring grace." "Nor can we understand here an instrumentality of bodies in producing spiritual effects (in effectione spiritualium). Aquinas would reply: 'What (Sacraments) do, they do not do through their own form, but through the form of the principal agent—i.e. God.' What is this if not to attribute the whole effect to God and nothing to the sacraments?"[5] The Sacraments are "means for obtaining grace, doubtless by a spontaneous ordinance of God Who decreed that further grace should be conferred upon those who practice grace". The two Sacraments "represent Christ as having suffered for us, so that in celebrating them the whole Gospel is practised. Hence we render praises and we pray, we make confession of faith and we practise charity: and by so great a number of acts of devotion we cannot fail to be more pleasing to God the giver; for He said: 'To him that hath it shall be given.' "[6] Boyle accepts the Scholastic view that the Christian Church is built up "through the Sacraments which flowed from the side of Christ as He hung upon the Cross". "For it is through Baptism that we are born again: it is through the Eucharist that we are fed."[7]

Other Irish Divines wrote on the efficacy of Sacraments with a variety of emphasis. Bishop Bedell held "the grace which the sacraments confer"

[1] Concil. Trident. Sess. vii. canon vi. "Si quis dixerit sacramenta novae legis non continere gratiam, quam significant, aut gratiam non ponentibus obicem non conferre, anathema sit."

[2] Ibid., can. viii.

[3] Op. cit., 271. "Sacramenta novae legis dicuntur conferre gratiam quam significant..."   [4] Ibid., 271 seq.

[5] Ibid., 272. "And indeed the Master of the Sentences says that a sacrament only shows what God does: of which later on the question of Absolution."

[6] Ibid.   [7] Ibid., 274.

to be, "first, the spiritual things which are proportional to the outward; second, the effects of these; third, the certification of the party in the lawful use of the outward, of the two former." [1] He did not disallow the definition of a Sacrament in the Catechism, but thought "incomparably better that of the apostle, 'that they be seals of the righteousness of faith'".[2] Bishop Mossom of Derry regarded the Sacraments as "no empty and bare signs to signify", but as "sacred and moral instruments to convey, real and effectual to confirm", and "gracious and evangelical pledges to assure".[3] To Ussher Sacraments were no bare signs. "Seals they are, as well as signs, of the Covenant of Grace", even "pledges and assurances of the interest which we have in the heavenly things that are represented by them". A picture of the French king is but a bare sign; but the King's Great Seal confirms "the title which he hath unto all the lands and livlihood which he doth enjoy". Although only ordinary wax is affixed to the Letters Patent, yet being applied to this use, it "is of more worth to the patentee than all the wax in the country beside".[4] In *A Form for Receiving Lapsed Protestants, or Reconciling Converted Papists to our Church*, the "two true and proper Sacraments of the Gospel", are declared by the person received to be "each of them means, by which the Holy Ghost does convey Grace".[5]

Two Irish Divines disown the theory of the *opus operatum*. A Sacrament in the hand of God, Taylor believed to be, "a proclamation of his graces". "He gives us notice that the springs of heaven are opened, and then is the time to draw living waters from the fountains of Salvation." [6] They are "instruments of grace in the hands of God, and by these His Holy Spirit changes our hearts and translates them into a divine nature; therefore the whole work is attributed to them by a synedoche." [7] But "the outward work is always the less principal". "God works in us His graces by the sacrament; but we must dispose ourselves to a reception of the divine blessing by moral instruments." [8] "For the rite is so wholly for the mystery, and the outward for the inward, that as no man is to rely upon the external as if the *opus operatum* would do the whole duty, so no man is to neglect the external because the internal is the more principal." [9] Christ's words of Institution, Charles Leslie believed, "*are spirit*, and

---

[1] Letter to Samuel Ward, 1630. E. S. Shuckbrough, *Two Biographies of William Bedell*, 319.

[2] Ibid., 321. Ward had recommended Hooker, who "doth truly explicate the efficacy of sacraments". Bedell replies: "Mr Hooker I have not." Ibid.

[3] *The Preacher's Tripartite*, III, 73.   [4] *Works*, II, 248.

[5] Larger Irish Prayer Books, 1700 to 1757.

[6] *Works*, VIII, 31.   [7] Ibid., 32.   [8] Ibid., 255.   [9] Ibid., V, 634.

G

therein consists the *Life* of all outward institutions, and not in the *opus operatum* of the letter, and of a form of words of human invention, to work like charms".[1]

Apart from Boyle, Taylor, and Leslie, Irish Divines do not appear to notice the *opus operatum* theory. They were far more concerned with the efficacy of Sacraments for personal righteousness. Most of them would agree with Hooker that Sacraments were "powerful instruments of God to eternal life". From Ussher to Jebb the Eucharist is regarded as a divinely appointed means of strengthening, continuing, and nourishing that "stock", "seed", or "principle" of life given in Baptism. This is admirably expressed by Philip Skelton in a sermon on "The Necessity and Efficacy of Spiritual Nourishment".

It is impossible, he should live for ever, who goes not thither; and most highly improbable, that he who goes but seldom should feed the principle of eternal life in himself during a long famine... A real Christian cannot be long absent from the Sacrament, because he knows, that without holiness no man shall see the Lord; that holiness without grace is impossible, and that grace is not to be expected from God, the only dispenser, but in the way of his own appointment. He is perfectly sensible of all this, and therefore never absents himself from the table of God.[2]

"In Baptism", affirms Jebb, "we originally received the gift of God: by the Sacrament of the Lord's supper, the gift then received, is renewed, enlarged, confirmed, strengthened, perfected. By Baptismal Grace, we first became properly, temples of the Holy Ghost: by the grace of the Eucharist we are made special temples, also, of the Son; an habitation meet for the whole three Persons of the ever blessed Trinity."[3]

(b) The Sacrament of Baptism

In the Baptismal controversy of the early nineteenth century writers appealed to the Caroline Divines, and among them Ussher and Taylor. *A Body of Divinity, or the Sum and Substance of the Christian Religion*, brought out under Ussher's name by John Downham, was sometimes cited, though Ussher himself declared that this book "was in divers places dissonant from his own judgement" and that it could not "by any means be owned by him".[4] Ussher's earliest teaching on the Sacraments is given in *The Principles of the Christian Religion*, written in 1603 but not published until 1654. Baptism is defined as "the Sacrament of our admis-

---

[1] *Works*, I, 507.   [2] *Works*, III, 124 sq.
[3] *Practical Theology*, I, 105; cf. 94: "In the former, we behold the divine seed ... in the latter, we may experience, the nourishment of that seed, and its radication in the heart."   [4] *Works*, I, 249.

sion into the Church, sealing unto us our new birth by the communion which we have with Christ Jesus". The water represents "the blood and Spirit of Christ Jesus our Lord"; the "cleansing of the soul by the forgiveness of sins and imputation of righteousness"; the being under the water and the freeing from it again "our dying unto sin by the force of Christ's death and rising again unto righteousness, through his resurrection".[1] Ussher's definition is incorporated in the eighty-ninth Irish Article of 1615: "...but much more a Sacrament of our admission into the Church sealing unto us our new birth (and consequently our Justification, Adoption, and Sanctification) by the communion which we have with Christ." In 1630 Ussher thanks Dr Samuel Ward for communicating to him the Bishop of Salisbury's and his own determination touching the efficacy of Baptism, "for it is an obscure point, and such as I desire to be taught in by such as you are, rather than deliver mine own opinion thereof". Bishop Downham of Derry, in a book ready for the press, "determineth that point of the efficacy of baptism far otherwise than you do: accommodating himself to the opinion more vulgarly received among us; to which he applieth sundry sentences out of St Augustine; and among others that *De baptismo*: 'Sacramentia in solis electis hoc vere efficient quod figurant.' "[2]

In 1630 Dr Ward also corresponded with Bishop Bedell on the efficacy of Baptism. Ward objects that Bedell appears to make the end and effect of all Sacraments to be obsignation, and all ablution of sin in infants to be only conditional and expectative, with no benefit till they believe and repent; whereby infants dying in infancy would appear to have no benefit by Baptism, and non-elect infants no benefit at all—and therefore there would be no necessity to baptize infants.[3] Bedell protests that infants are "received into the visible Church", and presently enter into covenant with God, "wherein God promises pardon of sin, and life eternal, upon their faith and repentance".[4] It is pious to believe that God takes the condition for performed if they die while it is in expectation. "All that come to the sacrament, elect and non-elect, receive the pardon of sin original and actual sacramentally; and whosoever performs the condition of the covenant, hath the fruit of that, whereof before he had the grant under seal." [5] The sacramental grace is "1. the blood and spirit of Christ; 2. the washing of sin, and new birth; 3. the obsignation to the party baptized, that by Christ's blood his sins are cleansed." [6]

---

[1] Ibid., XI, 193 seq. [2] Ibid., xv, 482; cf. XIII, 44.
[3] This correspondence is given in Ussher's *Works*, xv, 510.
[4] Ibid., 512. [5] Ibid., 513. [6] Ibid., 514.

Although Taylor's Discourse of Baptism in the *Great Exemplar* was appealed to in the controversy of the last century, his teaching cannot readily be accommodated to the case either for, or against, Baptismal regeneration. While with a weight of patristic evidence he emphasizes the great benefits conveyed in this "Divine evangelical institution",[1] and among them, the putting "into the order of eternal life", new birth, and entrance into a new creation, Taylor carefully distinguishes between Baptism and its effects, which "do not always go in conjunction". The effect may go before, as in the case of Cornelius, "and therefore much rather may it go after its susception".[2] "No disposition or act of man can deserve the first grace or grace of pardon." This being entirely the work of God, "faith and repentance are not necessary at first for the reception of the first grace, but by accident".[3] In Baptism "the seed of God is put into the ground of our hearts, and repentance waters it, and faith makes it *subractum solum*, the ground and furrows apt to produce fruits; and therefore faith and repentance are necessary to the effects of baptism, not to its susception; that is necessary to all those parts of life in which baptism does operate, not to the first sanction and entering into the covenant.[4]   The holy spirit which descends upon the waters of Baptism does not instantly produce its effects in the soul of the baptized, who is thereby admitted into the kingdom of God, which "cometh not with observation". "It is 'the seed of God', and it is no good argument to say, here is no seed in the bowels of the earth because there is nothing green upon the face of it." [5] Yet the Church rightly gives the Sacrament, though God does not always give the grace in the same instance, but afterwards.[6]

Taylor gives the real effects of Baptism, for which faith and repentance are necessary: (1) the separation from the unbelieving world as alienated from God, the Holy Spirit consigning us for God, "as sheep of His pasture, as the soldiers of His army, as the servants of His household" [7]; (2) the illumination of the Holy Spirit who becomes to us "the author of holy thoughts and firm persuasions", enabling God to sit in the soul "as if he sat in his Throne" [8]; (3) the descent of the Holy Spirit "to become the principle of a new life, to become a holy seed springing up to holiness" [9]; (4) participation in the victory of Christ and consignation to a holy resurrection;[10] (5) translation from death to life here, "the first resurrection", and preservation from the second death "to a glorious and eternal life".[11]

---

[1] *Works*, II, 234 seqq.   [2] Ibid., 248.   [3] Ibid., 252.
[4] Ibid., 253.   [5] Ibid.   [6] Ibid., 253 seq.   [7] Ibid., 241.
[8] Ibid., 242.   [9] Ibid., 242 seq.   [10] Ibid., 243 seq.   [11] Ibid., 244.

Taylor's teaching is given liturgical expression in the "Form of Administration of the Holy Sacrament of Baptism", contained in his *Collection of Offices*, published in 1658, the year in which he first settled in Ireland. Emphasis is given to the action of the Holy Spirit upon the waters of Baptism and upon the child baptized as well as to the great benefits conveyed thereby. The Holy Spirit descends "upon the waters of baptism that they may become to this infant a laver of regeneration, and a well of water springing up to eternal life",[1] and "be instrumental and effective of grace, of pardon, and sanctification".[2] Prayer is also made that the Holy Spirit "may be in this child as the seed of God springing up to eternal life, that the kingdom of God, which is within, and cometh not with observation", may prevent, work strongly in, and guard him "from the cradle to the grave";[3] and later, that the Holy Spirit may enlighten, and the Word of Christ instruct, the child's understanding, "that he may live by faith, and receive the secrets of Christ's Kingdom".[4] The only way in which children can be brought to Christ, the Minister explains after the Gospel, is "by this new birth and regeneration in the laver of baptism",[5] and the blessings of which the child is capable are "a title to the promises, and adoption to be the child of God, a sanctification of the Spirit, the designation to the service of Christ, and putting him into the order of eternal life".[6] God is called upon to adopt his child by creation into his covenant of grace and favour, and "let him be consigned with Thy Sacrament, admitted into Christ's kingdom, enter into His warfare, believe His doctrine, labour and hope for His promises".[7] Immediately before the Baptism prayer is made that "being buried with Christ in baptism, he may also rise with Him through the faith of the operation of God".[8] After the trine immersion (or dipping if any great cause intervene),[9] "the Priest" signs the child with the sign of the cross, enrols him a soldier under the banner of Christ, and admits him "into the communion of saints, into the bosom of the visible Church, the kingdom of grace, and the title to the promises evangelical and the hopes of glory"; and then declares him to be admitted also "into the covenant of faith and repentance, pardon and holiness".[10] A further prayer for the child consists of a beautiful passage in which Taylor has already described the baptismal benefit of new birth and entrance into the new creation.[11]

O God, be Thou his father for ever, Christ his elder brother and his Lord, the Church his mother; let the body of Christ be his food, the blood of Christ his

[1] Ibid., VIII, 631. [2] Ibid., 632. [3] Ibid., 636. [4] Ibid., 637.
[5] Ibid., 633. [6] Ibid., 634. [7] Ibid., 634 seq. [8] Ibid., 636.
[9] Ibid. [10] Ibid., 636 seq. [11] Ibid., II, 234 seq.

drink, and the Spirit the earnest of his inheritance. Let faith be his learning, religion his employment, his whole life be spiritual, heaven the object of his hopes and the end of his labours; let him be Thy servant in the kingdom of grace, and Thy son in the kingdom of glory, through Jesus Christ our Lord. *Amen.*[1]

Although this Office was drawn up for use during the Commonwealth, the Godparents are exhorted not to neglect "any opportunity of bringing him to the bishop, that he, by imposition of hands and invocation of the holy Spirit of God, may procure blessing and spiritual strength to this child".[2] The great emphasis Taylor gives to the action of the Holy Spirit in the Sacrament of Baptism should be kept in mind when we examine his teaching on the Rite of Confirmation.

In the second part of the *Dissuasive from Popery*, published after his death, Taylor sets forth, as wholly derived from Scripture, the proper reasons why the Church baptizes children, "even that children should be brought to Christ, should receive his blessing, should be adopted into the Kingdom of God, should be made members of the second Adam, and be translated from the death introduced by the first to the life revealed by the second, and that they may receive the Holy Spirit, and a title to the promises evangelical, and be born again, and admitted into a state of covenant in which they can receive the gift of eternal life." [3]

In a short Discourse *Of Persons Dying without Baptism* Bramhall distinguishes "the sole want of Baptism upon invincible necessity, and the contempt or wilful neglect of Baptism when it may be had", and also between the exterior sacramental ablution and the invisible grace of the Sacrament, interior regeneration. "We believe, that whosoever hath the former, hath the latter also; so that he do not put a bar against the efficacy of the Sacrament by his infidelity or hypocracy; of which the child is not capable." "Secondly, we believe, that without Baptismal grace, that is, regeneration, no man can enter into the kingdom of God." [4] In the case of children of Christian parents, who have a right to the Sacrament, but are defrauded of it through no fault of their own, "we believe, that God, Who hath not limited His grace to His outward ordinances, may and doth many times according to His good pleasure supply the defect of others, and operate in them the grace of the Sacrament by His Holy Spirit." [5] Bramhall gives at length the grounds for this belief, which he takes to be the doctrine of the soundest Anglican Divines, rejecting

---

[1] *Works*, VIII, 638.   [2] Ibid.   [3] Ibid., VI, 417.
[4] Ibid., V, 172.   [5] Ibid., 173.

St Austin as "a hard father to little children and innocents from actual sins" and the *Limbus Infantum* of the Romanists.

Bishop Berkeley left behind the outline of a sermon on Baptism preached at Newport on Rhode Island in 1729, in the presence of a number of unbaptized persons, from the text, "Repent, and be baptized everyone of you" (Acts 11. 38). Baptism is a "seal of God's promises—remission, justification, adoption. God binds Himself by free promise of grace on His part, on our part we become entitled to these promises, to the ordinances and the grace conferred by them." The inward grace is "New Life and regeneration. Rom. 6, 3, 4, 7; Mark 15, 16". Berkeley deals with the old objections to Infant Baptism, their lack of faith and the silence of Scripture. "Strictly speaking, it is not faith, but the application of Christ's righteousness that justifieth, and this may, if God please, be applied otherwise than by faith, e.g. by His sanctifying Spirit." Scripture is equally silent about "women receiving the Eucharist,—besides, it is said, several persons and all their households were baptized". The objection that Baptism makes slaves worse, "proceeds from an infidel mind; contrary shown; what they charge on baptism to be charged on their own unchristian life and neglect of instruction."

With apostolic plainness the philosopher gives the reasons why some of his hearers defer Baptism: through "supine negligence", despondency, the heresy of Novatian, a wrong notion of a covenant which they apprehend would entrap them, and an unwillingness to forsake sin. This last is "a cunning design of living to the world and dying to God; this is to say, I will wallow in vice and sin, cheat and purloin, indulge in gluttony and drunkenness, and deny nothing that any appetite leads to; the first-fruits, flower, prime to the devil, the fag-end, when faculty for good and evil is gone, to God."

Our Saviour's parable of those who came late in the day to work, not designed to encourage delay in believers, but to give comfort to those who had late means of instruction. But how do you know it is not late now? who hath given you a lease of life? who assured you that you shall live to be old, that you shall not die suddenly, that you shall not die to-morrow, or even this very day? Can you think that God, whom you never harkened to, will harken to your first call? When the fever is got into your head, when you can neither bend a knee nor lift an eye to heaven, when you cannot frame a prayer yourself or join with others, suppose Baptism conferred then and grace given, you have the talent without the time and opportunity to produce fruit or profit thereby. All things are ready; God now calls, but the devil causeth delay; to-day for me, to-morrow for the Lord. He is too cunning to suggest a resolution against ever doing what you know should be done, but stealing the present he stealeth day after day, till, &c. Be enrolled on earth in due time, that you may be written in the book of life in heaven.[1]

Elsewhere Berkeley, in a Confirmation address and in an impressive sermon on the "Mystery of Godliness", lays emphasis on Baptism as the translation from the kingdom of this world, estranged from God and where sin and death reign, into the peculiar kingdom of Christ, the Church, which is "reconciled to God by Christ, is justified by faith in him, redeemed by his sufferings, and sanctified by his Spirit: no longer subject to death, sin, or the devil, but made children of God and heirs of eternal life." [2]

We find a similar emphasis in Philip Skelton's Discourses. "So great is the change made in you by baptism, that, from the alien and enemy of God, from the outcast of heaven, you are become the brother of Christ, and the son of God; from the heir of that curse which fell on the first Adam and all his posterity, you are become a joint heir with Christ, the second Adam, of all the happiness and glory, which almighty love can bestow upon you. You are dead, and have passed from death unto life. You are a new creature. You are dead to this world and sin: and your life is hid with Christ in God." [3] "By the 'Covenant of peace' we are brought into the realm of eternal life, eternal happiness and glory" and "made one with Christ, as He is one with the Father", united "into one Church, or Spiritual Body, whereof 'He is head'. Thus joined to Him, who is by nature the Son of God, we also become, by a 'new birth in Baptism', the adopted sons or children of God." [4]

In the early nineteenth century the emphasis became centred on the question of Baptismal regeneration. John Jebb held that the Sacrament of Baptism "takes the great work of salvation, entirely out of the hands of man, and places it altogether in the hands of God." The inward Baptism, "with the Holy Ghost, imparts a virtue altogether super-human; a regeneration, in which is the power of God alone." [5] In 1810 Alexander Knox maintained in the *Eclectic Review* that, "in the judgment of the Church (ancient and Anglican), every one baptized in infancy, commences life in a justified state".[6] In his Bampton Lectures of 1804, Richard Laurence, later Archbishop of Cashel, demonstrated from the Anglican

---

[1] *Works* (ed. Luce), VII, 68 seq. The last section of the sermon outlined has been given at length to illustrate an impressive example of eighteenth-century evangelism, almost on the mission field, rather than to illustrate the doctrine of Baptism.

[2] Ibid., 168; cf. Sermon on the Mystery of Godliness, ibid., 89 seq.; cf. Report on *The Theology of Christian Initiation* (S.P.C.K., 1948), 21 seq.

[3] *Works*, III, 82 seq.   [4] Ibid., II, Discourse XXI.

[5] *Practical Theology*, I, 75.   [6] *Remains*, I, 281.

formularies, including the Baptism and Confirmation Offices, "that an actual regeneration always takes place".[1] Laurence later published *The Doctrine of Baptismal Regeneration contrasted with the Tenets of Calvin* in 1813 (2nd ed., 1827) and *Doctrine of the Church of England upon the Efficacy of Baptism vindicated from Misrepresentations* in 1816 (3rd ed., 1838). In his Bampton Lectures of 1812, Richard Mant strongly defended the doctrine of Baptismal regeneration, quoting at great length Bishop Taylor's Discourse of Baptism in the *Great Exemplar*. A storm of protest broke out when the S.P.C.K. published the two lectures on Baptism as *Two Tracts on Regeneration and Conversion*; and Daniel Wilson addressed *A Respectful Address to the Society on Certain Inconsistencies and Contradictions which have appeared in some of their Recent Books and Tracts*. Mant's Bampton Lectures, however, appear in the list of recommended books, appended to *The First Praelection* which Richard Graves gave as Professor of Divinity at Trinity College, Dublin, in 1814. It is generally agreed that the two Irish Prelates, Laurence and Mant, had an important part in the early stages of the Baptismal controversy of the last century.[2]

(c) *Sacrament of the Lord's Supper*

(i) *Introductory*

Irish Eucharistic teaching from Ussher to Palmer tends, on the one hand, to distinguish the central act of Christian worship from specific Roman Catholic definitions, and on the other to interpret the Anglican formularies in the light of what was believed to be the teaching of the primitive Church. "Transubstantiation and Zwinglianism", writes William Connor Magee in 1870, "are both definite and erroneous. Our formularies lie within these two boundaries, touching both because they are between them, and therefore 'ambiguous'—i.e., broad and catholic." [3] Bramhall claims that the Anglicans of his day stood with the primitive Church and ancient Fathers in avoiding over-definition. "We know what to think and what to say with probability, modesty, and submission,

[1] *An Attempt to illustrate those Articles of the Church of England which the Calvinists improperly consider as Calvinistical*, 180 seqq.

[2] For the teaching of other Divines, see Ezekiel Hopkins, *Works*, II, 413 seqq.; Robert Mossom, op. cit., III, 73 seq.; Roger Boyle, op. cit., 247 seq., where he holds the Baptismal grace to be inward conformity with the death, burial and resurrection of Christ; Thomas Wilson, who holds Baptism to separate us from Adam and engraft us into Christ: a resurrection from sin to grace; but although our sins die and are buried, the seed and root remain and have to be mortified all through life. *Works*, v, 947; cf. 333. Wilson also holds Taylor's view that in Baptism the Holy Spirit is communicated "for a principle of a new and spiritual life". *A Short and Plain Instruction ... of the Lord's Supper*, 1 seq.

[3] *The Life and Correspondence of William Connor Magee, Archbishop of York*, 253.

in the schools; but we dare neither screw up the question to such a height, nor dictate our opinions to others so magisterially as articles of Faith."[1] Caroline Divines had little intention of fitting their Eucharistic teaching into the well-known categories, and it would be precarious to attempt any such classification. It is possible, for example, to see in the teaching of Ussher certain parallels with the high sacramental teaching of Calvin: it is also possible to find many points at which he is altogether at variance with Calvin, particularly in his emphasis on the union of things heavenly and earthly in the Eucharistic action. Ussher, possibly more than any other Anglican of his day, had a thorough knowledge of the Fathers and of ancient liturgies; and it is more reasonable to suppose that he sought the ground for his Eucharistic belief in Scripture and antiquity than in sixteenth-century reformers.

Most Irish Divines held a balanced view of the Eucharist and its several aspects of Thanksgiving, Commemoration, Sacrifice, Mystery, Communion, and Fellowship, all of which are so clearly expressed in the Anglican Communion rite. Here we can only examine the main trend of Irish Eucharistic teaching under the two heads of the Eucharistic Offering and the Eucharistic Gift.

(ii) The Eucharistic Offering

Irish Divines from the time of Ussher laid great emphasis upon the Intercession of Christ as part of his heavenly Priesthood. Some of them do not appear to have regarded the Eucharist more than any other part of worship as being offered to God through Christ, while others thought of the Eucharist as being particularly, though not exclusively, connected with his heavenly ministry, and as a ritual enactment of what was said at the end of every prayer, "through Jesus Christ our Lord". Again, the Eucharist was often regarded as a sacramental commemoration of the Sacrifice of the death of Christ, made not only before men, but in the sight of God, and as a means of pleading the merits of that Sacrifice as well as of receiving its benefits. All Irish Divines were unanimously opposed to the "vulgar error", encouraged by such Romanist writers as Soto and Hardinge and denounced by the English Article 31, that the Eucharistic Sacrifice was equal to that of Christ on the cross, and was in fact a reiteration or a continuation of that Sacrifice. They were likewise opposed to the Romanist distinction between Sacrifice and Communion, or to the view that the Eucharistic Sacrifice apart from the act of Communion had a special value as an instrument of propitiation.

[1] Works, I, 22.

Sometimes Caroline Divines gave a sacrificial interpretation to ceremonies which had become general in the reign of Charles I in the absence
of any rubrical direction for the offering of the alms collected, the placing
or setting apart of the elements, or the breaking of the bread. The 1662
Prayer Book directed the alms collected to be presented and placed on
the Holy table, and when there was a Communion sufficient bread and
wine for the purpose to be placed on the table, though without using the
words "offer up" of the Scottish Liturgy of 1637. It also directed the
breaking of the bread during the Prayer of Consecration, but not the pre-
Caroline ceremony of pouring out the wine, which Ussher had interpreted as early as 1603 in the light of Isaiah 53. 5, 10, 12,[1] and which
continued in Ireland late into the eighteenth century, being mentioned
by Philip Skelton (d. 1787).

Ussher's view of the Eucharistic Sacrifice is given partly in his defence
of ancient Irish practices and partly in the symbolic interpretation he gives
to existing Caroline practices. In the former he maintains that the Romanist distinction between Sacrifice and Communion was unknown to the
Celtic Church. He sees a parallel between the Eucharistic Sacrifice and
the scriptural Sacrifice of communicating to the needs of the poor, in
which "we are taught to give both our selves and our alms, first unto the
Lord, and after unto our brethren by the will of God". Likewise, "in
this ministry of the blessed Sacrament, the service is first presented unto
God, (from which, as from a most principal part of the duty, the sacrament itself is called the *Eucharist*; because therein we offer a special sacrifice of praise and thanksgiving always unto God) and then communicated unto God's people." In the distribution of the Sacrament "both
the minister was said to *give*, and the communicant to *receive the Sacrifice*",
just as in the former part of the rite "they were said to *offer* the same unto
the Lord". The Celtic Church "did not distinguish the *Sacrifice* from
the *Sacrament*, as the Romanists do nowadays".[2] Ussher then gives
examples of the twofold use of the word "Sacrifice" [3] which made it
"appear that the Sacrifice of the elder times was not like unto the new

---

[1] *Works*, XI, 194 seq. Bishop Middleton, translated from Waterford to St Davids
in 1582, however, ordered his clergy not to "lift up or show unto the people the
bread and wine", but "let it lie upon the table until the distribution thereof, and then
break it, receive it himself, and then distribute it unto others, according to the orders
of the book without addition or detraction." *Injunctions*. Alcuin Club Collections,
XXVII, iii.

[2] Ibid., IV, 277.

[3] Ussher cites ancient Irish Synods which speak of the *giving* and *receiving* of the
Sacrifice, and the gloss of Sedulius upon 1 Cor. 11. 33, *Tarry one for another*, "that is
(saith he) *until you do receive the Sacrifice*".

mass of the Romanists, wherein the Priest doth eat and drink alone, the people being only lookers on; but unto our *Communion*, where all that are present at the holy action do eat of the Altar, as well as they that serve the Altar." [1] Ussher cites the testimony of Gallus that his master, Columbanus, was accustomed "to offer unto the Lord the Sacrifice of Salvation in brazen vessels", thus making it clear that "the Sacrifice of the elder times", which was like unto "our Communion", included the offering of the bread and wine. In addition to the Sacrifice of praise to God through Christ and of almsgiving (Heb. 13. 15, 16) Ussher appears to hold the primitive view of Irenaeus, Origen, and others that the bread and wine are first offered to God in thanksgiving. Likewise Ussher uses the word "Eucharist" in the twofold sense of a Sacrifice of praise and thanksgiving to God through Christ, and of what is received by the communicant. In the Irish Article 100 he defines a private mass as "the receiving of the *Eucharist* by the priest alone".[2] Thus far Ussher went beyond the teaching of Calvin, who excluded any offering of the bread and wine, and limited the Eucharistic Sacrifice to a thankful reception of all that is offered by the Sacrifice of the cross.[3]

Elsewhere Ussher in his treatment of the Eucharist repeatedly lays stress on the union of things heavenly and things earthly, which Calvin would regard as a confounding of heaven with earth. He applies Galatians 3. 1 to the Eucharistic action, in which Christ is "so represented as if his soul were before our eyes poured out unto death", and "heavenly things are, as it were, clothed in earthly garments".[4] The celebrant represents the person of Christ, and by the eyes of faith the communicant can see Christ in the breaking of the bread and the pouring out of the wine.[5] Thus God "represents to us the mystery of Christ offered for us, and offered to us".[6] The setting apart of the bread and wine, moreover, represents "how God from all eternity sets apart his Son for us", or the setting apart of the Lamb which was a type of Christ.[7] Some may see in Ussher's symbolic interpretation of the sacramental actions of the minister the influence of late medieval thought. It is equally possible to find a close parallel with a passage in St Chrysostom where he bids the worshippers at the time of

[1] Ibid., IV, 279.
[2] This, taken with Ussher's repeated insistence that the consecrated elements are no longer "common" food, may also suggest the influence of Irenaeus. "We offer to him that which is his own... For as the bread which comes from the earth, when it receives the invocation of God, is no longer *common* bread, but *eucharist*..." *Adv*. Haereses, IV. 18. 5.
[3] R. S. Wallace, *Calvin's Doctrine of the Word and Sacrament*, 214 seq.
[4] *Works*, XIII, 193.   [5] Ibid., 205.   [6] Ibid., 206.   [7] Ibid.

consecration see with the eye of faith Christ sacrificed and offered to them, and casting forth from their souls all carnal thoughts, to see with pure minds the things of heaven.[1] Ussher nowhere appears to connect the Eucharist more than any other part of prayer with the Intercession of Christ, which he nevertheless regards as part of his heavenly Priesthood, whereby he presents to his heavenly Father "both our persons and our imperfect obedience", making them, "by the merits of His satisfaction, to be acceptable in God's sight".[2]

In the seventeenth century Sacrificial language was by no means limited to "Arminian High Churchmen". Lewis Bayly, the puritanical Bishop of Bangor (1616–32), for example, held that "Christ was once in himself *really* offered; but as oft as the Sacrament is celebrated, so oft is he *spiritually* offered by the faithful. Hence the Lord's Supper is called a *propitiatory sacrifice*, not *properly*, or *really*, but *figuratively*, because it is a *memorial* of that propitiatory Sacrifice which Christ offered upon the Cross." [3] Likewise, Bishop Bedell of Kilmore (d. 1642), no "Arminian High Churchman", combined with a subjective view of the Sacraments a mystical interpretation of the Eucharistic Sacrifice. From the Epistle to the Hebrews and the Master of the Sentences he showed in what sense "we do offer Sacrifice for the Quick and Dead, remembering, representing, and mystically offering that sole Sacrifice for the Quick and Dead, by which all their sins are meritoriously expiated, and desiring that by the same, 'we and all the whole Church may obtain remission of sins, and all other benefits of Christ's Passion'." [4]

Bishop Henry Leslie of Down and Connor expressed in 1636 what we might term the classical Anglican view of the Eucharistic Sacrifice. The Eucharist is "our Christian Sacrifice, even a lively representation of the all-sufficient Sacrifice of Christ upon the Cross, and the means to make us partakers of the fruits thereof. And therein we resign ourselves unto the service of God, and offer our bodies a living sacrifice", and "we offer unto God our faith, our prayers, our thanksgiving, our alms-deeds, with a contrite and a broken heart; all which are spiritual sacrifices acceptable to God through Jesus Christ." [5] In the Sacrament, moreover, "we are petitioners unto Almighty God, that we may have an interest in that precious death, the remembrance whereof we then celebrate." [6]

---

[1] *De Sacerdot.*, iii, 4, 5; vi, 4.
[2] Op. cit., XI, 210.   [3] *The Practice of Piety* (1656 ed.), 461.
[4] Quoted from Bishop Burnet, *The Life of William Bedell*, 479; cf. 469.
[5] *An Answer to certain objections against the Orders of the Church*, especially kneeling at the Communion, appended to *A Treatise of the Authority of the Church* (Dublin, 1637), 186.   [6] Ibid., 188.

Three Irish Bishops expressed their views on the Eucharist shortly before coming over to Ireland. In 1636 Griffith Williams, Bishop of Ossory (1641–72), regarded the Eucharist as "*Sacrificium incruentum*, the unbloody Sacrifice of Christ, *non per oblationem sed per commemorationem*, not that we do herein offer up Christ to his Father, but do hereby commemorate that bloody sacrifice, which was made and offered by Christ himself, upon the altar of his cross, for appeasing of his Father's wrath".[1] As Dean of Bangor, Williams was regarded as a High Churchman in opposition to his puritanical Bishop, Lewis Bayly, who nevertheless held that in the Eucharist Christ was "spiritually offered" up to the Father.[2] In 1657 Robert Mossom, Bishop of Derry (1666–81), published the sermons he preached in London during the Commonwealth. In one of them he advised communicants to send up "this ejaculation of fervent prayer" after the Consecration:

Look down, oh look down, heavenly Father, from thy celestial Sanctuary, and behold the sacred Hoast, the death, the passion of my crucified Saviour; whose blood of sprinkling speaks better things than that of Abel, even things of grace and mercy, of pardon and peace.

From the Passion the communicant should "proceed in mediations of faith to his Resurrection, and behold him leading captivity captive, triumphing gloriously over sin and Satan, death and hell. From his Resurrection follow him to his Ascension, and raised by faith, behold him at the right hand of the Father in glory, where He ever lives to make intercession for us."[3] John Maxwell, who was translated from Ross in Scotland to Killala in 1640 and later became Archbishop of Tuam, is an interesting link between the Church of Ireland and the ill-fated Scottish Liturgy of 1637. According to Laud his "hand hath been as much in it as the most",[4] although Bishop Wedderburn is thought to have had a hand in drawing up the Communion Office. As Maxwell was an enthusiastic promoter of the Scottish Book, he must have approved the Sacrificial emphasis in the Communion Office.[5] In August 1637 Bramhall

---

[1] *The Best Religion*... (1636), 743.   [2] See above, p. 93.
[3] *The Preacher's Tripartite*, 35 seq.; cf. 80.   [4] *Works*, VI, 505.
[5] The Presbyter presents the alms "before the Lord" and then offers up and places the Bread and Wine upon the Lord's Table. In the Prayer for the Church the congregation is said to have assembled "to celebrate the commemoration of the most precious death and sacrifice" of Christ. Immediately after the Dominical words of Institution a memorial is made: "...we Thy humble servants do celebrate and make here before Thy divine Majesty, with these Thy holy gifts, the memorial which Thy Son hath willed us to make, having in remembrance His blessed passion, mighty resurrection, and glorious ascension..."

wrote to Archbishop Spottiswood of St Andrew's, thanking him for sending a copy of the new Prayer Book. "Glad I was to see it, and more glad to see it such as it is, to be envied in some things perhaps if one owned." [1]

Bramhall's own views on the Eucharistic Sacrifice were given during the Commonwealth. In answer to Romanist attacks he asserted that "all the essentials of their Sacrifice are contained in our celebration of the Holy Eucharist; that is, according to their schools, the consecration and consumption of the whole or part." The former we have "more purely than they, the latter more eminently than they"; for "with us both Priest and people do receive, with them the Priest only. It was truly said by the learned Bishop of Ely,—'Take away your Transubstantiation, and we shall have no difference about the Sacrifice'." [2] Nor have Protestants "pared off the pith of Christ's heavenly Priesthood...which is to make intercession and atonement for us to His Father, in respect whereof He is called our Passover, our Propitiation, our Advocate, our Mediator". It is the Romanists who "pare off the pith of Christ's heavenly Priesthood", "who daily make as many propitiatory Sacrifices as there are masses in the world; who mix up the sufferings of the saints with the Blood of Christ, to make up the treasury of the Church; who multiply their mediators, as the heathen did their tutelary Gods, begging at their hands to receive them at the hour of death, to reconcile them to God, to be their advocates, their mediators, their propitiation, and briefly, to do all those offices, which belong to the heavenly Priesthood of Christ." [3] The Easterns "know no new Sacrifice, but the commemoration, representation, and application, of the Sacrifice of the Cross".[4] Bramhall also gives a positive statement of what was generally held by Anglican Divines before the Restoration.

We acknowledge an Eucharistical Sacrifice of praise and thanksgiving; a commemorative Sacrifice, or a memorial of the Sacrifice of the Cross; a representative Sacrifice, or the representation of the Passion of Christ before the eyes of His Heavenly Father; an impetrative Sacrifice, or an impetration of the fruit and benefit of His Passion, by way of real prayer; and, lastly, an applicative Sacrifice, or an application of His merits unto our souls. Let him, that dare, go one step further than we do; and say that it is a suppletory Sacrifice, to supply the defects of the Sacrifice of the Cross. Or else let them hold their peace, and speak no more against us in the point of Sacrifice for ever.[5]

---

[1] *Works*, I, lxxxvi. Alexander Knox, Bishop Jebb, and Bishop Mant also expressed their regard for the Scottish Prayer Book of 1637.
[2] Ibid., v, 217. Bishop Andrewes of Ely is here referred to.
[3] Ibid., 220.   [4] Ibid., II, 62.   [5] Ibid., 276.

Jeremy Taylor's fullest treatment of the Eucharistic Sacrifice is given in *The Worthy Communicant* of 1660 and belongs to his Irish period. He claims that his teaching is plainly manifested in the Epistle to the Hebrews as understood by "the ancient and holy doctors of the Church", including St Ambrose, St Chrysostom, St Austin, and St Basil.[1] In *Clerus Domini* (1651), however, Taylor cites St Cyprian as setting forth the heavenly and eternal Priesthood, Sacrifice, and Intercession of Christ, who there perpetually presents the Sacrifice finished on the cross, and Gregory Nazianzen for the conception of the heavenly altar.[2] Already in the *Great Exemplar* (1649) Taylor had set forth his view of the celestial ministry of Christ, and, from 2 Corinthians 6. 1, of the earthly Eucharist being at one with the heavenly.[3] The Eucharistic action was not simply an imitation of what Christ did at the Last Supper, but an imitation of his celestial Priesthood and Intercession. The ministers of the Sacrament "do in a spiritual manner present to God the sacrifice of the cross by being imitators of Christ's intercession".[4] They do sacramentally and humbly what Christ performs in heaven "in a high and glorious manner".[5] In *The Worthy Communicant* Taylor maintains that Christ has commanded us to do on earth what he does in heaven; that is, "to represent his death, to commemorate the sacrifice, by humble prayer and thankful record; and by faithful manifestation and joyful eucharist, to lay it before the eyes of our heavenly Father, so ministering to his priesthood, and doing according to his commandment and his example." [6] Taylor then appears to express Nazianzen's distinction between the external and internal Sacrifice, the earthly ministry being a copy, imitation, or representation of the celestial, real, and archetypal offering perpetually presented at "the celestial altar". Taylor regards the church where the Eucharist is celebrated as "the image of heaven", the Priest as "the minister of Christ", the Holy table as "a copy of the celestial altar".[7] The Sacrifice of the Lamb slain from the beginning of the world is "always the same: it bleeds no more after the finishing of it on the cross; but it is wonderfully represented in heaven, and graciously represented here: by Christ's action there, by His com-

---

[1] *Works*, VIII, 39.   [2] Ibid., I, 32.

[3] "As Christ is a priest in heaven for ever, and yet does not sacrifice Himself afresh, nor yet without a sacrifice could He be a priest; but by a daily ministration and intercession represents His sacrifice to God, and offers Himself as sacrificed; so does He upon earth by the ministry of His servants; He is offered to God, that is, He is by prayers and the sacrament represented or offered up to God, as sacrificed; which in effect is a celebration of His death by... a ministry like to His in heaven." Ibid., II, 643.

[4] *Holy Living* (1650), ibid., III, 214 seq.   [5] Ibid., I, 32.

[6] Ibid., VIII, 37.   [7] Ibid., 38.

mandment here". [1] In the external ministry the earthly "ministers in that unchangeable priesthood" imitate "the prototype Melchisedec", who "brought forth bread and wine, and was the priest of the most high God". In the internal ministry they imitate "the antitype or substance, Christ himself, who offered up His body and blood for the atonement of us". [2] The Eucharist is "all but the representment of His death, in the way of prayer and interpellation, Christ as head, and we as members; He as high-priest, and we as servants His ministers". [3]

Taylor continually dwells upon the mystical union between Christ as Head and the Church as his Body in the Eucharistic action. The members of Christ's Body "present themselves to God with Christ, whom they have spiritually received". "The offering their bodies, and souls, and services to God in Him, and by Him, and with Him, who is the Father's well-beloved, and in whom He is well pleased, cannot but be accepted to all purposes of blessing, grace and glory." [4] Here we have an admirable commentary on the Prayer of Oblation after the Communion of the people in the Anglican Communion rite, as well as a clear exposition of the Augustinian view of the Eucharist as the Church's self-offering to God through Christ the Head. In his Communion Office of 1658 Taylor places a prayer of self-offering[5] after the Communion of the people, where he also places the Lord's Prayer and a "Prayer for the Catholic Church".[6] For Taylor held that the communicants being joined sacramentally to Christ, the High Priest, are admitted to intercede for others, joining their prayers to his Intercession.[7] "Having received Christ's body within us," Taylor said very simply in the Golden Grove, "we are sure to be accepted, and all the good prayers we make to God for ourselves and others are sure to be heard." [8]

Nor was the Eucharist the only imitation of Christ's eternal Intercession.

For what Christ did once upon the cross in real sacrifice, that He always does in heaven by perpetual representment and intercession: what Christ does by His supreme priesthood, that the Church doth by her ministerial; what He does in heaven, we do upon earth; what he performed at the right hand of God, is also represented and in one manner exhibited upon the holy table of the Lord: and what is done on altars upon solemn days, is done in our closets in our daily offices; that is, God is invocated, and God is appeased, and God is reconciled, and God gives us blessings and the fruits of Christ's passion in the virtue of the sacrificed lamb.[9]

[1] Ibid.   [2] Ibid.   [3] Ibid., 40.   [4] Ibid., III, 215.
[5] Ibid., VIII, 629, (First of "the Eucharistical Prayers").
[6] Ibid., 628. [7] Ibid., 226. [8] Ibid., VII, 598 seq. [9] Ibid., VIII, 73.

Hence we often find Eucharistic language in Taylor's ordinary prayers, or in his direction to the clergy of the diocese of Down and Connor to recite publically the daily Morning and Evening Prayer "that the daily sacrifice of praise and thanksgiving may never cease".[1]

The Prayer for the Dedication of "the Communion Table or Altar", in the Irish consecration form of 1666, first commemorates the fact that Christ, who was sent to be a Sacrifice for our sins, now sits at the right hand of God, and upon "the heavenly Altar" perpetually presents to Him "the Eternal Sacrifice, and a never-ceasing prayer". It then prays God to be present with his servants and to accept them in "the dedication of a Ministerial altar", which they humbly have provided for "the performance of this great Ministry, and in imitation of Christ's Eternal Priesthood", according to their duty and his commandment.[2] Here again the Eucharist is regarded as an imitation of Christ's celestial and eternal Priesthood and Intercession, and the Ministerial altar as a copy of the heavenly.

We find a similar emphasis in Henry Dodwell's *Discourse Concerning One Altar and One Priesthood* (1683), where he draws an interesting parallel between the Hellenist and early Christian conception of Sacrifice. To the Hellenists "the Archetypal High Priest was the λογος, the Adytum was Heaven, the Sacrifice that which was spiritually offered to the Father". This alone was the true Sacrifice, "as the Platonists used the term of Truth only concerning Archetypals, and the external Sacrifices themselves were no further thought to deserve the name of Sacrifices than as they *represented* and *transacted* and *applied* the Benefits of that *invisible Sacrifice*". If the Christian Eucharist "do perform the same office of *representing*, and *transacting*, and *applying* that *invisible Sacrifice*, this will have as just a claim to the name of a *Sacrifice* as those visible slaughters of beasts had".[3] We see a reflection of Jeremy Taylor's view of the Eucharist as an imitation of Christ's celestial and eternal Priesthood, Sacrifice, and Intercession in Dodwell's conception of the Eucharist "as a representation of the Heavenly Eucharist, or what is there transacted by the λογος in his own Person".[4]

Charles Leslie also regards the Eucharist as an earthly ministry performed in union with Christ's heavenly ministry. After the consecration "we may be said to offer the body and blood of Christ, while through

---

[1] *Holy Living* (1650), ibid., I, 113.   [2] Appendix: lines 393–402.
[3] Op. cit., 313 seq. Dodwell maintains that the language of the Hellenists is imitated by the sacred writers themselves, for example, in Heb. 8. 2; 9. 24; Luke 16. 11; John 1. 9; 6. 55. Ibid., 317 seqq.   [4] Ibid., 380.

the merits of his passion we intercede for mercy, and offer them to inter-
pose betwixt the justice of God and our sins". In this manner "Christ
does now offer them in heaven, and is for ever a Priest, though he is not
to be sacrificed again. Thus his priests do execute the same office and
priesthood upon earth which he does in heaven; and this makes them to
be priests in the most strict sense, even beyond the offering of the typical
sacrifices before his coming in the flesh." Besides our priests offer another
Sacrifice (Rom. 12. 1), "which the Church of Rome has forgot, and is
not to be found in all her canon of the mass, but in our office of Communion. The priest at the altar does in our names 'offer and present unto
God ourselves, our souls, and bodies, to be a reasonable, holy, and lively
sacrifice unto him'." [1] In the light of Leslie's Eucharistic teaching as a
whole it seems improbable that he meant to convey in this passage the
view that the Eucharistic action makes the ministers of the Sacrament
"sacrificing priests" in the Tridentine sense,[2] but makes them priests in a
strict sense because they minister "in that unchangeable priesthood" and
imitate Christ's heavenly Priesthood. Leslie seems to be following Taylor
and not Trent.

In Taylor, Dodwell, and Leslie, the emphasis is on the heavenly
ministry of Christ the High Priest, of which the earthly Eucharist is a
copy. In Bishop Wilson, however, we find an opposite emphasis. The
Eucharist is a representation of the death of Christ "not only to ourselves, but unto God the Father, that as the prayers and alms of Cornelius
are said to have 'gone up for a memorial before God', so this Service may
be an argument with His Divine Majesty to remember His Son's death
in heaven, as we do on earth, and for His sake to blot out our sins and to
give us all an interest in his merits".[3]

In *An Order or Method of Preparation for Weekly Communicants* (the
second edition appearing in 1703), Bishop Wetenhall provides prayers
with repeated references to the Intercession and heavenly Priesthood of
Christ.

. . . Thou who dyest for me, and now livest for ever, sitting at the Right Hand
of thy Father, to make Intercession for me. . . [4]

. . . where thou now sittest at the Right Hand of the Father, a merciful High
Priest, having made reconciliation by thy Blood.[5]

---

[1] *Works*, III, 531.
[2] Sess. xxii, can. ii. "Si quis dixerit. . . in illis verbis *Hoc facite in meam commemorationem,* Christum non instituisse Apostolos sacerdotes, aut non ordinasse, ut ipsi
aliique sacerdotes offerent Corpus et Sanguinem; anathema sit."
[3] *Works*, VII, 21.　　　[4] Op. cit., 41 seq.　　　[5] Ibid., 42 seq.

O thou who art entered within the Veil, into the true Holy of Holies, which is above, and ever livest to make Intercession for thine according to the Will of God: forasmuch as a clean thing cannot come out of an unclean, present, I pray thee, and offer up these my Prayers, with thy much Incense, unto Him thy Father.[1]

Bishop Peter Browne regarded the practice of drinking to the memory of the late King William III as a horrid profanation of "the most profound mystery of the Gospel".[2] For "the very essence of the Eucharistical Sacrifice" consists in "that action of eating and drinking to the memory of a Person once dead";[3] and "in this most solemn act of Christian worship" Christ is not only remembered as a Sacrifice offered on the cross for the atonement of our sin, but "as one who rose from the Dead, ascended alive into Heaven, and there makes intercession for us".[4] In Bishop Browne's manuscript book of private prayers, preserved in St Fin Barre's Cathedral, Cork, prayers are provided for the celebrant at "Approaching ye Altar", and at other points in the Eucharistic rite.

Placing the Elements.

This Bread and this Wine we sinners offer and present on thine Altar O Lord for a memorial of the All sufficient Sacrifice of thy Son Jesus;...And be thou Propitious and merciful unto us in contemplation of his Infinite merits and All powerful mediation and Intercession.

After eating ye Bread:

O Lord, Jesus Christ, As I am allowed ye Glorious Privilege of eating of that Sacrifice which was offered up for my sins, Let me thereby become one with it: and by the virtue of thy holy Institution make me partaker of ye ineffable union with thee which shall entitle me to ye Blessed and Everlasting Consequences of thy Precious Death and Agony.[5]

Among Caroline manuals expressing a similar view of the Eucharistic Sacrifice the following were published in Ireland, and thus made available to Church members: *The Whole Duty of Man*, Edward Lale's *Officium Eucharisticum* of 1673 (Dublin, 1683), the "old" *Week's Preparation* of 1678 (Dublin, 1715), copies of which were distributed by Philip Skelton

---

[1] Ibid., 44 seq.; cf. Wetenhall's meditations upon the Institution of the Sacrament in *A View of our Lord's Passion; with Meditations* (1710), 20 seq.

[2] *Of Drinking to the Memory of the Dead* (1713), 7.   [3] Ibid., 8.

[4] *A Second Part of Drinking in Remembrance of the Dead* (1714), 13; cf. *Sermons on Various Subjects* (ed. 1749), 41 seq.

[5] I am most grateful to His Grace the Archbishop of Armagh for drawing my attention to, and sending me a transcribed copy of, Peter Browne's Eucharistic devotions.

(d. 1787) to his young parishioners, and *The Countess of Morton's Daily Exercise* of 1665 (Dublin, 1723).

We must now examine the reaction against the Caroline view of the Eucharistic Sacrifice, which we have seen variously expressed. Bishop Roger Boyle, as early as 1681, would only acknowledge a spiritual Sacrifice, one of praise and thanksgiving, and of commemoration of the one sacrifice of propitiation. He rejected not only the Roman Sacrifice of the Mass,[1] but also the view that the Eucharist was a bloodless Sacrifice of propitiation for the living and the dead. While God has commanded us to pray for others, he has not commanded us to be baptized or receive the Eucharist for others, and so he will say, "Who hath required these things of you?" [2] Probably Bishop Boyle was only opposing medieval perversions of the Eucharistic Sacrifice which made it an instrument of propitiation, apart from the essential act of Communion, and not the primitive practice of making intercession at the Communion Service in union with the Intercession of Christ in heaven.

In 1718 Archbishop King takes an opposite view of the Offertory to that expressed by Charles Leslie, and later by Bishop Wilson, Bishop Mant, and John Jebb (junior). "We offer the elements", Charles Leslie held, "upon the holy table before the consecration: so it is directed in the rubric immediately before the prayer for the whole state of Christ's Church; then they are placed upon the table. After which done, the priest shall say, 'Lord, accept our alms and oblations.' *Alms* refer to the money given at the offertory; and *oblations*, I take it, to the elements then offered." The placing the elements upon God's holy table "is a solemn dedication of them to him; and the eating them from thence is a partaking of his table, and eating of his altar." [3] King, on the other hand, held that the 1662 rubric meant no more than that the bread and wine should by the care of the Priest be on the table at that time in order to determine how much should remain or be added for consecration. There was no intimation in the Liturgy, the Articles, or Canons, that the bread and wine should be offered up to God, the Restoration revisers having avoided the words "offer up" of the Scottish Liturgy.[4] Christian ministers, in spite of Dr Hickes, were God's ambassadors and representatives to men, but not representatives of the people to God. Since Christ has made the

---

[1] The outcome of the doctrine of transubstantiation. *Summa*, 268.   [2] Ibid., 270.
[3] *Works*, III, 529. Wilson regarded the placing of the bread and wine upon the altar as a solemn offering to God, the King of all the earth, and as an acknowledgment of our entire dependence upon his bounty. *Works*, VII, 20.
[4] Letter: King to Dr Maule, 29 Nov. 1718. T.C.D. MS.N. 3. 5, p. 72 seq.

perfect Sacrifice for the sins of the whole world, and there can be no more Sacrifice for sin, "all that the Minister and people do in the Sacrament of the Lord's Supper is to remember with thankfulness the infinite mercy of God, and to plead it for a satisfaction of their sins, which is no more to offer it as a Sacrifice than a malefactor placing the King's pardon is the granting of it or giving the price for it".[1] King owned "an offering at the Communion" of our selves, of praise and thanksgiving, of alms and oblations for the poor, but it was plain "these Sacrifices are performed by every Christian for himself; the Minister has no power over our souls and bodies to offer them; we ourselves must do it, and so in every other offering; and they are made acceptable by Christ our Priest's offering them to his Father, and not by act of the Ministers here, nor lastly are they properly Sacrifices." [2] Three years before King had expressed alarm at the doctrines of Dr Brett and others of that party who advanced "the Eucharist to be properly a propitiatory Sacrifice".[3] It would appear that distrust of the Non-juring party led to a reaction against the Sacrificial language used in Caroline times. Lewis Bayly had called the Lord's Supper "a propitiatory Sacrifice", and Jeremy Taylor had called it "ministerially and by application, an instrument propitiatory",[4] and "in genere orationis a sacrifice, and an instrument of propitiation",[5] but both writers had made it clear that they did not hold the views King thought the Non-jurors held. Although King made extensive use of the Irish consecration form of 1666 in his Dublin diocesan form of 1719, he altogether replaces the prayer for the dedication of the "Ministerial Altar", with its references to "the Heavenly Altar" and Christ's eternal Sacrifice, Priesthood, and Intercession, of which the earthly ministry is a copy.

Yet we find traces of the earlier emphasis at a later date. Philip Skelton held that in the Eucharist we "offer up on the altar of our great benefactor an act or proof of gratitude, required and accepted by him for the highest instance of mercy", and "we plead the great atonement", and "the merit of his Sacrifice" is directly applied to the soul of every worthy receiver.[6] In working out an analogy between Abel's sacrifice, the Mosaic sacrifice, and "the great Sacramental commemoration" of Christ's Sacrifice, William Magee in his Lectures on the Atonement in 1798–9, implies that the Eucharist is not a bare commemoration, but a "sacramental memorial" made before, and "acceptable to", God.[7] From

---

[1] Letter: King to Dr Maule, ibid., 76.   [2] Ibid.
[3] T.C.D., Transcript of King's Letters (N. 1. 8.), II, 259.
[4] *Works*, II, 643.   [5] Ibid., I, 33.   [6] *Works*, III, 120 seq.
[7] *Two Discourses on...Atonement and Sacrifice* (1801 ed.)., 62 seq; cf. 42 seq., where Magee deals with the Intercession of Christ.

1 Corinthians 10. 15-22, Alexander Knox in 1814 points to the Sacrificial character of the Christian Eucharist, and claims that Anglican Divines, in avoiding the extremes of Roman Catholic doctrine, on the one hand, and Bishop Hoadley's view of the Lord's Supper on the other, have extracted "what is Catholic from what is Roman".[1] William Palmer maintains that the thirty-first Article was directed against the "vulgar error", encouraged by Soto, Hardinge and others, that the sacrifice of the mass was "in every respect equal to that of Christ on the Cross; and that it was in fact either a reiteration or a continuation of that Sacrifice"; and he mentions Bramhall and Wilson among "our theologians" who "have always taught the doctrine of the eucharistic altar, sacrifice and oblation, according to Scripture and apostolical tradition".[2]

The continuance of Caroline piety is seen in *The New Manual of Devotion in Three Parts*, the twelfth edition appearing in Dublin in 1792. Immediately after the Consecration prayers adapted from Robert Nelson's *The Great Duty of Frequenting the Christian Sacrifice* are provided.

Accept, O eternal God, of that representation we make before thee, of that all sufficient Sacrifice which thy Son, our Lord Jesus Christ, made upon the cross: let the merit of it plead effectively for the pardon and forgiveness of all my sins, and render thee favourable and propitious to me a miserable sinner...and let the peace of it reconcile me unto thee...O Lamb of God, that takest away the sins of the world...[3]

Let me celebrate the Christian Sacrifice with purity of heart...[4]

Likewise in a Dublin edition of the *Book of Common Prayer*, appearing in 1808,[5] prayers from "A Companion to the Altar" are printed immediately after, and in the same type as, the Communion Office. The prayer beginning, "Now, O my God, though prostrate before thy altar...", appears to be another adaptation of Robert Nelson's prayer given above. *A New Week's Preparation*, designed in 1749 to replace the "old", was often printed in Ireland,[6] and so was Bishop Wilson's *A Short and Plain Instruction for the Better Understanding of the Lord's Supper.*[7]

---

[1] *Remains*, II, 253 seqq.
[2] *Treatise of the Church* (1842 ed.), II, 347 seq.
[3] Op. cit., 250; Robert Nelson, op. cit. (S.P.C.K., 1841), 73.
[4] Ibid., 251; cf. Nelson, ibid., 83.
[5] Dublin: Printed by Brett Smith, No. 38, Mary-Street. 1808.
[6] For example, Dublin, 1764; Cork, 1801 (18th ed.). This provides the prayer, "Now, O my God, prostrate before thine altar...", and "O Lamb of God that takest away the sins of the world...".
[7] For example, Dublin, 1791 (13th ed.) and 1812 (17th). "Indeed, if we should attempt to go to God, without an interest in Christ, we could hope for nothing but

(iii) *The Eucharistic Gift*

Caroline Divines were little interested in the *mode* of the Eucharistic Presence. Nowhere is the Caroline attitude better expressed than in a passage where Bramhall claims that the Anglicans of his day rested in the words of Christ, "This is My Body"—"leaving the manner to Him that made the Sacrament".

We know it is sacramental, and therefore efficacious, because God was never wanting to his own ordinances, where man did not set a bar against himself: but whether it be corporeally or spiritually (I mean not only after the manner of a Spirit, but in a spiritual sense[1]); whether it be in the soul only, or in the Host also; and if it be in the Host, whether by consubstantiation or transubstantiation; whether by production, or adduction, or conservation, or assumption, or by whatsoever other way bold and blind men dare conjecture;—we determine not. "*Motum sentimus, modum nescimus, Praesentiam credimus*".[2] This was the belief of the Primitive Church, this was the Faith of the ancient Fathers, who were never acquainted with these modern questions *de modo*, which edify not, but expose the Christian religion to contempt.[3]

The main Caroline emphasis on Communion with Christ implied Communion with all members of his mystical Body. In Caroline times this aspect of Fellowship was symbolized by the gathering together of the communicants in the chancel, or round the enclosure of the Communion table, for the Eucharistic action, and often by an unrubrical giving of alms on leaving the chancel between the Gloria in Excelsis and the Blessing[4] as a token of feeding the poorer members of the Body of Christ by whose Body they had been fed. "And what time is so seasonable", asks Jeremy Taylor, "to feed the members of Christ, as that when He gives His body to feed us, and that when we His members are met together to confess, to celebrate, to remember and to be joined to their Head and to one another?"[5]

Caroline Divines were primarily concerned with the Eucharistic Gift as a means of union with Christ and of promoting personal holiness.

to be rejected; but when we go to him, as *redeemed* by his own Son, and represent to him, as we do *in this holy Sacrament*, what he has done and suffered for us, we approach him as entirely reconciled to us." (Dublin, ed. 1812), 31.

[1] Bellarm, *De Sacram. Euchar.*, lib. i. c. 2. *Works* (L.A.C.T.), I, 22 n.1.
[2] Durandus. Ibid., n.k.   [3] Ibid.
[4] Bishop Andrewes, *Minor Works* (L.A.C.T.), 158.
[5] *Works*, VIII, 226. Cf. Bishop Wilson: "We do keep up a continual correspondence with our Lord in heaven; and hold communion with Him, and with all the members of His Body, which receive nourishment and growth from Him, as branches from the tree in which they are grafted." *Short and Plain Instruction* (Dublin, ed. 1812), 15.

This is seen in Ussher's earliest definition of the Eucharist in 1603 as "the Sacrament of our preservation in the Church, sealing unto us our spiritual nourishment and continual growth in Christ."[1] The Irish Article 92 of 1615 takes over this definition, while Article 94 contains the distinction which Ussher consistently makes elsewhere between the outward part of the Holy Communion, in which the Body and Blood of Christ are present symbolically and relatively, and the inward and spiritual part, in which they are "really and substantially presented unto all those who have grace to receive the Son of God", to whom they are "not only signified and offered, but also exhibited and communicated". Thu the Church of Ireland for the first nine years of the reign of Charles I was committed to the Eucharistic teaching of Ussher.

Later Ussher looked back upon his sermon before the English "Commons House" in 1620 as containing his fullest statement of "how far the real presence of the body of Christ in the Sacrament is allowed or disallowed by us".[2] In the outward part of this "mystical action" (*Sacramentum*), he there states, the presence of the Body and Blood of Christ is "relative and symbolical"; in the inward (*Rem Sacramenti*) "real and substantial".[3] But the Sacraments are no "bare signs": they are more than signs, "even pledges and assurances of the interest which we have in the heavenly things represented by them".[4] The elements are not changed in substance; "but in respect of the sacred use whereunto they are consecrated, such a change is now made that now they differ as much from common bread and wine, as heaven from earth."[5] They also exhibit the heavenly things they signify, being divinely appointed "means of conveying the same unto us, and putting us in actual possession thereof".[6] We receive not only "the benefits that flow from Christ, but the very Body and Blood of Christ, that is, Christ Himself crucified... We must have the Son before we have life".[7] And, therefore, we must "as truly be made partakers of Him as we are of our ordinary food, if we will live by Him. As there is a giving of Him on God's part, *for unto us a Son is given*, so there must be a receiving of Him on our part, *for as many as received Him, to them gave He power to become the sons of God*."[8]

[1] *Works*, XI, 194 seq. [2] Ibid., III, 52 (*Answer to a Jesuit*, 1625).
[3] Ibid., II, 426. [4] Ibid., 428.
[5] Ibid.; cf. "These elements are changed spiritually in their natures; not in substance, but in use, so that what was but now a common bread, becomes as far different as heaven is from earth, being altered in its use." Ibid., XIII, 192.
[6] Ibid. [7] Ibid., 429.
[8] Cf. "...this blessed bread and wine is termed a communion because it is an instrument whereby Christ instates me into himself, and whereby I have fellowship and Communion with him." Ibid., XIII, 194.

Our union with Christ being spiritual and supernatural requires "no local presence, no physical nor mathematical continuity or contiquity". The "spiritual ligatures" uniting us to Christ are "the quickening Spirit descending downward from the Head, to be in us the fountain of supernatural life; and a lively faith, wrought by the same Spirit, ascending from us upward, to lay hold upon Him *Who sitteth on the right hand of the Majesty on high.*" But the Spirit, thus uniting the earthly members to the heavenly Head, is received in divers measures; and "we that *receive out of His Fulness* have not our portion of grace delivered unto us all at once, but must daily look for the *supply of the Spirit of Jesus*". Having "received the Spirit and faith, and so spiritual life by their ministry, we are not there to rest", but we must desire to be fed at the Lord's table, be strengthened with that "spiritual repast" to do the Lord's work, and "continually be nourished up thereby in the life of glory".[1]

Ussher further emphasizes the Divine activity in the Eucharist, the heavenly treasure being presented to us "in earthen vessels, that the excellency of the power might be of God". God is the consecrator and the feeder. He does not feed us with the bare elements, but if we come worthily and with a living faith,

"the cup of blessing which He blesseth," will be unto us "the Communion of the Blood of Christ", and "the Bread which He breaketh the Communion of the Body of Christ"; of which precious Body and Blood we being really partakers (that is, in truth and indeed, and not in imagination only), although in a spiritual and not a corporal manner, the Lord doth "grant us according to the riches of His glory, to be strengthened with might by His Spirit in the inner man, that we may be filled with all the fulness of God". For the Sacraments, as well as the Word, be a part of that "ministration of the Spirit", which is committed to the "ministers of the New Testament"; forasmuch as "by one Spirit we have been all baptized into one Body, and have been all made to drink into one Spirit".[2]

Ussher, in a later sermon, dwells again on the relation between Baptism and the Eucharist. "And God hath appointed His Sacrament of the Lord's Supper to strengthen, and continue that life, which we received in Baptism, as by spiritual nourishment. In Baptism our stock of life is given us; by the Sacrament of the Holy Eucharist it is confirmed and continued." Unless Christ "be pleased to nourish that life, which he hath breathed into me in Baptism, and by his ordinances to give me a new supply and addition of grace, I am a dead man, I am gone for ever, upon the ground, that I receive not the never-perishing food, that endureth (as Christ who is himself that meat teachest us) unto 'everlasting life'." [3]

[1] Ibid., XI, 431 seqq.   [2] Ibid., 437.   [3] Ibid., XIII, 203.

In the third section[1] of his *Answer to a Jesuit* (1625) Ussher examines with great thoroughness the doctrine of transubstantiation in the light of Scripture and the ancient Fathers, together with its history. With pride Ussher shows the part played by an Irishman in the Eucharistic controversy. "The Emperor Charles, to whom the answer of Ratramus was directed, had then in his court a famous countryman of ours, called Johannes Scotus: who wrote a book of the same argument, and to the same effect, that the other had done." Nor do we find "any where that his book of the Sacrament was condemned before the days of Lanfranc, who was the first that leavened the Church of England afterward with this corrupt doctrine of the carnal presence. Till then, this question of the real presence continued still in debate: and it was free for any man to follow the doctrine of Ratramus or Johannes Scotus therein, as that of Paschasius Radbertus." [2]

Bishop Henry Leslie found much opposition in the diocese of Down and Connor to kneeling at the time of Communion. In 1636 he distinguishes between the Eucharistic practice of the Church of Rome and the Church of Ireland. "Their kneeling is the gesture of Papists, ours of Catholicks." [3] Ours "is directed to God alone, who vouchsafes to communicate himself unto us in these elements; yet out of that gesture directed to God reverence ariseth to the elements." [4] For as Athanasius says, " 'If the Jews did well to adore the Lord where the Ark and Cherubims were, shall we refuse to adore Christ where his body is present: shall we say, ...Keep thee from the Sacrament if thou wilt be worshipped?' " [5] In this Sacrament the signs of God's presence are "more glorious than the ark".[6] The Sacrament is "the conduit pipe of God's graces, the casket wherein a rich jewel is presented unto us from our heavenly Father: for in this Sacrament God 'offers unto us his own Son, in whom dwelleth the fulness of all grace': he is pleased to seal and deliver unto us the Charter of Redemption." [7]

In the same year Griffiths Williams, later Bishop of Ossory, affirms that the whole Christ is offered and received in the Sacrament. "Here is *all*

---

[1] Ibid., III, 52 seqq.

[2] Ibid., 84 seq.; cf. Jeremy Taylor: "...in the Church of England, Bertram's doctrine prevailed longer; and till Lanfranc's time it was permitted to follow Bertram or Paschasius." *Works*, VI, 160. This is one of the many points of contact between Taylor's *Real Presence* (1654) and the *Dissuasive from Popery*, Parts I (1614) and II (1667), and Ussher's *Answer to a Jesuit* (1625). In refuting the doctrine of transubstantiation Taylor uses many of Ussher's arguments and quotations.

[3] *An Answer to Certain Objections made against Kneeling at the Communion* (Dublin, 1637), 144.

[4] Ibid., 173.   [5] Ibid.   [6] Ibid., 185.   [7] Ibid., 186.

Christ undivided, his body by *consecration*, his blood by *connexion*, his soul by *conjunction*, and his Deity by *hypostatical* union."[1] There is no change of substance, but "an accession of *grace*".[2] They are changed "not in *nature*, but in *name*, *use*, and *estimation*". So "we deem them now as holy seals and symbols of most excellent graces". The heavenly graces so signified are "the body and blood of Christ, together with all the benefits of his Incarnation, and the merits of his death and passion, as especially, the remission of sins, the infusion of graces, and the possession of eternal joys".[3]

John Bramhall, Bishop of Derry (1634–61), distinguishes in 1653 between the doctrine of transubstantiation and "a true Real Presence, which no genuine son of the Church of England did ever deny".[4] With Hooker and Ussher he regrets the modern controversies about the "Sacrament of peace and unity",[5] for "we find no debates or disputes concerning the Presence of Christ's Body in the Sacrament, and much less concerning the manner of his Presence, for the first 800 years".[6] Bramhall then surveys the subsequent controversies which led to the formulation of the doctrine of transubstantiation,[7] and the differences arising from it. Regarding the adoration of the Sacrament "we deny not a venerable respect unto the consecrate Elements, not only as love-tokens sent us by our best Friend, but as the instruments ordained by our Saviour to convey to us the Merits of His Passion"; but we "dare not give Divine worship unto any creature, no, not to the very humanity of Christ in the abstract (much less to the Host), but to the *whole* Person of Christ, God and Man, by reason of the hypostatical union between the Child of the blessed Virgin Mary, and the Eternal Son". "Shew us such an union betwixt the Deity and the Elements, or accidents, and you say something."[8]

One outcome of the Romanist adoration of the Sacrament was the feast of Corpus Christi, "instituted about three hundred years since".[9] The Grecians "know no feast of Corpus Christi, nor carry the Sacrament up and down, nor elevate it to be adored. They adore Christ in the use of the Sacrament, so do we: they do not adore the Sacrament, no more than we."[10]

In the *Consecration and Succession of Protestant Bishops Justified* (1658), Bramhall maintains that ordained priests "ought to have power to consecrate the Sacrament of the Body and Blood of Christ, that is, to make

---

[1] *The Best Religion...*, 236.   [2] Ibid.   [3] Ibid., 238.
[4] *An Answer to M. de la Milletiere; Works*, I, 8.
[5] Ibid.   [6] Ibid., 9.   [7] Ibid., 10 seqq.
[8] Ibid., 21.   [9] Ibid., I, 21.   [10] Ibid., II, 634.

them present after such manner as They were present at the first institution". But our Church determines not whether the consecration of the elements is effected "by the enunciation of the words of Christ" as in the West, or by prayer as in the East, "or whether these two be both the same in effect, that is, that the forms of the Sacraments be mystical prayers, and implicit invocations". Our Church uses both forms; and "our consecration is a repetition of that which was done by Christ", the Priest consecrating "in the person of Christ", but Christ himself being "the chief consecrator still".[1]

Preaching as Primate of All Ireland before the Irish Commons on 16 July 1661, Bramhall maintains that after Baptismal grace "there is none more efficacious than the blessed Sacrament of the Body and Blood of Christ; the very conduit-pipe of grace to all worthy communicants, the manna of life and immortality, the precious antidote against the sting and infection of the Infernal Serpent;[2] that inestimable love-token, which Christ at his departure left to His Church, to keep in remembrance of Him; the true pool of Bethseda, wherein we may be cured of our infirmities." [3]

The Eucharistic teaching of Jeremy Taylor is contained in works written between 1649 and 1667. Taylor gives the subject devotional treatment in the *Great Exemplar* (1649), *Holy Living* (1650), and more fully in the *Worthy Communicant* (1660); doctrinal treatment in *Clerus Domini*; controversial treatment in the *Real Presence of Christ in the Blessed Sacrament* (1654) and in both parts of the *Dissuasive from Popery* (1664 and 1667); and liturgical expression in the *Collection of Offices* of 1658. It was natural that he should write with one emphasis in his devotional works and with another in his controversial; and of these it is important to distinguish between *The Real Presence*, written when he was a proscribed Anglican clergyman during the Commonwealth, and the *Dissuasive from Popery*, written when he was an Irish Bishop at the earnest request of the Irish House of Bishops.

In the *Worthy Communicant*, written in Ireland on the eve of the Restoration, Taylor develops and enlarges upon nearly all the aspects of the Eucharist contained in his earlier devotional works. For example, he develops his earlier view that the Eucharist continues the presence of Christ in the world, and cites, though without reference, the patristic

---

[1] Ibid., III, 163.
[2] The nineteenth-century editor cites Irenaeus, Ignatius, Athanasius, Optatus, and others. Ibid., V, 163 n.
[3] Ibid., 163.

designation of the Sacrament as "the extension of the Incarnation".[1] He develops the earlier view that in the Sacrament we become partakers of the Divine nature;[2] and that by faith and the Spirit being internally united to Christ and made partakers of his Body and Blood, "we are joined and made one with Him who did rise again", and that, therefore, "we shall rise again, and we shall enter into glory".[3] And he develops the earlier view that the heavenly ministry of Christ is "exhibited upon the holy table of the Lord".[4] On the other hand, Taylor for the first time lays stress on the duty of kneeling at the time of Communion, which he passes over in his earlier works.[5]

At one point Taylor appears to abandon his earlier well-known distinction in the *Real Presence of Christ* between the Roman and Anglican teaching that Christ's body is in the Sacrament "really, but spiritually", by spiritually, the Romans meaning "present after the manner of a spirit", the Anglicans "present to our spirits only".[6] In the *Worthy Communicant* Taylor declares our faith is not defective, "though we confess we do not understand how Christ's body is there incorporeally, that is, the body after the manner of a spirit".[7]

In the devotional works it is a matter for wonder "that He who cannot suffer any change or lessening should be broken into pieces, and enter into the body to support and nourish the spirit, and yet at the same time remain in heaven while he descends to thee upon earth".[8] For "every consecrated portion of bread and wine does exhibit Christ entirely to the faithful receiver; and yet Christ remains one, while He is wholly ministered in ten thousand pieces."[9] In the controversial works this wonderful fact becomes a major objection to the doctrine of transubstantiation. "For

---

[1] *Works*, VIII, 23; "He is the bread which came down from heaven; the bread which was born at Bethlehem, 'the house of bread', was given to us to be the food of our souls for ever." Ibid., 17. Cf. *Great Exemplar:* "Christ hath remained in the world by the communication of this sacrament." Ibid., II, 637.

[2] Ibid., VIII, 14 seqq.; cf. II, 642.

[3] Ibid., VIII, 40 seq.; cf. II, 645. "The Holy Sacrament is the pledge of glory and the earnest of immortality...and the consecrated symbols are like the seeds of an eternal duration, springing up to eternal life, nourishing our spirits with grace, which is but the prologue and the infancy of glory."

[4] Ibid., VIII, 73. At the Consecration "see Christ doing in His glorious manner the very thing which thou seest ministered and imitated upon the table of the Lord." VIII, 224. Cf. II, 640. "That body which is reigning in heaven is exposed upon the table of blessing."

[5] Ibid., 224 seq.

[6] Ibid., VI, 17; cf. Bramhall: "...whether it be corporally or spiritually (I mean not only after the manner of a spirit, but in a spiritual manner)." *Works*, I, 22.

[7] Ibid., VIII, 107.

[8] Ibid., III, 217 (*Holy Living*); cf, II, 640; VIII, 107.   [9] Ibid., II, 641.

Christ's body being in heaven, glorious, spiritual, and impassable, cannot be broken. And since by the Roman doctrine nothing is broken but that which cannot be broken, that is, the colour, the taste, and other accidents of the elements; yet if they could be broken, since the accidents of bread and wine are not the substance of Christ's body and blood; it is certain, on the altar, Christ's body naturally and properly cannot be broken." [1]

In the second part of the *Dissuasive* (1667), Taylor argues that if people in Peter Lombard's time who believed in Christ's Real Presence without determining the mode were "good Catholics", the Anglican Church is "as good a catholic Church as Rome was then, which had not determined the manner".[2] When the doctrine of transubstantiation was first formulated the doctors found it so intricate and involved that they "could not make anything distinctly of it". "However, whatever they did make of it, certain it is they agreed more with the present Church of England, than with the present Church of Rome; for we say as they said, Christ's body is truly there, and there is a conversion of the elements into Christ's body; for what before the consecration in all senses was bread, is, after consecration, in some sense, Christ's body; but they did not all of them say, that the substance of bread was destroyed; and some of them denied the conversion of the bread into the flesh of Christ; which whosoever shall now do, will be esteemed no Roman catholic." [3] This passage might suggest that Taylor had not altogether abandoned his earlier emphasis on the objectivity of the Sacramental Gift.[4]

Taylor's theory of consecration is perfectly consistent. "The Holy Ghost is the consecrator", and "he is called down by the prayers of the Church." [5] All liturgies in the world "do now, and did ever, mingle solemn prayers together with the recitation of Christ's words"; and the Anglican Church follows primitive precedent, always having believed "the consecration not to be a natural effect and change, finished in any one instant, but a Divine alteration consequent to the whole ministry; that is, the solemn prayer and invocation." [6] In the consecration of "the mysterious sacrament", Taylor claimed in an episcopal *Charge*, "the people have their portion; for the bishop or the priest blesses, and the people, by

---

[1] *Dissuasive* (I), ibid., VI, 207; cf. VI, 105 seq. 591.

[2] Ibid., VI, 576.   [3] Ibid., 576 seq.

[4] In an earlier letter of unknown date, published with the nineteenth-century title of *On the Reverence due to the Altar*, Taylor in a rhetorical comment on Chrysostom and Irenaeus, says: "We do believe that Christ is there really present in the Sacrament, there is the body and blood of Christ, which are 'verily and indeed' taken and received...shall not the Christian Altar be most holy where is present the blessed Body and Blood of the Son of God?" Ibid., v, 330.

[5] Ibid., I, 48.   [6] Ibid., I, 49; cf. VI, 44 seq.

saying 'Amen' to the mystic prayer, is partaker of the power, and the whole Church hath a share in the power of spiritual sacrifice." [1] In his Communion Office of 1658 Taylor introduces the Prayer of Consecration with an Invocation, adapted from an ancient Liturgy:

...send thy Holy Ghost upon our hearts, and let him also descend upon thy gifts, that by his good, his holy, his glorious presence, he may sanctify and enlighten our hearts, and he may bless and sanctify these gifts: That this bread may be the holy body of Christ *Amen*. And this Chalice may become the life-giving blood of Christ *Amen*. That it may become unto us all, that partake of it this day a blessed instrument of union with Christ, of pardon and peace, of health and blessing, of holiness and life eternal, through Jesus Christ our Lord *Amen*.[2]

The second part of the prayer for the dedication of "the Altar or Communion Table" in the Irish Consecration Form of 1666 asks that all the gifts which shall be presented on this table may be acceptable to God and become to his servants "a savour of life unto life"; that no unworthy receiver may ever taste "the holy body and blood which shall here be sacramentally represented and exhibited"; but that those who come hither with due preparation to receive "these mysteries" may "indeed partake of the Lord Jesus, and receive all the benefits of passion". Christ is "the Priest and the Sacrifice, the feeder and the food, the Physician and the physick of our souls".[3]

Dr Andrew Sall, the ex-Jesuit, who was received into the Church of Ireland in 1674, cites the Anglican formularies and Bishop Cosin's *Historia Transubstantionis Papalis* to show that Anglicans "believe and profess that Christ our Saviour is really and substantially present in the blessed Sacrament of the Eucharist, and his body and blood really and substantially received in it by the faithful". Our difference with the Church of Rome "is only regarding the *mode* of his presence". Protestants adore and reverence the "person of our Saviour, God and Man really present"; but to give the accidents the worship of *latria* "cannot with any colour of reason be excused from a formal idolatry".[4]

---

[1] Ibid., VIII, 504.   [2] Ibid., 624.   [3] Appendix: lines 402–16.
[4] *True Catholic and Apostolic Faith* (1846 ed.), 224 seq. At a much later date, however, Mortimer O'Sullivan, another ex-Romanist who joined the Church of Ireland, pointed to other differences. Both Churches "believe that the Sacrament is to be consecrated by a priest in the name and authority of Christ; but the Church of Rome affirms that the neglect or the malevolence of a minister may vitiate the form of consecration; the Church of England ascribes to her ministers no such power". This is interesting testimony to a Roman view, still held by some moral theologians, in the early nineteenth century. O'Sullivan cites Article 26 for the Anglican view. "Both Churches hold that the wicked and faithless eat to their condemnation; but the Church of Rome, in the doctrine of transubstantiation, teaches that the body and

Bishop Roger Boyle in 1681 regards the Eucharist as the sacrament of spiritual nourishment, just as Baptism is one of spiritual regeneration. "Faith within the soul in Christ crucified corresponds to the receiving of the body through hands and mouth; union with Christ through hope and love to the subsequent digestion of the elements." The grace manifested in the Eucharist is also unity of faithful people (1 Cor. 10. 17); for "Food is turned into body: therefore those whose food is one, their body is one also." [1] Boyle examines at length the doctrine of transubstantiation, which he shows to overthrow the nature of a sacrament.[2] Moreover, Romanists "look for nothing for which we do not look without any change of substance".[3] Boyle next dismisses the doctrine of consubstantiation. "Ubiquity abrogates the nature of a body and a creature, and so the Christ of the Ubiquitarians is not really a man"; and if Christ be present by reason of this ubiquity "then He is not more present in consecrated bread than in unconsecrated, nor can 'this is My Body' be more truly said of the bread than of the table".[4]

The key to the Eucharistic teaching of Bishop Ezekiel Hopkins, which stands quite apart in the post-Restoration period, lies in the meaning he gives to faith. Faith is "the soul's steward",[5] fetching in supplies of grace from Christ, making us "mystically one with Christ, lively members in his body, fruitful branches of that heavenly and spiritual vine".[6] Only acting faith fixed upon Christ the Mediator, as exhibited in his Body and Blood, can make this ordinance "beneficial to us, either as to its signifying or as to its sealing Office".[7] There is an external sealing by the Sacrament, and an internal sealing by the Spirit. By the Sacrament "God seals unto me, that, if I believe on the Lord Jesus, I shall be saved, and gives me a visible pledge of this promise, that, as sure as I eat of the sacramental bread and drink of the wine, so surely, upon my faith, I shall inherit eternal life". Yet the Sacrament "doth not properly seal and attest to me, that I do believe, and therefore shall be saved". But this is "the work of the Holy Ghost, the Spirit of Adoption, which seals us up unto the day of redemption; and works in the hearts of many believers a full assurance,

---

blood, soul, and divinity, of Christ are taken into the body of the guilty communicant, while the Church of England affirms, that the dishonour is done not to Christ, but to the symbols of his body and blood. In fine, both affirm that Christ instituted the sacrament in two kinds; the Church of England adheres to the rule thus divinely recommended: the Church of Rome, on her own authority, has altered it." *A Guide to an Irish Gentleman in his Search for a Religion*, 26 seq.

[1] *Summa Theologie Christianae*, 257 seq.
[2] Ibid., 262 seqq.   [3] Ibid., 264.   [4] Ibid., 267.
[5] *Works* (ed. J. Pratt, 1809), I, 225.   [6] Ibid., 325; cf. 291, 390.
[7] Ibid., II, 434.

I

that grace is already wrought in them, and that glory shall hereafter be bestowed upon them." [1]

The sacramental meditations of James Bonnell (d. 1699) may be some guide to what devout and intelligent lay people believed at the close of the seventeenth century. Bonnell distinguishes between the heavenly table and the earthly. "The table, which we call the holy altar, is but a shelf of wood: God's table is a spiritual thing." Those who are admitted to the divine feast sit at the heavenly table, though they kneel in the Church. The food which we receive comes from the heavenly table. "It is true, on our table, the holy elements are impregnated with the materials of life; like the first framing of a living creature, or embryo, before it is quickened: but they are quickened with spiritual life, only upon the faith of each receiver, which God hath appointed to be the concurring instrument, or means of the divine quickening. Then they become to us the seeds of glory, and the assured conveyances of spiritual nourishment and immortal happiness." The Gift comes from the heavenly table, and "while we sit with the Church triumphant, well may we be content to kneel with the Church militant".[2] In another meditation "composed upon his return home from that heavenly feast", Bonnell speaks of the work of the Holy Trinity in the Eucharist.

The glory of my God with his heavenly host, filled the place. God the Father, Son, and Holy Ghost, were all there... My Saviour impregnated the consecrated elements, and in a manner embodied himself there; yet still remaining where he was, filling heaven and earth, but more particularly our Chancel... I received my blessed Saviour into my heart, nay the whole Trinity; for the unity of the Father, and the power of the Spirit, accompanied the sacred action...[3]

Bishop William King in 1694 makes a lengthy defence of kneeling at the Communion,[4] and recommends a weekly celebration of the Eucharist, which Christ intended to be "a constant part of the ordinary worship". "To hold solemn assemblies of Christians without communicating is a corruption of popery." [5] The Presbyterian practice of allowing non-communicants to be present at the Sacrament "would have been reckoned a profanation of this Holy Mystery in primitive times; and is in earnest

---

[1] *Works* (ed. J. Pratt, 1809), 441 seq.

[2] William Hamilton, *Life of Bonnell*, 145 seq.

[3] Ibid., 154 seq.; cf. *The Harmony of the Gospels with Meditations*, 321 seq.; 325.

[4] *Inventions of Men in the Worship of God*, 158 seqq. He cites Mal. 1. 7; 2 Chron. 6. 12, 13; 1 Kings 8. 54; 2 Kings 18. 22; 1 Cor. 10. 16, 18, 21; and more curiously Ps. 22. 29, "All they that be fat upon earth, (that is, the favoured and happy Servants of God here, called in ver. 20 the *Meek*) shall Eat and Worship."

[5] Ibid., 211.

an abuse brought in by Popery." [1] As Archbishop of Dublin, King dealt more sympathetically with the doctrine of consubstantiation than some of his clergy who marked the accession of George I by preaching against it on the following Sunday. The Lutherans "seem not to mean a local presence but only a spiritual, by virtue of the reunion of the human with the divine person; for, say they, the divine person of our Saviour is everywhere, and he is nowhere without his humanity; which is true: but then, it is to be considered that the divine nature has no relation to place, not being an extended substance. But as thought is everywhere, and whatever I think of is really in my mind, without any local motion either of the mind or object, so by analogies I reckon the humanity of our Saviour is everywhere with his divinity without any relation to place." [2] King's prayer for the dedication of the altar in his Dublin diocesan consecration form of 1719 contains this petition:

...and forasmuch as thou, who fillest all Places, hast promised thy Presence in a more peculiar Manner, to those who approach thine holy Altar, let thy blessed Spirit, we beseech thee, be ever present with thy servants, when they come to this thy Table, to be fed with the Bread of Life, and to receive that spiritual food which thou hast provided for us...

Bishop Peter Browne and Bishop Wilson were not uninfluenced by the Eucharistic teaching of the English Non-jurors, which Archbishop King distrusted. Both provide in their private devotions at the Eucharist an invocation. At "Placing the elements" Bishop Browne prays that God will send down his Holy Spirit upon them "for a Divine and Quickening energy, that we may receive them again from thee as His Body and Blood". Bishop Wilson gives various forms of the invocation from the Clementine Liturgy in *Sacra Privata*[3] and the *Short and Plain Instruction*[4] for use "immediately after the Consecration". Charles Leslie, the Irish Non-juror, on the other hand, distrusted the tendency among the Non-jurors to introduce this kind of invocation. "In the collect just before the consecration, with us, we pray that we may eat the flesh of Christ, and drink his blood, which we are about to receive", which "no doubt is meant spiritually, according to John 6. 63. But they would have some wonderful transmutation in the very elements, which has introduced transubstantiation. Whither are we running?" [5]

In *The Case Stated between the Church of Rome and the Church of England*

---

[1] *Admonition to the Dissenting Inhabitants of the diocese of Derry*, 21.
[2] Quoted from C. S. King, *A Great Archbishop of Dublin*, 165 seq.
[3] *Works*, v, 73 seq.
[4] This Invocation appears in the 1781 collection of Wilson's works by Crutwell, but not in the editions by the S.P.C.K.   [5] *Works*, I, 506.

Leslie refutes the doctrine of transubstantiation. He cites a passage from Theodoret comparing this doctrine with the Eutychian view that the human nature of Christ was absorbed or swallowed up in his divinity.[1] Like Andrew Sall, Leslie appeals to Cosin's History of Transubstantiation, not yet answered, and he believed unanswerable, demonstrating the new doctrine to be against the Scriptures, primitive Church, and Fathers. Romanists have on their side nothing in the world but "an unintelligible jargon of metaphysics, upon which the schoolmen ring changes, all the noise of their bells having deafened common sense and reason".[2] Taking substance to be that which *sub stat*, and *essentis accidentis est inhaerentis*, Leslie concludes that when the substance is gone, the accidents are no more, "for their essence is gone, which is inherence, and they cannot inhere or stick in nothing".[3] In a recent work on Eucharistic teaching Leslie is said to have controverted Bishop Benjamin Hoadley's *A Plain Account of the Nature and End of the Sacrament of the Lord's Supper* (1735). No doubt he would have done so with great force and ability had he not died thirteen years before that book appeared.

In Hoadly's defence of *A Plain Account* severe criticisms are made of a devotional work by an Irish Bishop, Edward Wetenhall, *Concerning the Frequent and Holy Use of the Lord's Supper*, appended to *Enter into Thy Closet* (1666). Hoadly is shocked by the symbolism Wetenhall gives to the sacramental actions of the minister. "The Blessing the Bread and Wine represents God the Father sanctifying and furnishing our Lord Christ, as to his human nature, with all gifts necessary for the discharge of the office of our Redeemer; his blessing him *with the Spirit above measure*." [4] Hoadly was also shocked by Wetenhall's statement that by the consecrated elements God truly conveyed to the faithful receiver the Body and Blood of Christ, that is, "all the Effects, Powers, Virtues, Benefits and Fruits thereof", especially "of spiritual Strength, and pardon, and eternal life".[5] Hoadly particularly objected to Wetenhall's descrip-

---

[1] *Works*, III, 128.   [2] Ibid., 129.

[3] "Now to apply all this, when the substance of the bread and wine is gone, as you suppose, then their accidents are no more, for there cannot be accidents of nothing: nothing has no accidents: and they cannot be accidents of bread when there is no bread: and you will not endure they should be called the accidents of the body and blood of Christ: therefore they are accidents of nothing, that is they are accidents and no accidents: they are accidents without the essence of accidents which is inherence: there is roundness and nothing round, whiteness and nothing white, a taste and nothing tasted, liquidness and nothing liquid." Ibid., 129 seqq.

[4] Hoadly, *An Apologetical Defence...of a Late Book entitled a Plain Account...*, 20 (Wetenhall, op. cit., 1668 ed., 396).

[5] Ibid., 331 (ibid., 1676 ed., Append., 36).

tion of the Eucharist as "the chief of evangelical Ordinances, and the highest Advancement of the Christian soul on this side of Heaven".[1] In *Due Frequency of the Lord's Supper: Stated and Proved from Holy Scripture* (2nd ed., 1703) Wetenhall speaks of the Sacrament as "that Medicine of Immortality, that Seal or great earnest of our blessed Resurrection".[2]

A Plain Account had appeared anonymously in 1735, but everybody knew that Benjamin Hoadly was the author. Likewise everybody in Ireland knew that Philip Skelton was the author of a work which appeared in Dublin anonymously the following year—*A Vindication of the Right Rev. the Lord Bishop of Winchester against the Malicious Aspersion of those who uncharitably ascribe to His Lordship the Book entitled "A Plain Account of the Nature and End of the Sacrament of the Lord's Supper"*; the title-page bearing the text: "Who is this that darkeneth counsel by words without knowledge?" (Job 38. 2). Skelton knew not what part of the world the author lived in, but "next to the wickedness of the author, is the malice of those who would make us think it the work of so great and excellent a man as the bishop of Winchester. What a scandalous and uncharitable age is this that can ascribe such a work of darkness to an apostolical messenger of light! To a bishop! To a servant and successor of our Saviour! How is it possible that one who subscribes our articles, who engages to inculcate our Catechism, to administer the Church according to our Canons, and this Sacrament according to our rubric, should write one sentence of such a book?" Skelton could not join in the groundless and uncharitable imputation "that would fix one of the worst books ever wrote on one of the best bishops that ever adorned ours or any other Church, a bishop so learned and judicious, a bishop so sincere and in-genious, a bishop so sound and orthodox, a bishop, in short, so pious, so replete with the greatest abilities and highest virtues, so inspired, so fired, so almost consumed with Christian zeal."[3] Skelton then proceeds to attack what he asserts to be the author's main tenets: that the consecration of the elements is without scriptural precept or example;[4] that the rite is a bare commemoration;[5] that the only necessary preparation to a worthy reception of the Sacrament is a serious remembrance of our Saviour's death;[6] that there are no privileges peculiarly annexed to the worthy receiving of the Lord's Supper, no concomitant grace, no spiritual benefits, no communion with God, no renewal of our Baptismal vow, nor seal of the Christian Convenant;[7] and that the duty of communicating

---

[1] Ibid., 33 (ibid., 1668 ed., 357).   [2] Op. cit., Introd.
[3] *Works*, v, 213 seq.   [4] Ibid., 215 seqq.   [5] Ibid., 219 seqq.
[6] Ibid., 228 seqq.   [7] Ibid., 231 seqq.

is not so connected with other Christian duties, but that it may well be performed without them, or they without it, thereby making people more practically Christians, and greatly increasing the number of communicants.[1] Since it is at present inconvenient for the Convocation to meet, he hoped that the author would not go undetected and excommunicated and that his book would be censured and its doctrine condemned by Bishops in their Visitations. For "whom can it be more necessary to excommunicate, than him who has laboured to pervert and vilify the most sacred ordinance of our religion?"[2] Skelton's Diocesan, Bishop John Stearne of Clogher, was so pleased with this sly attack upon the Bishop of Winchester that he gave the author ten guineas.[3]

Skelton's Eucharistic doctrine may more readily be found in his discourse on "The Necessity and Efficacy of Spiritual Nourishment", parts of which are noticed elsewhere.[4] "The breaking and pouring out of the elements" convey a lively notion of our Saviour's sufferings. As common meat and drink they aptly figure "that heavenly food of God's grace, whereby our souls are nourished to eternal life". "Nor do they only represent, they also convey the food, and apply the merit of that Sacrifice to the soul of every worthy receiver."[5] The blessed Sacrament is not only "the formal act and seal, whereby Christ, in his last will and testament, bequeaths to us all our title to an inheritance in heaven, but also the chief means of imparting to us those aids of his Holy Spirit, without which it will be impossible to make good that title."[6] Skelton makes a plea for frequent Communion, and asks "whether it would not be happy for you, if you were to receive this blessed sacrament every day of your life?"[7]

The Collect for the Communion Service in *An Office for Consecration of Churches according to the Use of the Province of Dublin* of 1760 follows closely a Collect in the form used by Bishop Simon Patrick of Ely in the consecration of the Chapel of St Katherine's Hall, Cambridge, in 1704. It contains this petition:

Vouchsafe, we beseech thee, to make thyself spiritually present to us, both now and ever, when the holy Sacrament of thy blessed Body and Blood shall be prepared for us at this thy Table. Stir up in us, by the power of thy Holy Spirit, such heavenly thoughts and affections: Work in us such godly resolution to dedicate ourselves intirely to thee, that we may worthily commemorate thy wonderful Love in dying for us. And because Holiness becometh thine House for

[1] *Works*, v, 240 seqq.   [2] Ibid., 249.   [3] Ibid., I, xli.
[4] See above, p. 82; below, p. 162.
[5] Op. cit., III, 120 seq.   [6] Ibid., 126 seq.   [7] Ibid., 123.

ever, Consecrate us, both in Soul and Body, to be an holy Temple unto thee; that thou dwelling in our hearts by Faith and Love, we may be cleansed from all sinful affections, as to be devoutly given to serve thee in all good works to the Glory of thy Blessed Name...

This Collect was used in the consecration of the new Chapel of Trinity College, Dublin, in 1798.[1]

In 1819 Alexander Knox writes to Archdeacon Jebb of Emly "that the consecrated symbols are not merely (as Dr Waterland maintains) the signs and pledges of a concomitant blessing, but (as the old church taught, and as Dr Brett urges against Waterland) the actual vehicles, through which that blessing is conveyed".[2] In 1826 appeared Knox's *Treatise in the Use and Import of the Eucharistic Symbols*. In a prefatory letter Knox maintains that the Eucharistic teaching of Ridley, rather than of Cranmer, is embodied in our formularies. Ridley acknowledged Ratramus for his master, and his views emerged triumphant in the Elizabethan Prayer Book and were more perfectly expressed in the Scottish rite of 1637, which as far as was expedient provided the model for the rite of 1662.[3] In the *Treatise* Knox maintains that the "earthly elements" are "instruments of divine power", implying the presence of the Almighty agent. When we approach the table of the Lord we are admitted "into the presence-chamber of King Messiah". Let us recognize "the same spirit of meek majesty, which veiled its transcendent brightness, in the mystery of the Incarnation, as still continuing the like gracious condescension, in the mystery of the Eucharist".[4] In 1824 Jebb, now Bishop of Limerick, told Knox whose manuscript he had read that into a small compass he had "compressed more good sense and sound theology than are contained in any ten bulky volumes of former writers on the subject".[5]

One of Bishop Jebb's first Ordinands, William Palmer, deals at length with the doctrine of the Eucharist in his *Treatise of the Church of Christ* (1838). He maintains that the Anglican Church is "not in the slightest degree commited to the particular opinions of Archbishop Cranmer", whose books must not be confounded with her public and authorized

---

[1] *An Office used for the Consecration of the Chapel of Trinity College Dublin, on Sunday the 8th July, 1798* (Dublin, 1798), 12.

[2] *Thirty Years Correspondence*, etc., II, 356 seq. *Remains of Alexander Knox Esq.* (1857 ed.).

[3] Ibid., II, 151 seq. In the *Treatise* Knox says that Ridley's views are further embodied in Articles 25, 28, and 29, and in the Elizabethan addition to the Catechism. Ibid., 153 seq.

[4] Ibid., 220 seq.   [5] Ibid., IV, 409.

doctrine.[1] While the Catholic and Apostolic Church has always avoided the attempt "to determine too minutely the mode of the true presence in the holy eucharist", she believes that "the eucharist is not the sign of an *absent* body", but "that we receive in the eucharist, not only the flesh and blood of Christ, but Christ himself, both God and man". She holds "that the nature of the bread and wine continue after consecration: and therefore rejects transubstantiation". She holds "that the presence (and therefore the eating) of Christ's body and blood, though true, is altogether 'heavenly and spiritual'." She rejects "any such real presence of Christ's body and blood as is 'corporal' or organical: that is, according to the known and earthly mode of the existence of a body." Those who are totally devoid of a true and living faith, "do not partake of the holy flesh of Christ in the eucharist, God withdrawing from them so 'divine' a gift, and not permitting his enemies to partake of it". She holds such a faith to be "the means by which the body of Christ is received and eaten", "a necessary instrument in all these holy ceremonies". She believes that "the blessing" or "consecration" of the bread and wine "is not without effect, but that it operates a real change, for when the Sacrament is thus perfected, she regards it as so 'divine a thing' so 'heavenly a food' that we must not 'presume' to approach it with unprepared minds." [2] Palmer then returns to attack transubstantiation. Archbishop Yngve Brillioth sees "a reflection in Palmer of the Eucharistic doctrine of earlier High Anglicanism",[3] and asserts that "Palmer's book might just as well have been written before 1833".[4] And Palmer might just as well have provided the addition to the Catechism in the revised Irish Prayer Book of 1878.[5]

IV. CONFIRMATION

The Church of Ireland has made a rich contribution to the Anglican teaching on Confirmation. Jeremy Taylor's *Discourse of Confirmation* of 1663 has been praised as "a magnificent treatise",[6] "the high-water mark

---

[1] Op. cit. (1842 ed.), I, 391.   [2] Ibid., 401 seqq.
[3] *The Anglican Revival*, 317.   [4] Ibid., 202.
[5] "*Question*. After what manner are the Body and Blood of Christ taken and received in the Lord's Supper?
Answer. Only after a heavenly and spiritual manner; and the mean whereby they are taken and received is Faith."
The addition is of course taken almost verbally from Article 28.
[6] A. M. Ramsey, "The Doctrine of Confirmation", *Theology* (XLVIII), Sept. 1945, 198.

of the Caroline teaching",[1] "the greatest of all English books on Confirmation", "the fullest treatment of Confirmation, on its doctrinal, historical, and practical sides" put forth by any Anglican theologian,[2] and "by far the richest and most edifying work upon the subject" with which Dr A. J. Mason was acquainted.[3] The fact, however, that this publication was more than a private work has generally been overlooked. Taylor told the Duke of Ormonde, in his dedication, that he had only taken on the task at the entreaty of those who had "power to command" him;[4] and the title-page of the first Dublin edition of 1663 declares the work to be "Publish'd by Order of Convocation", making it clear that those who had "power to command" were the members at least of the Irish Upper House. The title-page, moreover, reveals that the book was not intended only for his own diocese, but "For the use of the Clergy and Instruction of the People of *Ireland*." We are fortunate too in knowing the views of Primate Bramhall, the President of the Upper House, and of Dean Mossom, the Prolocutor of the Lower. Both had preached on Confirmation during the Commonwealth.

Taylor says that Bramhall, when Bishop of Derry in exile on the Continent, "having usefully and wisely discoursed of the sacred rite of confirmation", imposed hands upon the Duke of York and Gloucester and the Princess Royal, "and ministered to them the promise of the holy Spirit, and ministerially established them in the religion and service of the Holy Jesus".[5] Taylor had evidently read this Discourse. It may have been similar to, or identical with, "A discourse made at Paris upon the confirmation of the Honourable ——, and sundry others", a large part of which survives in Bramhall's unmistakable hand among the Hastings papers in the custody of the Henry Huntington Library at San Marino, California. Unfortunately the discourse which Primate Ussher is said to have given at a Confirmation "concerning the antiquity and good use of it"[6] does not appear to have survived.

At a later date we find many publications on Confirmation: *An Exhortation to the Inhabitants of Down and Connor Concerning the Religious Education of their Children In general: and particularly in order to their being Confirmed* by Bishop Samuel Foley in 1695; *The Antiquity and Usefulness of Episcopal Confirmation* by Nicholas Brady in 1708; *A Discourse of*

---

[1] C. G. Richards, *Baptism and Confirmation*.
[2] S. L. Ollard, *Confirmation* (S.P.C.K.), I, 154; 162.
[3] *Relation of Confirmation to Baptism*, 380.
[4] *Works*, v, 609.   [5] Ibid., VIII, 418 seq.
[6] Nicholas Bernard, *Clavi Trabalis*, 63.

Confirmation in Dialogue by Archbishop Synge of Tuam, the second edition in 1740; "A Discourse of Confirmation" by Philip Skelton (d. 1787); *A Discourse of Confirmation* by Isaac Mann, Bishop of Cork and Ross, in 1785 ("Price Three Pence"); *An Address delivered before Confirmation throughout the Diocese of Meath* by Bishop O'Beirne in 1817; *Pastoral Advice to Young Persons before Confirmation*, twenty-fifth Dublin edition in 1821; *An Address to Parents and Sponsors on the Subject of Confirmation with Remarks on Infant Baptism* by Archdeacon Knox of Armagh in 1821; "The Church's Rite of Confirmation: its History and Value" by Bishop Mant; *Addresses to the Clergy of Dublin on Confirmation* by Archbishop Whately in 1832 and 1834.

All these Divines, while holding varying views on the scriptural ground for this rite,[1] are agreed upon its antiquity. Philip Skelton, for example, explained to his candidates that Confirmation was "practised universally by the apostles, bishops, and Christians, not only of the first and purest ages of the Church, but in all ages, from thence to the Reformation, when some of the Protestant Churches thought fit to discontinue it, on account of the superstitious ceremonies added to it in less enlightened times, which blessed be God, did not prevent ours from retaining a rite, in some sense necessary at the time that she pruned away the new-fangled additions".[2] The rite of Confirmation, Taylor maintained, was "ancient, and long before popery entered into the world", and "hath been more abused by popery than by anything; and to this day the bigots of the Roman Church are the greatest enemies to it; and from them the Presbyterians."[3] Bramhall also accused the Roman Church of meddling with this apostolic rite by investing Presbyters with power to confirm for avaricious ends, and without primitive precedent chalking out the way to innovators.[4]

Although Taylor thought the ancient and "not unreasonable" ceremony of anointing had been omitted "with sufficient authority" by our Church,[5] yet he laid great stress on the inward grace which it signified. In Confirmation "we receive the unction from above, that is, then we are most signally 'made kings and priests unto God, to offer up spiritual sacrifices'". Thus the early Church "made use of this allegory, and passed

---

[1] Among other passages given in support of this rite Jeremy Taylor cites John 3. 5; Acts 8. 14–17; 19. 1–6; and Heb. 6. 1–2; Bishop Wolley, Tit. 3. 5; Luke 24. 49; John 15. 26; Acts 1. 4; Bishop Roger Boyle, Matt. 7. 7; Skelton, Ephes. 3. 14–19; 6. 10 seqq.; Bishop Mant, Luke 11. 13; Archbishop Synge, Phil. 2. 13.

[2] *Works*, III, 83.   [3] *Works*, V, 613.

[4] *Works*, III, 26 seq.; cf. II, 71; V, 189; Taylor *Works*, V, 648 seq.

[5] *Works*, V, 653.

it into an external ceremony and representation of the mystery, to signify the inward grace.

> "*Post inscripta oleo frontis signacula, per quae*
> *Unguentum regale datum est, et chrisma perenne;*

'we are consigned on the forehead with oil, and a royal unction and an external chrism is given to us', so Prudentius gives testimony of the ministry of confirmation in his time." [1] Although Bramhall could understand the use of oil, he was absolutely at a stand for the use of balm, since all the balm of Judea, if there was any left at all, would scarcely suffice for one small diocese, and that brought from the newly discovered Indies was "a counterfeit mixed compound". The matter and form must be from heaven, and not from man. In espousing this captive rite the Anglican Church had reformed abuses and restored it to apostolical simplicity without tricking it out in the robe of a Sacrament. [2]

There was, however, a difference of emphasis on the blessings conveyed in this ancient and apostolical rite. Earlier Caroline Divines had the authority of the positive statement in the 1604 Prayer Book, omitted in 1662, that "Confirmation is ministered to them that be baptized, that by imposition of hands and prayer they may receive strength and defence against all temptations to sin and the assaults of the world and the devil". [3] In spite of this omission in 1662 the Anglican rite continued to imply that the Holy Spirit, the agent in Baptismal regeneration, further strengthens the baptized in Confirmation and daily increases in them the manifold gifts of Divine grace. "Our Church", explains Bishop Roger Boyle, "retains Confirmation as the prayer for grace because of the command of the Lord, 'Ask and ye shall receive'". There was no doubt that this apostolic rite had power "to confer increase of sanctifying grace (*gratiae gatum facientis*)". [4] Calvin, on the other hand, desired to retain this rite, "which existed in the early Church before the abortive mask of a sacrament appeared", but not such a rite, "which cannot even be named without injuring baptism". [5] He rejected any view which regarded Confirmation as perfecting Baptism. "Those anointers say that the Holy Spirit is given in baptism for righteousness, and in confirmation, for increase of grace, that in baptism we are regenerated for life, and in confirmation, equipped for contest." [6]

---

[1] Ibid., 652.   [2] MS. Sermon.
[3] Third rubric before the 1604 Confirmation rite.
[4] *Summa Theologie Christianae*, 276, seq.
[5] *Institutes*, IV, xix, 13 (ed. H. Beveridge, II, 632).   [6] Ibid., 8 (628).

Here the views of Calvin are in marked contrast with those of the Caroline Divines. He was citing a passage in an early Gallican homily on Pentecost, once attributed to Eusebius Emissenus, though Ussher regarded some of the homilies attributed to him as spurious,[1] and now ascribed by Dom G. Morin to Faustus of Riez. Hooker had given part of this passage: "The Holy Ghost which descendeth with saving influence upon the waters of baptism doth there give that fulness which sufficeth for innocency, and afterwards exhibiteth in confirmation an augmentation of further grace (*augmentum praestat ad gratiam*)." [2]   Cosin extends the passage: "In baptismo regeneramur ad vitam, post baptismum confirmamur ad pugnam: in baptismo alimur, post baptismum roboramur." Cosin claims that the whole passage sets forth "the virtue of the laying on of hands to the full".[3]

This view was fully shared by Irish Divines at the Restoration. Bramhall had worked out the military parallel at the Confirmation he held in Paris during the Commonwealth. The Holy Spirit is given in Baptism to regeneration: in Confirmation to corroboration. The Christians, quickened and made new creatures in Baptism, are newly armed and made fit soldiers in Confirmation to fight under Christ's banner. Those registered as Christ's soldiers at Baptism, and armed for all encounters at Confirmation, are by Ordination made leaders and commanders. Robert Mossom, the Prolocutor of the Lower House, had also fallen back upon the ancient homily on Pentecost. "In Baptism *regeneramur ad vitam*, we are regenerated to life; by imposition of hands, *confirmamur ad pugnam*, we are fortified to battle against the flesh, the world, and the devil; having given up our names unto Christ, and lifted ourselves under his banner." [4] A manuscript work on the ministry by Bishop Edward Wolley, Bishop of Clonfert (1665–84), has a section on Confirmation in which he cites the same passage from Eusebius Emissenus.[5]

Writing as a spokesman of the Irish Convocation Jeremy Taylor in 1663 describes the working of the Holy Spirit in the life of man. "In one mystery He illuminates and in another He feeds us; He begins in one and finishes and perfects in another. It is the same Spirit working divers operations." [6] "The Spirit moved a little upon the waters of baptism, and gave us the principles of life; but in confirmation he makes us able to move ourselves. In the first he is the Spirit of life; but in this he is the

---

[1] *Works*, XII, 277.   [2] *Ecclesiastical Polity*, v, lxvi, 4 (ed. J. Keble, 341).
[3] *Works* (L.A.C.T.), v, 195.
[4] *Preacher's Tripartite*.   [5] T.C.D., MS. N. 2. 10.
[6] *Works*, v, 616; cf. 615 seq.

spirit of strength and motion".[1] Confirmation is "the consummation and perfection, the corroboration and strength, of baptism and baptismal grace; for in baptism we undertake to do our duty, but in confirmation we receive strength to do it: in baptism others promise for us, in confirmation we undertake for ourselves." In Baptism "we give up our names to Christ, but in confirmation we put the seal to the profession, and God puts the seal to the promise".[2] " 'Spiritus sanctus in baptisterio plenitudinem tribuit ad innocentiam, sed in confirmatione augmentum praestat ad gratiam', said Eusebius Emissenus: in baptism we were made innocent, in confirmation we receive the increase of the Spirit of grace: in that we are regenerated unto life, in this we are strengthened unto battle."[3] Taylor also gives a similar passage from "a late synod of Rheims".[4] In Confirmation "we receive strength to do all that which was for us undertaken in baptism: for the apostles themselves (as the holy fathers observe) were timorous in the faith until they were confirmed in Pentecost, but after the reception of the Holy Ghost they waxed valiant in the faith and in all their spiritual combats."[5] In Confirmation, moreover, "we receive the Holy Ghost as the earnest of our inheritance, as the seal of our salvation": and "we are sealed for the service of God and unto the day of redemption".[6] The Holy Spirit is a witness to us that in Baptism we are made the sons of God. This is ὁ παράκλητος, the Holy Ghost the Comforter, this is He whom Christ promised and did send in Pentecost, and was afterwards ministered and conveyed by prayer and imposition of hands: and by this Spirit He makes the confessors bold and the martyrs valiant, and the tempted strong, and the virgins to persevere, and the widows to sing his praises, and His glories.[7] Taylor sees in 2 Cor. 1. 21, 22, a description of "the whole mysterious part of this rite".

God is the author of the grace: the apostles and all Christians are the suscipients, and receive this grace: by this grace we are adopted and incorporated into Christ; God hath anointed us; that is, He hath given us this unction from above, He hath "sealed us by His spirit", made us His own, bored our ears through, made us free by His perpetual service, and hath done all things in token of a greater; He hath given us His spirit to testify to us that He will give us of His glory. These words of

---

[1] Ibid. [2] Ibid., 656. [3] Ibid., 656 seq.
[4] Ibid., 657 seq. [5] Ibid., 658. [6] Ibid.
[7] Ibid., 659. Taylor deals with the still popular objection that confirmed people seem to be "the same after as before, no better and no wiser, not richer in gifts, not more adorned with grace...". The changes wrought upon our souls "are not after the manner of nature, visible and sensible, and with observation". The Holy Spirit is "received by moral instruments, and is intended only as a help to our endeavours, to our labours and our prayers, to our contentions and our mortifications, to our faith, and to our hope, to our patience and to our charity". Ibid., 659 seq.

S. Paul, besides that they evidently contain in them the spiritual part of this ritual, are also expounded of the rite and sacramental itself by S. Chrysostom, Theodoret and Thephylact, that I may name no more.[1]

A century later we find Philip Skelton, a country clergyman in the diocese of Clogher, conveying in simple and forceful language to his Confirmation candidates the teaching of Taylor and his Caroline contemporaries. In Confirmation, Skelton tells them, the baptized Christian confirms the Baptismal covenant, made in his name, and "the Spirit of God, communicated by the laying on of the bishop's hands, confirms the Christian".[2] "In baptism you was made, and are now going to be confirmed the child of God." God offers "his Holy Spirit by the hands of his appointed servant, first to guide you into all truth, that is, to assist both your understanding and heart, that you may believe aright; for faith, a truly Christian and lively faith, is not of yourself, it is the gift of God; and lastly, so to enliven and invigorate your conscience, that you may resolve and act up to the name and character of a real Christian, to the character of a candidate for eternal glory." [3] Then Skelton works out in Scriptural terms the military illustration given in the ancient homily on Pentecost.

By baptism you was enlisted into the army of Christ, the Captain of your Salvation. But that was done for you by suretees when you was yet a child. You are now going in person to be attested and sworn into his service. You are going to be trained to the exercise and discipline of a Christian soldier; to put on the helmet of salvation, the breastplate of righteousness, and the girdle of truth; to take the shield of faith and the sword of the Spirit, at the armory of God. You are going in a little time to be fed at the table and magazine of your Lord with the bread of Life. Religion, truth, virtue, heaven, Christ, God, your soul, are all to be

---

[1] *Works*, v, 660 seq. It is impossible here to give an adequate impression of this great work, which is divided into an Introduction and seven sections: "1. The divine original, warranty and institution of the holy rite of confirmation; 2. That this rite was to be a perpetual and never-ceasing ministration; 3. That it was actually continued and practiced by all succeeding ages of the purest and primitive churches; 4. That this rite was appropriate to the ministry of bishops; 5. That prayer and imposition of the bishop's hands did make the whole ritual; and though other things were added, yet they were not necessary, or anything of institution; 6. That many great graces and blessings were consequent to the worthy reception and due ministration of it; 7. I shall add something of the manner of preparation to it, and reception of it." Ibid., 618.

[2] *Works*, III, 83. "Do not hope that the Holy Spirit will, by his grace alone and without your concurrence, enable you to renounce, to believe, and do, as you have vowed... You are commanded to work out your own salvation with fear and trembling, though you are, at the same time assured, that it is God that worketh in you, both to will and to do..." Ibid., 84.   [3] Ibid., 86.

fought for. See that you behave yourself in a manner worthy of such a cause and such a captain. Keep close to the standard, and firm in your rank. It is safest fighting in a body. Single combat hath more danger in it. Forsake not, therefore, the assemblies of the faithful, as the manner of some is ... Above all, go constantly to God's house and table. Here you converse with God by prayer, and he with you by his word. Here you may kindle your devotion at the fire of others, and light your candle at those which shine around you. You may take a useful example from the army of your enemy. He, you see, keeps up the spirit of discipline of his service by assemblies in those churches of his contrivance.[1]...

Thus it is that the enemy prepares for battle. In assemblies of an opposite kind, and by exercises of a contrary nature, but still in assembling, and by exercising, must you prepare on your part. Nothing in your power is able to give you so much skill, strength, and courage, in the spiritual warfare....

See how the good Christians of your aquaintance advance steadily on the enemy, and put to flight the armies of the aliens! See how the martyrs break through fire and blood to take the kingdom of God by violence! Above all, see how Christ, your captain, lays round him with his cross, levels whole ranks at one with every stroke of his two-edged sword! His almighty hand rises to heaven, and crushes to hell, at every blow. How can you be dismayed, or draw back, in such company, with such a leader, and such a prize in view? Shew the proof of your armour and the vigour of your feeding. Quit you like a man, be strong.[2]

Skelton then describes in a way worthy of Bunyan the narrow way and the broad, and the people who travel on each. Towards the close he again stresses the value of Church membership, of the Communion of Saints, of the table which the Holy Spirit spreads for refreshment on the difficult upward journey.

But move a little further up to the point of victory, where triumph and exultation shall begin; where you shall be crowned, and surrounded with the natives of heaven, with saints, martyrs, Christian heroes, angels, archangels, principalities, powers, thrones, through the loud hallelujahs of whom, you shall pass into the immediate presence of God, your Father, your Saviour, your Comforter. You shall see him. You shall see his countenance all covered with smiles and love. You shall hear him say, "Well done, thou good and faithful servant; enter thou into the joy of thy Lord." [3]

[1] "...playhouses, gaming houses, taverns, drums, &c., in higher life; and in fairs, horse-races, cock-fights, dram shops, whiskey-houses in lower life, where his veteran soldiers, and raw recruits, meet to exercise one another, in lying, cheating, swearing, lewd jesting, infidel haranging, and sneering at religion, and, in all these, giving vogue and fashion to wickedness."

[2] Ibid., 87 seqq.   [3] Ibid., 92.

Skelton concludes this very striking Confirmation sermon with Ephesians 3. 14–21, bringing it in thus:

And now, my dear children, whom I have faithfully laboured to train up in the way that ye should go, "I bow my knees unto the Father of our Lord Jesus Christ...to be strengthened with might by his Spirit in the inner man...that ye might be filled with all the fulness of God..." [1]

Side by side with the rich teaching we find in Jeremy Taylor and his Caroline contemporaries, and in Philip Skelton and Bishop Wilson[2] in the next century, we find a tendency to minimize the blessings conveyed in Confirmation. The distinction is made between the miraculous effects of the Spirit attending this rite in primitive times, and the "usual" or "ordinary" graces and assistances of the Holy Spirit.[3] A representative example of this treatment may be seen in the popular tract, "2d. or 12s. per Hundred", by Archbishop Synge of Tuam, the second and corrected edition appearing in 1740. *A Discourse of Confirmation in a Dialogue between the Minister of the Parish and a young Servant Maid named Sarah*, "Containing proper Instructions for such Persons as are to be confirmed". The young Servant Maid, having informed her parish Minister that she can neither read nor write, proceeds to deliver this weighty pronouncement on the rite of Confirmation.

As to what related to Confirmation, I have heard it plainly suggested from two or three passages of the New Testament: particularly from Acts 8. 15, 16, 17 and Acts 19. 6, that the Apostles used to lay their Hands upon Persons who had been baptized, and to pray for them that they might receive the Holy Ghost. And

---

[1] *Works*, III, 92.

[2] The effect and blessing of Confirmation, Wilson held, is "to convey the inestimable blessing of the Holy Spirit of God, by prayer, and the imposition of the hands of God's minister, that He may dwell in you, and keep you from the temptation of the world, the flesh, and the devil. Confirmation is the perfection of Baptism. The Holy Ghost descends invisibly upon such as are rightly prepared to receive such a blessing, as at first He came visibly upon those that had been baptized. By the imposition of the hands of God's minister, God takes as it were possession of you as His own peculiar treasure; He sanctifies and consecrates you again to Himself—and makes us partakers of the divine graces and virtues". *Works*, V, 76 seq. By Confirmation "God unites to Himself by His Spirit", that he will keep "us under his protection". Ibid.

[3] This distinction is made by Roger Boyle, Nicholas Brady, Mant, and others. Taylor, however, held: "This power from on high, which is the proper blessing of confirmation, was expressed not only in speaking with tongues and doing miracles, for much of this they had before they received the Holy Ghost, but it was effected in spiritual and internal strengths; they...were indued with courage and wisdom and christian fortitude and boldness to confess the faith of Christ crucified, and unity of heart and mind, singleness of heart, and joy in God." *Works*, V, 655.

altho' the miraculous Gifts, which thereupon followed, have long since ceased; yet since all Christians ought to believe that *it is God which worketh in us both to will and to do, of His Pleasure*, Phip. 2. 13, and that therefore the Grace and Assistance of His Holy Spirit is to be sought for, in order to our leading a Holy Life: I cannot but conclude that this Laying on of Hands upon Persons that have been baptized, together with Prayer, for their growth in Grace, (which we call Confirmation) is a Godly custom, and ever fit to be continued in the Christian Church; altho' I do not take it upon me to condemn those Churches, where it is not administered in the same manner as it is in ours.[1]

This statement is substantially the same as Archbishop Synge's view of Confirmation in *A Gentleman's Religion in Three Parts*, though he dare not hastily condemn those Churches where Confirmation is disused or intermitted.[2] Sarah, however, condemns not those Churches where it is administered in another manner, including presumably the Church of Rome. This statement is also in line with the teaching of Nicholas Brady and Bishop Mant, who, however, insist that Bishops, as successors of the Apostles, are the only proper ministers of Confirmation.[3]

V. "THE SPECIAL MINISTRY OF RECONCILIATION"

The ancient Celtic Church is generally thought to have brought about a revolution in the penitential system of the western Church in the seventh century, by extending to the continent of Europe through the influence of her missionaries, particularly St Columbanus, a system of private, instead of public, penance, imposed by the confessor and performed privately by the penitent, of which "the essential was prayer, mortification, and good works, the amount being proportioned to the number and character of sins in accordance with a fixed tariff set down in the penitential books".[4] An old Irish Penitential, drawn up by "the venerable of Ireland from the rules of Scripture", for "the annuling and remedy of

---

[1] Op. cit., 7 seq.   [2] Op. cit., 239 seq.

[3] Brady, *The Antiquity and Usefulness of Episcopal Confirmation* (1708), 3; Mant, "The Church's Rite of Confirmation, its History and Value", *The Church and Her Ministrations*, 293. Another expression of this view may be seen in Robert Nelson's *Instructions for them that come to be Confirmed by Way of Question and Answer* (Dublin, ed. 1728). Bishop Wetenhall conceives the inward effect to be "more grace given by God for perseverence", *The Catechism...with Marginal Notes*, 51 seq. Bishop Mann has on the title-page of his *Discourse of Confirmation*, "Then laid they their Hands upon them, and they received the Holy Ghost. Acts 8, 17."

[4] J. E. Kenney, *The Sources for the Early History of Ireland (Ecclesiastical)*, 238; cf. 188.

K

every sin both small and great", appoints "the eight chief virtues, with their subdivisions" for the curing and healing of "the eight chief vices, with whatsoever springs therefrom".[1] Ussher points to an old Irish Canon which required penance to be performed first, and Absolution to be withheld until the sincerity of repentance had been proved. By the new device, however, of sacramental penance the sinner by the power of the keys is "instantly of attrite made contrite," and after Absolution "some sorry penance is imposed, which upon better consideration may be converted into pence".[2]

In his *Answer to a Jesuit* (1625) Ussher cites the first Exhortation in the Communion Office to show that after the manner of the doctors, pastors, and Fathers of the primitive Church, the Anglican Church exhorts the people "to confess their sins unto their ghostly fathers". "No kind of confession, either public or private, is disallowed by us, that is any way requisite for the due execution of that power of the keys, which Christ bestowed upon his Church." But we reject "that new pick-lock of sacramental confession, obtruded upon men's consciences, as a matter necessary to Salvation, by the Canons of the late Conventicle of Trent, where those good fathers put their curse upon every one, that either shall 'deny that sacramental confession was ordained by divine right, and is by the same right necessary to Salvation'. Council Trident. sess. 14. can. 6: or shall 'affirm that, in the sacrament of penance, it is not by the ordinance of God...' Ibid., can. 7. This doctrine, I say, we cannot but reject: as being repugnant to that which we have learned both from the Scriptures, and from the fathers."[3] Ussher also points out that up to the twelfth century the Church used the form, "Absolutionem et remissionem tribuat tibi omnipotens Deus", and finds in the ancient rituals, the new Roman Pontifical, and in the present practice of the Greek Church "the absolution expressed in the third person, and attributed wholly to God; and not in the first, as if it came from the priest himself."[4]

The Irish Canon 19 of 1634 went beyond other Anglican formularies as well in directing the bell to be tolled the evening before the Eucharist for the receiving of confessions as in recommending, on the one hand, "the special Ministry of reconciliation" not only to those who were "much troubled in mind", but to those who upon self-examination found

---

[1] J. E. Kenney, ibid., 242. For other Penitentials and disciplinary Canons, drawn up under Celtic influence, see op. cit., 235 seqq.

[2] *Works*, IV, 287 seqq.   [3] Ibid., III, 90 seq.

[4] Ibid., 135; cf. 133 seqq. Ussher gives a great weight of evidence to show that among the doctors of the Church the view of the Master of the Sentences that Absolution was ministerial and declarative continued to be held. Ibid., 176 seqq.

themselves "extreme dull", and on the other "advice and counsel" not only for "avoiding all scruple and doubtfulness", but for "the quickening their dead hearts, and the subduing of those corruptions whereunto they have been subject". The Irish Canon 64, like the English 113, admonished the minister not to reveal "any crime, or offence so committed to his trust and secrecy (except they be such crimes, as by the Laws of the Realm his own life may be called into question for concealing the same) under pain of irregularity".

Bramhall acknowledged that in penitence "the pastors of the Church have a dependent ministerial power of loosing from sin". God's "primitive imperial power" is absolute, "—ad sententiandum simpliciter,—without ifs; man's power is conditional,—ad sententiandum si,—to loose a man, if he be truly contrite and aptly disposed." [1] But Bramhall objected to the doctrine and practice of the Roman Church. They had "tricked it up with the robes of a sacrament, obtruding it upon the world as absolutely necessary to salvation, and that by Divine institution, contrary to their own schools". They had "restrained it to a particular and plenary enumeration of all sins"; whereas "Christ said not, 'What sins ye remit', but 'whose sins'; giving this caution to the Presbyters, to attend more to the contrition and capacity of their confitents, than to the number and nature of their sins." And they had made it "to be meritorious at the hands of God, and satisfactory for sins, not only by way of complacence only, but even in justice." [2] In practice, "they first absolve a man, and then bind him to make satisfaction; quite contrary to reason and the practice of the ancient Church"; and they impose "ludibrious penances as a few Paternosters for the most enormous sins".[3] Hence it is "reduced to a customary formality, as if it were the ending of an old score to begin a new".[4] Preaching before the Irish Commons at the Restoration Primate Bramhall recommends confession, which "with its requisites, contrition and amendment of life" makes "complete repentance; which some Fathers style a 'second table after shipwreck', others a 'Baptism of pain and tears'." "Let confession and repentance have their due; but let them not thrust Christ out of the chair, from Whose grace they flow, from Whose acceptance they have their efficacy." [5] Having repeated his earlier objections to the Roman doctrine and practice, Bramhall complains that "our Protestant confessions are for the most part too general" and "a little too

[1] *Works*, v, 190.   [2] Ibid., v, 222 seq.
[3] Ibid., 190; 224; "As Chauser saith of the friar, that 'he knew how to impose an easy penance where he looked for a good pittance' "; cf. 160.
[4] Ibid., 191; 224; 160.   [5] Ibid., 158.

presumptuous". They who dare not dispense with the advice of a lawyer or physician are "wise enough for their souls without direction". Again, confessions are "a little too careless, as if we were telling a story of a third person that concerned us not", and "we conceal and cover with as much art as may be", and "even whilst we are confessing, we are too often a mind to return with 'the dog to his vomit', and with 'the sow to her wallowing in the mire'. What is this but a plain mocking of God?"[1]

In the Preface of his *Ductor Dubitantium* of 1660, Jeremy Taylor complains of the great scarcity of books of conscience in the reformed Churches. Some Lutherans and Anglicans had indeed, "done something in this kind which is well". "But yet our needs remain; and we cannot be well supplied out of the Roman store-houses; for although there the staple is, and very many excellent things are exposed to view; yet we have found the merchants to be deceivers, and the wares too often falsified."[2] Taylor had already in the *Unum Necessarium* (1655) made an exhaustive examination of confession on its historical, doctrinal, and practical side, condemning the Roman doctrine and practice as strongly as Ussher and Bramhall. The primitive practice was further distorted by the giving of Absolution[3] before the work of repentance was done, and by the claim that bare attrition was sufficient on the part of the penitent.[4] The new Roman doctrine was hugely distant from "the spirit of Christianity" and from "the doctrine and practice of the apostolical and succeeding ages of the Church", and "a perfect destruction to the necessity of a holy life".[5] In the *Dissuasive from Popery* Taylor claims that confession, as practised by pious Anglicans, might be made of excellent use; "but by the doctrines and practices of the Church of Rome it is not made the remedy of sins by proper energy, but the excuse, the alleviation, the confidence, the ritual, external and sacramental remedy, and serves instead of the labours of a holy and a regular life; and yet is so entangled with innumerable and inextricable cases of conscience, orders, human prescripts, and great and little artifices, that scruples are more increased than sins are lessened."[6] Taylor, in his *Rules and Advices*, required every minister of his diocese to "exhort his people to a frequent confession of their sins, and a declaration of the state of their souls",[7] and also to study "the ancient canons of the Church, especially the penitentials of the Eastern and Western Churches".[8]

---

[1] *Works*, v, 160.   [2] Ibid., IX, vi.
[3] Ibid. Like Ussher Taylor regards Absolution as being ministerial and declarative; I, 12 seqq.; III, 416 seqq.; V, 251; VI, 515 seqq.; VII, 447; 451 seqq; 453.
[4] Ibid., VII, 459; cf. the Council of Trent's definition "that bare attrition doth sufficiently dispose a man to receive Grace in that sacrament". Sess. 7, can. 4.
[5] Ibid., 462.   [6] Ibid., VI, 241.   [7] Ibid., I, 112.   [8] Ibid., 114.

In the first of *Two Letters of Advice* (1673), that "For the Susception of Holy Orders", Henry Dodwell urges the too much neglected study of "Casuistical Divinity" [1] and the duty of instructing the people "in the art of holy meditation and mental prayer" and of stirring them up to a frequent Communion and to seek spiritual advice. [2] He thought the order of the Irish Canon 19 should be revived "for tolling your Parish Bell the Evening before the Eucharist, and waiting for such in Church as are desirous to confess themselves, and ask your Ghostly Counsel, withal warning them of those crimes which you are not obliged to conceal, that they may not think themselves betrayed under pretence of Religion". [3]

William King, in his *Answer to Peter Manby* (1687), having read many "Protestant books" and consulted both Divines and Bishops, concluded that they were well agreed in these things. Confession should be made to God of every sin with sorrow, and sin should be forsaken before pardon could be expected; in the case of injury to others, confession should also be made to the injured person with restitution; in the case of injury to the Church, submission must be made to her discipline before Absolution could be given; in the case of scruple a spiritual guide should be repaired to for his "resolution, counsel, and direction", in case of a heavy sense of guilt recourse should be made to a spiritual physician for the ministry of Absolution; confession to a priest is a great mortification "and of great use in most cases" (Canon 19), and "it is counted a great wickedness for a Priest to reveal any such confession" (Canon 64), but it is "not necessary by any divine command, that a man should discover every sin to a Priest, though this may be had". From this harmony among "our Bishops and Divines", King concluded that it could no more be said that confession to a Priest was wanting in the Church of Ireland, "because she doth not oblige all people to it under penalty of damnation, than a City can be said to want water, where the fountains are full and open, only because men are not obliged under pain of death to use them". [4]

At Easter 1638 most of the parishioners of Gowran, Co. Kilkenny, had gone to confession. [5] In 1661 Primate Bramhall assumed that members of the Irish House of Commons were not unfamiliar with this ministry of the Church, and that some of them were capable of making careless or formal confessions. In 1676 Andrew Sall testified that private confession was "practiced by many, if neglected by others". [6] In 1692 Bishop Richard Tennison said it was "still observed by those humble and devout Christians

---

[1] Op. cit. (1691 ed.), 46.   [2] Ibid., 98.
[3] Ibid., 102.   [4] Op. cit., 41 seq.   [5] See above, p. 16.
[6] *True Catholic and Apostolic Faith maintained...* (1846 ed.), 254.

who are dubious and afraid that their heart, the true Christian Sacrifice, is
not so fit to be offered as it should be." [1]

During the seventeenth century what the Irish Canon 19 called "the
special Ministry of Reconciliation" was not a matter of party contention.
Laud thanked Ussher as well as Bramhall for this Canon "about confession".[2] Bishop Downham (d. 1633), whose Augustinian theology was
frowned upon by Laud, cites Chrysostom and Theophlect on the ministerial commission to absolve to support his contention that we are bound
to hear and to receive God's ministers "not only as angels of God, but
even as Christ Jesus".[3] Bishop Bedell (d. 1642) tells an ex-Anglican to be
content with "the Pontifical of the Church wherein you were ordained;
wherein is verbatim all that your Pontificals had well taken out of the
holy words of our Saviour, *Accipe Spiritum Sanctum quorum remiseris
peccata remittuntur*... which methinks you should rather account to contain the essential Form of Priesthood than the former, both because they
are Christ's own words... and do express the worthiest and principallest
part of your commission, which the Apostle calls the *Ministry of Reconciliation*." [4] This ministry is also taken for granted by Bishop Ezekiel
Hopkins,[5] Bishop Roger Boyle,[6] Bishop Wetenhall,[7] Bishop Richard
Tennison,[8] Archbishop Narcissus Marsh,[9] and Archbishop Vesey of
Tuam.[10] One of the most remarkable treatments of the subject is by
Bishop William Sheridan of Kilmore, before he was deprived as a Non-

---

[1] *A Sermon Preached at Christ's Church, Dublin, On Sunday, November 13, 1692,
Before His Excellency the Lord Lieutenant*, 12. "And therefore our Church, who lays
the efficacy of Absolution on the sincerity of the penitent's contrition and faith, and
tells her people that her Absolution is only conditional, deals more severely, and
sincerely too, with her penitents, than the *Roman* Church, who leaves the chief
stress on the outward Absolution of the Priest." Ibid., 53.

[2] See above, p. 15.

[3] *Two Sermons, the One Commenting the Ministrie in General*..., 57 seqq.

[4] Burnet's *Life of Bishop Bedell*, 477 seq.; Bedell is said to have "sent a strange
absolution to an Irish recusant, in a letter (using many good instructions, for the man
was sick) in this form: 'If you be content to receive Christ, and believe in him, by
the authority given to me, I absolve you from all your sins you have confessed to
Almighty God, in the Name of the Father, Son, and Holy Ghost. Amen.'" Ussher,
Works, xv, 459 seq.

[5] *Works* (1809 ed.), I, 128 seq.

[6] *Summa Theologie Christianae*, "De Poenitentia" (Pars. v, XIV), 283 seqq.

[7] *Enter into Thy Closet* (1668 ed.), 420 seq.; (1846 ed.), 254; *Be ye also Ready* (1694),
99 seqq.; *The Protestant Peace Maker* (1682), 86 seqq.

[8] *A Sermon preached at Christ's Church, Dublin, On Sunday, November 13, 1692,
Before His Excellency the Lord Lieutenant of Ireland*, 11 seq.

[9] See above, p. 45, n. 5.

[10] *Visitation of John, Archbishop of Tuam, 1705.* "We must be faithful Physicians and
search their Diseases to the very bottom: we must not heal their sores slightly..."

juror in 1693, in a sermon preached "before the State" in one of the Dublin cathedrals.[1] The sermon, however, may be composite, as at least four pages of it are taken verbatim from Bramhall, particularly from the sermon he preached as Primate before the Irish Commons in 1661. Sheridan claims that "there is no such sovereign 'Balm in Gilead' as a sacerdotal Absolution", distinguishes the moral and material integrity of a confession, and shows what things "the seal of confession may not keep secret".

The fullest treatment of the subject on its practical side is given in *Tractatus de Visitatione Infirmorum*... (1697) by John Stearne, Vicar of Trim, and later successively Bishop of Dromore and Clogher (d. 1745). Stearne recommends rather subtle ways of moving the sick person to make a special confession of sin, advising the forms of questions from Archbishops Anselm and Laud.[2] Absolution should be explained to the penitent as being "absolute" regarding offences bringing scandal upon the Church, as "authoritative" with respect of all other sins, and "as securing the grace of God towards those who have perfected their repentance".[3] While there is no divine command that all secret sins should be confessed to the Priest, yet wholesome advice cannot be expected from the spiritual physician if any of the diseases of the soul are concealed.[4] The penitent should be put in mind, by extempory prayer fitted to his condition, not only of the heavier crimes, but of anger, pride, envy, slander, dishonesty in buying and selling of merchandise, neglect of public prayers, Holy Communion, works of charity, paying debts, and other sins of omission.[5] The minister should also warn the penitent that certain crimes, including murder and treason, should not be disclosed directly, but that advice concerning them should be made indirectly by a third person, or by an anonymous epistle, or by asking advice as if it concerned a third person.[6] Ten pages at the end of the Dublin edition of 1697 are occupied by books which Stearne commends for the use of the clergy. These include the *Ductor Dubitantium*, the *Unum Necessarium*, and other works of Taylor; Gerson's *De arti audiendi confessiones*; Soto's *Methodus Confessioni*; Polanco's *Directorium breve ad confessorii et confitentis manus recte obeundum*; Benardinus, *De Officii curati*; "Azorius, Filiucius, Navarrus, Toletus, and other Popish Casuists"; Amesius, *De Casibus Conscientiae*; works by Andrewes, Hammond, Laud, Kettlewell, Saunderson; *The*

---

[1] *Several Discourses...All Preach'd...before the State in the Cathedrals of St Patrick and Christ Church, Dublin*, 1, 36 seqq.
[2] Op. cit. (19th cent. translation), 27 seq.
[3] Ibid., 54.　　　[4] Ibid., 91.　　　[5] Ibid., 101.　　　[6] Ibid., 108 seqq.

Whole Duty of Man; and for books *de absolutione* Hammond's *Power of the Keys*, and Ussher's *Answer to a Jesuit*.[1] This selection from the books recommended by Stearne would suggest that moral theology was by no means a neglected subject at the end of the seventeenth century in Ireland. Stearne's tract was commended to ordinands by Bishop Jebb and Dean Graves, and praised by Bishop Mant, early in the nineteenth century.

In the next century this ministry was recommended with greater caution. In 1715 Archbishop King expressed alarm at some of the doctrines of the English Non-jurors, and accused them of teaching the necessity of confession to a Priest and of sacerdotal Absolution. Archbishop Synge of Tuam (d. 1742) acknowledged the usefulness in some cases of private confession,[2] though his successor, Archbishop Hort, expressed alarm in 1742 at the practice whereby wicked livers received the Communion and Absolution "as a kind of passport, which they hope will do their business at once, and carry them by a short way to heaven". For this reason the minister "ought not to be so ready with his absolutions".[3] In 1741 Bishop Berkeley tells Sir John James that confession may be had in the Church of Ireland, "by any who please to have it; and I admit, it may be very usefully practised. But as it is managed in the Church of Rome, I apprehend it doth infinitely more mischief than good. Their casuistry seemeth a disgrace, not only to Christianity, but even to the light of nature."[4] At the primary Visitation of Archbishop Laurence of Cashel in 1822 Archdeacon Jebb held that the reading of the Exhortation giving warning of Communion laid upon the clergy a tremendous responsibility, and they could not be prepared to give spiritual counsel and advice without "the recourse of Christian meditation" and asking for "the preventing and assisting grace of God's holy Spirit".[5]

Archbishop King had attached more value to public than to private confession and Absolution, especially in the exercise of the Church's discipline. We have already noticed that as late as 1724 King wrote to Bishop Wilson of Man urging him to continue steadfast in the exercise of ecclesiastical discipline in spite of the fact that he had recently been imprisoned for excommunicating the Governor's wife for slander, and complaining that the English Bishops had almost laid all thoughts of it aside.[6] Apparently the Irish Bishops had not yet abandoned it. All Caroline Divines would agree with King that "the true intention of confession,

---

[1] Op. cit. (ed. 1697), 109 seqq.
[2] *A Gentleman's Religion*, 262 seq.; cf. *Catholick Christianity*, 33.
[3] Primary Visitation Charge (1742).
[4] *Works*, (ed. A. A. Luce), VII, 153.
[5] *Practical Theology*, II, 187.   [6] See above, p. 44 seq.,

and of all other parts of Christian discipline, is the amendment of people's lives".[1] To them public Absolution was as valid as private.

Brief notice should be taken of forms of Absolution. They were contained in offices for receiving "Lapsed Protestants" or converted Romanists. Bramhall used such a form in 1640, in admitting Mr Matthews to the Communion of the Church of Ireland, at which Ussher greatly rejoiced when he received a copy of "the solemnity used in his reception".[2] Another appearing in 1691 was *A Form of Reconciliation of Lapsed Protestants and of Admission of Romanists To the Communion of the Church of Ireland, Written by the Right Reverend Anthony Lord Bishop of Meath*. It contained the following form of Absolution.

Then let the Priest stand up (the Penitent kneeling) and lay his hand on his head saying:
"By vertue of the Authority, to me committed, by our Lord and Saviour Jesus Christ, I do readmit this person into the Communion of the Church, and restore him to the prayers of the Church, and the participating of the Eucharist, and to all other Rites and Symbols of Communion, in the Name of the Father, and of the Son, and of the Holy Ghost, *Amen*.[3]

Bishop Anthony Dopping's form has often been confused with the altogether different *Form of Receiving Lapsed Protestants, or Reconciling Converted Papists to our Church*, bound with larger Irish Prayer Books from 1700 to 1757,[4] which contains another form of Absolution.[5]

In the Convocational *Form of Prayer for the Visitation of Prisoners* (1711) the minister is directed to examine prisoners and exhort them if they have any scruples to declare the same. The minister is further directed to exhort a criminal under sentence of death "to a particular confession of the sin for which he is condemned", and

after his confession the Priest shall absolve him (if he humbly and heartily desire it) either in the Form which is appointed in the Visitation of the Sick, or in that used in the Communion Service. After Absolution shall be said the Collect following.

O Holy Jesus, who of thine infinite goodness didst accept the conversion of a

---

[1] *Answer to Peter Manby*, 52.   [2] *H.M.C., Hastings*, IV, 89.

[3] Op. cit., 24 seq.

[4] This form, for example, is ascribed to Bishop Dopping by Bishop Frere in *A New History of the Book of Common Prayer*, 234.

[5] "Our Lord Jesus Christ, who hath commanded, that Repentance and Remission of sins should be published in his name among all Nations, of his great mercy give unto thee true Repentance and forgive thee all thy sins. And I his Minister, by the Authority committed unto me, Do absolve thee from all Ecclesiastical censures, which thou hast, or may'st have incurred, by reason of thy former Errors, Schisms and Heresies: and I restore thee to full Communion of the Catholick Church, in the Name of the Father..."

sinner on the Cross, open thine eyes of mercy upon this thy Servant; who desireth pardon and forgiveness, though in the latest hour he turneth unto thee...

The remainder of this Collect follows closely the ancient precatory form of Absolution directed to be said after the declarative form in the English Book of Common Prayer.

Caroline Divines would interpret the declarative form of Absolution in the light of the precatory, which they knew to be the more ancient. They would agree with Bishop Ezekiel Hopkins that "it is God only who pardons sinners: the Minister's part, is, in a solemn and official manner, to pronounce and proclaim his pardon, to all that shall accept it upon the terms in which it is offered by God," [1] or with John Stearne that no grace could be secured by Absolution until repentance had been perfected. Just as King was disturbed by the tendency of English Non-jurors to teach the necessity of confession to a Priest and of sacerdotal Absolution, so Irish Churchmen in the nineteenth century were disturbed by a similar tendency in English High-Church circles. Thus the Preface to the Irish Book of Common Prayer of 1878 explains:

The Special Absolution in the Office for the Visitation of the Sick has been the cause of offence to many; and as it is a form unknown to the Church in ancient times, and as we saw no adequate reason for its retention, and no ground for asserting that its removal would make any change in the doctrine of the Church, we deemed it fitting that, in the special cases contemplated in this Office, and in that for the Visitation of Prisoners, absolution should be pronounced to penitents in the form appointed in the Office for the Holy Communion.

As the Church of Ireland introduced the system of private confession into the Western Church in the first place, it was quite within her competence to regulate its practice and to prescribe a precatory form of Absolution, which was the only form known to the Christian Church for the first twelve centuries. "With regard to the varieties of the *form*", writes William Palmer, the Irish Tractarian, "it does not appear that they were formerly considered of any importance. A benediction seems to have been regarded as equally valid, whether it was conveyed in the form of a petition or a declaration, whether in the optative or the indicative mood, whether in the active or passive voice, whether in the first, second, or third person." [2]

[1] *Works*, I, 129.
[2] *Origines Liturgicae* (1839 ed.), I, 215. "It is true that a direct prayer to God is a more ancient form of blessing; but the use of a Precatory, or an optative form, by no means warrants the inference, that the person who uses it is devoid of any divinely instituted authority to bless and absolve in the congregation of God." Ibid.

3

CAROLINE WORSHIP IN IRELAND

I. "A HOLY LITURGY, EXCELLENT PRAYERS, PERFECT SACRAMENTS"

BROADLY speaking the Church of Ireland has from the twelfth century adopted the liturgical use of the Church of England. The Synod of Cashel in 1172 decreed that "all sacred offices be henceforth performed everywhere in Ireland according to the usages of Holy Church as observed in the Church of England (*ecclesia Anglicana*)".[1] In the next century the use, which had taken shape at Sarum *c.* 1210, gradually extended through most of Ireland, though in some parts particularly of the province of Tuam Celtic usages lingered on. From the Reformation the Church of Ireland received all the English Prayer Books but the second of King Edward VI.

The basis of Caroline worship before the Commonwealth was the English Prayer Book as revised in 1604. When called upon by the Parliamentary Commissioners in 1647 to discontinue its use, a group of Caroline Churchmen in Dublin declared that they were still bound by the Act of Uniformity, by the second Canon of 1634, and by their solemn oaths to use none other; and that the citizens of Dublin "for the most part generally do love it, have been edified by it, are loth to part from it, and earnestly desire the continuance of it".[2] In the same year Jeremy Taylor published his *Apology for Authorized and Set Forms of Liturgy*, and just before first settling in Ireland in 1658 claimed that in the 1604 Book Anglicans had "a holy liturgy, excellent prayers, perfect sacraments".

Many of the Irish Restoration Bishops had kept up the use of the 1604 Prayer Book during the Commonwealth. Between 26 August and 2 September 1662, Primate Bramhall, with his preference for the Scottish Book of 1637,[3] Taylor with his wide knowledge of ancient liturgies, and

---

[1] Giraldus Cambrensis, *Expugnatio*, lxxxiv.
[2] *A Declaration of the Protestant Clergie...1647.*
[3] *Works,* I, lxxxvi. Letter Bramhall to Archbishop Spottiswood, 1637. In 1661 Bramhall claimed that the restored Anglican religion was "neither garish with superfluous ceremonies, nor yet sluttish and void of all order, decency, and majesty in the service of God". (Ibid., v, 123.)

the other Irish Bishops examined the revised Prayer Book lately published in London, and found it, in a few particulars, different from that which had hitherto been used in Ireland, and that there seemed no reason to find fault with it (*non reprobanda videatur*). Partly for this reason and partly for the sake of concord between the Churches of Ireland and England, they commended it for use in Ireland. The revised English Book of 1661–2 was finally agreed upon by both Houses of Convocation on 11 November 1662, four years before it was given temporal enforcement by the Irish Act of Uniformity. The records make it quite clear that full synodical consent was given to the English Prayer Book as lately published in London[1] without omissions, but with the proposed addition of a Service for 23 October and a Prayer for the Lord-Lieutenant. The claim that the Irish Convocation intended the omission of the preface *Concerning the Service of the Church* and of the *Ornaments Rubric* was made in the mistaken belief that the manuscript copy of the Prayer Book, from which they are missing, was originally annexed to the Irish Act of Uniformity of 1666. Bishop Reeves has demonstrated that this imperfect manuscript was attached instead to a rejected Transmiss of 1663 and that the introductory matter was missing "through accident, not design".[2] Moreover, the missing items were included in every Irish edition of the Prayer Book from 1666 to 1846, when Bishop Stopford brought out a curious edition, adopted by the Ecclesiastical Commissioners, based upon the imperfect manuscript annexed to the abortive Transmiss of 1663, claiming that it expressed the mind of the Irish Convocation of 1661–6.[3] No Caroline precedent, however, can justly be claimed for the omission of the direction for daily Service or of the Ornaments Rubric.

The Prayer Book of 1662, like that of 1604, was loved by the clergy and people, and became sanctified by centuries of use. Laymen, like Bonnell, Edmund Burke, and Alexander Knox, expressed their veneration for it; and Philip Skelton declared it to be "the best Liturgy any Church was ever blessed with".[4] Nor was the Church of Ireland lacking in liturgical writers. We have *An Answer to Certain Objections made to the Orders of the Church* by Bishop Henry Leslie, appended to his *Treatise of the Authority of the Church* of 1637; *A Sermon in Defence of the Liturgy of the Church*, preached at Whitehall by Richard Lingard, Dean of Lismore,

---

[1] "Liturgiam Anglicanum nuper Londoni editam." *Journal*, 11 Nov. 1662.
[2] *The Book of Common Prayer according to the Use of the Church of Ireland* (1871), 29 seq. This is an effective and devastating reply to *The Book of Common Prayer: printed from the Manuscript originally annexed to Stat. 17 & 18, Car. II c. 6, and preserved in the Rolls Office Dublin*.
[3] J. B. Garstin, *The Book of Common Prayer in Ireland*, 37 seq.   [4] *Works*, II, 361.

in 1668; *Of the Gifts and Offices in the Public Worship of God*, by Bishop Wetenhall in 1678, then Chantor of Christ Church in Dublin; *The Inventions of Men in the Worship of God* by Bishop King in 1693; *Lectures on the Art of Reading*, particularly on the reading of the Liturgy, by Thomas Sheridan Esq., in 1775; Bishop Jebb's Sermons on the Liturgy;[1] *The Choral Service of the United Church of England and Ireland* by John Jebb, the Bishop's nephew in 1843, up to which time he had been a Prebendary of Limerick; and *Origines Liturgicae* by William Palmer, one of Bishop Jebb's first ordinands at Limerick, who was drawn by the Bishop's set syllabus to an interest in liturgiology.

The Prayer Books in use in Caroline times required the Morning and Evening Prayer to be said daily, with the administration of Holy Baptism after the last Lesson upon Sundays and Holy Days. The Morning Prayer was to be followed, after an interval in 1604,[2] by the Litany every Sunday, Wednesday, and Friday, and by the Communion Service, at least as far as "the general Prayer", with a sermon or homily, every Sunday and Holy Day, and with the administration of the Holy Communion at regular intervals. Children were to be catechized, in 1604 "upon Sundays and Holy Days half an hour before Evensong", in 1662 "after the second Lesson at Evening Prayer". Our inquiry will be to find out how Divine Service was performed in Ireland, with what frequency the Holy Communion was celebrated, to what extent the daily Morning and Evening Prayer were provided, and what Ornaments were prescribed for, and used by the ministers. Let us begin by reconstructing, as far as contemporary evidence allows, the services provided in Ireland on some Sunday or other Holy Day, assuming it also to be a Communion Day.

II. WORSHIP ON SUNDAY AND OTHER HOLY DAYS

(a) *Introductory*

The Irish Canons of 1634 made it a matter of obligation that "all manner of persons" should "celebrate and keep the Lord's Day and other Holy Days, according to the orders of the Church",[3] and that the clergy should celebrate Divine Service on them "at convenient and usual times of the day".[4] In 1636 Wentworth told Laud that he had been misinformed about a "general neglect of keeping holy days", and later that with the

---

[1] *Practical Theology*, I, 1–116.
[2] 1604 Prayer Book: first rubric before the Communion Office; rubric before the Commination.   [3] Canon 6.   [4] Canon 7.

co-operation of Primate Ussher direction had been given through the four Archbishops to the Bishops of their provinces for a stricter observance in cases where they had been neglected.[1] From the Restoration Bishops urged the strict observance of Holy Days other than Sundays together with daily prayers in towns and populous places. Archbishop Narcissus Marsh required the performance of Divine Service throughout the province of Cashel in 1692, and of Dublin in 1694, "both in the Aforenoon and Afternoon of every Sunday and Holy Day: as the 6th and 7th Canons, and the Act of Uniformity do injoin".[2] As Primate of All Ireland he was able to tell the Archbishop of Canterbury in 1706 that throughout his province of Armagh "Divine Service is duly and very regularly performed in every Church twice every Sunday (and on Holy Days) except in some places, where the Ministers serve two cures".[3] Holy Days were observed, though less extensively, all through the eighteenth century,[4] and early in the nineteenth we find them better observed in the south than in the north.[5] But we find nothing in Ireland as deplorable as the diocese of Rochester in 1800 when Bishop Horsley found it necessary to point out that there could be "no excuse for the neglect of the feast of our Lord's Nativity, and such stated fasts of Ash Wednesday and Good Friday, even in the smallest country parishes".[6]

In Caroline times the clergy were admonished to declare the Fasts as well as the Festivals to the people, and these were very strictly observed by Ussher, Bedell, Dodwell, Bonnell, Hewetson, and others. Ussher "fasted till evening" on Good Friday,[7] and in the middle of the next century the Delaneys fasted till 5 p.m. on Ash Wednesday and certain other days.[8] Near the beginning of Lent, 2 March 1728/9, Dean Berkeley preached a forceful sermon on fasting at Long Island.[9] Later Dr Delaney, in a Lenten sermon, commended the primitive practice of fasting on Wednesdays and Fridays till 3 p.m. or, if too severe "for the imitation of a

---

[1] Laud, Works (L.A.C.T.), vii, 299, 305; Wentworth, Letters and Dispatches, ii, 42.
[2] Visitation Charge.
[3] Quoted from E. F. Carpenter, Thomas Tenison, 384.
[4] The evidence is very scattered. Watson's Almanack is silent about Holy Days which Vestry Books tell us were observed in Dublin churches. Wesley often preached at Divine Service on Holy Days. A New Companion for the Festivals and Fasts of the Church...with devotions proper to each Solemnity, Revised and Corrected by Leo Howard, Chaplain to the Lord Deputy, appeared in 1774.
[5] As at eight churches at least in the scattered diocese of Killaloe in 1820 (N.L.I. MS. 352) and at the city churches of Limerick and Cork in 1824.
[6] Quoted from Legg, Eng. Ch. Life, 222; cf. 210.
[7] N. Bernard, Clavi Trabalis, 63.
[8] Autobiography and Correspondence of Mrs Delaney (1st Series), iii, 212 and passim.
[9] Works (ed. A. A. Luce), vii, 56 seq.

degenerate age, at least half their discipline cannot be thought too much by any that profess themselves Christians".[1]

(b) Hours of Divine Service

When Sir William Brereton visited Dublin in 1635 he found that Primate Ussher, when in town, preached every Sunday in St Audoen's at 8 a.m.,[2] and Dr Hoyle in St Werburgh's at 10 a.m. and 3 p.m.,[3] and that there were sermons at St Nicholas Without at 10 a.m. and in the Choir of St Patrick's at 1 p.m.[4] "You may with ease and convenience", he observes, "hear four sermons every Lord's Day, and, as I was informed, six sermons may be heard in one day."[5] The times of Divine Service appear to have varied in different city churches. When Wentworth first came to Ireland two years before he found "no second Service, at all, no epistle nor gospel".[6] This suggests the continuance in Ireland of the earlier Anglican separation of the Second Service from the First, which had been normal in England before Archbishop Grindal's direction of 1571, which did not extend to Ireland, for the continuous performance of Morning Prayer, Litany, and Communion Service. There was still an interval between the First and Second Service at Christ Church in 1638, when the Chapter gave order for the entry of the Choir "for the Second Service and Communion on the first Sunday of the month".[7] Wentworth may have gone in state to Christ Church at an earlier hour for Morning Prayer, or First Service, at which the sermon was often preached in the reign of Charles I, and come away before the Second Service began. The 1662 Prayer Book no longer required the interval after Morning Prayer implied by the first rubric before the 1604 Communion Office; and by the end of the century it had become normal in Ireland for the Litany and Second Service to follow Morning Prayer without any break.

From 1736 we find in some Dublin churches a duplication of Sunday morning worship. In addition to the normal forenoon Service with a monthly Sacrament there are Early Prayers, Sermon, and monthly Sacrament, though on another Sunday of the month, at 6 a.m. A decade later we find a similar duplication in the city churches of Cork. This provision may go back long before our information becomes available into the seventeenth century.[8]

[1] Quoted from R. Mant, *Feriae Anniversariae*, II, 159 seq.
[2] *Travels* (Chetham Society), 139, 143.
[3] Ibid., 139, 144.   [4] Ibid., 138.   [5] Ibid., 144.
[6] *Tanner Letters*, 8.   [7] Chapter Book.
[8] The information for Dublin is given in Watson's *Almanack* from 1736. At St Andrew's there was a Reader of 6 a.m. prayers from at least 1728 (Vestry Book),

Otherwise our little information suggests that the hour of morning worship was earlier in Caroline times than it was a century later. Primate Bramhall ordered the procession for the consecration of the twelve Bishops in 1661 to assemble at 7 a.m., and the consecration form of 1666 the Bishops and clergy to assemble at the new Church "between eight and ten in the morning". In 1706 Primate Marsh told the Archbishop of Canterbury how difficult it was for people in the province of Armagh to attend evening as well as morning worship, many of them living from two to four miles from their parish church. He had, therefore, enjoined the clergy, who had not practised it before, "to make a pause half an hour or an hour after morning service and sermon is over, which never ends betwixt twelve and one of the clock, and then assemble the congregation again, and read the evening service and catechize their children before they depart, by which means catechizing will be practised in every Church; as it is in most Churches throughout the year".[1] Thus it appears that throughout the province of Armagh at the turn of the century Morning Prayer, Litany, Second Service, and sermon, judging from its great length, began at least by 10 a.m. and Evening Prayer with catechizing between 1 and 2 p.m. As distances increased with the union of benefices the time of forenoon Service gradually became later until it reached noon, which John Wesley found "the usual hour in Ireland".[2] The time of Evening Prayer, which had varied from one to five in Caroline times, had become later in many town churches by the opening of the nineteenth century[3] when we also find Evening Prayer at Christ Church in Dublin performed by candlelight and "greatly crowded".[4]

(c) The Christian Assembly

"If I look at the people flocking to their public Churches on Holy Days", observed the ex-Jesuit, Andrew Sall, of Dublin Anglicans in 1676, "the very silence and modesty of their carriage in the streets gives me a testimony of their inward good disposition; and when they are come to

and it may be possible to trace other cases to an earlier date. In England we find some cases of Morning Prayer at an early hour but without Sermon. *Hierurgia Anglicana*, III, 299 seqq.

[1] Quoted from E. F. Carpenter, op. cit., 384.

[2] *Journal, passim*, though Wesley often found the hour was 11.

[3] The accounts of St Peter's, Dublin, show that a stipend was paid from *c.* 1735 "to the Curate for Reading Sunday Evening Prayers", and from 1764 the words "at 7 o'clock" are added (Accounts and Vestry Book). The time was changed from 5 to 6 at St Werburgh's, Dublin, in 1809. In 1828 the normal time in Dublin churches was 7.

[4] *Ecclesiologist* (CXLIV), Oct. 1862, 252; *Watson's Almanack* (1815).

A CONJECTURAL RECONSTRUCTION OF AN IRISH
CAROLINE CHURCH

(*facing p.* 144)

The author offers this conjectural reconstruction of a Caroline Church as suggested by the rubrics of the Irish Form of Consecration of Churches (1666) and other contemporary evidence. The "Coemetery" or "Dormitory" which the Bishop dedicates in that rite is beneath the south transept, the floor of which is raised high above the level of the nave, and which is occupied by large family pews.

the Church each one retires to his own respective seat, all decently severed to avoid confusion." [1] "When we come into the public Assemblies", writes Bishop King in 1694, "we believe ourselves to come into Christ's presence (Matt. 18. 20) and...it is our custom to bow our bodies before Him. This bowing our bodies, when we come into the Assembly of Christians met together in Christ's Name, and for His service, though it be not enjoined by any Constitution of our Church, is generally practiced by good people, as very decent in itself, and edifying to others." [2] Having made their reverence towards the East, members of the congregation knelt down in private prayer. The prayers composed for this purpose by James, Duke of Ormonde, the Caroline Lord-Lieutenant, and by James Bonnell, are still extant.[3] In churches with organs a voluntary is played, we are told in 1678, "immediately before the Service, while the chief of the congregation are taking their places".[4]

Until recent times the singers usually went to their places either in a gallery, a special pew, or the Cathedral Choir, individually before the Service began. At St Patrick's Cathedral, for example, the vicars, already in their places, stood up by special Statute of 1692, "at the entrance of the Dean (or in his absence of the Sub-dean) into the Choir",[5] though on special occasions, as before the opening of Parliament in 1634[6] or for the consecration of the twelve Bishops in 1661, the Choir proceeded two by two from the west door into the choir singing Te Deum Laudamus.[7] As late as 1843 Christ Church, Dublin, was one of the few Anglican cathedrals

---

[1] *True Catholic and Apostolic Faith maintained in the Church of England* (ed. J. Allport, 1846), 256.

[2] *Of the Inventions of Men in the Worship of God*, 113 seq. King reproves the Presbyterians for omitting this custom, and forbidding it in their *Directory*. "The Scriptures say, O come, let us kneel before the Lord our Maker. Your *Directory* says, Let us enter the Assembly without Adoration, or Bowing." Ibid., 127 seq. In the Exhortation appended to his consecration office of 1719, King says: "Hence the primitive Christians used to prostrate themselves, when they came into their religious Assemblies, and this even in the Apostles' time, as will appear probable" from 1 Cor. 14. 25, "where speaking of a Heathen convinced by coming into a Christian Assembly, the Apostle adds, that *Falling down on his face, he will worship God*, which would never have been expected from a converted Heathen, if the Christians themselves had not used to do so." Bishop Anthony Dopping, junior, defended the same practice in a sermon of 1716, repeated in 1727, 1729, and 1731. (Professor R. R. Hartford, "An Eighteenth-Century Sermon", *Hermathena*, No. LVI, Nov. 1940, 40 seqq.) This practice, defended by Jeremy Taylor (*Works*, V, 317 seqq.) and Bramhall (*Works*, V, 77), required by the Statutes of St Patrick's Cathedral (ibid.), observed by Dean Swift (d. 1745) and the Knights of St Patrick in 1783, continued in some places into the nineteenth century.

[3] T. Carte, *Life of Ormonde*, V, 196; W. Hamilton, *Life of Bonnell*, 118 seq.

[4] E. Wetenhall, *Of the Gifts and Offices in the Worship of God...*, 399.

[5] W. Monck Mason, op. cit., 91, n.m.   [6] Ibid., 186.   [7] Ibid., 193.

L

where the Choir went in procession two by two before every Service.[1] In parish churches the minister often ascended the reading-desk while the congregation was still assembling, and began the opening sentence at the hour of Service. In country churches lacking a vestry the minister often put on "his clerical dress in the Reading-desk, before the people".[2]

Although the parish clerk, sitting below the minister, was appointed partly for "his competant skill in music",[3] there were from Caroline times in Ireland "singing boys", "singing men", and "singing women". In Primate Ussher's time there was a Choir and organ at St Peter's, Drogheda, and "on Sunday the Service was sung before him, as is used in the Cathedrals of England".[4] Bishop Bedell "never went about to set up a queere of quyristers of singing men and women".[5] "He was much displeased with the pompous service at Christ's Church in Dublin, which was attended and celebrated with all manner of instrumental musick, as organs, sackbutts, cornets, violls, &c, as if it had been the dedication of Nebuchadnezer's golden image in the plain of Dura."[6] The organ, provided in many town churches before the Commonwealth, became more general after the Restoration, and was often placed with the singers in a western gallery. "Our Church", observed Bishop King in 1694, "permits the use of some grave musical instruments, to regulate the voices of them that sing", a provision "more requisite in northern counties where generally people's voices are more harsh and untuneable than in other places".[7] A barrel-organ was sometimes used in the eighteenth century, and one was still used at Collon in the nineteenth, capable of playing eighteen hymn tunes and, to the depression of speech-rhythm, two chants.[8] Early in the last century the singing in St Nicholas, Galway, was accompanied by two ladies playing harps.[9] Often the singing was led by the children of the parochial charity school; and the stated duties of the organists of at least four Dublin churches in the 1720s was to train these

[1] J. Jebb, *Choral Service*, 229.
[2] Bishop Jebb, *Practical Theology*, I, 407.   [3] Canon 86.
[4] *Works*, I, 147.   [5] E. S. Shuckbrough, op. cit., 154.
[6] Ibid. Sackbutts and cornets were actually used in Caroline worship. In 1634, for example, the Dean and Chapter of Canterbury reported that in place of a deacon and sub-deacon "are substituted two corniters and two sackbutters, whom we do willingly maintain for the decorum of our quire." (*H.M.C.*, Fourth Report, Pt I, 125b.)
[7] *Inventions of Men in the Worship of God.*
[8] J. B. Leslie, *Armagh Clergy and Parishes*, under Collon.
[9] J. F. Berry, *St Nicholas's Collegiate Church Galway*, 53. At another date the Choir sat by the organ in the south transept, and walked out in front whenever their time for singing came. Ibid., 54.

children to sing Psalm tunes.[1] There may have been a surpliced Choir at St Michan's, Dublin, when Robert Woffington was organist (1725–57), for the vestry in 1731 "agreed that a sum not exceeding 3l. 12s. per annum be henceforth allowed for washing 134 surplices".[2] This Choir consisted of the charity children "and other Persons chosen by the Minister and Churchwardens".[3] In 1773 John Wesley greatly admired "the excellent singing by forty or fifty voices, half men and half women", at Tanderagee. A little later Hillsborough had a stipendiary Choir of men and boys; and between 1820 and 1832 Prebendary John Fitzgibbon "instituted a small choir of men and boys" at St John's, Limerick, who "were habited and arranged according to the best choral precedent"[4] . . .

No picture of Irish Caroline worship would be complete without some account of the people assembled and met together in their high box pews. Often these had seats on three sides with a door on the fourth opening to a passage, making it necessary for a third of the congregation to face westward. For this reason no doubt Michael Hewetson, later Archdeacon of Armagh, advised Thomas Wilson never to "turn his back upon the Altar in Service time, nor upon the Minister, if it can be avoided".[5] At the same time Hewetson drew Wilson's attention to devout customs which he claimed to be general in the Church of Ireland in 1686. "To stand at the Lessons and Epistle, as well as at the Gospel, and especially when a Psalm is sung; to bow reverently at the name of Jesus, whenever it is mentioned in any of the Church's offices; to turn towards the East when the *Gloria Patri* and the Creeds are rehearsing; and, to make obeisance at coming into and going out of the Church, and at going up to and coming down from the Altar,—are all ancient, commendable, and devout usages, which thousands of good people of our Church practise at this day."[6] On the other hand, there was less uniformity in congregational usage where Presbyterian influences were strong. Bishop Roger Boyle in 1681, from his experience in the diocese of Down and Connor, and later of Clogher, wished for more explicit canonical direction as to when people should stand, sit, and kneel; "for what is more absurd", he asks, "than a congregation performing the same ceremonies, in which some are seated and perhaps snoring, some are standing, some are kneeling,

---

[1] Vestry Books.
[2] Vestry Book. In 1744 £3 12s. is paid "for washing Church linen".
[3] "Memorial of St Michan's", 107.
[4] J. Jebb, *Choral Service*, 512 seq. This was probably the first Anglican parish church in the last century to introduce a surpliced Choir together with choir-stalls.
[5] J. Keble, *Life of Bishop Wilson* (L.A.C.T.), I, 22.
[6] Ibid., 22 seq.

and a number of women are rolling flat on the ground and groaning under their veils (*complures muliercules obnucilatis capitibus gemant?*)." [1]

"Divine Office", observes Andrew Sall in 1676, "is performed in a most grave and devout manner, all fitted to the benefit and spiritual food of souls, so as if any Hymn or Psalm is sung, with more exquisite music, the Chanter or some other of the Choir informs the people what Psalm or verse is to be sung, that seeing it in their books they may be furnished with the sense, that thereby the music may work better in their minds to devotion, so great care is taken, that in all we pay to God *rationabile obsequium*, a rational service with grace and feeling of what we do, may be rendered." [2] In this way Irish congregations were not only encouraged to "join in the Liturgy",[3] but were provided with the words of anthems and metrical Psalms and informed what was to be sung.

One of the earliest printed collections for regular use was *Anthems to be Sung At the Celebration of Divine Service in the Cathedrall of the Holy and Undivided Trinity in DUBLIN, Printed Anno Domini, 1662*. In addition to anthems for festivals, including the Epiphany (No. 4) and the Ascension (35), Dean Fuller's curious anthem of 1661 is provided "after the consecration" (50),[4] together with another almost as quaint for use on national occasions (51). The words of this anthem are:

> O God that art the well-spring of all Peace,
> Make all thy gifts in Charles his Raign increase.
> England preserve, Scotland protect,
> Make Ireland in thy Service perfect.
> That all these Kingdoms under Great Britains King
> May still be watered with the Gospel Spring.
> Oh never let unhallowed breath have space
> To {Blight / Blast} these blooming buds of union;
> But let us all with mutual love embrace,
> One Name, one King, and one Religion.
> Ah let this Peace be thought the only Gemme
> That can adorn King Charles his Diadem.
> Hallelujah, Hallelujah &c.
> Hallelujah, Hallelujah. Amen.

---

[1] *Summa Theologie Christianae*, 290, seq. Boyle had succeeded Jeremy Taylor in the difficult see of Down and Connor, where an earlier Bishop, Henry Leslie, had told the Presbyterians: "The lifting up of the eyes to heaven, the spreading out of the hands, the knocking on the breast, sighing and groaning in God's Service, are ceremonies, used by none so much, as by yourselves." *Treatise of the Authority of the Church*, 49 seq.   [2] Op. cit., 256.
[3] E. Wetenhall, *Enter into Thy Closet*, 395.   [4] See above, p. 32.

Wetenhall held that the diocesan Bishop should control the matter of anthems in his Cathedral Church,[1] and John Jebb that the matter should fit the liturgical season or harmonize with the Service of the day.[2]

The Whole Book of Psalms, Collected into English Metre, By Thomas Sternhold, John Hopkins, and Others, Conferred with the Hebrew, set forth in England in 1560, "and allowed to be sung in all Churches, of all the people together",[3] was often printed in Ireland separately or with some editions of the Prayer Book printed in Dublin.[4] Wetenhall, as a Hebrewist, strongly objected to this translation, which "must needs flatten and nauseate men's minds in the heavenly exercise of singing to God".[5] He thought a new translation was long overdue.[6] In 1696 Nicholas Brady, who had been Bishop Wetenhall's chaplain at Cork, brought out with another Irishman, Nahum Tate, the Poet Laureate, *A New Version of the Psalms*, "allowed and permitted" by the Crown. Perhaps the Bishop had inspired Brady with a desire to bring out a new version. Wetenhall held that the choice of the Psalm should in no case be left to the parish clerk, "a person commonly of as little judgement as most of the people, but of much more conceitedness and pertness".[7] Instead the minister should choose a Psalm "suitable to the time, or subject of the Sermon".[8] The choice was not always left to the parish clerk; for in 1714 Archbishop King complained that many of his clergy had marked the accession of George I by choosing Psalm 137 and preaching against consubstantiation.[9] As late as 1821 Bishop Mant admonished the clergy of Killaloe to keep either to the Old or the New Version of the Psalms, and banish from public worship "all that variety of modern compositions under the name of hymns", which too frequently could only be considered "as tricking out the chaste and matronly simplicity of the Church with the meretricious trappings of the conventicle".[10]

Although Mant repeated his views on hymns verbatim in 1830,[11] he himself made a valuable contribution to Anglican hymnody in 1836 by his publication of *Ancient Hymns from the Roman Breviary, to which Original Hymns are Appended*. Mant divides the hymns of "the Romish Church" into three classes: "some altogether scriptural and

[1] *Gifts and Offices*, 565.   [2] Op. cit., 375.
[3] "Before and After Morning and Evening Prayer; and also before and after Sermons." There is little evidence that in Caroline times they were sung before and after the offices, but much that they were sung before and after sermons.
[4] As in some copies of 1621, 1666, 1680, and Rhames editions of 1712, 1714.
[5] Op. cit., 422.   [6] Ibid., 564.   [7] Ibid., 422.
[8] Ibid., 564.   [9] Mant, II, 291, 275.
[10] *Charge* (Killaloe, 1821), 37 seq.   [11] *Clergyman's Obligations*, 81.

unexceptionable: others debased by a sprinkly of error and corruption: others again corrupt and unsound throughout." He therefore selects from the first two classes. Some of his translations have passed into modern Hymnals: others have been adapted by later compilers. Of his original hymns that "commemorative of the Triune Holy" was intended to be sung at the Eucharist, the missing quatrain being:

> Ever thus in God's high praises,
> Brethren, let our tongues unite;
> Chief the heart when duty raises
> Godward at His mystic rite.

Many of them popularize High Church teaching of the pre-Tractarian type, and though they have little of the conventicle about them, they are for the most part of too controversial a character to be sung in churches.[1] The original hymns of Nicholas Brady (1659-1726) and Nahum Tate (1652-1712) are almost the only traces of Irish hymnody near the Caroline period. The hymns of Jeremy Taylor in *The Golden Grove* are difficult to adapt for congregational use, though his second Advent hymn has been adapted in two English collections.[2] The connection of John Quarles with Ireland as Primate Ussher's secretary was short lived. It is outside the Caroline period that we must look for the rich contribution which the Church of Ireland has made to Christian hymnody.[3]

(d) The Celebration of Morning and Evening Prayer

No evidence has come to notice in Ireland of an English custom before the revision of 1661, whereby a junior minister often read the opening Sentence, Exhortation, and Confession at the Litany-desk, and a senior minister read the Absolution at the reading-desk.[4] The 1666 consecration form, requiring the presence of the diocesan clergy at the new church, appoints the Dean "to read the Morning Prayer, or first Service,

---

[1] Some refer repeatedly to the "Apostolic Succession" with the recurring phrase, "In one unbroken line"; some are in thanksgiving for the Church's Creeds, Liturgy, Sacraments, Moderation, Reformation; some again denounce superstition, schism, false zeal, enthusiasm.

[2] As an Advent hymn in *Church Hymns* (1874 ed.), No. 66; another, shorter adaptation for Palm Sunday in the revised edition of *Hymns A & M*, 599 (cf. *Works*, VII, 550).

[3] See J. H. Bernard and R. Atkinson, *The Irish Liber Hymnorum* (H.B.S. XIII, XVI); J. K. Kenney, *The Sources for the Early History of Ireland*, I, *passim*. Later hymn-writers include Thomas Kelly (1769-1854), Henry Francis Lyte (1793-1847), John Samuel Burly Monsell (1811-75), and Cecil Frances Alexander (1823-95).

[4] Legg, *Eng. Ch. Orders*, 60 seq., 163, 212, 221.

in the Reading Desk".[1] Likewise for the consecration of the twelve
Bishops in 1661 Primate Bramhall ordered "that the office of morning
prayer be solemnly celebrated by the Dean" of St Patrick's, and at the
consecration of Kildare Cathedral in 1686 Morning Prayer was read by
the Dean. The assigning of the office to a senior minister was an Irish
custom which persisted into the nineteenth century. In 1843 John Jebb
distinguished between the presbyterial and diaconal parts of Divine
Service, maintaining that a senior minister should read the office and latter
Litany, and a junior the Lessons and the former Litany.[2] The universal
custom in Irish parish churches, he observed, was to assign the Lessons,
and sometimes the Litany, to the assisting minister, while the general
English custom was to assign the whole performance of Divine Service to
the end of the Litany to a junior minister, often a deacon, although a
senior minister was present in the family pew waiting to take over at the
Second Service.[3]

The Irish Canons of 1634 directed that the Confession and Absolution
"where the people all, or most are Irish, shall be used in English, first,
and after in Irish";[4] but "where the Minister is an Englishman, and many
Irish in the Parish" the parish clerk should be able "to read those parts
of the Service which shall be appointed to be read in Irish".[5] This was
not a lay invasion of a ministerial function, but the interpretation in Irish
of one already performed in English.

"The Versicles and responsory Petitions, in the daily Morning and
Evening Office" are in 1678 "generally modulated in a very plain way,
and at more solemn seasons sometimes sung after the newer figurative
mode."[6] The peculiar Irish use for the responses was described by Dr
P. R. Stewart as "a distinct form of ancient plain chant" and as "being in
use in all Cathedrals throughout the land".[7]

In 1678 "plain Tones" are used for the Psalms and "too very often for
our most usual Hymns, the *Te Deum*, *Magnificat*, and the rest".[8] The
use of plain-song in Ireland appears to have persisted side by side with
the use of Anglican chants and settings to the hymns, many of which
were put forth by Irish composers from the late seventeenth century.[9]

[1] Appendix 1, 638–40. [2] *Choral Service*, 241. [3] Ibid.
[4] Canon 8. [5] Canon 86.
[6] E. Wetenhall, *Of the Gifts and Offices...*, 333. Dean Lingard of Lismore in 1668
saw scriptural precedent for singing responses and prayers in the "Penitential Psalms",
in Psalms 86, 102, 142, and the Psalmist's frequent addresses to hear his prayers.
Op. cit., 20.
[7] *Report of Church Congress in Dublin, 1868*, 426. [8] E. Wetenhall, op. cit., 489.
[9] John Jebb made an admirable defence of the Anglican chant when promoters of
the revival of plain-song in England were advocating its exclusive use. Op. cit., 290.

In parish churches the Psalms were often read by the minister and people.[1]

In 1678 there is a voluntary "betwixt the Psalms and the first Lesson",[2] and in 1725 the new organist of St Michan's, Dublin, is directed to play "a grave solemn composition or Voluntary immediately before the First Lesson, to hold four minutes on Week Days and eight minutes on Sundays and Holy-Days, rarely exceeding or falling short".[3] A voluntary at this point was long kept up in the two Dublin cathedrals and in many parish churches,[4] though it was sometimes omitted on Sacrament Sundays.[5]

The Irish Canon 8 directed the minister reading the Lessons to turn himself to the people, and this suggests that the minister did not face west for the prayers. Lecterns in parish churches were exceptional in Caroline times, and the Lessons were generally read from the reading-desk, often large enough to accommodate more than one minister, with one shelf for the Prayer Books and another facing west for the Bible. At Christ Church, Dublin, in 1633 lay vicars read "the First Lesson and the Epistle at the Communion Table",[6] which for the first part of that year stood lengthwise in the choir, but which was restored "to its ancient place" by 10 August.[7] The more general practice in larger Irish cathedrals was for a junior vicar to read the Lessons at a lectern in the choir.[8]

In 1821, and again in 1830, Bishop Mant notices the survival of an older Anglican practice, long disused in England, of singing a metrical Psalm between the second Lesson and Canticle of both Morning and Evening Prayer.[9] In 1716 this practice was still kept up in some English parishes, and Thomas Bisse objected to it as adding "Hymn to Hymn".[10] Possibly it had been introduced in Caroline times to cover the movement of the minister and clerk to the font for the Baptism Office, or with the 1662 Book as an introduction to the public catechizing at Evening Prayer.

---

[1] There are still a variety of ways of reading the Psalms in Ireland. In one church the minister and the people on the side of the reading-desk read one verse, and the people on the opposite side the other. In another church the minister reads each verse as far as the colon: the people read what follows the colon.

[2] E. Wetenhall, op. cit., 399.

[3] "Memorial of St Michan's" (MS. in Vestry), 106.

[4] J. Jebb, op. cit., 317n.

[5] *Eccles.*, Vol. XXIII, Oct. 1862, 252 seq. The new organist of St Peter's, Dublin, in 1757 was directed to play "four Voluntaries on each Sunday in every year, except Sacrament Sundays".

[6] H. Cotton, *Fasti Eccles. Hibern.*, II, 84.   [7] Bramhall, *Works*, I, lxxix, lxxxi.

[8] Every Vicar of St Patrick's at his going to read any Lesson, and at his return, had to bow to the Dean, by Statute of 1692. (W. M. Mason, op. cit., 92.)

[9] *Charge* (Killaloe), 1821, 47; *Clergyman's Obligations Considered* (1830), 93.

[10] *The Beauty of Holiness* (1716 ed.), 115.

There had probably been no conscious imitation of the Office hymns at Lauds and Compline, and the revival of Office hymns in England after the Tractarian Movement no doubt led to the disuse in Ireland of this Caroline practice. In 1843 Jebb mentions the general Irish custom, again long disused in England, of singing the Gloria Patri after every metrical Psalm.[1] We have already noticed the Irish Caroline custom of standing for the Psalms, the hymns, the Lessons, and Epistle, and of turning to the East at the Gloria Patri and the Creeds.

Caroline Divines attached no sacerdotal significance to the rubrical direction for the Priest to stand up, after the second Lord's Prayer, for the Preces. "The purpose of it is", explains Jeremy Taylor in the *Ductor Dubitantium*, "that the people who are concerned to answer may better hear." [2] "All our Collects", observes Wetenhall, "and such like prayers, are only read in a distinct, plain, and audible voice" with a "variation of a note in the close of the Prayer, for retaining or exciting the attention of the people, that all may be ready to give their *Amen*." [3]

The anthem had no fixed place before the Commonwealth. Often it had been substituted for one of the metrical Psalms allowed to be sung "before or after Sermons", and the sermon was often preached after the Litany. At St Peter's, Drogheda, in Primate Ussher's time "Anthems were sung very frequently, and often instead of a Psalm before Sermon".[4] At the consecration of the twelve Bishops in 1661 a metrical Psalm was sung between the third Collect and the sermon; an anthem followed the sermon; then a voluntary while the Lord Primate and Bishops "ascend into the enclosure within the rails" for the Second Service, Consecration Office with Litany, and the Communion.[5] In spite of the new rubric of 1662 prescribing its use after the third Collect, the anthem was still sung in its earlier Caroline position after the sermon in both Dublin cathedrals in 1843.[6] A metrical Psalm was sung "immediately after the third Collect at Morning and Evening Prayer" in St Michan's, Dublin, in 1725,[7] but this practice did not become general in Anglican worship until the nineteenth century.

In Caroline times the Irish custom had been to chant the Litany, excepting at festivals, "in a very plain way".[8] "The ancient method" at Christ Church in Dublin had been for a junior vicar to chant the former Litany

---

[1] Op. cit., 398. [2] *Works*, x, 391. [3] Op. cit., 332.

[4] Ussher, *Works*, I, 147.

[5] Bramhall's directions are given in *The Pillars of Priesthood and Orthodoxy Shaken* (ed. Rich. Baron), II, 338 seqq.

[6] J. Jebb, op. cit., 371, 374. [7] "Memorial of St Michan's", 106.

[8] E. Wetenhall, op. cit., 333.

"on one unvaried note throughout" and a senior vicar the latter Litany with "the usual cadences".[1] The use of the Litany-desk, required for several decades after the Restoration,[2] survived at Christ Church into the nineteenth century.[3] After the prayer, *We humbly beseech Thee*, etc., a prayer for the Chief Governor was added, being composed at the request of the Irish Convocation at the Restoration possibly by Bishop Taylor.[4]

From 1662 "the five Prayers" following the anthem were regarded as an integral part of the Office when the Litany was not used, being connected like the three daily Collects with the preceding Preces; *O Lord, shew thy mercy upon us . . .*, relating to the Sunday Collect; *O Lord, save the King . . .*, the prayers for the King and Royal Family; *Endue thy ministers with righteousness . . .* and *O Lord, save thy people*, the prayer for the Clergy and People; *Give peace in our time, O Lord . . .*, the daily Collects for Peace; *O God, make clean our hearts within us . . .*, the daily Collects for Grace.[5] Although it was an old Anglican custom to insert the Churching Office either before or after the General Thanksgiving at Morning or Evening Prayer,[6] Bishop Peter Brown required "Churching at the rails of the Chancel; the rubric always read to the women" who were to be "put in mind of preparation for the Communion before they are Churched, and on Sunday morning".[7] The sexton of St Michan's, Dublin, in 1724 was required "to have cushions before the Communion rail" for the Churching Office.[8]

---

[1] J. Jebb, op. cit., 439, 445, 449.   [2] See below, p. 231.   [3] J. Jebb, op. cit., 435.
[4] On an inserted leaf in one of the few extant copies of the Prayer Book printed in Dublin in 1666 (R.C.B.L., Dublin: 45) is printed the following "Prayer for his Grace the Lord Lieutenant":
"Almighty God, in whose hand all earthly Power doth consist, we humbly beseech thee, to bless the Most Honourable James Duke of Ormonde his Grace, Lord Lieutenant General, and Governor of this Kingdom: and grant that the Sword which our dread Sovereign Lord the King hath committed into his hand, he may wield in thy faith and fear, and use according to thy blessed Will and Word; Let thy Grace enlighten him, thy goodness confirm him, and thy Providence protect him. Bless, we beseech thee, the whole Council, direct their consultations to the advancement of thy Glory, the good of thy Church, the honour of his Sacred Majesty, and the safety and welfare of this Kingdom. Grant this, O heavenly Father, for Jesus Christ his sake, our only Saviour and Redeemer. Amen."
This prayer, though obviously contemporary, is an insertion and not part of the text of the 1666 Irish Prayer Book. It appeared for the first time in 1700, and from 1721 was printed as the second alternative prayer for the Chief Governor, with a blank left for the name of the Lord-Lieutenant, "to be used after the Prayer for the Royal Family, in the Morning and Evening Service; or, when the *Litany* is used, after the Prayer (We humbly beseech thee, &c)".
[5] See Wheatley and Mant on the Prayer Book.
[6] C. Wheatley, *A Rational Illustration* (1840 ed.), 486; J. Jebb, op. cit., 532.
[7] Quoted from C. A. Webster, *Diocese of Cork*, 309.   [8] Op. cit., 19.

Although in Caroline times the morning sermon often followed the metrical Psalm sung after the Grace, by the close of the seventeenth century it normally followed that sung after the Nicene Creed. In either place, it was required on Holy Days as well as Sundays, and we have evidence that sermons on Holy Days were kept up, as at Limerick Cathedral[1] and Christ Church, Dublin,[2] into the nineteenth century. In 1758 we find a sermon in Irish "every day in Passion Week" at St Patrick's Cathedral,[3] and in 1800 Peter Roe at St Mary's, Kilkenny, preaching daily not only in Holy Week but in the week preceding Whitsunday. He also preached on all Holy Days drawing "a number which astonished many".[4]

Afternoon sermons though not required by the rubric, were provided in many cathedrals and town churches. Against the objection that they were introduced by "English Puritan Overdoo's" Wetenhall in 1678 argued that the Fathers preached in afternoon assemblies.[5] "We can get people to Church twice in the day", he claims, "and keep them there too, and have full congregations, if we so often preach diligently to them."[6] Not one in twenty who now frequent alehouses, taverns, public games, and sports would do so if Sunday afternoon Sermons were provided.[7] A proper place for them in the Liturgy, he thought, was "after the second Lesson".[8] Collections were taken at Evening Prayer in some churches.[9]

(e) The Ministration of the Public Baptism of Infants

On Sundays and Holy Days the public Baptism of infants was ordered to take place after the last Lesson of Morning or Evening Prayer; and from the time of Ussher Bishops urged that it should not be administered apart from the public Service. "Have you a Font of stone set in the usual place, and doth your Minister Baptize there publickly?",[10] asked Archbishop Narcissus Marsh. An interesting link with the 1549 rubrical direction for the woman that is Churched to "offer her Crysome and other accustomed offerings" is to be found in an item mentioned in the petition of the Lower House of Convocation in 1662 based upon the tithing table of Ulster for which Ussher had obtained Royal authority in 1630[11] and which Bramhall wanted to extend to the whole of Ireland.[12] "For the

[1] Bishop Jebb, op. cit., II, 383 seq.
[2] *Ecclesiologist* (N.S. CXLV), Aug. 1862, 254.   [3] *Pue's Occurances*, 11 Feb. 1758.
[4] Samuel Madden, *Memoir of...Peter Roe*.   [5] Op. cit., 722.
[6] Ibid.   [7] Ibid.   [8] Ibid., 782.
[9] See below, p. 178, n. 2.   [10] Visitation Articles Cashel, 1692, Dublin, 1694.
[11] *Works*, XV, 477.   [12] *H.M.C., Hastings*, IV, xxx.

Chrysome Cloath and all other Duties at every Churching...to the Parson, Vicar, or Curate 1s. 6d. and to the Clerk 8d. without paying any thing for the Sacrament of Baptism." [1] It would appear that the baptismal Chrysome veil to be thus returned at the Churching was actually used in Ussher's time in Ireland, although it had long been disused in England. "Here in Ireland", wrote Jeremy Taylor in *Ductor Dubitantium*, "there is a custom of receiving oblations at the baptism of infants." [2] In the same work he advocated Baptism with "Trine Immersion". [3] Peter Browne, Bishop of Cork and Ross (1710–35), required "Public Baptism on Sundays and Holy Days, yet never without the Public Service with Trine Immersion; Private Baptisms registered as such; the water poured into the Font at the time of Baptizing; the same water never consecrated twice, but always poured out after Baptizing is over." [4] The Lower House of Convocation in 1703 petitioned for the enforcement of the rubrical direction that children privately baptized be brought in due time to the church and publicly received into the congregation of Christ's flock. [5]

(f) The Catechizing of Children

Before 1662 the children of the parish were catechized upon Sundays and Holy Days half an hour before Evensong by former rubrical direction, or "for half an hour, or more" by order of Canon 11; and Jeremy Taylor in 1661 had directed the bell to be tolled "when the catechizing is to begin". [6] Primate Ussher had required catechizing not only before Evening Prayer, but also for half an hour after the first and second Lesson. [7] "For the better grounding of the people in the principles of the Christian Religion", Canon 12 directed "that the heads of the Cathechism being divided into as many parts as there are Sundays in the year, shall be explained to the people in every Parish Church". The 1662 Prayer Book directed children to be catechized after the second Lesson of Evening Prayer with the dual purpose, repeatedly emphasized by Bishops in their Charges, of instructing the children and reminding the adult members present of the principles of their religion. In 1694 Bishop King told the dissenters of the diocese of Derry that catechizing was constantly performed "in our Solemn Worship" every Sunday and Holy Day. [8] In the middle of the next century Philip Skelton used to expound the Catechism for half an hour every Sunday afternoon in summer; and "when he had

---

[1] Journal, 11 Nov. 1662.   [2] *Works*, x, 366.   [3] Ibid., 371.
[4] Manuscript Book of Prayers; quoted from C. A. Webster, *Diocese of Cork*, 309.
[5] T.C.D., MS. F. 3. 24.   [6] *Works*, i, 111.
[7] Mant, i, 440.   [8] Op. cit., 106.

reason to suppose the grownup people were tolerably well acquainted with their duty", he locked the church door without warning "and examined them all to see what progress they had made under his care in religious knowledge".[1] In 1678 the minister catechized from the reading-desk,[2] but in 1724 the sexton of St Michan's, Dublin, was required "to have the Moving Desk placed in the Body of the Church with cushions, stools, and forms before it when Persons are to be married, Converts to be reconciled, or Children catechized".[3] No doubt the children of the parish came out from the high box pews and grouped themselves in "order'd files".[4]

(g) The Rite of Confirmation

A rubric in the Irish consecration form of 1666 directs the Bishop to administer the rite of Confirmation between the Litany and Communion Service.[5] At the consecration of Kildare Cathedral in 1686 "the Bishop confirmed a great number", but after the second Lesson, as the Litany occurred in the Ordination Office which preceded the Communion.[6] Bishop Peter Browne required Confirmation "on Sundays with Communion".[7] Bishop Jemmet Browne administered this rite before the Eucharist in Cork Cathedral every Whitsunday; and in 1762 "he laid his hands crossed on the heads of about 200 young persons", and afterwards "administered the Communion to every one of them all".[8] A Confirmation in Waterford Cathedral on 12 December 1813 preceded the Eucharist at which 350 communicated.[9] Two Broad Churchmen of the nineteenth century, Archbishop Whately of Dublin and Bishop Fitzgerald of Cork, made it a rule to administer the rite of Confirmation before the Eucharist.[10] Confirmation sermons were sometimes given by Bishops, as by Ussher, Bramhall, King, Berkeley, and O'Beirne, but they were often delegated to priests such as Nicholas Brady, Philip Skelton, Peter Roe, and John Jebb (senior).[11]

(h) The Communion Service

We have already noticed that the Chapter of Christ Church in 1638 ordered the Choir to go "by two and two into the Choir for the Second

---

[1] Life in Works, I, lxix.   [2] E. Wetenhall, op. cit., 782.   [3] Op. cit., 19.
[4] J. Keble, "Cathechism" in The Christian Year.   [5] Appendix 1, 646–7.
[6] J. Keble, Life of Bishop Wilson (L.A.C.T.), I, 21.
[7] C. A. Webster, op. cit., 309.
[8] R. Cauldfield, Annals of St Finbarre's, Cork, 72.   [9] Preacher's Book.
[10] E. J. Whately, Life and Correspondence of Richard Whately, I, 64; C. A. Webster, op. cit., 349.
[11] The sermons of Brady and Skelton at Confirmations are extant. Peter Roe preached at a Confirmation c. 1800, and John Jebb at Cashel in 1805 and 1806.

Service and Communion", and that in earlier Caroline times there was often an interval between the First and Second Service. In 1678, however, Wetenhall speaks of a voluntary "betwixt the first and second Service while those, who officiate at the Communion Service, are going up to the Altar".[1] Although the English custom was often to read the Second Service in the reading-desk,[2] no contemporary evidence for this un-rubrical practice in Ireland has come to notice. The Irish Canon 94 fixed the altar at the east end of the chancel; and in 1639 the Archbishop of Dublin asked the churchwardens of St Audoen's Church, Dublin, to take down the ancient rood loft, partly because it was decayed and might endanger the people sitting nearby, and partly because "it depriveth the rest of the congregation of the sight of the east window and Holy Table, causing the Minister's voice performing the Second Service there to be less audible".[3] Likewise Bishop Jebb in the early nineteenth century speaks of "the Scriptures, which are read from the reading-desk, and the communion table",[4] implying that the Epistle and Gospel are not read in the reading-desk.

In 1678 Wetenhall observed that a Sanctus was sometimes sung instead of a voluntary before the Communion Service and wished "that practice were general, or else that some Versical (or Heavenly strain) out of the Psalms were used." [5] In 1725 there was "a Solemn Introit or Doxology" at St Michan's, Dublin, "upon the morning of Sundays and Holy Days" immediately after the Grace.[6] By the end of the century the practice of singing the Sanctus for the Introit in Cathedrals had become general, though in parish churches a metrical Psalm was sung instead. The Caroline practice had been to sing Psalms before and after the sermon, and during the Communion of the people.[7] It is uncertain how much of the Communion Service was sung. On Easter Day 1568 Archbishop Loftus dispensed with "the curious singing, which at other times is used" at the Communion; the presence of the Choir at the Communion was required by the Chapter of Cork in 1634, and by the Chapter of Christ Church in 1638. There is a tradition that Benjamin Rogers who was admitted organist of Christ Church in 1639 was commissioned by the Chapter to compose a setting for the Communion Service.[8] The same Chapter in 1699 commissioned David Rosingrave to compose "two Creeds and two

---

[1] Op. cit., 399.   [2] *Hierurgia Anglicana*, II, 304.
[3] Marsh Library, Dublin, MS. Memorial of St Audoen's, Vol. II, p. 34.
[4] *Practical Theology*, I, 3.
[5] Op. cit., 562.   [6] Op. cit., 107.
[7] *Hierurgia Anglicana*, II, 225; E. Wetenhall, *Enter into thy Closet*, 401 seq.
[8] I am indebted for this information to the Dean of Cashel.

Services".[1] The incompleteness of the great English settings of Gibbons, Farrant, and Aldrich suggests that the later Sanctus and Gloria in Excelsis were seldom sung, though Wetenhall says "the Versicles and responsory Petitions" in "the Communion Service" are in 1678, excepting at festivals, "modulated in a very plain way".[2] The earliest complete setting of Irish origin appears to be the one in manuscript, preserved in the Chapter Room at Cashel, by Robert Shenton (d. 1798), Treasurer of Kildare, who had been Dean's Vicar at Christ Church from 1757, and at St Patrick's from 1783. It may have been composed for one of the Dublin cathedrals, but it is to be found with the manuscript music at Cashel which was in use in Archbishop Agar's time (1779-1801). It provides music for the Sanctus (Introit), Kyrie eleison, "after the naming of the Gospel", Credo, Responses before the Sanctus, Sanctus (a repetition of the first), and Gloria in Excelsis. The Sanctus and Gloria in Excelsis were also sung at St John's, Limerick, before 1832, two decades before the same usage at Leeds Parish Church.[3] The fact that the Eucharist was sung in Irish cathedrals later in the nineteenth century when fear of Puseyism was greatest may suggest that the practice had been traditional from Caroline times.[4]

During the voluntary or the opening Sanctus the clergy approached the altar. It was the Caroline custom not only for the clergy to make adorations[5] on their approach, but also for the celebrant to begin the Communion Service "at the North side of the Table". "The more general position", writes Dr J. H. Srawley, "which Andrewes, and Laud after him, adopted, was at the north end, and this position gradually became general until modern times, when the eastward position was revived."[6] The rubrics in the Restoration consecration forms make it quite clear what the Restoration revisers meant by "the north end". In Bishop Cosin's form, drawn up at the request of the English Convocation, the Bishop's chaplains, "placing themselves at each end of the Table where he that is at the North, shall begin the Communion Service".[7] In the

[1] Grove's *Dictionary of Music*.
[2] Op. cit., 333.   [3] J. Jebb, op. cit., 512 seq.
[4] The Eucharist was sung at Christ Church *c.* 1840 (Walcott) and weekly from at least 1878 (*Irish Times*); at the dedication of the organ of St Mary's, Donnybrook, in 1866; before the Church Congress in 1868; in Cork *c.* 1873; at the consecration of the Cathedrals of Cork (1870) and Kildare (1896).
[5] Andrewes, op. cit., 150; cp. Hewetson's advice to Wilson in 1686 (p. 147, above) and an account of Cathedral Service *c.* 1780 in *Christ Church Cathedral Dublin... Year Book 1957.*
[6] "The Holy Communion Service", in *Liturgy and Worship*, 308 seq.
[7] Legg, *Eng. Ch. Orders*, 253; cf. Juxton's form of 1663: "One of the Chaplayns kneeling on the South, and the other on the North side of the Holy Table, or Altar, and saying, Our Father..." Ibid., 213.

Irish consecration form of 1666, the Bishop kneels "before the Altar or Communion Table" to dedicate it, and stands "his face being Eastward" to dedicate the plate, but he goes "to the North end of the H. Table" for the solemn prayers which follow.[1] In no Anglican formulary is the sacrificial aspect of the Eucharist more fully stated than in this form[2] which allows the northward position for solemn prayers, and which like Cosin's form demonstrates that "the North side of the Table" can in no sense be the west side. If the Lincoln Judgement held that by the north side the west side was really intended, Bishop Mant shared Wheatley's belief that "wherever, in the ancient Liturgies, the Minister is directed to stand *before* the altar, the north side of it is always meant".[3] Mant thought it most important that a new church should be oriented so that the Priest stands at the north side of the altar, "the right hand or upper side of it, that being deemed the station of preeminence, and therefore the most proper for the officiating priest, that so the assisting minister, if there be one, may occupy the inferior station on the left hand, or lower side".[4] The present Irish rubrical and canonical insistence on the northward position should be regarded as a perpetuation of traditional Anglican usage, which cannot be condemned without condemning the Caroline Divines and early Tractarians who used it.

If there were two assisting ministers they stood at the south side of the altar,[5] though if one of them was a deacon he knelt at the door of the Septum.[6] The Irish Canon 8 directed that the minister reading the Ten Commandments, the Epistle, and Gospel, "shall so place himself, and so turn himself to the people, as they may best harken thereunto". According to Bishop Andrewes' use the celebrant descended to the door of the Septum to read the Ten Commandments, and the assisting minister read the Epistle and Gospel in the same place.[7] The dedication of "Books for the Communion" in the Irish consecration form of 1666[8] suggests that the celebrant was normally assisted by at least one minister. The marginal scribblings in one of the extant copies of this form assign the readings of the Epistle to the Bishop of Leighlin and the Gospel to the Bishop of Kildare. Another Irish Office of 1756 and the Dublin provincial Office of 1760 for Consecration of Churches provide the rubric: "The Bishop, attended by two Priests, beginneth the Communion Service." In the former the "Junior Priest readeth the Epistle" and the "Senior Priest" the

---

[1] Appendix 1, lines 391, 425–7, 448.   [2] Ibid., 393 seqq.
[3] *Book of Common Prayer, with Notes* (1820).
[4] *Church Architecture Considered*, 6.
[5] *Ecclesiologist* (CXLII), Oct. 1862, 253 seq.
[6] Bishop Andrewes, *Minor Works*, 153.   [7] Ibid., 162.   [8] Appendix 1, 420.

THE COMMUNION TABLE OF CASHEL CATHEDRAL

(facing p. 160)

This shows the Communion Table of Cashel Cathedral, which was formerly the metropolitan church of the province of Cashel. The Communion plate consists of a Caroline flagon, chalice, and paten given in memory of Archbishop Thomas Fulwar (1661–7) and an early eighteenth-century set comprising flagon, two chalices, and two patens, given in memory of Archbishop William Palliser (1694–1727). The silver-gilt candlesticks and the red leather Dublin-bound service-books are Georgian. The alms-bason is late sixteenth or early seventeenth century. The carpet of green and gold damask is in the Caroline tradition.

Gospel. In 1717 the Chapter of St Patrick's enacted that two of the senior dignitaries should always assist the Dean at the Christmas Day Eucharist,[1] and the ancient usage of Christ Church was for two of the senior members to act as Epistoller and Gospeller.[2] From the middle of the eighteenth century Irish Churchmen often spoke of "the Epistle side" and "the Gospel side",[3] but the Caroline custom had been to read both Lections in the centre.[4] In Ireland the assistance of the parish clerk was sometimes necessary "where the Minister is an English man, and many Irish in the parish";[5] for "all the Second Service, (at or before the Communion, to the Homily or Sermon)" had to be repeated in Irish.[6]

A peculiar Irish custom, long disused in England, was the weekly collection for the poor; and this was made between the Nicene Creed and the sermon, the Priest first saying, "Pray remember the poor".[7] This was normally in addition to the rubrical collection at the Offertory.[8] "Let a collection be made every Lord's Day", Jeremy Taylor advised his clergy in 1661, "and upon all solemn meetings, and at every Communion."[9] In 1745 Dr Delaney wrote of the "weekly and monthly collections of the Church",[10] and in 1824 Bishop Jebb of the "Alms collected weekly, and at Sacraments".[11] "In Ireland", Bishop Jebb told the House of Lords in 1824, "we have no legal fund for the poor", but "in all our Churches, on the first day of the week, after the manner of primitive times, a collection is made for the relief of the poor."[12] The considerable sum raised was generally applied "in aid of the Roman Catholic poor".[13] Lord John Manners complained of two collections at Killarney on a Communion Sunday in 1846; but however unrubrical he and other English visitors thought this weekly collection made before the sermon, the usage was one of which it could be claimed that charity is above rubrics. A metrical Psalm was sung before the sermon.

"Doth your Minister declare to the People every Sunday at the time

---

[1] R. Wyse Jackson, *Jonathan Swift, Dean and Pastor*, 97.

[2] J. Jebb, op. cit., 479; cf. p. 58, where he suggests that this usage is general in Irish Cathedrals.

[3] In 1744 and 1750 Dr Charles Smith speaks of "the Gospel side" of the altar; in 1751 Bishop Pococke of "the Epistle side"; in 1843 Bishop Mant of "the Gospel side".

[4] Legg, *Eng. Ch. Orders*, 64, 167, 213.   [5] Canon 86.

[6] Canon 8.

[7] J. Jebb, op. cit., 489. By the 1604 rubric the curate was earnestly to exhort the people "to remember the poore".

[8] For an exception see below, p. 178, n. 2.

[9] *Works*, I, 114. In the context, the collection is for the poor.

[10] *Reflections upon the Present Neglect of a Public Worship of God*, 12.

[11] *Practical Theology*, II, 385.   [12] Ibid., 386 seq.   [13] Ibid.

M

appointed in the Communion Service, the several Holy days and Fasting days in the week following: and doth he observe them?", asked Archbishop Narcissus Marsh in his Visitation Articles.[1] The unwarranted alteration made in two rubrics in English Prayer Books, permitting banns to be read after the second Lesson (26 Geo. II, c. 33), was never made in the Irish, and banns continued to be published after the Nicene Creed.[2] The Bidding Prayer, prescribed by the English Canon 55, unadopted in the Irish code of 1634, but agreed upon by the Irish Convocation at the Restoration,[3] was constantly used in Ireland, so Archbishop King told Dean Maule, from that time to the Revolution, when it generally fell into disuse.[4] King believed that the Irish clergy were still bound by Act of Parliament (28 Hen. VIII, c. 13) "to bid beads in the English tongue".[5] The prayers before sermon of Primate Ussher[6] and of Jeremy Taylor[7] were drawn up for use during the Commonwealth. Before the Commonwealth the Invocation may have been used in some places, as Bishop Bedell instructed his clergy that "if at the saying the name of the Father and of the Son etc. any of the people did cross themselves, the Minister should tell them it was not amiss if they did so, provided they put no confidence in the sign but in Him that died on the Cross."[8]

On Sacrament Days the preacher sometimes exhorted the congregation not to turn their backs upon and forsake the table of the Lord. "If while you are being addressed", admonished Philip Skelton,

you are preparing to quit the house, and forsake the Table of your Redeemer, go, since you are able; go, return to those sinful pursuits, whatever they are, which are dearer to you, it seems, than the Son of God, after all you have suffered by them, and he hath suffered for you. But know this, that you leave the love of Almighty God, ungrateful as you are, and the necessary means of your salvation, foolish as you are, behind you. Go, and leave us, who, I trust in God, are not cursed with hearts so very stony, to meet the Lamb of our Salvation with love resembling his own; to feast on the miracles of his mercy, and to put forth all the ardour of our hearts in a grateful act of devotion, inspired by our Comforter, recommended by

[1] For the province of Cashel, 1692, of Dublin, 1694.
[2] J. Jebb, op. cit., 489. The unaltered rubric before the Marriage Service orders publication of banns "immediately before the Sentences for the Offertory". Although at variance with the rubric in the Communion Service, the revisers of 1662 probably had in mind the widespread, though unrubrical, practice of placing the sermon after the Litany.
[3] Journal, 5 Feb. 1662/3.
[4] Letter, 29 Nov. 1718. T.C.D., MS. N. 34, 82 seq.
[5] Ibid.   [6] C.U.L., MS.   [7] Works, I, 64; VIII, 595.
[8] E. S. Shuckburgh, Two Biographies of William Bedell, 317.

our Redeemer, and returned into our souls by our heavenly Father in grace, mercy, and peace, without end.[1]

The ascription of praise was usually woven into the final sentence of the sermon, as in George Rust's sermon at Jeremy Taylor's funeral:

...which God grant for His infinite mercies in Jesus Christ: to whom, with the Father, through the eternal Spirit, be ascribed all honour and glory, worship and thanksgiving, love and obedience, now and for evermore. Amen.[2]

"After the Sermon or Homily ended" the First Exhortation was still read in full in many Irish churches on the Sunday before the Eucharist early in the nineteenth century.[3]

On Sacrament Days the rubrical collection followed the sermon even though the weekly collection for the poor may have preceded it. The 1604 Prayer Book had directed the devotions of the people being gathered to be put into "the poormen's box" without any offering, but the Caroline custom had grown up whereby the people came up to the door of the Septum and made their individual offerings. The clergy often made their offerings individually at the altar, kneeling in prayer, and then returning to their places. There was "a solemn Offertory" at the consecration of the twelve Bishops in 1661.[4] With the 1662 Book, however, the custom became established whereby the alms were gathered from the people, brought to the Priest in a decent bason, and by him humbly presented and placed upon the Holy table.

The collection for the poor took place not before, but after charity sermons which were designed to raise considerable sums.[5] Often leading citizens, their wives, or even Bishops, were employed to gather the Alms

---

[1] *Works*, III, 133. Skelton cites the example of an incumbent who, observing almost the whole congregation leaving church after the sermon on a Sacrament Day, called them back and reproved them for turning their back upon Christ and facing about to the world which they had renounced in Baptism. Ibid., 130 seq.

[2] Taylor, *Works*, I, cccxxvii. Many of Taylor's own sermons end in this way. (Ibid., VIII, 283, 330, 391, 423, 570.) Some of Swift's and some of Skelton's sermons also. Berkeley sometimes used this ending (*Works*, ed. Luce, VII, 39, 92, 128): sometimes the ascription, "Now to God the Father..." (Ibid., 113, 138.)

[3] Bishop Jebb, *Practical Theology*, II, 187; J. Jebb, op. cit., 500.

[4] Dudley Loftus, op. cit., 7.

[5] Edward Wakefield wrote: "When a charity sermon is preached, the collection is not made until the feelings of the congregation have been roused by the pathos and eloquence of the preacher." Dean Kirwan "would get £1000 or £1200 at a sermon, and his hearers, not content with emptying their purses into the plate, sometimes threw in jewels or watches, as earnest of further benefactions." Quoted from Constantia Maxwell, *Dublin under the Georges*, 142 seq.

on these occasions,[1] while curious compositions, often containing a
solemn invocation of the wealthy members of the congregation, were
sung by the poor charity children.[2]

The 1604 Prayer Book had contained no direction for placing the
elements upon the altar, though the Irish[3] and English Canons required
the Wine to be brought to the Communion table in a metal stoup (i.e.
flagon). The two new rubrics of 1662 were no doubt designed to cover
the chief uses which had grown up during the previous reign. Immediately after the revised rubric for placing the alms there now appeared:
"And *when* there is a Communion, the Priest shall *then* place upon the
Table so much Bread and Wine as he shall think sufficient." The italics
have been introduced to illustrate the ambiguity some later Caroline
Churchmen found in this rubric, some laying the emphasis on "when",
others on "then". Of the former, Archbishop King thought that the
rubric intimated no more than that *"when* there is a Communion", the
Bread and Wine should by the care of the Priest be on the table at that
time so that he could order the elements according to the later rubric
before the Prayer of Consecration.[4] King's view was widely held for it
had long been the custom in many churches to place the elements upon
the altar before the beginning of Morning Prayer. Hence Hewetson
advised Thomas Wilson in 1686 "not to turn his back when he sees the
Holy Elements upon the Altar, though he knew not there would be a
Communion till he came into Church".[5]

---

[1] At St John's, Dublin, the Lady Mayoress and the wives of the Recorder and
Sheriffs collected in 1786, and the collectors of 1788 included the Bishop of Elphin
and the Lord Mayor. (C. S. Hughes, op. cit., 39.)
[2] The hymn "during the Collection" at St Ann's, Dublin in 1796:

I.	2
Guardian guides of innocence,	Friendless, helpless, did we stray:
Almoners of Providence:	No one mark'd to Heaven our way:
Hither turn your Eyes, and view	Now through you our God we bless,
Infant hands held up for you.	Through you a Saviour's name confess.

3.

Blessings, blessings, then receive.
We have nothing else to give:
Better far than India's store
Is the blessings of the Poor.

*Psalms and Hymns to be sung by the Children of St Anne's Parish on Sunday the 28th of
February, 1796.*
[3] Canon 95.
[4] Letter: King to Dean Maule 29 Nov. 1718 (T.C.D., MS. N. 35, 72 seqq.).
[5] J. Keble, *Life of Bishop Wilson*, I, 23.

Other Divines like Charles Leslie and Thomas Wilson, however, attached great importance to the offering of the elements before the general Prayer with its petition for the acceptance of the "oblations", which they identified with the elements, but which King with Cosin[1] and others identified with monetary offerings.[2] In a Charge at Killaloe in 1822 Bishop Mant quotes Bishop Simon Patrick's *Christian Sacrifice*: "By the word 'oblations' are to be understood, according to the style of the ancient Church, the elements of bread and wine, which the Priest then offers solemnly to God."[3] Accordingly the rubric was taken to mean that after the placing of the alms, "the Priest shall *then* place upon the Table" the elements. The parish clerk of St Michan's, Dublin, in 1724, for example, was directed "when there is a Communion to go into the Vestry after the Sermon, and put the Bread Scored on the Paten, and pour out the Wine into the Flaggons; and carry them in the Cistern provided for that purpose (being covered with a decent cloth) to the officiating Priest, immediately after he hath presented and placed ye Alms and Devotions of ye People upon the Holy Table: to the end he may then place upon the Table so much Bread and Wine as he shall think sufficient."[4] A similar practice seems to have survived elsewhere, for a letter in *The Tablet* of 22 July 1888 makes a contemptuous reference to a former practice in Headford Church, Co. Galway, where "during the last incumbency the elements for Holy Communion used to be carried from the vestry up to the Communion Table in an old clothes-basket covered with a patchwork quilt".[5] An analogue of this wicker basket was suggested to Dr J. Wickham Legg in Bishop Andrewes's "Canistor for wafers like a wicker basket, and lined with Cambrick laced".[6] John Jebb in 1843 pointed to Caroline precedent for a "Credential" or side-table, but thought there was "a closer analogy to primitive practice observed by bringing the Elements from the Vestry, which answers to the ancient Chapel of Prothesis".[7] In the same year Bishop Mant advised the clergy of Down and Connor to be guided by local circumstances; "either causing the bread and wine to be brought to him, as well as 'the alms and other devotions of the people', at the appointed time, or previously depositing them near at hand, on

---

[1] Rubric in Cosin's Convocational consecration form: "Then shall the Bishop reverently offer upon the Lord's Table...the Bread and Wine for the Communion, and then his own alms and *oblations*." Legg, *Eng. Ch. Orders*, 253. The elements were offered *before* the alms.

[2] Bishop Dowden, *Further Studies in the Prayer Book*, 176 seq. "Oblation" is used in a wide sense in the Irish consecration form (1666). See Appendix 1, 808.

[3] *The Rule of Ministerial Duty Enforced and Illustrated*, 24.

[4] "Memorial of St Michan's", 18.

[5] Quoted from Legg, *Eng. Ch. Life*, 194.   [6] Ibid.   [7] Op. cit., 498.

a small table for instance, as is always done in the Church of the parish where I reside, or in a recess such as I found useful and commodious in Killaloe, having been in old time an aumbrey if not a provision for this very purpose".[1]

The custom whereby the communicants entered the chancel after the sermon, or at the Invitation, was no doubt restricted by the shallow chancels of so many Irish churches. A sacramental meditation of James Bonnell (d. 1699) implies that the communicants were in the chancel for the Prayer of Consecration,[2] and a sermon early in the nineteenth century that the communicants have already approached the altar and are kneeling before it for the Prayer of Humble Access.[3] A rubric in *A Form for Receiving Lapsed Protestants*, bound in Irish Prayer Books from 1700 to 1757, is plainer. "Then shall the Absolved Penitent rise, and go and take his place in the Church, or if there be (as is requisite) a Communion, at the Communion Table, amongst the rest of the Congregation." "Having gone through the forgoing Service of God in the Church (prayers and Sermon)", writes Wetenhall, "coming now up towards the Lord's Table, I gravely take my place, and till the assembly be placed, it is better for me to be on my knees."[4] It is still the custom in many churches to stand up for the shorter Exhortation. The Caroline custom of assigning to assisting ministers parts of the Communion Service other than the Epistle and Gospel[5] long survived.[6]

Robert Shenton's setting to the Communion Service includes "Responses in the Communion Service (belonging to and intended for the following Sanctus and Gloria &c)":

N.B. for Precentor or Priest. Lift up your hearts...

N.B. Precentor or Priest. Let us give thanks...

N.B. Precentor or Priest. It is very meet &c. org chor, senza organs.

The music for these Responses is very elaborate compared with the "very plain way" in which Wetenhall said they were "modulated" in 1678. Irish Divines saw no difficulty in the sudden translation from exultation in the Sanctus to penitence in the Prayer of Humble Access, but

---

[1] *Church Architecture Considered*, 55 seq.

[2] See above, p. 114.   [3] Bishop Jebb, *Practical Theology*, I, 110 seq.

[4] *Enter into Thy Closet*, 395.   [5] Legg, *Eng. Ch. Orders*, 71, 176, 214 seq.

[6] At Christ Church, Dublin, early in the last century the Epistoller read the general Prayer (*Eccles.*, CXII, Oct. 1862, 253); and at the consecration of Cork Cathedral (1870) the Dean read the Ante-Communion Office, the Bishop of Tuam the Offertory Sentences, the Bishop of Down the Exhortation, the Bishop of Limerick led the Confession, and the diocesan Bishop took over at the Absolution and celebrated the Communion. (R. Cauldfield, *Annals of St Finbarre's Cathedral, Cork*, 120.)

"the happy union of Christian lowliness, with Christian exultation",[1] an imitation of "the mingled exultation and abasement of the Cherubim, who stood around the throne".[2] Ussher compares the petition in this prayer with a passage in Gregory Nazianzen.[3]

The 1604 Prayer Book had given no direction for manual acts at the Consecration, but Caroline Divines attached great importance to the sacramental actions of the minister. Ussher gave a mystical interpretation to the setting apart of the elements, and to the breaking of the Bread and pouring out of the Wine.[4] Before 1662 the Bread had been broken and the Wine poured from the flagon into the chalice, sometimes immediately before,[5] and sometimes during, the Prayer of Consecration. Jeremy Taylor seems to refer to the latter practice in *The Worthy Communicant* of 1660.[6] With the 1662 direction for breaking the Bread during the Prayer of Consecration, the pouring the Wine into the chalice, though unauthorized, took place after the breaking of the Bread. This Caroline practice continued in Ireland far into the eighteenth century, being mentioned by Dr Delaney in 1765[7] and by Philip Skelton who died in 1787.[8] Wetenhall had urged the communicant "to join in the Liturgy" and attend to "every passage and particular ceremony in the Consecration".[9] "And thus in the consecration of the mysterious sacrament", Jeremy Taylor told his clergy at a Visitation, "the people have their portion; for the bishop or the priest blesses, and the people by saying 'Amen' to the mystic prayer is partaker of the power, and the whole church hath a share in the power of spiritual sacrifice." [10]

Andrew Sall thus describes the distribution of the Sacrament in Christ Church in Dublin on Easter Day 1675.

The most Reverend the Lord Archbishop of Dublin, Chancellor of Ireland,[11] having performed the Communion Office with singular decency and good order, he himself reverently took the Sacred Communion and gave it to the Ministers of the Altar, then to the Lord Lieutenant, to the Peers and Royal Council, and to a

[1] Bishop Jebb, *Practical Theology*, I, 112.   [2] Ibid., II, 90.
[3] *Works*, XVI, 163.   [4] See above, p. 92.
[5] Legg, *Eng. Ch. Orders*, 71, 177.
[6] *Works*, VIII, 224. "When the holy man reaches forth his hands upon the symbols and prays over them, and intercedes for the sins of the people, and breaks the holy bread and pours forth the sacred chalice, place thyself by faith and meditation in heaven."
[7] *Doctrine of Transubstantiation Confuted*, 7.
[8] *Works*, III, 121. Bishop Wilson also makes it quite clear that the Wine is poured out during the Prayer of Consecration. *Works* (L.A.C.T.), IV, 275.
[9] *Enter into Thy Closet*, 395; 396.
[10] *Works*, VIII, 504.   [11] Dr Michael Boyle.

numerous concourse: all receiving it with singular devotion; having for associates in giving it the most Reverend the Archbishop of Armagh, Primate of all Ireland, the Right Reverend the Bishop of Meath, the chief of the Bishops of Ireland; after the Metropolitans and three Dignitaries of the Church, there were Doctors in Divinity to administer the Cup, each one making a godly brief exhortation to the receiver for a due receiving of it, the Lord Archbishop having read at the Communion Table a grave and pious Homily, exhorting to a right preparation for receiving that venerable Sacrament, as is usually done in all Churches upon such an occasion.[1]

Sall found far greater devotion and reverence among Irish Anglicans than he had found among Romans, "though pretending to believe something more (they knew not themselves what) about the presence of our Saviour in that Sacrament, than Protestants do".[2]

Caroline Divines saw nothing unfitting in the use of the Lord's Prayer after the Communion of the people. From Ussher onwards they connected the receiving of Christ by faith in the sacramental action with John I. 12,[3] and, therefore, it was fitting for the sons of God, now made at one with Christ, to call upon the heavenly Father.[4] Moreover, the Lord's Prayer was not regarded simply as a petition for spiritual nourishment, but as a great act of intercession and thanksgiving on the part of those who had become one with the celestial High Priest and thereby "admitted to interceed for others, even for all mankind", their intercession being united to his intercession.[5] This was Taylor's view, and the "Post-Communion" of his Communion Office of 1658 begins with the Lord's Prayer and is followed by a prayer "for the Catholic Church" and by a prayer of self-offering.[6] For when the communicants receive the Sacrament worthily "they receive Christ within them, and therefore may also offer Him to God, while in their sacrifice of obedience and thanksgiving, they present themselves to God with Christ, whom they have spiritually received, that is, themselves with that which will make them gracious and acceptable. The offering their bodies and souls and services to God, in Him, and with Him, who is the Father's well-beloved, and in whom He is well pleased, cannot but be accepted to all purposes of blessing, grace, and glory." [7] In Caroline times the first of the alternate

---

[1] Op. cit., 256 seq. [2] Ibid. [3] *Works*, II, 429.

[4] cf. Thomas Comber, *A Companion to the Altar*, 301, and Bishop Wilson, *Plain Instruction* (Dublin, ed. 1812), 103.

[5] Taylor, *Works*, VIII, 226.

[6] Ibid., 628 seq. In the Prayer Book revision of the 1870s Irish High Churchmen powerfully resisted the proposal, sponsored by Broad Churchmen, to place the Lord's Prayer before the Communion of the people.

[7] Ibid., III, 215.

prayers in the Post-Communion seems to have been more generally used.[1]

Although the laudable custom prevails in most Irish country parishes at least whereby the communicants remain kneeling at the rails until all who are kneeling with them have communicated, the earlier practice had been to remain either at the rails or elsewhere in the chancel until the end of the Gloria in excelsis. "And though", writes Wetenhall, "I should not before have sung an hymn,[2] yet do I not depart from the Lord's Table without a very Seraphical Hymn, if I devoutly join in the Church's prayers: for such is that which is sung or said after the administration, Glory be to God on high, &c".[3] Just as Caroline Divines compared this hymn with that at the end of the Last Supper,[4] so it was the Caroline custom to go out, as from the Upper Room, into the body of the Church when they had sung this hymn, and before the final Blessing. "Here the congregation ariseth", notes Bishop Andrewes, "and having made their adoration[5] they go towards their seats", making a further offering "in their way at the foot of the Choir".[6] Taylor, in the *Worthy Communicant*, rather implies that an offering was made after the Communion by Irish Anglicans during the Commonwealth.[7] After the Blessing which then followed, a voluntary was sometimes played, but at the consecration of the twelve Bishops in 1661 the *Laetificatur cor regis* was sung "before the Lord Primate, as he goeth from the Choir to the outward part of the Church".[8]

"We come not from Church on Sunday (and haply from the Communion too) to the Market", observes Wetenhall, "nor buy there our dinners, and go then in the next tavern we can get them dressed in... And, as from Church we go gravely home to our private and modest and necessary refreshments, so after them, soberly to Church again." [9]

Little information regarding the number of communicants becomes available before the closing decades of the eighteenth century, though the steady expenditure on sacramental elements often shown in vestry accounts from the late seventeenth century to the early nineteenth may suggest that the available figures have some continuity with the earlier period. In the 1780's Philip Skelton writes of "the numbers who crowd

---

[1] Legg, *Eng. Ch. Orders*, 72, 178, 215, etc.
[2] Wetenhall has already said that there is no need to join in the metrical Psalm during the Communion unless it makes sense.
[3] Op. cit., 404.   [4] T. Comber, op. cit., 343; T. Wilson, op. cit., 105.
[5] A widespread Irish Church custom in 1676, see above, p. 147.
[6] *Minor Works*, 158.   [7] Works, VIII, 226; see above, p. 104.
[8] Op. cit.   [9] *Gifts and Offices*, 768 seq.

this Sacrament at Christmas and Easter",[1] and in 1814 Alexander Knox
of "the crowds who throng our Altars at festivals".[2] On Whitsunday
1785 John Wesley records that the Service in Limerick Cathedral lasted
from 11 to 3 concluding "a little sooner by my assisting at the Lord's
Supper".[3] On Easter Day 1800, when there were only six communicants
at St Paul's Cathedral, London,[4] there were 311 at St Mary's, Kilkenny,
where, the year before there had been 280 at Whitsun and 520 at Christmas.[5] Among the remarkable figures given by Bishop Jebb in the House
of Lords in 1824 are 2100 at festivals and 480 monthly at St Mary's,
Dublin, and 2000 "last Easter Day" at St Peter's, Dublin.[6] Yet Jebb's
figures for 1824 show a gap between the numbers at festivals and the
numbers at the monthly Sacrament, though not as serious as that shown
at St Peter's, Drogheda, in 1802.[7] At St Mary's, Dublin, for example,
less than a quarter of the number at festivals communicated monthly, in
six other Dublin city churches less than a fifth,[8] in seven Cork city churches
less than a third.[9] Shortly before his death in 1787 Skelton had complained
of the large numbers who only communicated at festivals and absented
themselves "ten or twelve times every year".[10] He exhorted his people
to communicate frequently[11] and his influence lasted, for as late as 1830
more than half the number at festivals communicated monthly in his
former parish of Findonagh.[12]

[1] "Senilia", *Works*, VI, 102.   [2] *Remains*, III, 257.
[3] *Journal*; cf. Palm Sunday 1787, "above 500" at St Patrick's; Easter Day 1789,
"7–800" at a Dublin church.
[4] Abbey and Overton, *The English Church in the Eighteenth Century*, 454.
[5] Ossory Visitation Report (R.C.B.).
[6] *Practical Theology*, II, 382 seqq.
[7] 800 Fest., 100 monthly (R.D. Rep.).   [8] 6650 F, 1165 M.
[9] 2205 F, 692 M.   [10] Op. cit., VI, 102 seq.   [11] See above, p. 118.
[12] 120 F, 60–100 M; cf. 1825 "very numerous" M (Clogher V.R. in N.L.I.).
Other figures include: [Abbreviations: Good Friday GF, Easter E, Whitsun W,
Christmas C, Festivals F, Monthly M] *1813*, Waterford Cathedral 35 GF, 156 E,
135 W, 270 C, 350 at a Confirmation, *c.* 33 each fortnight; *1820,* Roscrea 100–150 F,
30–40 M; Kilrush *c.* 150 E, C, *c.* 70 W & Michaelmas, *c.* 40 M (early); Nenagh
150–200 F, 40–60 M; *1824*, 9 parishes of Ferns and Leighlin 1816 F; 8 towns of the
diocese of Cork 3360 M; *1825*, Athlone 402 C; *1828*, Newry 268 E, 375 last C;
1829, Waterford Cathedral 70 GF, 145 E, 140 Low S, 94 W, 190 C, *c.* 48 a fortnight;
1830, Clogher Cathedral 84 GF, 280 E, 320 last C; Devenish (another of Skelton's
former parishes) 101–6 F, 21 (lowest), 61 (highest) M; *1833*, Clones with two
chapels 180, 190, 70 F, 60, 69, 30 M; Enniskillen 350 E, 95 W, 455 last C, 73 M.
(Clogher V.R. in N.L.I.)
I am grateful to Dr J. Wyse Jackson for extracts from the Preachers' Books of
Waterford Cathedral (1811–38).

III. THE FREQUENCY OF HOLY COMMUNION IN IRELAND

(a) Introductory

The eighteenth Irish Canon of 1634 laid down a minimum rule that the Holy Communion should be administered "in every Cathedral and Collegiate Church at least once a month" and in every parish church and chapel where Sacraments are to be administered "so often, and at such times as every Parishioner may communicate at least three times in the year". The Caroline Statutes of Trinity College, Dublin, required the Eucharist to be celebrated on Christmas Day, Easter Day, Whitsunday, and Trinity Sunday, and "at least the second Sunday in every term".[1] The clergy of the diocese of Down and Connor in 1661 were directed by Bishop Jeremy Taylor to "exhort and press the people to a devout and periodical Communion, at least three times in the year, at the great festivals; but the devouter sort and they who have leisure, are to be invited to a frequent Communion."[2] The clergy of the province of Cashel in 1692, and of Dublin in 1694, were directed by Archbishop Narcissus Marsh to administer the Eucharist frequently "once a month, if may be: at least once every Quarter of the Year."[3] The Lower House of the Irish Convocation (1703–11) petitioned the Bishops to recommend monthly Sacraments to the Ministers of all parishes. Monthly Communion, as we shall see, became increasingly the rule until it became fixed as the minimum standard, beside "the days for which Proper Prefaces are provided", by the fifteenth Victorian Canon.

Side by side with this standard was the strong recommendation of weekly Communion, the neglect of which William King, Bishop of Derry, in 1694 declared to be "the most defective part of the Reformation".[4] Yet every endeavour had been made, and King believed "that by God's assistance, we should have brought our people before now to the Scripture Order of Constant Weekly Communicating, had not the ill example and obstinacy of those, that separate from our Church, encouraged their negligence, and weakened our discipline."[5] Likewise Bishop Wetenhall maintained that it was "closely and most evidently concluded from Scripture, that to receive the Lord's Supper, every Lord's Day, is such a duty, that no serious and conscientious Christian, who has

[1] R. Bolton, A Translation of the... Statutes of Trinity College Dublin, 48.
[2] Works, I, 113 seq.
[3] The Charge given by Narcissus Lord Archbishop of Cashel...1692, and given in 1694 to the clergy of the province of Dublin.
[4] Inventions of Man in the Worship of God, 208.   [5] Ibid., 210 seq.

opportunity and leisure can ordinarily omit." [1] Late in the eighteenth
century, Philip Skelton, in denouncing the numbers who communicated
at the Festivals only, observed that all Christians, "in the time of the
apostles, when the Spirit of God immediately governed the Church,
when the nature and use of the ordinance were best understood, and for
three or four centuries afterward, communicated at the Lord's table every
day. *In tempora devenimus!*" [2]

Before examining the opportunities for monthly or weekly Communion, we should notice the celebration of the Holy Communion on
special occasions and on Holy Days other than Sundays. The Eucharist
was celebrated at the opening of the Synod of Kilmore in 1638, before
the opening of Convocation in May 1661, for the corporate communion
of the Irish House of Commons on 16 June 1661, at the consecration of
new churches, and often at Confirmations; and in 1696 Anthony Dopping, Bishop of Meath, maintained that a Bishop in his diocesan Visitation should celebrate the Eucharist and that his clergy should communicate with him.[3] In 1660 Jeremy Taylor referred to the practice of communicating at marriages and at the visitation of the sick; and the rubrics
before 1662 required a celebration at marriages and "a good number to
receive the Communion with the sick person". The celebration of the
Eucharist on Christmas Day appears to have been universal; but for other
Holy Days falling on week-days our evidence is extremely meagre. The
Commemoration of King Charles, 30 January, was observed as a "general
Communion Day" at St Catherine's, Dublin, in 1664.[4] The Caroline
custom of celebrating the Communion on Good Friday was continued
well into the nineteenth century;[5] and we notice a celebration on Ascension Day in Dublin, at St John's in 1719 and 1721, at St Mary's from 1833,
at St Stephen's from 1841, and Christ Church Cathedral by 1842.

Three decades after the Restoration we are given a clear picture of the
general practice of the Church of Ireland. "As to our practice," observes
Bishop King in 1694, "we have prevailed so far, that universally the Lord's
Supper is celebrated thrice every year; and where either our persuasions,
arguments, or entreaties can prevail with our people, we have Monthly

[1] *Due Frequency of the Lord's Supper stated and Proved from Holy Scripture* (Dublin, 1703), 46.
[2] *Works*, VI, 103.
[3] *Tractatus de Visitationibus Episcopalibus* (Dublini, 1696), 28.
[4] Vestry Book (R.C.B.L.).
[5] As in a number of churches in the diocese of Dublin and in the cathedrals of Waterford and Clogher. Four Dublin churches had a Eucharist on Good Friday 1956 (*Irish Times* of preceding day).

Communions: and in Cities and large Towns, by changing the Monthly Days in several Churches, people that are devoutly disposed, have opportunities of receiving weekly: and we have reason to bless God that our Church wants not some, and I hope I may say many such." [1] Taking this statement as a basis for our inquiry, first let us see to what extent monthly Communions were provided in Ireland, and then examine what seems to have been a Caroline practice peculiar to Ireland, the provision for weekly Communion in cities and large towns "by changing the Monthly Days in several Churches".

(b) Monthly Communion

In 1647 the leading clergy of Dublin presented a petition to the Parliamentary Commissioners, that they might continue the use of the Book of Common Prayer "in their several Cathedral and Parish Churches" and keep the monthly fast on the last Friday of each month, "being a day of preparation for the monthly Communion, according to our custom these past five years". [2] On the eve of the Restoration Jeremy Taylor implies that there are Irish Anglicans "who communicate every month, and upon the great festivals besides". [3] At the Restoration the monthly Communion appears to have been revived immediately in Dublin churches. At St Catherine's, for example, it was celebrated on the first Sunday of every month, besides Christmas Day, New Year's Day, 30 January, Easter Day, Low Sunday, and Whitsunday. [4] In 1706 Primate Narcissus Marsh, who in his former provinces of Cashel and Dublin had encouraged monthly Communion, told Archbishop Tenison of Canterbury that in the ten dioceses of the province of Armagh he had for the most part found already practised "Monthly Communions in all Towns and quarterly in all villages". [5] Although we have no contemporary account for the other three provinces, apart from King's general statement that monthly Sacraments by 1694 had been provided where possible, the figures for the year 1833 in the Commissioners' Report[6] show a much higher standard in the provinces of Dublin and Cashel, and this may suggest a correspondingly higher standard in the southern provinces at the end of the seventeenth

[1] Op cit., 210.
[2] A Declaration of the Protestant Clergie of the City of Dublin....
[3] Works, VIII, 191.   [4] Vestry Book.
[5] Quoted from E. F. Carpenter, Thomas Tenison, 384.
[6] Third and Fourth Report on Ecclesiastical Revenue and Patronage in Ireland (1836–7), I, 505 seqq., 615 seqq.; II, 283 seqq., 671 seqq. The Articles of Inquiry were sent out by the Royal Commission (15 Aug. 1833), and the church accounts and other statistics are for the year 1833, though the Third Report (Armagh and Tuam) was published in 1836 and the Fourth (Dublin and Cashel) in 1837.

century. The figures for the four provinces in 1833 may be tabulated thus:

Frequency of the Holy Communion	ARMAGH	TUAM	DUBLIN	CASHEL	Total
At least TWELVE times in the year	174	37	189	218	615
From FIVE TO ELEVEN times in the year	263	23	73	87	446
FOUR times in the year or less	100	45	24	47	216

In view of the popular belief that, excepting in large towns, the Anglican custom was to celebrate the Eucharist as infrequently as three or four times a year until the religious movement which began in Oxford in the year 1833, it is good to know that in the Irish portion of the then United Church of England and Ireland, and in that very year, only one-sixth of the total number of churches had the Eucharist as infrequently, while just over a third had it from five to eleven times a year, and nearly half the number had it at least once a month. Moreover, in 1833, the standard was still rising. When in 1824 Peter Roe became Rector of Odagh, a country parish near Kilkenny, he announced his intention in his first sermon of having the Eucharist "regularly once a month, besides the three great festivals", agreeably to the publicly expressed wishes of the Bishop and "to the general custom of our Church".

In England, on the other hand, Communion only three or four times a year was the general custom in the opening decades of the nineteenth century;[1] and as late as 1865 Archbishop Trench, in his primary Charge to the clergy of the provinces of Dublin and Cashel, rejoiced "that the rare celebration of the Holy Communion only four times in the year, which used to be so common in the country districts of England, and has by no means yet disappeared, is almost unknown in these dioceses".[2] In 1743

---

[1] J. H. Overton, The English Church in the Nineteenth Century, 127.

[2] Charge (1865), 8. The separate diocesan summaries given in the Commissioners' Report reveal that in 1833 the Eucharist was far more frequent in the south of Ireland than in the north, where Presbyterian influence was strong and the Church people reluctant to communicate frequently. Of the 154 churches in the southern dioceses of Waterford, Cork, Ross, Ardfert, and Limerick, 122 provided the Sacrament at least once a month, and only 13 once a quarter; but of the 199 churches in the northern dioceses of Raphoe, Derry, Connor, Down, and Dromore, only 45 had monthly Communion and as many as 56 quarterly. While quarterly Communion was almost unknown in the dioceses of Cork and Ross, it prevailed in as many as 35 churches in the diocese of Derry.

only 72 out of 1036 churches of the diocese of York had monthly Communion, while 571 had it four times or less;[1] and during the period 1705–23 only 32 out of 627 parishes in the two Lincolnshire archdeaconries had monthly Communion, while the majority had it only three or four times a year.[2]

The figures for 1833 also show that provision for fortnightly Communion was made in ten city churches of Dublin, five city churches of Cork, at Waterford Cathedral, St Iberius, Wexford, the two parish churches in the town of Bandon, at Clonmel, and at Kinsale. In Dublin and Cork fortnightly Communion[3] was firmly established by the first half of the eighteenth century when we find no trace of it in the diocese of York. There were also cases where the Eucharist was celebrated twice on the same Sunday of the month,[4] and where monthly Communion was provided at several churches within the same Union.[5]

(c) Weekly Communion

When King spoke of the provision of weekly Communion in cities and large towns he was no doubt speaking from his experience of Church life in Dublin when he was Minister of St Werburgh's (1678–89) and later Dean of St Patrick's. One of the "devoutly disposed persons" who made use of this provision was King's friend, James Bonnell, who on his return to Dublin in 1684 as Accomptant-General found that he was able to communicate in this city every Sunday by the changing of the monthly days at several churches. "He used to wish that there was some Church in Dublin, wherein the Holy Sacrament was administered every Lord's Day; 'for going about from Church to Church', he said, 'had something

---

[1] *Archbishop Herring's Visitation Returns*, 1743, I, xvi seq.

[2] *Speculum Dioceseseos Lincolniensis sub Episcopis Gul: Wake et Edm: Gibson A.D. 1705–1723*, xx.

[3] Provided by a monthly early Sacrament in addition to the monthly forenoon Sacrament which was more normal. At St Kevin's Chapel, Dublin, there was early Sacrament only (1763–1824), and at Kilrush, Co. Clare, in 1820 a well attended monthly early Sacrament, but only "after regular Service" four times a year.

[4] St Matthew's, Ringsend, Sandford Chapel, and Castledermot in the diocese of Dublin.

[5] Armagh Cathedral and five daughter churches; Clones and two chapels; Wicklow and two chapels; Sligo, seventeen times a year, and Calrey (half a mile away) fifteen times; St Peter's, Dublin, fortnightly, St Stephen's Chapel, fortnightly, and five other daughter churches, monthly. At Leeds, in 1743, there was monthly Communion at the parish church, but no celebration whatever at St John's and Holy Trinity. The weekly Eucharist at Holy Trinity, Hull, in 1743, was not designed to encourage weekly communion, but to split the parish into four groups of monthly communicants for more convenient administration.

of ostentation in it'; and it was with some difficulty that he at last con-
quered this scruple." [1] About the time of Bonnell's death in 1699 a visitor
to Dublin, John Dunton, observed that the Holy Sacrament was administered in some one of the Dublin churches every Sunday in the year. [2]
In 1703 William King was translated from Derry to Dublin, and, in order
to encourage what he believed to be "the Scripture-Order of Constant
Weekly Communicating", he would extend this already existing Caroline
provision to the new churches which he made it his care to erect in the
growing parts of the city. Although within a decade of King's death we
find that devoutly disposed Dubliners could "by going from Church to
Church" attend an early Sacrament at 6 on the first, second, third, and
last Sundays of the month, it is not until later that we find the details of the
provision for the Sacrament at the forenoon Service by "changing the
Monthly Days in several Churches".

From 1743 to 1775 John Watson's *The Gentlemen and Citizen's Almanack*
gives this rather vague information: "The Holy Communion celebrated
in the Churches of Dublin, on the (1st, 2d, 3d, 4th, or + last) Sundays of
the Month." The symbol before the word "last" strongly suggests that a
list already existing was intended to follow this statement, but held over
for lack of space. In 1776, for the first time, the statement is elucidated by
the following list of churches with the Sacrament Sunday in brackets:

St Andrew's, (2); St Ann's, (1); St Audoen's, (1); St Bridget's, (1); St Cath-
erine's, (1); Christ Church, (1); St James's, (3); St John's, (4); St Luke's, (1);
St Mark's, (+); St Mary's, (2); St Michael's, (2); St Michan's, (1); St Nicholas
Within, (1); St Nicholas Without, (1); St Patrick's, 1, 2, 3, 4, (+); St Paul's, (3);
St Peter's, (3); St Thomas's, (1); St Werburgh's, (+).

St Thomas's, consecrated in 1762, would be the only church added to
the list already existing in 1743.

While thus withholding details of the late Sacrament until 1776,
Watson's *Almanack* gives full information from 1736 of "Early Hours of
Divine Service on Sunday in the Churches of Dublin, where Masters of
Families may send their Servants, whom they cannot spare from home
at the more stated times". "Prayers, Sermon, and Sacrament" are provided at an early hour at St James's, St Ann's, St Andrew's, and St Audoen's
on fixed monthly days from 1736 to at least 1824; at St Kevin's from 1760,
at St Werburgh's (without sermon) from 1766, St Catherine's from 1766,
St Peter's from 1784, St Bridget's from 1798, St Thomas's from 1802,

---

[1] Wm Hamilton, *The Exemplary Life...of James Bonnell Esq.*, 92 seq.
[2] R. Wyse Jackson, *Scenes from Irish Clerical Life in the Seventeenth and Eighteenth
Centuries*, 22 seq.

St George's from 1828, St Stephen's from 1833. Before 1765 there had
been a number of short-lived experiments, the most interesting being the
twice-monthly early Sacrament at St Ann's (1738–40) and at St Catherine's
(1744–52). If we tabulate the monthly days for the early Sacrament beside

Sunday of the Month	EARLY SACRAMENT 1736 to 1833 (with dates)	LATE SACRAMENT 1776–1833 (alterations noted)
FIRST	St James's (1736–1824) St Ann's (1738–40) St Mark's (1752–5) St Kevin's Chapel, in St Peter's parish (1760–1824) *St Peter's* (1784–1833)	St Patrick's Cathedral Christ Church Cathedral *St Ann's* *St Audoen's* *St Bridget's* *St Catherine's* St Luke's St Michan's St Nicholas Within St Nicholas Without *St Thomas's* St James's (after 1824 when the Early Sacrament was discontinued)
SECOND	St Catherine's (1738–52) St Bridget's (1765) *St Werburgh's* (1766–1833) *St Mark's* (1825–33) *St Stephen's* (1833)	St Patrick's Cathedral *St Andrew's* St Michael's St Mary's *St George's* (from 1802) St Kevin's (from 1824) Kirwan House (from 1818)
THIRD	*St Ann's* (1736–1824) *St Audoen's* (1736–1824) St Catherine's (1776–1833) *St Bridget's* (1798–1833) *St Thomas's* (1802–33)	St Patrick's Cathedral *St James's* *St Peter's* St Paul's
FOURTH	St Catherine's (1744–52) *St George's* (1828–33)	St Patrick's Cathedral St John's
LAST	St Catherine's (1744–52) *St Andrew's* (1736–1833)	St Patrick's Cathedral *St Werburgh's* *St Mark's* *St Stephen's* (from 1824)

N

the monthly days for the late Sacrament, we notice at once that at the churches printed in italics in the table above, the monthly days for the early and late Sacraments fall into a well-ordered provision for fortnightly Communion, either on the first and third, or on the second and last Sundays of the month.

If from 1776 the monthly days for the late Sacrament thus bore an orderly relation to the monthly days for the early Sacrament, there is good reason to suggest that they may have had the same relation in 1736 when our evidence for the early Sacrament first becomes available. In several cases we can trace the Sunday of the month for the late Sacrament to an earlier date than 1776. John Wesley, for example, complained of the bad behaviour of the communicants at St Peter's on the third Sunday of April 1758;[1] the weekly Sacrament at St Patrick's became firmly established in the second decade of the eighteenth century; the Sacrament on the first Sunday at Christ Church is mentioned in 1678 and in 1638, at St Catherine's from 1663, at St Michan's from c. 1724, and at most of the Dublin churches in 1647. The Sacrament of St John's on the fourth Sunday is mentioned continuously from 1700.[2] The strong probability that the last Sunday of the month was the Sacrament Day at St Werburgh's during the incumbency of William King (1679–89) is suggested by the fact that during his imprisonment in Dublin Castle he fell back upon the last Sunday of each month to "administer the Holy Sacrament" to his fellow-prisoners.

If we assume that the monthly days for the late Sacrament go back beyond 1736 into the seventeenth century, the Table of 1776 at once becomes self-explanatory. By excluding the churches of new parishes created from 1697 we have a list of the eleven parish churches which James Bonnell knew when he made his Communion every Sunday "by going from Church to Church". In five near the centre of the city and in St Michan's on the north of the river, the Eucharist is celebrated on the first Sunday of the month; in St Andrew's and St Michael's on the second Sunday; in St Peter's on the third; in St John's on the fourth; in St Werburgh's on the last. In 1697 St Michan's parish, the only parish on the north side of the river, was divided into three. The new parish churches of St Mary and St Paul entered into the scheme, so that weekly communicants on the north side could go to St Michan's on the first Sunday,

---

[1] *Journal*, 16 April 1758 (Easter III).

[2] "The Poore Book" of St John's (begun 1700) enters a "Collection" every Sunday morning and evening, excepting the morning of the fourth Sunday of each month, when there was an "Offertory". By the end of the century there was a "Collection" and Offertory on Sacrament Days.

St Mary's on the second, St Paul's on the third, and, by crossing any of the then existing bridges, at the nearby churches of St John on the fourth Sunday or of St Werburgh on the last. The new churches provided by Archbishop King also entered into the scheme. People, for example, in the new part of the city to the east, already provided at St Andrew's on the second Sunday and at St Peter's on the third, could now communicate at St Ann's on the first Sunday and at St Mark's on the last. Likewise people on the west side of the city found provision on the third Sunday, nearer than St Peter's, at the new parish church of St James; while people on the south side could attend the weekly Eucharist in St Patrick's Cathedral.

It is easier to believe that the Table of 1776 represents the careful extension in Archbishop King's time (1703–29) of an existing Caroline custom than that the monthly days became fixed for the first time in 1776. All we can say with certainty is that the Table of 1776 has continuity in principle, if not in detail, with the practice Bonnell found in Dublin at the end of the reign of Charles II. The practice may have taken shape for the first time soon after the Restoration, or it may have continuity with an earlier Caroline use before the Commonwealth.

The evidence for the same use in the city of Cork is more disjointed, and it is only at the end of the eighteenth century that we begin to get fuller information. Edward Wetenhall, Bishop of Cork and Ross (1679–99), implies this Caroline provision in his *Declaratio recognitio et Protestatio...circu acta et gesta Arthuri Pomeroy, Decani Cork*. In spite of his dispute with Dean Pomeroy of Cork he declared himself to be in charity with all men, his accuser not excepted, and that on the next Lord's Day he would communicate "in the next parish Church where the Lord's Supper, according to our use, is celebrated".[1] The Bishop's intention is easy to understand if this Caroline use was firmly established in Cork, as it was in Dublin, by the end of the reign of Charles II. In 1750 Dr Charles Smith, the antiquary, testifies to an arrangement, no doubt of long standing, whereby there are "Early Prayers and Sacrament" at St Mary's, Shandon "the second Sunday of every month",[2] at St Peter's "the third Sunday of the month",[3] and at Christ Church[4] and St Nicholas "the fourth Sunday of every month".[5] With one exception Cork Almanacks from 1798 (Nixon's) to 1827 (Finny's) give information about services in city churches under the two headings of "Early Services" and

---

[1] Quoted from W. M. Brady, *Records of Cork, Ross, and Cloyne*, I, 285 seq.
[2] *The Ancient and Present State of the County and City of Cork* (1750 ed.), I, 382.
[3] Ibid., 385.   [4] Ibid.   [5] Ibid., 387.

"Administration of the Sacrament" without stating that the Sacrament is also administered at "Early Services". *The Cork Almanack for the Year of Our Lord MDCCXXV*, however, in giving fuller information makes it quite clear that the Sacrament is administered at every Early Service, excepting at St Mary's on the first Sunday when the Thresher Lecture (founded 1737) is still given; and Bishop Jebb had told the House of Lords the year before that some of the city churches had fortnightly Communion.[1] If we tabulate our accumulated evidence, with that of Dr Charles Smith in italics, we get the following curious result:

Sunday of the Month	EARLY SERVICE and SACRAMENT		LATE SERVICE and SACRAMENT
FIRST	St Nicholas		St Finbarry's Cathedral St Ann's, Shandon St Paul's
SECOND	St Peter's (*St Mary's, Shandon, 1750*)		St Mary's, Shandon St Nicholas
THIRD	Christ Church (*St Peter's, 1750*)		St Peter's
FOURTH	St Mary's, Shandon (*Christ Church, 1750*) (*St Nicholas, 1750*)	LAST	Christ Church
FIFTH	St Paul's		

It will be noticed that in the case of St Mary's, Shandon, St Peter's, and Christ Church, Dr Smith gives for the early Sacrament *c*. 1750 the monthly days for the late Sacrament which remained fixed from 1798 to at least 1827. It is just possible that Dr Smith, a layman living in Lismore, while giving valuable evidence for the provision of early prayers and Sacrament in the middle of the century, has assigned to them by mistake the monthly days for the late Sacrament. If this was the case the Tables from 1798 have far greater interest and continuity. In any case, the "changing the Monthly Days in several Churches" goes back in principle to Caroline times, and enabled Bishop Wetenhall to declare his intention

[1] *Practical Theology*, II, 384.

"next Lord's Day, in the next parish Church where the Lord's Supper, according to our use, is celebrated" to receive "the Holy Communion".

King rather implies that this Caroline use was general "in cities and large towns"; and in 1694 Waterford, Galway, and Limerick were regarded as being more important than Cork. Galway had only the collegiate Church of St Nicholas, and if ever the Caroline custom was established at Limerick it had fallen into disuse by 1769.[1] Only in Waterford do we find what may have been a mutilation of an earlier provision. In 1833 the Sacrament was administered, besides festivals, on the first and third Sundays of the month at the Cathedral, once a month in St Olave's, and "every three weeks" in St Patrick's. Good as this provision was at that time, it does not cover every Sunday "by changing the Monthly Days in several Churches". It is doubtful whether King was thinking of cities and large towns outside Ireland. There is no trace of the custom in Lincolnshire between 1705 and 1723, or in the diocese of York in 1743. The nearest approach to this Irish Caroline use is one which Archbishop Yngve Brillioth, Primate of All Sweden, said prevailed in the city of Basel c. 1930, when there was "a celebration in one or other of the Churches every Sunday".[2]

Of the provision for weekly Communion in one cathedral or parish church we find little evidence before the nineteenth century. At Waterford Cathedral the Eucharist seems to have been celebrated with great frequency by the Restoration Bishop, George Baker (1661–5), who generally preached there once every Sunday besides festivals, and we gather from his funeral sermon, celebrated the Eucharist as often as he preached, though only "half a score or less" remained for the celebration.[3] In 1811, however, the Eucharist was celebrated here but twice a month besides festivals, the average number of communicants being twenty-two. On 7 April 1719 the Dean and Chapter of Cork decreed, "That a Weekly Sacrament be constantly administered for the future, of which the Chapter and Vicars Choral are to take notice."[4] This weekly Sacrament, however, did not survive the century. Shortly after becoming Dean of St Patrick's in 1714 Swift established a weekly Eucharist in that Cathedral[5] which has continued ever since. In 1754 Dr Delaney observed

---

[1] *Limerick Directory for 1769.*
[2] *Eucharistic Faith and Practice Evangelical and Catholic*, 183.
[3] Daniel Burston, *Christ's Last Call to His Glorified Saints*, 35 seq.
[4] R. Cauldfield, *Annals* (Cork), 58. Jemmet Browne, Bishop of Cork (1745–52), generally attended the Cathedral on Sunday mornings "and read the Second Service".
[5] W. M. Mason, *History of St Patrick's*, 420.

that St Patrick's was "the only Church in the city wherein the primitive practice of receiving the Sacrament every Lord's Day was renewed, and is still continued".[1] Henry Echlin, Rector of St Catherine's, Dublin (1716–52), had, however, nearly established the practice during the last eight years of his incumbency. In addition to the monthly Sacrament on the first Sunday of the month he had early prayers and Sacrament on "the Second, Fourth, and the Last Sunday of every Month at 6 in the morning".[2] There may have been other short-lived experiments before 1736.[3] In 1710 Bishop Wetenhall, who was then living in Dublin, published *A View of our Lord's Passion: with Meditations*. In the Advertisement he writes of "the larger congregations for the Weekly or Monthly Sacraments within this city". In the nineteenth century we find a weekly Eucharist at St Luke's, Dublin, from 1837, at St Stephen's Chapel from 1841, at Glasnevin from 1842, at five Dublin churches in 1865, at thirteen in 1869, and eighteen in 1879.[4]

IV. THE DAILY MORNING AND EVENING PRAYER IN IRELAND

"Since my coming to the Protestant Church", declared Andrew Sall within two years of his reception into the Church of Ireland in 1674,

my constant habitation has been in Trinity College of Dublin, where I see more practice of sobriety, devotion, and piety, than ever I saw in a College of so many young men on the Romish side. Three times a day they all go to prayers to the Chapel, at six in the morning, ten at noon, and four in the evening, with admirable reverence and attention: their Prayers most grave and pious for all purposes, and for all sorts of persons, they say kneeling; the Psalms standing; and the sacred Lectures they hear sitting reverently and bare headed, with a respect due to the Lessons used by them, sacred indeed, as taken out of those blessed fountains of living waters of the Old and New Testaments, not out of the broken cisterns of Romantic legends; all being read in a voice audible, and language intelligible, and thereby suitable to the edification and instruction of all the people present.[5]

---

[1] W. M. Mason, *History of St Patrick's*, 420.   [2] Watson's *Almanack*, 1744–52.

[3] From *c.* 1718 to *c.* 1730 the Vestry Book of St Andrew's enters the cost of the elements "for the frequent Communions", which may have been more frequent than in the next decade when they were fortnightly.

[4] Ibid. (1837); Post Office Directory (1841–2); Archbishop Trench's Charges of 1865 and 1879. A number of larger churches in the diocese of Dublin have retained the eighteenth-century duplication of Divine Service, though at 10 and 11.30, with a monthly Sacrament at each, in addition to a weekly Sacrament at 8.

[5] *True Catholic and Apostolic Faith maintained in the Church of England* (new ed. of 1846), 255.

The same order and style [Sall continues], I see observed in the Palaces of Princes and Prelates, and in the houses of gentlemen and godly persons, all the family being called to pray together in the Chapel or other decent room of the house, after the manner now described. When I come to the Royal Castle or Palace of Dublin, there I see the Lord Lieutenant of Ireland (to whom a judicious French writer gives the chief place among all Viceroys of Europe) with all his flourishing family, and many Nobles attending on his Excellency, break off discourses and business, though weighty and serious, and answer the sound of a Bell calling all at set hours to Prayers in the Chapel, which they assist with singular piety and gravity.[1]

Two years before Sall had declared that Protestants generally "have the word of God clearly and intelligently beaten into their ears daily in their Liturgy".[2]

This remarkable testimony of an ex-Jesuit to the use of the daily offices in Ireland after the Restoration may well serve as the basis of our inquiry noticing the part they played in the life of Trinity College, Dublin, and other seminaries of learning, in the lives of Bishops and private families, and finally in the worship of Cathedrals and parish churches.

The Caroline Statutes of Trinity College, Dublin, of 1637 ordered public prayers to be "offered up to God thrice every ordinary Day", short prayers at 6 a.m.,[3] Morning Prayer at 10 a.m. and Evening Prayer at 4 p.m. Anthony Martin, Bishop of Meath, "continued to read the Liturgy in the college chapel in accordance with the Statutes" for three years after the Prayer Book had been forbidden by the Parliamentary Commissioners in 1647.[4] At the Restoration Jeremy Taylor, now Vice-Chancellor, visited the college and made known the Duke of Ormonde's desires "of their regular comportment to the laws of the Church, and the particular statutes of the house".[5] So the three daily services became firmly established again and continued to be held at 6, 10, and 4 well into the nineteenth century. Primate Margetson, who succeeded Jeremy

---

[1] Ibid. [2] *A Sermon Preached at Christ Church in Dublin...1674* (1840 ed.), 61.
[3] The 6 o'clock prayers consisted of Sentence, Exhortation, Confession, Absolution, Lord's Prayer, Apostle's Creed, Versicles and Responses, Collects for Peace and Grace, Prayer for Blessing on Studies, Prayers for the King's Safety, for the Queen and Royal Issue, Prayer of St Chrysostom and Shorter Blessing. That for blessing on Studies was:
"O Lord Jesu Christ, who art the Wisdom of the Father, we beseech Thee to assist us with thy heavenly Grace, that we may be blessed in our Studies this Day, and above all things, may attain the knowledge of thee, whom to know is Life Eternal: and that, according to the Example of thy most holy Childhood, we may grow in Wisdom and Years and in Favour with God and Man. Amen."
R. Bolton, *Translation of the Charter and Statutes of Trinity College Dublin*, 43 seqq.
[4] Mant, I, 586 seq.   [5] *Works*, I, xciv.

Taylor as Vice-Chancellor in 1667, strongly recommended to Divinity students in 1672 *Two Letters of Advice* by Henry Dodwell.[1] In the first letter Dodwell maintains that it was the intention of the Church to supplement the recitation of the daily offices by the study of Scripture "to make amends for the length of the Roman Offices (imposed by them on their Clergy under pain of mortal sin) above that of our Liturgy".[2] In the second letter Theological students are advised daily to follow "the Lessons at Public Prayers in your Greek and Hebrew Bible".[3] The atmosphere of the college chapel, described by Andrew Sall in 1676, had a profound influence upon the future Irish clergy and contributed largely to the continuance of Caroline Churchmanship and piety in Ireland into the nineteenth century. If as a medical student Thomas Wilson had been fined between fifty and sixty times for non-attendance at the three statutory daily services in the chapel,[4] as Bishop of Sodor and Man he was most regular at daily prayers in his chapel, and required his clergy to offer the Prayers of the Church daily on behalf of their own flocks. George Berkeley no doubt remembered the chapel bell at Trinity when he finished the first of the *Three Dialogues between Hylos and Philonous*:

> *Phil.* Hark; is not this the college bell?
> *Hyl.* It rings for prayers.
> *Phil.* We will go in then if you please, and meet here again to-morrow morning.

The daily Morning and Evening Prayer also played an important part in the life of Irish schools, such as the Hospital of Charles II, Dublin,[5] of Kilkenny College,[6] of the Green-Coat Hospital, Cork,[7] of the Female Orphan-House, Dublin, now more happily named Kirwan House,[8] and of St Columba's College, founded at Stackallen, Co. Meath, in 1844, "on the model of Eton", where from the beginning the greatest care was taken with the singing of the daily Psalms and Canticles and with the chanting of the Litany on Wednesdays and Fridays.[9]

Andrew Sall testified to the regularity with which Bishops attended

---

[1] Imprimatur in the first edition of 1672.

[2] Op. cit., 36 seq. (1672); 28 seq. (1691).

[3] Ibid., 298 (1672); 238 (1691).   [4] *Works* (ed. J. Keble), I, 14.

[5] At 10 a.m. and 4 p.m. F. R. Falkiner, *The Foundation of the Hospital of Charles II Dublin*, 44.

[6] Statutes of 1684, given in Edward Ledwich, *History and Antiquities of Irishtown and Kilkenny*, 509 seq.

[7] Trustees' decision of 1716. *Pietas Corcagiensis*, 32.

[8] In 1818 John Jebb said that the daily offices had been said in the house since 1780. *Practical Theology*, II, 88.

[9] Precentor's Weekly Table (184): copy in C.U.L. (Hib. O. 844. 1). This college was later moved to Rathfarnham, near Dublin.

daily prayers. James Ussher, Archbishop of Armagh (1625–56), "had prayers four times a day, at 6 a.m. and 8 p.m., and Chapel Service before dinner and supper".[1] Bishop Berkeley said of him, as of Henry Dodwell, that his piety was equal to his learning.[2] Izaak Walton said that William Bedell, as Provost of Trinity (1627–9) and as Bishop of Kilmore (1629–42), "observed besides his private devotions the Canonical Hours of Prayer very strictly".[3] His chaplain, Alexander Clogie, testified that in addition to the public prayers which he said in church, Bedell read the Psalms of each day in the Hebrew Psalter and had prayers in his family thrice every day.[4] George Baker, Bishop of Waterford and Lismore (1661–5), who had been domestic chaplain to Primate Ussher, had prayers four times a day, "twice by the Church's prayers" and "twice by his private meditations in his closet".[5] When George Wilde, Bishop of Derry (1661–6), laid the foundation stone of his private chapel at Faughan in 1665, he prayed that when built and consecrated he might "go often into it as Aaron into the Tabernacle", and that "all our prayers may be heard for this Parish, this Diocese, this Church, this Kingdom, for the King's Majesty and all his Realm, for all Christian people. . ." [6] At the funeral of Jeremy Taylor in 1667 George Rust spoke of his "extraordinary piety", believing "he spent the greatest part of his time in heaven" and "his solemn hours of prayer took up a considerable portion of his life".[7] All these Bishops had died before Andrew Sall joined the Church of Ireland and observed the same piety among Irish Bishops in the 1670s. He regarded Primate Margetson as "a most renowned and perfect Prelate",[8] of whom Bishop Henry Jones said that his house was "an Oratory for constant and frequent Devotions, public in the use of the Church Offices, and in private Prayers also".[9] We find the same standard of piety in Archbishop Francis Marsh,[10] Jeremy Taylor's son-in-law, in Bishop Wetenhall, who in 1695 was daily either in his closet, chapel, or cathedral, "or in all three successively, praying for the success of his Majesty's arms",[11] in William King, who during his imprisonment in Dublin Castle read the daily offices with his fellow prisoners,[12] in Peter Browne, whose manuscript book of private prayers is still preserved in Cork Cathedral, and a

[1] J. A. Carr, *Life and Times of James Ussher*, 242 seq.
[2] *Works* (ed. A. C. Fraser), IV, 529.　　　[3] *Lives* (London, 1847), 153.
[4] E. S. Shuckborough, op. cit., 155.
[5] Daniel Burston, *Funeral Sermon* (1665), 31.
[6] Legg, *Eng. Ch. Orders*, 295.　　　[7] Jeremy Taylor, *Works*, I, cccxxvi seq.
[8] Op. cit., 162.　　　[9] *Funeral Sermon* (1679), 43.
[10] *Funeral Sermon* (1694), 19.　　　[11] *Hexapla Jacoboca*, Preface.
[12] *Diary of William King Kept during his Imprisonment in Dublin Castle* (ed. H. J. Lawlor), 65 & n.

century later, in Bishop Jebb, Bishop Mant, Archbishop Broderick, and Primate Lord John George Beresford. Charles Broderick, Archbishop of Cashel (1801–22), besides his daily devotions, read the New Testament daily "in the original, as a scholar, as a divine, and, above all, as a devout and humble Christian", commonly adding "some portion of the Greek and Latin Fathers".[1] After his munificent restoration of Armagh Cathedral (1831–7), Primate Beresford constantly attended its daily worship with his family.[2]

Andrew Sall found the daily offices used in private families either "in the Chapel or other decent room in the house". In the early seventeenth century most noblemen in Ireland had private chaplains who read the daily prayers.[3] The Irish Canon 21 of 1634, by requiring private chaplains to officiate in their chapels, "very seldom upon Sundays and Holy Days", implies that their main duty is to read the Morning and Evening Prayer on other week-days, leaving the families whom they serve free to attend their parish church on Sundays and Holy Days. During the Commonwealth Anglican worship had been kept up as far as possible in private families, as in the family of Dr Alexander Colville at Galgorm Castle, of Major Rawdon at Lisburn, and of Colonel Hill at Hillsborough Castle. Among the Duke of Ormonde's books at Kilkenny Castle in 1685 were thirty-one richly bound copies of the Book of Common Prayer, suggesting their use in household worship.[4] In 1691 Bishop Wetenhall advised the laity of the diocese of Cork, who had not leisure to attend the daily public prayers in church, to set up the worship of God in their homes, using parts of the Prayer Book.[5] Three years later Bishop King advised the laity of the diocese of Derry to do the same, "not least to use such set hymns and collects as seem most adapted to that purpose".[6] In the next century we find the daily offices kept up in families. The Delaneys had constant prayers in their various homes, before breakfast[7] and again in the evening,[8] the hour of prayer being announced by "the prayer-bell".[9] Mrs Delaney also testifies in 1758 to the "constant prayers" at Moira, the seat in Co. Antrim of Baron John Rawdon.[10] In 1778 Lady Carlow visited Carton House, the seat of the Duke of Leinster in Kildare, and noticed that the Duke's chaplain, who lived in the house, read prayers every morning.[11] Garret Wellesley, first Earl of Morning-

---

[1] J. Jebb, *Practical Theology*, II, 202.   [2] R. Mant, *Religio Quotidianum*, 7.
[3] E. S. Shuckburgh, op. cit., 156.   [4] *H.M.C., Ormonde*, N.S., VII, 526 seq.
[5] *Pastoral Admonitions....*, viii.   [6] *Inventions of Man in the Worship of God.*
[7] *Autobiography and Correspondence...of Mrs Delaney* (First Series), III, 597.
[8] Ibid., II, 363; III, 231, 234.   [9] Ibid., III, 50, 597.
[10] Ibid., III, 526.   [11] Constantia Maxwell, *Dublin under the Georges*, 91.

ton (1735–81) "had a full Choir in his Chapel at Dangan Castle, in Meath".[1] Daily prayers were also the rule in many institutions, as in Kingston College, near Boyle, founded in 1698,[2] and in Wilson's Hospital, Multifarnham, founded in 1724.[3]

The daily prayers were long kept up in the chapel of Dublin Castle, though on Sundays and Holy Days the Lord Deputy went in state to Christ Church Cathedral, and on Wednesdays in Lent to St Patrick's. Some eighteenth-century Lord Deputies lacked the piety of Sir Henry Sidney, of Thomas Wentworth, Earl of Strafford, of James, Duke of Ormonde, or of Henry Hyde, second Earl of Clarendon, in the seventeenth century. In 1710, for example, Swift complained of the irreverent behaviour of Thomas, Earl of Wharton, who "goes constantly to prayers in the forms of the place, and will talk bawdy and blasphemy at the Chapel door".[4] James, Duke of Ormonde, on the other hand, found in the daily offices a source of strength in his difficult post in which he was so often misrepresented and from which he was more than once unjustly recalled. This is part of a prayer in his own hand which he used during his tenure of office.

...Particularly, O Lord, be gracious unto me in the administration of the office I am in, guide my intentions, that they may aim at thy glory, and at the honest, uncorrupt, dispassionate, and diligent discharge of my duty. Endue me with courage, sincerity, and a love of justice; with humility, compassion, mercy, and charity towards the poor, the fatherless, the widow, and desolate and the oppressed. If it be thy holy will, bless and prosper my endeavours and undertakings. And whensoever I shall be removed from the place I am in, let me carry with me the testimony of a good conscience, and leave behind me that of a good name. Pardon, O Lord, all my most malicious and causeless enemies, and all that ignorantly and unchristianly culminate me, my intentions, and my actions; and let me look upon them as instruments of thy justice, layed for the punishment of my sins, which have justly deserved much severer inflictions. Relieve all that are in affliction or distress of any kind. Fit us all, from the highest to the lowest, for thy mercies temporal and eternal, and that for the sake of thy dear Son and our only Saviour, Jesus Christ the righteous.[5]

On the last day of his life the Duke of Ormond went to prayers with his family at the set hours of 10 and 3, and "at prayers he answered distinctly, and near as loud as he was wont".[6]

The provision of Daily Choral Service in Irish cathedrals must be

---

[1] J. Jebb, *Choral Service*, 152.   [2] Erk's *Register*, 253.
[3] J. Healey, *Diocese of Meath*, II, 95 seq.
[4] *Works* (ed. J. Hawkesworth, 1767), III, 374.
[5] T. Carte, *The Life of James Duke of Ormonde*, V, 188 seq.   [6] Ibid., IV, 16.

regarded as exceptional; for although there were thirty-two cathedrals only a third of them had any choral foundation at all. Many of them had lost their statutes and their endowments, and in most cases the Precentor, Treasurer, Chancellor, and Archdeacon resided not near the Cathedral, but in the parishes of which they were Incumbents. In the province of Armagh only Armagh Cathedral had vicars-choral until the provision of lay vicars at Downpatrick in 1790; in the province of Tuam one vicar-choral at the metropolitical church and two vicars at the collegiate church of Galway were the sole survivors in 1830 of former colleges; in the province of Dublin there were only three choral foundations, and of these Kilkenny had suffered greatly during the Commonwealth; in the province of Cashel there were in 1830 more choral foundations than there were in the other three provinces put together, though the College of Youghal had been despoiled before Caroline times and Ross and Ardfert had but one vicar-choral each, sole survivors of former colleges. Most Irish cathedrals were also parish churches, and in many cases they were for practical purposes served by a rector, who was not always dean, and a reader, preacher, or curate.[1] Derry, for example, had neither precentor nor vicars-choral, and in the seventeenth century was served by the dean and a curate; and yet we find the Cathedral "Cathedrally served" at the Restoration, daily prayers kept up during the siege, two daily services in 1693 and 1733, and again in the later nineteenth century when they were well attended.[2]

In cathedrals with choral foundations, moreover, we do not always find continuity in the provision of daily worship. After the restoration of Armagh Cathedral by Primate Margetson (d. 1679) "the Service of God in its several ministrations" was restored and "constantly attended",[3] and still performed twice a day in 1693 and 1700, but only on Wednesdays and Fridays c. 1830. After its restoration by Primate Lord Beresford (1831–7), the Choral Service was daily performed "with a scientific skill and religious decorum in every respect exemplary"[4] and "with a precision and reverence which leaves the Cathedral of Armagh second to none in England".[5]

At Limerick, where "daily Prayers have never been disused",[6] we find

[1] John Jebb, *Choral Service*, 54 seqq.; 103 seqq. Erck's *Register, passim.*
[2] Derry now has one of the most proficient Choirs in the British Isles. Likewise Waterford, without choral foundation, kept up daily prayers both in the Cathedral and nearby Church of St Olave which it served.
[3] *Funeral Sermon* (1679), 39.
[4] John Jebb, op. cit., 105.   [5] *Eccles.* (N.S., LXX), Feb. 1855, 14.
[6] Ibid. (N.S., CXI), Dec. 1861, 34.

in 1615 a college of seven vicars, residing next to the Cathedral, and assisting at the daily Morning and Evening Prayer;[1] in 1749 John Wesley going to prayers on a Saturday morning; in 1769 three daily services at 6, 11, and 3.30, though without early prayers on Sundays and Holy Days;[2] at the opening of the nineteenth century two daily services at 8 and 11 attended by many; and in the middle of the century daily Choral Service in the morning and afternoon.

At Cork the Dean in 1634 placed a copy of a monition over the stall of every vicar-choral in the choir, requiring him to perform his office "according to the praiseworthy custom of all Cathedral Churches, especially in imitation of the Metropolitical Church of Cashel." [3] "Every day within the canonical hours of Morning and Evening Prayer, the Vicars were solemnly, devoutly, and in their decent habits of gowns and surplices, to read or sing Service in the Choir", each taking weekly turns, "the others attending at the canonical hours." [4] From 1679 to 1699 Bishop Wetenhall took active steps to improve the daily Choral Service here. Not only were the vicars-choral, organist, and choir to attend daily and perform the Service "in the best melody they can according to Cathedral Use",[5] but the dignitaries and prebendaries were admonished to attend daily Morning and Evening Prayer "during their four months' residence".[6] In 1740 Bishop Peter Browne admonished a vicar-choral of Cork "for neglecting to attend the Service some days this week".[7]

At Lismore there was daily Choral Service in 1615; Richard Lingard, the Restoration Dean, was a great promoter of Choral Service; and Charles Agar, Bishop of Cloyne (1768–79) and Archbishop of Cashel (1779–1801), did much to improve the Choral Service both at Cloyne and at Cashel, which in 1634 had set the standard for the province. Daily Choral Service at Cloyne continued for some time after his translation to Cashel,[8] where although daily services survived his time they were only choral on Sundays, Fridays, and Holy Days.[9]

At Kilkenny before 1641 the vicars-choral lived collegiately in a common hall, keeping good hospitality, but the chief part of their revenue

---

[1] J. C. Erck, *Ecclesiastical Register*, 162. There was also "a college of six Vicars-choral in the town of Killotie in this diocese... who were bound to attend service in the pa ochia church". Ibid. [2] *Limerick Directory for the year 1769*.
[3] C. A. Webster, *Diocese of Cork*, 105. [4] Ibid.
[5] R. Cauldfield, *Annals of St Fin Barre's Cork*, 46.
[6] Ibid., 42 seq. [7] W. M. Brady, *Records of Cork*, I, 268.
[8] R. Cauldfield, *Annals of St Coleman*, Cloyne, 36. In 1783 Bishop Woodward gave the organist leave to employ a deputy "on all days, Sundays and Holy Days excepted".
[9] John Jebb, "Cathedrals of Ireland V", *Eccles.*, July 1867.

was swallowed up by the soldiers and adventurers, leaving a very scanty maintenance for the three surviving vicars-choral.[1] In 1622 eight singing ministers and four choristers daily serve the Cathedral Church;[2] in 1679 the vicars-choral, stipendiaries, and choristers are required to attend the daily services; and in 1731 there are two daily services in summer, and one in winter.[3]

In the two cathedrals of Dublin daily worship was firmly established long before the Commonwealth.[4] When required in 1647 to discontinue the Prayer Book and use the Directory, the Deans of Christ Church and St Patrick's, together with the Bishop of Killaloe and fifteen of the Dublin clergy, expressed their great grief, "on their own account and for their people, for the want of the daily accustomed Service of God in the two Cathedrals and Parish Churches of this city", and for "their people being lately deprived of them and their ministry."[5] James Margetson, who as Dean of Christ Church, signed this Declaration, would, as Archbishop of Dublin (1661–3), make it his care to restore the daily worship "in the two Cathedrals and Parish Churches of this city". At Christ Church the three daily services continued into the nineteenth century. Towards the end of the seventeenth century they were performed at 6, 10, and 4:[6] in 1815 Choral Service was at 11 and 4, and early Divine Service in St Mary's Chapel at 6 in summer, and 8 in winter.[7] The vicars-choral of St Patrick's, by special Statutes of 1692 rigidly enforced until 1786, had diligently to "attend divine Offices in the Church, both forenoon and afternoon, at the canonical hours, every day".[8] Those who came not into the church till after the Confession were fined 2d., if not till after the Psalms 4d., if not till after the first Lesson 6d., and if negligently absent from the whole Service 12d.[9] Jonathan Swift, Dean of St Patrick's (1713–45), "went to Prayers every morning at 9 o'clock, and often at three in the afternoon".[10] In addition to the Service of the Choir, there was early Morning Prayer at six for the greater part of the century in the Church of St Nicholas Without in the north transept. The Choral Service which had given way to the reading of prayers twice daily by the beginning of the nineteenth century, was revived after the restoration

[1] J. C. Erck, op. cit., 113.
[2] MS. The Bishop of Ossory's Certificate of the estate of that Diocese 1622. Cf. Visitation of 1615.
[3] Ossory Visitation Books.   [4] Visitation of 1615.
[5] *A Declaration of the Protestant Clergy of the City of Dublin...July 9, 1647*, 1.
[6] Dunton's *Letters*, quoted from R. Wyse Jackson, *Scenes of Irish Clerical Life*, 22.
[7] Watson's *Almanack*, 1815.   [8] W. Monck Mason, op. cit., 91, n.m.   [9] Ibid.
[10] Ibid., 420, n.w. Swift told Lady Carteret that the merit of a vicar-choral "would be brought to test every day". Ibid., n.x.

of the Cathedral in the middle of the century. Archbishop Trench in his Charge of 1865 said that there was "an average attendance of 148 a day, or 74 at each Service". In 1843 the Ante-Communion was still performed in this cathedral on Wednesdays and Fridays of Lent.[1] Choral Service is still performed twice every day in the two cathedrals.

The provision of daily prayers in parish churches had greater continuity in Dublin than elsewhere in Ireland. As we have seen the daily prayers were not only provided in the parish churches, as well as in the two cathedrals of Dublin, before the Commonwealth, but greatly valued, attended, and missed when taken away suddenly in 1647. The citizens of Dublin were again, though for a shorter time, deprived of Anglican worship by a proclamation of 1690, up to which time most of the Dublin churches "were frequented twice every day at Prayers".[2] At the end of the same decade John Dunton observed one thing very commendable in Dublin, "that a man may spend nine hours every day in public prayers at the several Churches".[3]

James Bonnell, the Accomptant-General, who resided in Dublin from 1684 to his death in 1699, attended public prayers "twice every day", excepting when want of health kept him back. "And when the hurry of business hindered him from keeping constantly to one Church, and hour of public prayer, he would use all his art to get prayers at some Church or other, though not exactly at the time which he desired them most."[4] "If you are subject to spiritual pride", Bonnell advised, "go to prayers to Churches where you are not known; and shift Churches, that you may not seem constant. But if you have surmounted this weakness, keep to the same Church where you are known: that your example may edify others, as well as the prayers edify yourself."[5]

On his translation from Derry to Dublin in 1703 Archbishop King would find daily prayers provided in the existing Dublin churches at hours varying according to the needs of the citizens. Already a promoter of daily prayers,[6] King required their provision in the new

[1] J. Jebb, *Choral Service*, 471.
[2] "A True and Perfect Journal of the Affair in Ireland..." Quoted from C. S. King, *A Great Archbishop of Dublin*, 24, n. 2.
[3] R. Wyse Jackson, op. cit., 22. No information seems available for the hours of daily service other than in the two cathedrals: 6, 9, 10, 3, 4. Times of daily Service in London at this period were: Morning, 6, 7, 8, 9, 10, 11; Evening, 2, 3, 4, 5, 6, 7, 8. Legg. *Eng. Ch. Life*, 108 seq.
[4] W. Hamilton, *Life of James Bonnell*, 117.   [5] Ibid., 88 seq.
[6] As Commissary for Archbishop Francis Marsh King had insisted on daily prayers at St John's Dublin, as Bishop of Derry in the towns of that diocese, as Commissary for Primate Boyle in towns of the province of Armagh.

churches which were being built in the growing parts of the city. In the *Discourse* appended to, and for use at, his Office of Consecration of a new Church, agreed to at a Synod of the diocese of Dublin in 1719, King emphasizes the part the daily offices should take in the newly consecrated church:

We ought to use them as often as we can conveniently: this we are taught by the example of the Disciples (Acts 2. 46), who "assembled daily in the Temple". Now, in conformity to this practice, our Church has appointed, that in every Church, "the Morning and Evening Prayer shall be used, and that the Minister shall cause a Bell to be tolled thereunto, a convenient time before he begin, that the people may come to hear God's Word, and to pray with him"; an Order so holy and excellent, that whenever it is observed duly, it begetteth and awakeneth devotion in the people; and the strict observation of it would go near to restore a holy disposition in the hearts of men. It is true, the people are not obliged to come to Church except on Sundays and Holy Days; but they are exhorted to attend it, and ought to have opportunity given them, if so disposed; and those of our Communion who have any true sense of Religion, embrace it as often as they can conveniently; for nothing can excuse them from attending the public Service of God, except the necessary offices of life, which cannot consist with such attendance, or the infirmities of our bodies, that disable us...[1]

The spirit of Bonnell and King lived on. Both had encouraged the formation of Religious Societies in Ireland. In 1746 there was printed in Dublin, together with the *Rules and Orders Observed by the Religious Society of St Catherine's*, which King had founded, *A Friendly Letter to All Young Men who are desirous to live godly lives*, from which we gather that a number of young Dubliners in the middle of the eighteenth century made it their business to frequent "the public Prayers every Day".[2] The *Rules* and *Letter* were reprinted in Dublin in 1790.

In the 1720s the organists of at least four Dublin churches were required to attend the daily Morning and Evening Prayer, and the organist of St Michan's to play a voluntary holding four minutes before the First Lesson and a Psalm after the third Collect.[3] In 1757 the new organist of St Peter's was required to "attend in person Divine Service every day at the usual hours appointed".[4]

From 1752 we have information of weekly lectures given in some Dub-

---

[1] *Offices to be Used For the Consecration of a Church new built* (1719), 45.
[2] Op cit., 14.
[3] "Memorial of St Michan's". In 1730 this organist was "indulged to serve on week-days by a sufficient deputy provided he be careful to attend his duty in person on Sundays and Holy Days". (Vestry Book.)
[4] Vestry Book.

THE HEAVENLY ALTAR

(*facing p.* 192)

This gives a representation of the Communion Service according to the older Anglican use common to England and Ireland, from the frontispiece to the second edition of C. Wheatly, *A Rational Illustration of the Book of Common Prayer* (1714). The communicants are conveniently placed in the chancel, having left their seats either after the sermon or the general prayer. The representation of Christ as High Priest making intercession at the celestial altar suggests that the northward position of the celebrant is perfectly consistent with the view alike of Jeremy Taylor, Henry Dodwell, and the Irish consecration form of 1666 that the earthly eucharist is an imitation of the heavenly Priesthood, Sacrifice, and Intercession of Christ our High Priest. (See pp. 96ff, 159f, 308.)

lin churches either at Morning or Evening Prayer on week-days. Thus Sterne's catechetical lectures were given weekly from Easter to Michaelmas at St Werburgh's and at St Nicholas Without at 8 a.m. A weekly lecture at St John's was given at 5 p.m. to c. 1788, and Ramsay's lecture was given at St Mary's at 5 p.m. By 1813, however, all these lectures were given at 11 o'clock prayers, though Southwell's lecture continued to be given at St Werburgh's every second Wednesday with Evening Prayer[1] at 5 p.m. In the 1830s lectures were given in some Dublin churches on Wednesdays and Fridays of Lent.

In 1821 "Divine Service is celebrated in every Church in Dublin at eleven o'clock every day, except Sunday, when it commences at twelve";[2] but in St Audoen's and St Thomas's it is "performed here every day at the usual hours",[3] suggesting the provision of daily Evening Prayer as well. Daily Service at St George's, moreover, "in consequence of the respectability and number of inhabitants is generally well attended".[4] The provision of daily prayers in eighteen Dublin churches in 1821 compares favourably with the same provision in nine churches only of the city of London, where it had been made in seventy-three in 1714.[5] The falling away from the standard of 1714 was far less serious in Dublin, although the times of daily prayers no longer varied, as they did in the time of Bonnell and of King, according to the needs of the citizens.[6] There was, however, a falling off in Dublin in the next decade, but a remarkable revival in the decades preceding and following the Disestablishment.[7] And day by day *The Irish Times* publishes the hours of what Dublin Caroline Churchmen called "the daily accustomed Service of God in the two Cathedrals and Parish Churches of this City".

Outside the city of Dublin we find many attempts to provide daily prayers at least in large towns. Early in 1633 the Archbishop of Cashel tells Laud that he has urged the Lord President of Munster to take steps towards

[1] These Lectures are advertised in Watson's *Almanack* from c. 1752. The former times may suggest the hours of Morning or Evening Prayer at these churches from the middle of the century. The weekly lecture at St Andrew's at Evening Prayer was given up c. 1785.

[2] G. N. Wright, *The Historical Guide to Ancient and Modern Dublin* (1821), 152.

[3] Ibid., 139, 159.   [4] Ibid., 157.

[5] Legg, *Eng. Ch. Life*, 108 seqq. Compare the Tables for the years 1714 and 1824.

[6] A tract, *A Discourse Concerning Publick Prayer*, published in Dublin in the 1720s, implies that public prayers are provided "twice or thrice a day" (p. 65), suggesting the provision of Morning Prayer at 6 a.m. as well as at a later hour, or alternatively the duplication of Evening Prayer at a later hour.

[7] *Commissioners' Report* (1836-7); Archbishop Trench's Charges of 1865 and 1879. Besides the two cathedrals there were daily prayers in four Dublin churches in 1865, and in ten in 1879.

recovering Church manses and glebes so that there can be resident clergy throughout the province "by whom the daily Service may be performed".[1] In 1661 Jeremy Taylor, in his *Rules and Advices* to the clergy of Down and Connor, reminded them that "every minister is obliged publicly or privately to read the common prayers every day of the week, at morning and evening". He further insisted that "in great towns and populous places conveniently inhabited, it must be read in Churches, that the daily sacrifice of praise and thanksgiving may never cease".[2] In 1692 Archbishop Narcissus Marsh charged the clergy of the province of Cashel not only to have Divine Service twice every Sunday and Holy Day, but "that you read Prayers publicly in your Churches on other weekdays (especially on Wednesdays and Fridays) in all Towns and other Places, where your Churches stand so conveniently that you have a congregation".[3] He gave the same Charge to the clergy of the province of Dublin in 1694. As Primate of All Ireland, Marsh wrote to Archbishop Tenison of the state of the ten dioceses of the province of Armagh. "In all considerable Towns, I have found or enjoined Prayers to be read in the Churches every day of the week (indeed in most of them I found it done...) and in all other places where any conformists live near enough to the Church, I have enjoined Prayers to be read on Wednesday and Friday, where I found it not done before." [4]

In 1703 Bishop Wetenhall blesses God that the daily Service "in cities and great towns is much observed at present: in country villages indeed it cannot generally be practised with convenience to people's labours".[5] In 1745 Dean Delaney writes of "those most edifying and most enobling lectures of heavenly wisdom weekly and daily published in the Church, in the Hymns and Psalms, the Liturgy and Litany, in the Epistles and Gospels of the day".[6] In 1767 Philip Skelton implies that the daily offices are still recited even by the unorthodox clergyman, whose double dealing is shown "by his every day repeating the Creeds in Church, or by his continually offering up his public devotions to two persons, whom he herein expressly calls God, though he believes them to be but creatures, and, as such, wholly unworthy of prayer and adoration".[7] Philip Skelton, as a curate at Monaghan, had thirty or forty at week-day prayers,[8] and John Wesley often preached at week-day prayers in Irish country parishes.

[1] *H.M.C.*, *Cowper*, II, 12th Report, App. 2.
[2] *Works*, I, 113.   [3] Op. cit., 19.
[4] Quoted from E. F. Carpenter, *Thomas Tenison*, 384.
[5] *An Order or Method of Preparation for Weekly Communicants*, 12.
[6] *Reflections upon the Present Neglect of Publick Worship*, 12.
[7] *Works*, III, 391.   [8] Ibid., I, xxxvii.

Our little information suggests that daily prayers were often kept up late into the eighteenth century in places where they were wanting in 1833, by which date we also find the falling away from a higher standard. Divine Service, for example, is only performed in 1833 on four week-days at Wexford, where it had been performed daily in 1688.[1]

In the city of Cork, Christ Church was seized on Saturday, 24 October 1689 during prayers,[2] there were daily prayers in two city churches "at least" in 1691,[3] at St Mary's, Shandon, in 1716,[4] and in some of the city churches in 1824 "every day in each alternate week".[5]

The most remarkable case of continuity, however, is the provision of daily prayers in St Olave's, Waterford, a plate at the west end testifying to the value set on them by Bishop Thomas Milles:

That the inhabitants of the city of Waterford might have a convenient and decent place, to offer up their morning and evening devotions to God, this Church was rebuilt, and consecrated on the 29th day of July, 1734, by Thomas Milles, S.T.P., Bishop of Waterford and Lismore.

Psalm LV. 17. 18

As for me, I will call upon God: and the Lord shall save me. In the evening and morning, and at noon day will I pray, and that instantly: and he shall hear my voice.

This church was provided with free seats for 500 and to the north of the front row with a Bishop's throne, where no doubt Bishop Milles often joined the poorer inhabitants of Waterford in their morning and evening devotions. In 1824 "Divine Service is performed here twice every day, at hours intended to accommodate those whose time it is for the most part occupied in daily labour".[6] "I have been told", wrote John Jebb in 1867 "on the evidence of a friend now many years at rest, a man of the strictest truth and piety, that formerly there was an early daily service in one of the Churches of Waterford (St Olave's, I think) to which working men used to resort with their tools under their arms." [7]

In the first decade of the nineteenth century the elder John Jebb preached a remarkable sermon on the daily Morning and Evening Prayer in Cashel Cathedral implying as well as recommending their use.[8] He illustrated from the third morning Collect, the Venite, and the Te Deum, how the

---

[1] W. King, State of Protestants, 395.
[2] W. King, Diary Kept during his Imprisonment, 71.
[3] Bishop Wetenhall, Pastoral Admonitions, viii.
[4] Pietas Corcagiensis, 32.   [5] Bishop Jebb, Practical Theology, II, 383.
[6] R. H. Ryland, The History, Topography, and Antiquities of... Waterford (1824), 156.
[7] Eccles. (N.S., CXLVII), Dec. 1867, 360.   [8] Practical Theology, I, 55 seqq.

Morning Prayer is a preparation for the activities, problems, difficulties, and temptations of each day.[1] Nor does holy activity "more visibly distinguish the one service, than an air of home-felt happiness, of heavenly benignity, and of contemplative rest, diffuses itself over the other".[2] In the second evening hymn the venerable Symeon instructs us "with what feelings we should pass from the activities of the day, to the quiet of the evening"; for "the state of our mind at the end of each day, is ever liable to be our state for eternity".[3] The spirit of the Liturgy "will accompany us, in leisure or in business; in private, or in public; when we rise up, and when we lie down; far from disqualifying us for active pursuits, it will give us such vigour, such alertness, such calm, but persevering activity, as will enable us to excel even the worldling, in what he deems his own peculiar province; as will secure, the prompt, and effectual performance of whatever is really conducive, to our temporal well-being." [4] "The devotion of our Liturgy" should become "the very element we breathe".[5]

Jebb's sermon not only reveals the attitude of pre-Tractarian Irish Churchmen to the daily offices, but gives an insight into that Caroline piety which found in them the sanctification of each day's occupation; a piety we have seen exemplified in the lives of Irish Divines from Primate Ussher to Primate Beresford, in the lives of James Duke of Ormonde and the Lord-Lieutenants of Caroline times, of noblemen and private families, of James Bonnell and busy officials, of young men in the city of Dublin, and Waterford working-men who went to early prayers "with their tools under their arms".

It is fitting that Hillsborough, with its memories of Jeremy Taylor, should have been the scene of an interesting revival of daily prayer. In 1846 the Rector, Archdeacon Mant, sent a circular letter to his parishioners, giving notice of the provision of daily Morning Prayer, regretting that he had hitherto omitted this part of his public duty, and trusting that a considerable number would attend. Extracts are then given from the Preface, *Concerning the Service of the Church*, from his father's Charge of 1842,[6] and from Bishop Taylor's *Rules and Advices* of

---

[1] *Practical Theology*, 57 seq.; 63 seq.

[2] Ibid., 64 seq.   [3] Ibid.   [4] Ibid., 70.   [5] Ibid.

[6] Bishop Mant continually urged the provision of daily prayers. He appealed not to Tractarian tenets which he lived to criticize in his later Charges, but to the Caroline Churchmanship of the past. Thus Primate Beresford, by attending daily prayers, was following the example of Ussher and Bramhall, the clergy who were promoting them were "like the Patricks and Beveridges of a better age", and the people who attended them "like the Waltons, the Evelyns, and the Nelsons, and the Bonnells of the same age, and the Stevensons and Parks of the generation now passing away." This comparison was made in a sermon preached at the opening of the Magdalen

1661 requiring the provision of daily prayers in populous places "that the daily sacrifice of prayer and thanksgiving may never cease".

V. PRAYER FOR THE DEAD

The fullest Caroline treatment of prayer for the dead is given in Ussher's *Answer to a Jesuit*, the relevant section being reprinted in 1836 as one of the *Tracts for the Times*. From the fathers and ancient liturgies Ussher shows that the Church made prayer and offering for the dead long before "the discovery of this new found creek of purgatory",[1] which he has already demonstrated to be an addition to the Catholic faith.[2] From the answer of Epiphanius to Aerius, who saw no profit to the dead in the ancient practice, Ussher shows that there are "other profits that redound from thence unto the living; partly by the public signification of their faith, hope, and charity toward the deceased; partly by the honour that they did unto the Lord Jesus, in exempting him from the common condition of the rest of mankind." [3] The Romans who reject "that kind of praying and offering for the dead, which was practised by the Church in the days of Aerius, are in that point flat Aerians".[4] Elsewhere Ussher shows that the ancient Irish offered the Eucharist for the dead, as "a sacrifice of thanksgiving for their salvation rather than of propitiation for their sins",[5] and that none of their prayers or oblations had "any necessary relation to the belief in purgatory".[6] Writing nearly forty years later at the request of the Irish Bishops, Jeremy Taylor uses many of Ussher's arguments and citations.[7] Such general prayers as were anciently used, Taylor maintains, the Anglican Church "did never condemn by any express article, but left it in the middle; and by her practice declares her faith of the resurrection of the dead, and her interest in the communion of saints, and that the saints departed are a portion of the catholic Church,

---

Episcopal Chapel, Belfast, where Morning Prayer daily at 8 a.m. had been well attended from the beginning of 1845. The sermon is given in *Religio Quotidiana*, which Mant published in 1846, giving an exhaustive account of the part played by the daily offices in the Church of England, but giving little information of daily worship in Ireland. For other information regarding daily worship in England, see Legg, *Eng. Ch. Life*, Ch. 4.

[1] *Works*, III, 197; 198 seqq.

[2] Ibid., 177 seqq.; cf. Bramhall, *Works*, I, 26, 65 ("Your new Roman Purgatory, whereof the Pope keeps the keys"); II, 241; V, 192. Bishop Berkeley thought that here and there one could see in the fathers "something like a Platonic or Pythagorean Purgatory" but nothing like "a Romish Purgatory whereof the Pope has the Key" (*Works*, ed. Luce, VII, 144).

[3] Ibid., 269.   [4] Ibid.   [5] Ibid., IV, 269.

[6] Ibid., 271.   [7] Particularly in Part II of the *Dissuasive* (*Works*, VI, 543 seqq.).

parts and members of the body of Christ; but expressly condemns the doctrine of purgatory, and consequently all prayers for the dead relating to it." [1] With Andrewes and Cosin, Bishop Bedell applies to the dead as well as the living the petition in the Anglican Communion Service, that "we and all thy whole Church may obtain remission of our sins".[2]

VI. THE ORNAMENTS OF THE MINISTERS

The English Prayer Book of 1549, first introduced into Ireland in 1551, prescribed most of the Ornaments of the ministers which had already been in use there from at least the twelfth century.[3] Surplices were to be worn at Mattins, Evensong, Baptizing, and Burying, with hoods in cathedrals and colleges, and elsewhere for preaching.[4] The celebrant at the Holy Communion was to wear "a white alb plain, with a vestment or cope", and the assistant ministers "albs with tunicles".[5] The Bishop in celebrating the Communion or executing any other public ministration "shall have upon him, besides his rochet, a surplice or alb, and a cope or vestment, and also his pastoral staff in his hand, or else born and holden by his chaplain".[6] All these Ornaments, with the exception of the surplice, rochet, and pastoral staff, were expressly forbidden in the second English Prayer Book of 1552.[7]

The second Edwardian Prayer Book of 1552, however, never received legal sanction in Ireland, and when Bishop Bale, acting on his own authority, commanded the clergy of his diocese of Ossory to use it, "they would not, and alleged the evil example of the Archbishop of Dublin, and want of copies of the Book; and they said their own justices and lawyers had not consented thereto." [8] The clergy of Ossory were making their stand by the first Prayer Book of 1549, and they in turn tried to make Bishop Bale use the Ornaments which that Book prescribed. "What ado had I that day with the Prebendaries", Bale records, "about wearing cope, crozier, and mitre in the procession! I told them I was not Moses's minister, but Christ's... They got two disguised priests (that

---

[1] *Works*, VI, 196; cf. Bramhall, *Works*, I, 59 seq.; II, 633 seq.
[2] See p. 93; cf. Cosin, *Works* (L.A.C.T.), V, 351 seq.
[3] For an account of earlier liturgical dress in Ireland, see F. E. Warren, *The Liturgy and Ritual of the Celtic Church*, 110 seqq.; W. Alison Philips, op. cit., I, 397 seqq.
[4] "Certain Notes" at the end of the 1549 Prayer Book.
[5] Fourth rubric before the Communion Office of 1549.   [6] "Certain Notes".
[7] Second rubric before Morning Prayer (1552).
[8] *Vocacyon of Johan Bale*, quoted from R. W. Dixon, *History of the Church of England*, III, 499 seq.

is what I call priests in their habits), the one to bear the mitre above me, the other the crozier before me, making three pageants instead of one." [1]

The Irish Act of Uniformity of 1560 (2 Eliz. I, c. 2) directed: "Such Ornaments of the Church, and of the Ministers thereof, shall be retained and be in use, as was in the Church of *England*, by the Statute of 2 and 3 Ed. 6. c. 1. until the Queen shall take other Order, by the advice of her Commissioners..." [2] It was further enacted (2 Eliz. I, c. 4) that the consecrating Archbishops and Bishops give to the person consecrated "his Pall and all other Benedictions, Ceremonies and things requisite for the same, without procuring any Bulls or other things, by or from any foreign Power". [3]

Archbishop Parker's *Advertisements* of 1566 were not published outside the province of Canterbury; and the Irish Canons of 1634 do not, like the English twenty-fourth of 1604, quote these *Advertisements*, which had been designed to authorize a minimum standard of decency in face of Puritan opposition. The Irish Canons 7 and 13 of 1634 direct the clergy to use and observe all "Rites, Ornaments, and Ceremonies prescribed in the Book of Common Prayer, and in the Act of Uniformity printed therewith". Unlike the English, the Irish Canons contain the word "Ornaments", and appeal to the authority of the Act (2 Eliz. I, c. 2) which prescribes the Ornaments in use by the Statute 2 & 3 Ed. VI, c. 1, which enforced the use of the first Prayer Book of 1549.

In 1770 Dr Edward Bullingbrooke, Vicar-General to Primate Robinson, gave his opinion on the legal Ornaments of the Irish clergy in *Ecclesiastical Law...of the Church of Ireland*. He gives a list of the Ornaments prescribed in the 1549 Prayer Book and the Elizabethan Act of Uniformity, together with this comment on the words, *until further order*: "Which *further order* (at least in the method prescribed by this act) was never yet made: and therefore, *legally*, the ornaments of ministers in performing divine service, are the same now, as they were in 2 E. 6. And by the Irish Statute 17 and 18 C. 2. c. 6. 'And *here be it noted* that such ornaments of the Church and of the ministers thereof at all times of their ministration, shall be retained and be in use, as were in the Church of England in the second year of the reign of king Edward the sixth'." [4] Bullingbrooke, in support of this view, further cites the Irish Canons 7 and 13 of 1634. In 1822 Bishop Mant, in a Charge to his clergy of Killaloe, pointed to "the considerable probability" of the view that the

[1] Ibid., 500 seq.
[2] Quoted from N. Robins, *Irish Statutes*, 337.   [3] Ibid., 28.
[4] Op. cit., I, 375 seq.; cf. I, 274.

Ornaments Rubric "must be understood as prescribing the use of all ancient ministerial habits, injoined by the first book of King Edward the sixth".[1]

Of the rubrics in the first and second Prayer Books of King Edward VI Archdeacon Stopford observed in 1861: "Our present rubric makes the former our legal rule; but the universal practice of the Church, with the local consent of our ecclesiastical rulers, has adopted the latter for ministration at the Communion." [2] The only question of vestment to trouble the Church of Ireland, Stopford maintained, was that of preaching in a surplice or a gown. Both, he argued, were "equally agreeable or equally contrary to the law"; for "the legal dress" for the preacher, if he be celebrant, is "a white alb, plain, with vestment or cope", or if an assisting minister, "an alb with tunicle".[3] Stopford, however, overlooked the "Certain Notes" at the end of the 1549 Book which direct the preacher, presumably not the celebrant, Gospeller, or Epistoler, to wear surplice with hood.

It is doubtful whether the use of the legal vestments survived the sixteenth century to any extent. When the Lord Deputy, Sir Henry Sidney, visited Munster and Connaught in 1567, he was received by the Bishop of Limerick "in full Pontificals...and all the rest of the priests and clerks in copes", with "a cross borne before them", and later by the Archbishop of Tuam, "in his pontificals, accompanied with divers priests in copes, singing".[4] If monuments are any guide, those of two Archbishops of Cashel in Cashel Cathedral deserve attention. One is the effigy of that unsatisfactory Anglican prelate, Archbishop Miler Magrath (d. 1622), on the south side of the ruined choir, representing him in full pontificals, with chasuble over dalmatic, tunicle, and apparelled alb, with mitre on his head and a primatial cross in the left of his gloved hands. The other is the much defaced tomb of Archbishop Malcolm Hamilton (d. 1629) on the north side. In 1681 Thomas Dinely made a sketch of the matrix of the monumental brass which had been removed from this tomb during the civil wars. It is sufficiently clear to reveal a mitred figure holding a primatial cross.[5] We know more certainly that the Bishops of the province of Armagh had scarlet chimeres in the reign of James I. For the opening of Convocation in 1613 Primate Hampton and his suffragans "were provided of scarlet robes", but finding the Archbishop of Dublin

---

[1] *The Rule of Ministerial Duty Inforced and Illustrated*, 25.
[2] *A Hand-Book of Ecclesiastical Law and Duty for the Use of the Clergy*, 296 seq.
[3] Ibid.   [4] W. M. Brady, *Irish Reformation*, 139, 150.
[5] The sketch is reproduced in his *Observations in a Voyage through the Kingdom of Ireland in the Year 1681*, 93.

(the Lord Chancellor) "unfurnished thereof", Hampton persuaded his suffragans "to leave their scarlets at home, and go to Convocation in our rochets to cover my Lord Chancellor and his omission".[1]

Although the Irish Caroline Canons 7 and 13 clearly prescribed the legal vestments of the 1549 Book, it was difficult enough to enforce the minimum Anglican usage of the 1552 Book. In 1636, for example, Primate Ussher wrote to the other three metropolitans directing them to require the Bishops of their provinces "not one of them to be at public prayers or to preach but in his episcopal form and habit", and "to take order that all the rest of the clergy shall read public prayers and administer the Sacraments duly in their surplices".[2] The following year, however, a postscript to an Order in Council required the Mayor of Waterford to restore to the Cathedral "certain copes and vestments, which he had in his custody".[3] An Anglican prebendary of Waterford, in 1824, believed these copes and vestments to be those which were handed over by Richard Chevenix, Bishop of Waterford and Lismore (1746-79), to Dr Hussy, the Roman Catholic Titular Bishop, and which have since been preserved among the treasures of the Roman Catholic Cathedral there.[4] There is no evidence that these copes and vestments were worn in the Anglican Cathedral between 1637 and their curious transfer to the representatives of another Church over a century later.

At the Restoration Primate Bramhall, who had been largely responsible for drawing up the Caroline Canons of 1634, seems to have taken some steps towards bringing in the legal Ornaments of the ministers. In his directions for the consecration of the twelve Bishops in 1661, "all the bishops consecrators" were to assemble "in their corned caps, rochets and chimers", the deans and other clergy in "their respective formalities", but "the bishops elect in their albs"; and although the Jacobean Prayer Book, still in use, gave no direction for "the rest of the

---

[1] Quoted from J. A. Carr, *Life and Times of James Ussher*, 105 seq.

[2] Letter of Ussher to the Archbishops of Dublin, Cashel, and Tuam, 20 Nov. 1636 (Chetham Library, Manchester, M.A. 677).

[3] R. H. Ryland, *History...of Waterford*, 136, 162 seq. Prebendary Ryland describes the five copes and set of chasuble, dalmatic, and tunicle with stoles and maniples. "Three of the copes are of crimson and two of green velvet, and are almost entirely covered with gold embroidery... A broad band of highly finished work, representing various parts of scripture history, occupies the larger side of the cope: the figures are admirably executed and the countenances are remarkable for a great variety of expression." The vestments are quaintly described as "close dresses" and "the Dalmatics are like the vestments, except that they have sleeves". "Each Dalmatic", writes Patrick Power, "has twenty panels of saints with figures seven inches high". *Waterford and Lismore*, 279.

[4] Ibid., 162 seq.

episcopal habit", Bramhall directed "that while *veni creator* is singing, the bishops to be consecrated shall have their rochets and chimers put on".[1] The "albs" are therefore distinct from the "rochets" and from the "formalities" (surplices and hoods) of the other clergy.

Two years later the Upper House of Convocation, with Bramhall presiding, agreed upon regulations for the everyday apparel of the episcopal order, while making it clear "that nothing on that account should be changed in the habit of the said Archbishops and Bishops in the solemn celebration of Divine Service, but that they may use those vestments hitherto enjoined; and when they in person celebrate the Eucharist or the Confirmation of Children they may freely use Pontificals: for in Divine Religion, as Jerome says, there is one dress for ministering, and another for common use." [2]

References to episcopal Ornaments, however, are very meagre. When Primate Bramhall died in 1663, "his Crozier staff was buried with him".[3] "The crozier and pastoral staff, both gilt" and "the miter" were carried in the funeral procession of Primate Lindsay in 1724,[4] and "the crozier" and "the miter" at the funeral of Bishop Ellis of Meath ten years later.[5] Pectoral crosses appear to have been worn by Thomas Milles, Bishop of Waterford (1708–40)[6] and by Charles Lindsay, Bishop of Kildare (1802–46).[7] At the funeral of Mrs Matthews at Thomastown, near Cashel, in 1781, Charles Agar, Archbishop of Cashel, "dressed in full Pontificals, with a miter on his head, accompanied by a long train of his diocesan clergy, appeared and joined the solemn march".[8]

From the seventeenth century we find many contemporary references to "vestments", but these should be read in the light of modern Irish usage. The Irish clerical Tailor advertises as "vestments" what the English clerical Tailor advertises as "robes", that is, surplice, hood, and scarf. Bishop Jebb, in his Charge of 1824, required every member of his diocese to provide himself with "a decent black gown" and suggested

---

[1] *The Manner of the Consecration of Bishops in Dublin*, given in *Pillars of Priestcraft and Orthodoxy Shaken* (ed. R. Baron), II, 338 seqq.

[2] "Predicte tamen ita voluerunt intelligi dicti Patres ut nihil propterea immutetur quod habitum que vestitum dictorum Archiepiscoperumque Episcoper[um] in solonni divinorum celebratione quin tunc utantur hactenus iis—injunctis vestimentis et quando—Eucharistiam vel Confirmationem pussillorum ipsi celebraverint pontificalibus uti liberum sit. Religio enim divina, ut inquit Hieronimus, alterum habet in ministerio alterum in usu communi." *Journal*, under 5 Feb. 1662–3.

[3] "Brief Occurances touching Ireland begun 25 March 1661 to Oct. 29 1666" (B.M. MS. Vol. 20, Clarendon MS. 4784, 249 seqq.).

[4] Mant, II, 407.   [5] Ibid., 528.   [6] Ibid., 198.

[7] Copies of portrait at Clarisford House and Christ Church, Dublin.

[8] *Gentlemen's Magazine*, under July 1781.

that all beneficed clergymen being "masters of arts, or of any superior degree" might "with their surplices wear scarfs or tippets".[1] The decent black gown may have meant a preaching gown, for which there was some Caroline precedent,[2] or, according to Caroline terminology, a cassock. Bishop Mant, who in a Charge at Killaloe of 1822, had suggested the strong probability that the legally required vestments were those of the 1549 Prayer Book, in a Charge to the clergy of Down and Connor twenty years later recommended preachers to wear surplices in the pulpit in parish churches as well as in cathedrals and colleges. There is no evidence that the legal vestments were revived between the Tractarian Movement in England and the drawing up of the new Irish Canons in the 1870s by which they were expressly forbidden.

This brief survey has shown that while the Irish Caroline Canon Law of 1634 was less at variance with the Statute Law than the English Jacobean Canon Law of 1603, in practice the Church of Ireland has generally from Caroline times adopted the minimum Anglican usage in ministerial vesture. When at her Disestablishment the Church of Ireland became independent of the State and a self-governing portion of the Church Catholic, she was no longer bound by the Statute Law. She was free to give sanction to the Ornaments prescribed by the 1552 Prayer Book which had never received legal sanction in Ireland. The intention, however, of her fourth Victorian Canon was to perpetuate what was at the time of Disestablishment the normal usage of the hitherto "United Church of England and Ireland". Every Archbishop and Bishop was to use in his public ministrations "the Customary Ecclesiastical Apparel of his Order", and every presbyter and deacon to wear surplice, hood and scarf, though to be at liberty to wear a plain black gown when preaching.

[1] *Practical Theology*, I, 376 seq.
[2] Vestry Book of St Catherine's, Dublin (R.C.B.).

4

CAROLINE CHURCHES IN IRELAND

I. CHURCH FABRICS AND ARCHITECTURE

"OUR WARS OF THE ROSES lasted on to the reign of William III",
declared Professor George Salmon at the Dublin Church Congress in
1868: "Those ages which raised the noble Cathedrals of England and the
numberless fine old parish Churches...were with us times of strife and
turbulance." The *Annals of the Four Masters* bear repeated witness to the
wanton destruction of churches in the Middle Ages, particularly during
the century which followed the Anglo-Norman occupation. The Irish
in turn often burnt churches "to prevent the English from quartering in
them", while the invading army of Edward Bruce from 1314 to 1318
burnt and plundered churches wherever it penetrated. The Court of
Rome appears to have taken the destruction of churches in Ireland for
granted. Thus a papal faculty was granted to John de St Paul, Archbishop
of Dublin (1349–63), "in accordance with that granted by Nicholas IV
to his predecessor, Archbishop John,[1] to absolve those clerks and laymen
who in that distant part of the world, where wars are almost continually
being waged, have incurred excommunication by taking part in the
destruction of Churches, towns, and other places, burning, slaying of
ecclesiastics, and public spoliations".[2] Primate Prene (1439–44) complained of the ruined state of churches in his province of Armagh, and the
Bishop of Derry in 1469 that his cathedral was roofless. In 1407 an unbaptized marauder destroyed forty churches. In 1503 the Earl of Kildare
burnt Cashel Cathedral in the mistaken belief that the Archbishop was
inside; and in 1538 the Lord Deputy wantonly destroyed the stately
Cathedral of Down. On the eve of the Reformation the churches in the
territory of O'Neill were in ruins, those in Counties Kilkenny and
Tipperary "in such extreme decay that no divine service is kept there",
while the Cathedrals of Clonmacnoise and Ardagh were almost in
ruins, and the metropolitical church of Tuam had been used as a barracks

---

[1] John de Saundford (1286–96).
[2] *Calendar of Papal...Letters* (ed. W. Bliss), III, 606. The province of Dublin at
that time was almost entirely within the Pale.

for three centuries.[1] Monastic houses, moreover, had long neglected to keep in repair their very numerous "appropriate Churches".[2]

In consequence, the Church of Ireland at the Reformation took over a great number of ruined or decayed churches; and the task of rebuilding them was made more difficult because the lay impropriators responsible for the repair of churches of impropriate parishes sat in the Irish Parliament. "They were not going to vote for inroads on their gains," writes Dr G. V. Jourdan, "either in the days of Elizabeth or, as we shall see, in those of James or Charles." [3] It was left to the Lord Deputy and Council and to individual Bishops to take what steps they could towards supplying the want of churches. In the 1690s Edmund Spencer deplores the scarcity of churches in Ireland "whereof the most part lie even with the ground". And some, he adds, "that have been lately repaired, and so unhandsomely patched and thatched, that men do even shun the places for the uncomeliness thereof".[4] In the reign of James I the reports of Sir Arthur Chichester in 1607 and of the Regal Visitations of 1615 and 1622 tell a similar story. Yet great energy had been shown by some Jacobean Bishops. Thomas Ram, Bishop of Ferns and Leighlin (1605–1635), had by 1615 put the great majority of his churches into good repair.[5] Although in 1622 only 166 of the original churches in the province of Armagh were in repair, and 426 in ruins or decay, yet 48 churches were either "now built", "in building", or "almost finished".[6]

Greater energy was shown in the reign of Charles I. "Commissions for the repair of Churches", Wentworth informed Archbishop Laud at the end of 1633, "are issued all over the Kingdom, and all the life shall be given to it that possibly I can".[7] The Irish Convocation in 1634, moreover, had in mind not only the restoration of ruined churches, but the building of new ones on entirely new sites; for Canon 43 directed the consecration of churches as often as they are "newly built, where formerly they were not", provided "the ancient Churches shall not be put to any

---

[1] Mant, I, 102 seq., 104; W. Alison Philips, op. cit., II, 211, 183, 230; J. T. Ball, *The Reformed Church of Ireland*, 334; T. M. Fallow, *The Cathedrals of Ireland*, 13.

[2] C. A. Webster, *Diocese of Cork*, 212; "The Reformation", *The Church of Ireland, 432–1932 Report*, 122.   [3] W. Alison Philips, op. cit., II, 348.

[4] *View of the State of Ireland, written Dialoguewise between Eudoxus and Ireneus* (1750 ed.), 212.

[5] Regal Visitation Report (MS. T.C.D.). All sixteen churches, for example, of the parishes, seven of them impropriate, into which the present Union of Kilscoran was then divided, were reported by him to be in good repair with the exception of the chancel of one. (Ibid.) The ruins of twelve of these churches, often less than a mile apart, can still be seen. Six of them have a small nave with western bell-turret and a low eastern arch leading to a smaller chancel.

[6] Mant, I, 396 seqq.   [7] Ibid., 473.

base and unworthy use". During the reign twenty churches were rebuilt and many more repaired in the diocese of Derry alone, Derry Cathedral was built on a new site, while the Cathedrals of Kilmore, Cloyne, and Lismore were rebuilt, and the renovation of Downpatrick and Christ Church, Dublin, considered.[1] Indeed, Wentworth's energy in rebuilding churches was one of the charges brought against him at his trial.[2]

Few of the new churches built during the reign of Charles I survived the civil wars. Of these Derry Cathedral (1628–33) is traditional in plan and an interesting example of late perpendicular architecture. With its battlemented tower, clerestory, aisles, porches, and eastern aisle turrets it has superficially the appearance of a fifteenth-century church.[3] Although until 1887 it lacked a chancel, part of the original scheme, Richard Pococke in 1752 thought it "something like many churches in large country towns in England".[4]

Although some churches were destroyed in the Rebellion of 1641, the Roman Catholic Confederates were still agitating for the possession of churches in 1645.[5] It is doubtful, therefore, whether the widespread destruction of churches which they wanted to possess took place until the Cromwellian occupation of Ireland from 1649. At the Restoration, however, the vast majority of Irish churches were lying "in ruinous heaps".[6]

Primate Bramhall, who found all the churches of his diocese "ruined or inclining to ruin",[7] greatly desired to put into execution the Act (14 & 15 Charles II, c. 10) for uniting smaller parishes and dividing greater. His biographer, Archbishop Vesey, had seen "a map of the diocese of Armagh which his grace had drawn up for this end, intending to distribute it parochially and appoint places for the building of Churches, with more advantage to the Minister and People; Plantations being moveable things and not nailed to a place especially after a long and destructive civil war." [8] The act was only operative for twenty years. In Jeremy Taylor's dioceses the existing Cathedral of Dromore was rebuilt, but Hillsborough (1663) and the Middle Church of Ballinderry (1665–8) were built on entirely new sites.

The Irish Restoration Bishops appear to have envisaged the traditional

---

[1] W. Alison Philips, op. cit., III, 29.   [2] Ibid.
[3] The windows of clerestory and aisles, however, are more austere; and the capitals of the pillars in the nave arcades of seven bays are similar to those of the same date in St John's, Leeds. The roofs, leaded without, were originally vaulted within with a plaster ceiling.
[4] *Tour in Ireland in 1752*, 43.   [5] W. Alison Philips, op. cit., III, 102 seq.
[6] For evidence, see below, p. 267 seq.   [7] *Works*, I, cix.
[8] Life, prefixed to *The Works of John Bramhall* (1676), no pagination.

plan for a new church.[1] Jeremy Taylor had spoken of the altar as being the *terminus* of reconciliation in primitive times, the several degrees of approximation to it being the several stations of penitents in "the Church-porch", "by the reading place", "at the Chancel door", and finally "up to the very rails".[2] The "Chancel door" was distinct from, and westward of, the door of the rails. Likewise *A Form of Consecration or Dedication of Churches and Chappels* "according to the Use of the Church of Ireland", published in 1666, the year in which the fire of London opened the door for bold experiments in Anglican church architecture, gives the impression of a church of the traditional type. There is a central passage from "the West Door" to "the Chancel door"; there are passages, if not aisles, to the north and south, so that the Bishop with his clergy can "go in procession round about the Church within", and steps to the east so that later passing through the Chancel door they can "ascend to the Communion Table".[3]

The need for new churches, however, was so great that simple aisleless buildings, either cruciform or on the plan of a plain rectangle, often had to suffice. Hillsborough, as built in 1663, was a plain cruciform church with "a handsome Gothick Portal" at the west entrance.[4] Ballinderry (1668), on the plan of a rectangle seventy-one feet by twenty-nine, has walls three feet thick and windows of oak with mullions and circular heads, and transomes in the east.[5] The nave of Waringstown (1681) retains its original oak roof with finely carved hammer beams.[6] Of the seven Dublin churches which were rebuilt between 1660 and 1689 only St Michan's remains much as it was when rebuilt in 1685-6. It is a spacious cruciform church, which until 1828 had a wide but shallow eastern recess, named on the plan of 1724 "Place of ye Altar". Its fine western doorway and its main features are classical.

Between the Restoration and the Revolution churches were gradually built or rebuilt;[7] and it was strongly represented to James II "that all the

---

[1] The traditional plan of an Irish church was broadly speaking simpler than the English. Often larger medieval churches and some cathedrals were simple cruciform buildings without aisles; and churches with aisles often lacked a clerestory. Most country churches had small rectangular Chancels, though some of them were built on the plan of a plain rectangle.

[2] *Works*, v, 328.   [3] Appendix 1, 32, 70-2, 207-9, 335, 368-9.

[4] *The Ancient and Present State of the County of Down* (1744), 96. This church was rebuilt 1772-4.

[5] The east window has five lights: the others three.

[6] This church has had many additions and undergone many alterations.

[7] Only the eastern part of St Peter's, Drogheda, and the Choir of Kildare Cathedral were rebuilt in 1666 and 1686. The beautiful Chapel of the Royal Hospital of Kilmainham was consecrated in 1687 in honour of St Charles.

Churches of Ireland were in manner ruined" between 1641 and 1660, and "that it was with great difficulty and cost that the Protestants had new built and repaired them".[1] All the churches of the diocese of Armagh, for example, were "in extraordinary good repair being all either rebuilt or repaired since the Restoration",[2] and then many of them suffered again when a large part of the diocese was laid waste by the garrison of Charlemont. But the diocese of Derry suffered most. The majority of churches, in ruins at the Restoration, had been rebuilt by 1689. In 1693, however, Bishop King reported that a large number had been "defaced", "burnt", "demolished", or "ruined" by King James's army, or had "suffered in the late troubles". At the same time he was able to report that most of these churches had been put into "tolerable repair".[3] Little help at that time could be expected from the government, and five years later King complained bitterly to the Bishop of Down that "more care seems to be employed towards settling a Jewish synagogue than a Christian church, because Jews are traders".[4]

As Archbishop of Dublin (1703-29) King "procured fourteen Churches to be repaired, seven to be rebuilt, and nineteen to be erected in places where no divine service had been performed since the reformation".[5] He also drew up *Offices to be Used For the Consecration of a Church new built, and Restauration of a Church rebuilt in the Diocese of Dublin*, which were agreed to at a diocesan Synod in 1719. The rubrics show that the plan of a new church has already become modified and the chancel a shallow recess; for the "Chancel doors" of 1666 become "the Doors of the Rails enclosing the Communion Table". Indeed King maintained "that we ought to multiply the number of our Churches than make them magnificent".[6] St Mary's, Dublin, already built just before King's time, is a well proportioned classical church with a nave curving inwards to a shallow chancel.[7] But of the city churches provided by King, which were not rebuilt or taken down at a later date, only St Luke's, St Ann's, and St Mark's remain. St Werburgh's, rebuilt and handsomely furnished (1715-19),[8] was extensively damaged by fire in 1754 and later rebuilt. Its inventory of church goods in 1767 is sadly shorter than that of 1731, which is a valuable guide to how a new church was furnished in King's time.

---

[1] William King, *State of Protestants in Ireland*, 210.
[2] "State of the Diocese of Armagh 1693" (P.R.O.N.I., T. 505, 19).
[3] "State of the Diocese of Derry 1693" (ibid., *passim*).
[4] Mant, II, 97.   [5] Ibid., 152.   [6] Ibid., 350.
[7] The nave, with semicircular vault, is separated from the flat-ceiled aisles by oak pillars which incorporate the galleries as in the later Church of St Peter, Drogheda.
[8] Under the care of Chancellor Theophilus Bolton.

ST OLAVE'S CHURCH, WATERFORD

(facing p. 208)

St Olave's Church, Waterford was rebuilt and consecrated by Bishop Milles on St Olave's Day, 29 July 1734. The altarpiece, bishop's throne, pulpit, single seats all facing east for men on the north side and women on the south, together with the black and white marble paving, were accurately described by Dr Charles Smith in 1746 and more generally by Richard Pococke in 1752. This testimony and the expert opinion that the throne, altarpiece, and pulpit agree in design and proportion should be set against a local tradition that the throne, if not the pulpit as well, came out of the nearby cathedral. The desks for minister and clerk agree in design, not with the pulpit, but with the other seats. The brass gas-fittings appear to have been adapted from the original branches, each bearing a mitre. Note the upward curve of the handsome rails at the corners and gates of the Septem, with floor inlaid in geometrical figures; and also the tetragrammaton in a Glory above the altar with *mensa* of black marble. (See pp. 195, 209, 215–39 *passim*.)

Of the Cork city churches provided by Bishop Peter Browne only St Ann's, Shandon, and St Paul's, now a Synod Hall, remain. But the two Waterford city churches provided by Bishop Thomas Milles both remain. To-day St Olave's, Waterford is perhaps the most unspoilt church in the whole of Ireland. It is the reconstruction of the old Norse Church, but on the plan of a plain rectangle and in the classical style. Though built (1734) to accommodate the poor in free seats, it has a handsome altarpiece, and richly carved rails, pulpit, throne, and western screen, all in perfect proportion to the building. Few, however, of the churches built in this period have retained their original form. Many, like the large cruciform churches by Richard Cassels (d. 1751) at Sligo and Castlebar, were rebuilt in the next century.[1]

During the century a large number of existing churches were abandoned, and new churches more central and convenient to newly constituted Unions built on entirely new sites. Little use had been made of the Caroline Act for this purpose, but special Acts providing for at least thirty-four churches on new sites were passed in the reign of Queen Anne. One of these (9 Anne, c. 12) also gave the parishioners of any newly constituted Union of parishes permission to "make use of the Materials of every ancient Church" in the Union "towards building such new-intended Churches, and for no other Use whatsoever".[2] A general enactment followed in 1715 (2 Geo. I, c. 14), and altogether we can account for at least 143 new churches built on new sites during the century, leaving in every case two or more existing churches to fall into decay.[3]

In 1760 there appeared *An Office for Consecration of Churches According to the Use of the Province of Dublin*, based largely upon Bishop Simon Patrick's form of 1704. Its rubrics are very meagre and tell us little about the new church. The Bishop, having received the Petition of Consecration at "the West Door," then "proceedeth, attended by his Chancellor,

---

[1] Richard Pococke admired these two churches (*Tour in Ireland in 1752*, 75, 82). Churches (1710-60) which remain include Mourne Abbey Church (1717), Moira (1724) and parts of Inch (1742) and Knockbreda, probably by Cassels (1737), Co. Down, St Peter's, Drogheda (1752), Clonderhorky (Ballymore), which Pococke saw in building when he passed through Donegal (op. cit., 57), Ballycastle, Co. Antrim (1756), and St Werburgh's, Dublin (1759). Clogher Cathedral was built by Bishop Stearne (1717-45) "in a quasi-medieval style of architecture, but remodelled as a classical building by dean Bagwell in 1818". (T. M. Fallow, op. cit., 8.)

[2] N. Robins, *Abridgment of Irish Statutes*, 189 seqq.

[3] Between 1719 and 1800 Mant accounts for a further 109 churches built on new sites; 39 in the province of Armagh, 22 in that of Dublin, 23 in Cashel, 24 in Tuam (op. cit., II, 307).

P

Clergy, and Officers, to the Communion Table", saying, for the first time in any Anglican printed form, " 'Peace be to this House, and to all assembled therein'." Elsewhere the Caroline form of 1666 appears to have been used in some places.[1]

The speed of church building and restoration increased when in the second half of the century the Commissioners of First Fruits were supplied with government grants for the purpose, and became greater after 1807 when government grants or loans were advanced to them as required (48 & 49 Geo. III). In 1829 Henry Newland claimed that by 1830 the Irish Bishops would have accomplished since the Act of Union "nearly as much as had been effected in the space of three centuries".[2] This exaggerated claim is gravely unjust to those Jacobean, Caroline, and later Bishops who strove so courageously to provide new churches and to restore those which had been demolished or defaced in civil war long before government aid became available.

In his primary Charge of 1865 Archbishop Trench, who had been Dean of Westminster, spoke of "the extraordinary unsightliness of many of our Churches, indeed almost all that were built in the last century, or during the first decades of the present".[3] But Irish churches of this period must be seen against the background, not of Westminster Abbey, but of Irish history, remembering that Irish church architecture like the Church of Ireland has a history and development of its own. Although a number of utility churches were built, particularly after 1807, many churches of great merit were built between 1700 and 1837, and a number of interesting changes took place during that period. The simple rectangular churches which were given classical details in the 1730s[4] often became elaborately gothic eighty years later.[5] The wide nave, at least twice the

---

[1] *An Essay on Church Consecration* by "Z" (Dublin, 1777) implies that the 1666 form is still used in some places (p. 56), and it said that this form continued in use in some places into the nineteenth century.

[2] *An Apology for the Established Church in Ireland*, 136. Newland bases his claim on the number of churches in 1800 which he gives as 689, and that 312 churches will have been built between 1801 and 1830. He seems to have reached his figure for 1800 by subtracting the number of new churches not from the total number for 1830, but from the official number of churches in 1792, which D. A. Beaufort gives as 1001 (*Memoir of a Map of Ireland*, 137). Thus 1001 − 312 = 689! In 1830 J. C. Erck claims that 474 churches were erected since 1800. He probably includes the 64 ordered to be built October 1828 and 99 enlarged. Newland excludes the 99, but adds the 64 to his 312 together with 242 rebuilt churches and gets a total of 618 (ibid.).

[3] Op. cit., 25.

[4] St Olave's, Waterford (1734), Downpatrick (1735).

[5] Collon, Co. Lough; Swords, Co. Dublin.

width of the tower, of classical proportions with ceiled roof and elaborate cornice, remains, but it is frequently given gothic windows with cases and mullions of wood painted white.[1] Primate Robinson (d. 1785) employed as architects, first Thomas Cooley (d. 1784), who designed the chaste Palace Chapel of Armagh (1771), together with Grange (1773) and other churches, and later Francis Johnson (d. 1824), who designed Ballymakenny (c. 1785), and who was equally happy in his classical Church of St George, Dublin (1813), and his gothic Chapel of Dublin Castle (1814). Bishop Jebb believed Johnson's simpler gothic Chapel of Kirwan House (1818) to exemplify the Anglican spirit; "that is, on the one hand to avoid all ostentatious ornament and show, but, on the other, to shun all sordid and unseemly negligence". The church building should be "answerable to the service of our Church", which above all other in the world "is, at once, cheerful, simple, and majestic".[2] This is equally true of Hillsborough, rebuilt 1772–4 much on the plan and with some of the material of the earlier church of 1663. It is a magnificent example of late eighteenth-century gothic. Apart from the sanctuary the church retains its original furniture perfectly proportioned to a noble building, its original richly coloured glass, and its Communion silver dedicated by Jeremy Taylor in 1663. Hillsborough conveys a Caroline atmosphere with the impression that the church has been built and furnished for Anglican worship.

II. THE ORNAMENTS OF THE CHURCH

(a) Introductory

There is evidence that in some places pre-Reformation Ornaments remained either in use or in private hands well into the reign of Elizabeth. In 1577, for example, the Lord President of Munster complained to Walsingham that "the proud and undutiful citizens of Waterford have their altars, painted images and candlesticks, in derision of the Gospel, every day in their synagogues".[3] In the same year the Dean and Chapter of Waterford alienated to the Mayor, Sheriffs, and citizens the following: two standing crosses, four candlesticks, two standing cups, five censers, and "a monstrant with two angels of silver gilt", with other Ornaments of silver weighing altogether 487 ounces.[4] In 1612 the widow of the

---

[1] Kilscoran, Co. Wexford (1818), and many other examples.
[2] Practical Theology, ii, 95.
[3] W. M. Brady, State Papers concerning the Irish Church, 22 seqq.
[4] R. H. Ryland, op. cit., 135 seq.

Archdeacon of Cork restored "to the use of the Cathedrall Church of Saynte Barrys" one censer, two chalices and their patens, and one pyx, "all belonging to the said Church." [1] In the same year we read that incense was used at the funeral of Luke Chaloner in Trinity College Chapel, Dublin.[2] Rood-lofts with wooden crosses also remained in some places up to 1634 when the ninety-seventh Irish Canon ordered their removal.

The Irish Canons of 1634 give a clear idea of what minimum Caroline requirements were before the Commonwealth. Like the English Canons of 1603 they direct the churchwardens to provide, at the common charge of the parish, the reading-desk, the pulpit, the font, the Communion table with its carpet and communion cloth,[3] a "stoup" or flagon,[4] the Table of Marriage,[5] and the alms chest;[6] but the Bible was to be "of the last translation" (1611) instead of "the Great Bible", and a Prayer Book was to be provided for the clerk as well as for the minister;[7] and "where all, or the most part of the people are Irish, they shall also provide the said Books in the Irish Tongue".[8] Unlike the English Canons, the Irish direct the "fair Table to be placed at the East end of the Church or Chancel" without permission for its removal at the time of the Communion, or direction for the Decalogue to be set up on the eastern wall.[9] They further direct the provision, omitted in the English code, of "a cup of Silver for the Celebration of the Holy Communion".[10] The Irish Canons further imply the provision of a bell[11] and of seats,[12] together with the Ornaments prescribed in the first Edwardian Prayer Book of 1549.[13] The only Ornaments of 1549 not mentioned in the Irish Code of 1634 are the Book of Homilies, the corporas, the paten, and the choir door; and of these the paten was no doubt thought of as the cover to the "cup of Silver".

The Irish Caroline Canons were taken very seriously until the Act of Union at least, when the English Canons were sometimes regarded as having equal if not greater authority. In his Visitation Articles for the provinces of Cashel in 1692 and of Dublin in 1694, Archbishop Narcissus Marsh asked "Have you a fit Seat (or Pew) for the Minister, with a decent Pulpit conveniently placed: A large English Bible, and two Books of Common Prayer...? Have you a Font of Stone set in the usual place...?

---

[1] C. A. Webster, *Diocese of Cork*, 172–4.
[2] *Hierurgia Anglicana*, II, 176.   [3] Irish Canon 94: 81–3.
[4] Canon 95 (Ir.): 20 (Eng.).   [5] Canon 47 (Ir.): 99 (Eng.).
[6] Canon 96 (Ir.): 84 (Eng.).   [7] Canon 94 (Ir.): 80 (Eng.).
[8] Canon 94 (Ir.).   [9] Canon 94 (Ir.); cp. Canon 82 (Eng.).
[10] Canon 94 (Ir.).   [11] Canon 19 (Ir.).
[12] Canon 91 (Ir.).   [13] Canons 7 and 13 (Ir.).

Have you a Communion-Table, standing at the *East end* of the Church; a Silver cup or Chalice; a fair *Carpet* and a *white linnen cloth* to cover it with for the Celebration of the Holy Communion (Can. 94)?" [1] Anthony Dopping, Bishop of Meath, provides in 1696 an *Index Rerum visitandarum* in a Bishop's Visitation. This includes *Septum Altaris*, seats, alms chest, *campanae*, Books of Homilies and Canons, and a Register of Communicants. [2]

Greater light is thrown upon Irish ecclesiology at the Restoration by the rubrics in *A Form of Consecration of Churches*, published in Dublin in 1666, under the sanction of the Primate and the Archbishop of Dublin, and claiming to be "according to the use of the Church of Ireland". The "Chancel Door" and the "Napkins" answer to the "Choir Door" and the "Corporas" of the 1549 Book. In addition to the chalice and paten, "the other Vessels, Books, and Utensils for the Communion" are presented and dedicated. There is a chair on the south side of the altar and a Litany-stool before the chancel door. [3] All these Ornaments reappear in the Dublin diocesan offices of 1719 with the sole exception of the chancel door. For a further reconstruction of an Irish church in Caroline times or wherever the Caroline tradition continued, we must rely upon contemporary description, [4] parish accounts, inventories, Visitation and other reports, and upon plans and sketches, and be guided by Irish expositions of Caroline ecclesiology. For we can seldom, if ever, step into an Irish church to-day which has retained all its Caroline furniture and Ornaments.

With this help let us go back in time and enter the west door of an Irish Church in the post-Restoration period. We notice the alms chest with three locks, the Table of Marriage, the Royal arms either above the chancel door or in the centre of the western gallery, [5] and at a later period the Benefaction Boards. [6] The wide central passage is paved perhaps with black and white marble; the walls are wainscoted; the windows with cases and mullions of wood or stone are glazed with sheet glass or at a

---

[1] *The Charge...together with Articles of Visitation 1692.* He also asks whether the seats are in good repair.
[2] *Tractatus de Visitationibus Episcopalibus* (Dublinii, 1696), 25 seq.
[3] Appendix 1, *passim.*
[4] Dr Charles Smith's county histories describe churches as they were in the middle of the eighteenth century. For convenience his long titles are abbreviated. Thus *The Ancient and Present State of the County and City of Waterford* is given C. Smith, *Waterford.*
[5] At Ballinderry (Middle Church) they were formerly set over the east window.
[6] Recommended by the Lower House of the Convocation of Canterbury in 1710, they came to Ireland a little later. They were set up in St John's, Dublin, in 1732.

later period with richly coloured glass;[1] the roof of Irish oak is either uncovered, revealing finely carved hammer beams,[2] or plastered and sometimes richly decorated with stucco work,[3] and from it are suspended the branches in the centre and in the transepts.[4] Let us in turn examine the font, the seats, the pulpit and reading-desk, the Litany-stool, the chancel screen, the *Septum Altaris*, and the Communion table with its furniture.

(b) The Font

The Irish Canon 94 of 1634 required "a Font of Stone set in the ancient usual place". It would, however, be difficult to determine what exactly was the ancient usual place in Ireland, for a Provincial Synod of Dublin in 1186, among other Canons directed against former Celtic usage, enacted that every church should have an immovable font so contrived that the Paschal procession could conveniently pass round it. Such is the Romanesque font in St Audoen's, Dublin, placed there a few years later. If before the reforms of the twelfth century movable fonts had been in use,[5] then no "ancient usual place" could be determined, and ancient precedent can be claimed for the movable fonts which became increasingly common from the late seventeenth century. But the intention of the Caroline Canon was to fix the font at the west end of the church.

Of the few remaining Caroline fonts that at Loughilly is "of an octagon-pear shape tapering to a short shaft", seven of the faces having "a sunk panel, on five of which is an inscription in high relief: GE: SINGE. P. ROBER. STURG. TH. WRENCH. CHURCH WA. 1637." [6] In the same year a stone font with a lead cover was erected in St John's, Dublin.[7] A very small font at Enniskillen has "an interlaced border round the rim, and bears upon its

---

[1] Sheet glass in the windows of solid oak at Ballinderry (1665-8), and richly coloured glass at Hillsborough (1774).

[2] Waringstown (1681).

[3] Chapel of King Charles the Martyr, Kilmainham Hospital (1686).

[4] St Catherine's, Dublin, had a "great hanging Candlestick" in 1661; St Werburgh's, Dublin, had in 1731 "two brass Branches with eighteen sockets each; twenty side Branches; and thirty seven brass candlesticks for the seats". St Michan's, Dublin, in 1724 had large branches in the centre of the nave and of each transept. Most cathedrals and town churches had them, and we find frequent parish expenditure "for cleaning the Branches". Limerick Cathedral still retains three fine branches of the mid-eighteenth century.

[5] Although the dedication of the font was given prominence in an old Celtic rite described in the *Leabhar Breac*, the Irish name assigned to it means "ox-tub", which rather suggests a movable font.

[6] J. B. Leslie, *Armagh Clergy and Parishes*, 356 seq.

[7] C. S. Hughes, *Church of St John Dublin*, 22.

upper edge the following inscription in raised capitals: 'the gift of William Vincent, Rector of the Church, A.D. 1666' ".[1] The font in the Middle Church of Ballinderry (1668) is a circular stone bason, standing on a pedestal made out of one piece of solid oak, and it has an oak cover with wrought iron fittings.

Early in the next century care was still often taken to place the font at the west end. When Christ Church, Cork, was rebuilt in 1720 the vestry decided to build the font in the place laid out for it "at ye wester end of ye Church".[2] The font standing in the centre of the western narthex of St Olave's, Waterford (1734), is of black marble supported by a fluted pillar, and it has an attractive cover of white and black marble, which was originally surmounted by a brass cross.[3] Many font covers, however, have disappeared like that in Mourne Abbey Church (1717) which in 1750 was said to be "neatly carved and gilded".[4] Often the font was placed in a large and specially constructed pew, at the west end usually on the south side. This was its position at Moira, Co. Down (1724), elsewhere, and in the plans of new churches drawn for Primate Robinson after 1765 by Thomas Cooley (1740–84). The font, however, was often moved to make room for additional seating. In 1761 the vestry of Dundalk, for example, permitted a seat to be erected "where the Font stands, and the Font to be removed, and fixed in another place".[5] Later in the century there was a tendency to fix the font immediately in front of the reading-desk, whether it stood half-way down the church or towards the east end; or in cruciform churches, like Hillsborough in 1844, "at the central point of intersection of the passages from the door to the Chancel, and through the transepts".[6] This indeed was the only place where Baptism could be administered in the view of the whole congregation, in the transepts as well as in the nave.[7]

[1] *The Old Enniskillen Vestry Book (1666–1797)*, 139.

[2] Notes by W. A. Copinger in annotated ed. of C. Smith, *Cork* (1893).

[3] C. Smith, *Waterford* (1774 ed.), 178.

[4] C. Smith, *Cork* (1750 ed.), I, 182.   [5] J. B. Leslie, op. cit., 286.

[6] "Memoir of Hillsborough Church", Feb. 1844 ("Stray Papers" 16, Down, Connor, and Dromore Diocesan Library). The writer, probably Archdeacon Mant, maintains that what is lost in symbolism is gained by the opportunity given to every member of the congregation "of witnessing the ceremony of admission into the Christian Covenant".

[7] Eighteenth-century fonts were often circular or oval basins on slender columns, executed in marble. That in Inch Church, Co. Down (*c.* 1744), is of red marble, 3 ft. in height, with a basin 1 ft. 9 in. diameter and 4 in. deep. That at Hillsborough (*c.* 1774) was described in 1844 as a circular basin of grey marble; 12 in. in diameter on the inside, and 6 in. deep, finished with convex fluting on the outside, and standing on eight oaken pillars clustered together on an octagonal base.

Movable fonts became common from the later seventeenth century. That in St John's, Dublin (rebuilt in 1681), "was affixed to No 13 [pew] when required for Baptisms".[1] In 1724 the sexton of St Michan's, Dublin, was required "upon Notice of Baptism to have the Font brought out against the end of the second Lesson into the Middle Isle in the range of seats at the west end of the western extremity of the Church".[2] He was also required to place cushions and also "the moving stool or Desk" which the vestry had provided that year "to be placed before the font for the minister to stand and kneel on in the administration of Baptism to the end that he may be better seen and heard."[3] The plan of the church in 1724 shows that the font otherwise stood in a pew at the west end on the south side. In some other cases the font with its pedestal was kept in the vestry when not in use.

When Bishops, in their Charges,[4] complained of the absence of fonts in some of the churches within their dioceses, they most probably meant that these churches contained no immovable font; for while there is evidence that the setting up of a movable font for Baptisms on the Communion table continued within living memory[5] that of placing it upon a movable pedestal in the nave has not altogether died out.

Bishop Mant, who was an exponent of traditional Anglican ecclesiology, insisted that "the ancient usual place" for the font was at the west end of the church, "and not in the modern unusual place, not at the upper end of the Church, not in the Chancel, not hard by or within the rails of the Communion Table, thus confounding the entrance into the Church mystical with a confirmed and mature establishment in it".[6] The font should also be of stone "with reference to the 'rock', from which the water, typical of baptism flowed in the wilderness; and to the 'corner-stone' and the 'rock', which are scriptural emblems of our blessed Lord, who gave forth the living water."[7] The font should be "large enough for immersion".[8] But "the shape of the bason is left, by the judgment of the Church, indifferent and indefinite". Mant could see no value belong-

---

[1] E. S. Hughes, op. cit., 30.   [2] "Memorial of St Michan's", 19.
[3] Vestry Book.
[4] Bishop Mant; Visitation Charge at Killaloe, 1820; Archbishop Trench's charge at Dublin, 1879.
[5] In 1826 it was reported of a church in the Kilsaran Union of Parishes that there was no font, but that the children were "baptized at the Altar". J. B. Leslie, History of the Kilsaran Union of Parishes, 160. This was the practice, within living memory, at a church, built in the nineteenth century, in the diocese of Dublin.
[6] R. Mant, Church Architecture Considered, 11. In two churches of the diocese of Down the font had recently been moved to "the ancient usual place". Ibid., 12.
[7] Ibid., 10.   [8] Ibid., 14.

ing to "the symbolical argument for an octagon, as put forth by the Cambridge Camden Society";[1] but he thought the font should stand upon two or three steps, and mentioned with approval the "elevated font" in the restored Cathedral of Armagh.[2]

(c) The Seats

When Sir William Brereton visited Dublin in 1635 he noticed that a church recently taken over from the Jesuits and not yet adapted for Anglican worship had "no fastened seats in the middle or body thereof",[3] but that the Parish Church of St Nicholas Without (in the north transept of St Patrick's Cathedral) was capable of receiving a great congregation "by reason of capacious galleries round about, wherein are abundance of seats placed one above another with great advantage of room".[4] The Irish Canon 91 takes the provision of seats in churches for granted in directing churchwardens to warn the people not to bring to the church "children which are not so nurtured, as they can be kept quiet in their seats, without running up and down".

In addition to seats in the body of the church there were seats in the chancel of St John's, Dublin, in 1632,[5] "seats in ye Chancell" of St Catherine's, Dublin, in 1661,[6] and a few years later "benches, desks, and footstools with the seats in the Chancel" were made for Holy Trinity, Cork.[7] James Bonnell (d. 1699), who received the Sacrament weekly in Dublin by going "from Church to Church", implies that the communicants were conveniently placed in the chancel before the Consecration.[8] Although, after the seventeenth century, the chancel of a new Irish church was normally too small for additional benches, considerable space was often left for the gathering together of communicants in front of the Communion rails as at St Michan's, Dublin, in 1724[9] and Hillsborough in 1774.[10]

The tenth Canon of the diocesan Synod of Kilmore, which Bishop Bedell held in 1638, directed that the women should not sit "in sacrario", but outside the chancel and apart from the men, giving as authority; "Concil. Laodicen, 44, Concil. Aquisgran, 82; Capitular Car. I. 1, c. 17;

---

[1] Ibid., 14.   [2] Ibid., 11 seq.   [3] *Travels*, 142.   [4] Ibid., 138.
[5] S. C. Hughes, op. cit., 18.   [6] Vestry Book.
[7] R. Cauldfield, *Extracts from the Parish Books.*
[8] See above, p. 114.   [9] Plan in "Memorial of St Michan's".
[10] "Memoir of Hillsborough Church", Feb. 1844. "There is an open space 10 ft. from east to west, and 20 north to south, in front of the rails of the Communion Table, unoccupied except by one or two open benches. This is a great advantage at times of the Administration of the Communion."

Ve Concil. Turonen, 2, c. 4, Ut laici, &c." This was the only Canon which did not receive full assent, as Dr Faithfull Teate "had ordered a new seat for his wife in the chancel but a little before, and was loathe to remove it".[1] Both Dr Charles Smith in 1746 and Richard Pococke in 1752 witness to a similar separation of sexes in St Olave's and St Patrick's, Waterford, both restored and furnished by Bishop Thomas Milles *c.* 1734, the women sitting "on the right, and the men on the left of the Isle".[2] There was a similar custom "established from the first" at Grange, built by Primate Robinson and consecrated in 1773 as a Chapel-of-Ease to Armagh.[3]

Of the few seats in Ireland surviving from Caroline times those in the Middle Church of Ballinderry (1668), furnished by Bishop Taylor, and Killala Cathedral (*c.* 1671) are square and extend from the north and south walls to the central passage. Those at Ballinderry were described in 1897 as being "made of Irish oak, framed and panelled, relieved with fine delicately-worked mouldings, the panels being selected for the rich wavy graining oak, and the frames held together with oak pins".[4] "The two front pews are larger and more elaborate in workmanship."[5] Fashions in church seating changed rapidly. In 1672, for example, the vestry of St Audoen's, Dublin, decided to re-seat the church entirely "according to the form and model of the seats of St Werburgh's, Dublin", and the next year ordered the joiner "to raise the seats that are most remote to the profit of the hearers".[6] We do not know what the "form and model" was because St Werburgh's was entirely rebuilt and refurnished in 1719 and the present seats in St Audoen's are of later date. In 1674, however, the seats of Dublin churches were said to be "all decently severed to avoid confusion and disorder",[7] and in 1686 it was difficult to avoid turning one's "back on the Altar in Service time, or on the Minister".[8] This strongly suggests that square pews with seats on three sides and a door on the fourth were common in the late seventeenth century.

In the early part of the next century square pews continued to be employed particularly in country churches. Where the building was cruci-

---

[1] *A True Relation of the Life and Death of William Bedell*, ed. T. W. Jones (Camden Society), 162 seqq.
[2] C. Smith, *Waterford* (1746), 180; R. Pococke, *Tour in Ireland*, 178 seq.
[3] J. B. Leslie, *Armagh...*, 307. R.D. Report 17 (N.L.I.).
[4] F. J. Bigger and W. J. Fennell, "The Middle Church of Ballinderry and Bishop Jeremy Taylor", *Ulster Journ. of Archaeology*, III (1897), 17.
[5] Ibid.
[6] "Memorial of St Audoen's", II. Every man was to give 5s. "per yard square" for the wainscot of the fronts and 3s. 6d. "per yard square for the backs and sides of the sayd seats."
[7] See above, p. 144.   [8] See above, p. 147.

form and without aisles the square pews were often extended symmetrically into the transepts, short passages leading to the end pews of
each, and against the walls of the nave and transepts panelling in perfect
proportion to that of the pews rose high above their level and was continued round the wall of the chancel. This is the attractive arrangement at
Hollymount, Co. Mayo (1714 but rebuilt 1816). When the transepts were
added in 1830 to Inch Church, Co. Down (1742), the square pews were
extended into them in the same way as in Hollymount. The plan of the
larger cruciform Church of St Michan, Dublin in 1724 shows that the
square pews extended not only into the transepts but into the eastern arm,
leaving a clear passage all round the walls of the outer chancel, the transepts and the nave, and a considerable space between the front seats and
the "Place of ye Altar". The seats thus set cruciform were divided into
four blocks by the central passage from west to east and by the passage
through the centre of the transepts.

In his county histories Dr Charles Smith often speaks of town churches
being furnished with "double rows of pews", suggesting the more modern
division into four blocks separated by central and side passages, but
often in this period the seats in the aisles or under the galleries faced
inwards.[1] In the middle of the century it was still unusual for all the seats
to face east. Dr Smith and Richard Pococke noticed not only the separation of the men from the women in St Olave's and St Patrick's, Waterford, but the fact that all the seats were so arranged "that the whole
congregation can only face east".[2] Pococke points out that this arrangement as well as the separation of the sexes was ordered by his uncle,
Bishop Thomas Milles.

Contemporary descriptions are sometimes misleading. In 1744, for
example, it was said that Down Parish Church, rebuilt in 1735, "was
adorned with a neat Pulpit, reading desk, and rows of seats regularly laid
out", rather giving the picture of a town church with a pulpit and reading-
desk each side of the central passage towards the east. The Plan of 1734,
however, gives a very different picture. The pulpit and reading-desk
stand together near the west end on the south side; eight square pews stand
along the west wall, and the rest of the rectangular church is arranged as a
college chapel with two rows of oblong pews on each side facing inwards
to the central passage, and behind them lateral seats for the poor, the

[1] In St Mary's, Dublin (c. 1697), there are lateral seats set in the three window
recesses to the north and south of the nave; and in old St Thomas's, Dublin (1762),
there were lateral seats under the galleries.
[2] C. Smith, op. cit., 180; R. Pococke, op. cit., 178 seq.

hospital, and the Latin school. Outside the enclosure of the Communion table on either side are four stalls with desks, no doubt intended for the Chapter of the Cathedral, which was still in ruins. Single seats facing east have since been substituted, but interesting examples of the college chapel arrangement survive at Glenealy (1783) with canopied stalls against the north and south walls and western screen, at Kilbixy (1798), and at Collon (1813).

In the later eighteenth century single seats facing east became increasingly common. The nave of Hillsborough Church (1774) is filled with such seats, three and a half feet in height and three from back to back, and the backs and sides handsomely panelled in oak. In the transepts, attractively raised six steps above the floor of the nave, are four large square pews, in the north two for the Marquis of Downshire and his family, and in the south one formerly occupied by the Sovereign and Burgesses of Hillsborough, and one by the Bishop of the diocese. Behind these large pews are single seats in both transepts, at the extremities of which are tower spaces formerly appropriated to the children of the parochial schools.[1] In his *Charge to the Clergy of the Diocese of Killaloe* in 1821 Bishop Mant required that every new church in the diocese should have single seats facing the Communion Table.[2]

Most churches had a western gallery, sometimes with the Royal arms carved in the centre, and town churches often had parallel galleries as well. Where they were part of the original plan they were well proportioned to the building, which often had larger windows above, and smaller below, their level. Sometimes the galleries and pews were painted white.[3]

The original symmetry was often disturbed by the provision of additional seats or by the raising of existing seats to extraordinary heights. Thus the vestry of Dundalk in 1784 resolved "that the ground now possest of the Pulpit and Reading Desk be divided into two seats",[4] and in 1786 allowed "the raising of Captain Morton's seat, so to shelter his family from the wind of the door".[5] The vestry of St Peter's, Dublin, in the 1770s allowed several seats to be raised to the height of "exactly 6 feet 6 inches from the ground".[6] On the other hand, the vestry of Enniscorthy in 1824 requested Caesar Colclough "to lower the seat, which has been raised above the level of the rest in the Chancel, as the clergy and

---

[1] "Memoir of Hillsborough Church." Likewise Thomas Cooley, in his twelve plans for churches (1765–84), provides, with the exception of the two front seats, single seats facing east, the minimum space from back to back being 3 ft. 1½ ins. The backs and sides are well panelled.

[2] Op. cit., 14.   [3] St Peter's, Dublin, before 1821.

[4] J. B. Leslie, op. cit., 286.   [5] Ibid.   [6] Vestry Book.

congregation are greatly inconvenienced by its elevation".[1] The large oak canopied pews in Larne Church were taken down in 1840. Besides family pews, public bodies often rented special pews. Thus the Corporation of Shoe-Makers had a pew in St Michael's, Dublin, and the Corporation of Tailors, which had a Guild Chapel in St John's, Dublin, in 1417, rented a pew in that church and had their arms suspended from the northern gallery.[2]

In 1843 Bishop Mant recommended that the seats, all single and facing east, should be separated by a central passage to allow the minds and thoughts of the people entering the church "to be directed at once to the Sanctuary".[3] "Since there meet together 'high and low, rich and poor, one with another', all in order to the worshipping of the same common Father through the same common Redeemer", the church architect should not "lavish, for the ostentatious indulgence of the opulent few, space which might be beneficially bestowed for the comfort and improvement of the low and indigent many".[4] The purposes of religious worship for which churches are built "are not best answered by spacious rooms, inclosed with lofts, partitions, and secluded from common observation, however convenient they may be for concealing the apathy of the indevout, the slumbers of the indolent, the playfulness of the young, the sallies of the witty, and the whispers and smiles of the gay and fashionable".[5]

Provision for kneeling was repeatedly recommended though often wanting. Occasionally we find parish expenditure on kneeling forms,[6] and they were included in Thomas Cooley's estimate of quantities. Mant, who had insisted on provision for kneeling in new churches in the diocese of Killaloe in 1821,[7] later declared: "No Church can be built as a Church should be unless it contain facilities for kneeling."[8] Although devout

---

[1] J. B. Leslie, *Ferns*, 154.

[2] With this motto in Latin, "I was naked, and ye clothed me"; no doubt chosen originally to remind the Guild of its solemn responsibility to clothe the poorer members of the Body of Christ at a just price.

[3] *Church Architecture Considered*, 35 seq.

[4] Ibid., 36. When Mant became Bishop of Down and Connor in 1823, Belfast had but two churches: St Ann's with accommodation for 990 persons exclusively in private pews, and St George's with accommodation for 1300 but with only six seats for the free accommodation of the poor, who were not provided for, as in Dublin and Cork churches, by early Divine Service. Mant set out to reform this abuse, and as a first step consecrated Christ Church with free seats for a thousand persons in 1833, just a century after Bishop Milles had provided two churches in Waterford with free seats for 500 in each. [5] Ibid.

[6] I.e., "for covering several kneeling forms". (Vestry Book of St Michan's, Dublin, under 1724.) [7] Op. cit., 14. [8] *Church Architecture Considered*, 37.

people made their own provision, there was seldom general provision for the use of the congregation. This want led to "a habit which prevails among our congregations, who in assuming the attitude of prayer, are accustomed to turn themselves half round in their places, and thus lean their bodies over the backs of their pews, and to rest their knees, or a knee, upon the seats." [1] This posture, contrary to the Church's direction of meekly kneeling upon our knees, encouraged the congregation in general to turn their backs upon the Altar, and disturbed the devotions of any in the pew behind who wished "to direct their faces towards the holy table".[2] The proper provision for kneeling in a new church had been given prominence in Archbishop King's "Discource concerning the Consecration of Churches", appointed to be read in the Dublin diocesan *Office for the Consecration of a Church* of 1719: "Since People are so careful to provide Seats for their Ease, so there ought to be care taken in the Contrivance of our Churches, that they may, in the most solemn Acts of Worship, fall down before their Maker."

Seats in Cathedrals

Of the many Irish cathedrals only Killala (*c.* 1671), Downpatrick (1818), and Achonry (1823) have retained anything like their original arrangements, and even at Downpatrick the necessary provision of additional seats within a short time of its restoration led to the insertion of a central block of single seats in what must have been a most impressive open space eighteen feet wide. Up to the middle of the last century the larger Irish cathedrals retained the traditional arrangements of the choir, though the need for additional seating had led to many experiments: first to the provision of galleries, and then to the extension of the choir either to the west of the crossing,[3] or further westward into the nave,[4] the Chapter stalls being moved westward to the new entrance into the choir, and finally, under the influence of the Irish liturgical writer, John Jebb, the traditional arrangements were abandoned and the whole cathedral thrown into one, as at St Paul's, Salisbury, Ely, Durham, and elsewhere in England, being treated as a large parish church, with the congregation in the nave and the Chapter stalls facing inwards in the choir.[5] An early Irish instance of this arrangement was at Raphoe where the nave was filled with high pews and the stalls stood on the north side of the choir

---

[1] *Church Architecture Considered*, 38. [2] Ibid.
[3] As at St Patrick's, Dublin, Kilkenny, and Leighlin.
[4] As at Limerick, Cloyne, and Ross.
[5] *Choral Service*, 204 seqq., where he recommends the removal of choir screens and "throwing open the Nave to the Congregation during Divine Service".

and the throne on the south side "with another smaller one for the Dean nearer the Altar".[1] More often the tradition that the Chapter stalls should face east was preserved until the middle of the last century.

When the choir of the small Cathedral of Clonfert was found too confined for the congregation early in the last century, the nave was fitted up for service "after the manner of a Cathedral Choir".[2] The stalls were placed on either side at the west end of the nave and the throne in the middle of the north wall.[3] A similar arrangement had prevailed from the first, though with the throne on the south side, at Cork (1735), Waterford (c. 1775), Cashel (1788), and Achonry (1823). It was introduced at Derry about 1855, where the stalls then erected at the west end have, like the western stalls at Cashel, been left undisturbed, though in both cathedrals later chancels with stalls facing inwards have been added. In 1813 the stalls at Killala stood each side without the enclosure of the altar; but they were moved c. 1824 to the west end in the belief that this was their original position c. 1681. In this case there is Caroline precedent for this arrangement.

Before the restoration of Armagh (1834–7) the nave was used for larger congregations and the choir for smaller, the central crossing serving as a vestibule to each. The nave had an altar decently covered against the west door,[4] a throne, a large pew for the Chapter and priest-vicars, a gallery for the lay-vicars, and it was heavily pewed throughout.[5] After 1837 the crossing was filled with choir seats facing inwards, the choir with congregational seats also facing inwards, with the pulpit and throne to the north and south of its entrance. The easternmost bay of the nave was filled with single seats facing east, and behind them stood the Chapter stalls against a stone screen. The four western bays were left unoccupied.[6] Thackeray thought the Cathedral at this time "as neat and trim as a lady's drawing room".[7]

Before 1844 the arrangements of Derry were most curious. Richard

---

[1] T. M. Fallow, *The Cathedral Churches of Ireland*, 182.
[2] Samuel Lewis, *Topographical Dictionary* (1837), I, 364a.
[3] T. M. Fallow, op. cit., 82.
[4] This is an early and interesting use of a nave altar. There was at the time an altar each end of the Cathedral as at Trier. This arrangement is attributed to Primate Stuart. The nave, however, had been used separately from the choir at an earlier date. In 1700 the choir was found to be too small for the congregation, and it was ordered that a pulpit, reading-desk, "and other conveniences for ye people shou'd be placed in the body of the Church as before the wars".
[5] John Jebb, *Choral Service*, 210; and the picture in the Chapter Room.
[6] *Eccles.*, Feb. 1855, 11 seqq.; and another picture in the Chapter Room.
[7] *The Irish Sketch Book of 1842*, 287.

Pococke visited the Cathedral in 1752 when they were being made. "The Bishop's and Dean's seats are pointing to the west, on each side to the opening of the Chancel, and the stalls of the Prebends are to be in line with them." [1] Early in the last century, however, there were large Chapter stalls each side of the quasi-chancel facing west, and the throne was on the north side of the nave. [2]

The Bishop's throne normally stood on the south side of the choir, but at Kilmore before the Commonwealth it stood in the centre of the east wall facing west, and at Downpatrick it stood on the north side of the choir. The Chapter of Cloyne in 1679 ordered the erection of a new throne for "the next coming Bishop and his lady". [3] Thirty years later the throne in this Cathedral had damask curtains and a velvet cushion with "gold tassels". [4]

A Bishop's throne was sometimes set up in a Parish church. In 1752 Richard Pococke said that both St Patrick's and St Olave's, Waterford, were adorned with thrones; [5] and six years before Dr Charles Smith had described "the Bishop's Throne" in St Olave's as being of oak and having a canopy "well executed". [6] This throne, on the north side opposite the pulpit, in proportion and design, shows every sign of being part of the original furniture of the church, and not as has been thought the throne removed from the modern Cathedral, which Street described as "an odd little pagan temple, with pillars and pediment, and painted white". [7] A Bishop's throne is mentioned in 1751 and 1769 at Christ Church, Cork. [8] At Hillsborough (1772–4) a Bishop's chair carved with a mitre under a richly carved canopy stands in a large pew in the south transept facing east. Thomas Lewis O'Beirne, Bishop of Meath (1798–1823), placed a wooden mitre over a chair in Navan parish church, which was recently given to the newly constituted Cathedral of Trim for the diocese of Meath, where it stands behind the throne to the north. [9]

(d) The Pulpit and Reading-Desk

The Irish Canon 94 orders the provision of "a fit Seat for the Minister to read Service in" and "a comely and decent pulpit, to be set in a con-

---

[1] *Tour in Ireland in 1752*, 43.   [2] Picture in the Chapter Room.
[3] T. M. Fallow, op. cit., 46.
[4] Richard Cauldfield, *Annals of the Cathedral of St Coleman, Cloyne.*
[5] Tour in *Ireland*, 132.   [6] *Waterford* (1746), 178.
[7] G. W. O. Addleshaw and F. Etchells, *The Architectural Setting of Anglican Worship*, 198n.
[8] C. A. Webster, *Diocese of Cork*, 134.
[9] There are also thrones in the Collegiate Churches of Galway and Youghal.

venient place for the preaching of God's Word". By fixing the Communion table at the east end of the church the same Canon rules out the nineteenth-century arrangement of placing the pulpit at the east end behind the Communion table. The rubrics of the *Irish Form of Consecration of Churches* (1666) make it quite clear that the pulpit is intended to stand in the body of the church, for it is dedicated immediately before the solemn entrance into the chancel,[1] and that it cannot stand where it sometimes stood in England in post-Restoration times "in the middle alley in front of the Chancel gates",[2] because the Bishop, attended by his clergy, is directed to kneel "in the body of the church, before the chancel door, at a convenient distance".[3] Likewise a Dublin diocesan Office of 1719 directs the Bishop to "kneel down in the body of the Church, with his face towards the Altar". The rubrics of 1666 and 1719 imply that the pulpit is set at one side and does not obstruct a view of the chancel door or of the altar.

The position of the pulpit and reading-desk depended partly upon the plan of the church and partly upon the seating arrangements. It required one treatment in small aisleless churches, another in cruciform churches, another in churches with aisles or parallel galleries, another in cathedrals. Again, the position depended upon whether the church was provided with square pews having seats on three sides facing no particular direction, whether the seats were all facing the east, or whether they were facing inwards as in a college chapel. In small churches without transepts, aisles, or parallel galleries, and furnished with square pews, the pulpit often stood in the middle of the north or south wall of the nave, with the lower desks for the minister and clerk extending inwards to the central passage.[4] In similar churches furnished with single seats all facing the altar the pulpit more often stood on one side to the east of the seats with the desks either below in a variety of positions or on the opposite side of the church.[5] In churches arranged as a college chapel there was no fixed rule. At

---

[1] Appendix I, lines 297–8, 335–6.

[2] G. W. O. Addleshaw and F. Etchells, op. cit., 76, where this position is said to have become "increasingly common from the Restoration onwards". See, however, Legg, *Eng. Ch. Life*, I, 148.

[3] Appendix I, 70–3.

[4] Against the north wall of the Middle Church of Ballinderry (1668): against the south wall in most of the churches of the diocese of Meath at the beginning of the eighteenth century. J. Healy, op. cit., II, 57.

[5] Sometimes the reading-desk had a shelf facing inwards for the Prayer Book, and one for the Bible. Thomas Cooley's designs for Church furnishing (below, p. 227 seq.), giving great variety to the position of the pulpit and reading-desk, probably incorporate many post-Restoration experiments.

Q

Downpatrick Parish Church (1735) the pulpit and desks stood against the south wall near the west end facing north; at Collon (1813) in the centre of the west wall facing east;[1] and at Kilbixy (1798) in an eastern corner. In cruciform churches the pulpit stood near the crossing, sometimes at the angle of the chancel and one of the transepts with the reading-desk below or at the opposite angle. In large town churches with parallel galleries the pulpit was often placed at one side of the central passage with the desks for the minister and clerk either below or on the opposite side. Such churches sometimes had a "moving pulpit", as at St Michan's, Dublin (from 1726),[2] Athlone (c. 1733), and St Peter's, Drogheda, "provided by way of trial" in 1757.

Of the few remaining pulpits of the seventeenth century, the threefold structure in the Middle Church of Ballinderry (1668) still stands half-way down the church against the north wall extending inwards to the central passage. The pulpit, with its canopy, and desks are square, and simply panelled; and there are double candlesticks for each. The pulpit and canopy of Waringstown (1681), without attendant desks, are elaborately carved, and there is a handsome rail to the curved staircase.[3] Of the next century the richly carved pulpit of St Olave's, Waterford (1734), stands against the south wall east of the single seats which all face the altar. It is unconnected in design and structure with the desks beneath which extend inwards to the central passage; but it is clearly connected in design with the throne opposite and with the altarpiece. The gilded dove of wood now detached and lying on the base of the pulpit may have adorned the canopy. Hillsborough (c. 1772) has a fine hexagonal pulpit at the south-eastern angle of the outer chancel, well panelled in the perpendicular style, with a richly canopied sounding board standing upon two pillars. The square reading-desk, with similar panelling, stands at the opposite angle, raised three steps above the floor of the chancel, with shelves facing south and west.[4]

Kilbixy (1798), and later, Littleton and Rathaspeck, have two pulpits of equal height, one for preaching and the other for reading the Service in, after the seventeenth-century example of Halsted in Kent (1609) and

[1] In 1894 this pulpit was removed and a western entrance made. A new pulpit now stands in the centre towards the east facing west, with modern reading-desks at the eastern extremity of the stalls facing west. This is the position of the reading-desk at Glenealy, also arranged as a college chapel.

[2] "for Moving the Pulpit" is an item frequently mentioned in parish accounts from 1726 (Vestry Book).

[3] There is a gilded dove beneath the canopy at the back.

[4] Of the nineteenth century the fine pulpit designed by Francis Johnson for Dublin Castle Chapel now stands in St Werburgh's, Dublin.

Layton Ecclesia (Leighton Bromswold) in Huntingdonshire (c. 1627).[1] Bishop Mant appears to have known other cases surviving into his time, for he thought that church architects had betrayed "much insensibility of the Church's spirit by elevating the Minister's seat into a second pulpit".[2]

From contemporary accounts we gather that pulpits from Caroline times had sounding-boards, though by the opening of the nineteenth century many of them had fallen down or into extreme decay.[3] The sounding-board of Mourne Abbey Church (1717) was "neatly carved and gilded".[4] From the Restoration we frequently read of "double candlesticks", cushions for the pulpit and lower desks, and pulpit cloths. St Werburgh's, Dublin, had in 1671 a new pulpit cushion costing £9, and in 1731 velvet cushions and a pulpit cloth, which like the "Carpet for the Altar" was of velvet "with gold lace and binding".[5] There was a "Bible for the Pulpit" of St Audoen's in 1672, and an hour-glass for that of St John's, Dublin, in 1742.[6]

In his twelve plans and elevations of new churches drawn for Primate Robinson between 1765 and 1784 Thomas Cooley gives interesting variations of the position of the pulpit and reading-desk in a parish church either as a single unit with clerk's desk added or in separation on opposite sides of the building. In one case only (No. 7) does the pulpit stand further west than the front seats, and here it extends inwards with lower desks from the south wall to the central passage. The threefold pulpit otherwise stands facing west, either at the south-east corner (1), along the north wall (6) or just left of the central passage (9). Each pulpit has six or seven sides and the lower desks are square. In two cases (6 and 9) the same staircase leads to the two desks and pulpit, and in one of these (9) it is curved to balance the curved corner of the pew on the opposite side of the central passage. In the other eight plans the pulpit and reading-desk are placed symmetrically each side of the Church: in one each side of the enclosure of the altar; in others westward of the rails, either against

---

[1] Legg, *Eng. Ch. Orders*, liii.

[2] Op. cit., 32. Mant cannot have meant the octagonal reading-desk raised by two or three steps, for he provides one in his "Plan of a Church agreeable to the principles of the United Church of England and Ireland". Ibid., facing p. 5. He may have had in mind the gigantic reading-desk in Christ Church, Belfast (1833), towering to the height of a chancel screen and ascended by a spiral staircase continuing helterskelter-wise to the pulpit above. A similar structure appeared in Trinity, Belfast, in 1843.

[3] St J. D. Seymour, *Diocese of Emly*, 251, 254, etc. One was "totally broke" in 1791; another "had fallen and lay on the floor".

[4] A modern pulpit has been substituted.   [5] Vestry Book.

[6] "Memories of St Audoen's", 63; C. S. Hughes, op. cit., 34.

the north and south walls (5), between the walls and the central passage (10 and 12), or each side of it (3 and 8). As separate units the pulpit and reading-desk are usually both hexagonal or octagonal, the one raised seven or eight steps, and the other three, above the floor.[1] The panelling of each is in good proportion to that of the pews, and the balusters of the pulpit stairway to those of the Communion rail. All twelve pulpits have neatly panelled sounding-boards usually standing on two pillars. Although most of Cooley's furniture where adopted has been replaced,[2] his designs may be regarded as conservative experiments in ecclesiology, and the positions chosen for the pulpit and reading-desk as influenced by precedents reaching back in some cases to Caroline times. In no case are they placed in the centre, either before or behind the Communion table.

Traditional Anglican ecclesiology was again promoted a few decades later by Bishop Mant. In his *Charge to the Clergy of the diocese of Killaloe* in 1821, Mant directed that the pulpit and reading-desk of a new church should be "towards the eastern extremity of the building", but not "within the rails of the Communion Table",[3] nor obstructing its view.[4] Later in the diocese of Down and Connor Mant maintained that they should stand, not in front of the Communion table, but on either side of it; "westward, at the same time, of the Chancel and Chancel-screen, in advance of the holy table, so as to concede to it its pre-eminence against the eastern wall".[5]

The fixing of the pulpit, often with lower desks, in the centre of the church, though common in Dublin and other towns early in the nineteenth century, seems to have been a late development borrowed from England, where "of late years", it was complained in 1804, "the pulpit obstructs the altar in many newly repaired churches", and the pulpit in St Paul's Cathedral moved from where Wren placed it "in the new-fangled way, directly in the centre",[6] but where the new position was

---

[1] In his design for the chapel in Phoenix Park of 1771 Cooley has a reading-desk with five steps making it almost as high as the pulpit with seven (Architectural Drawings in Murray Collection (N.L.I.)).

[2] As in Grange and Lisnadill, Co. Armagh, built by Primate Robinson.

[3] In the Kilscoran Union, Co. Wexford, the pulpit in Carne Church stands within the rails to the north of the altar, and in the Parish Church the staircase and half the pulpit are within the rails to the north.

[4] *Church Architecture Considered*, 15.

[5] Ibid., 31. In spite of Mant's strong objection to fixing the pulpit in front of the altar, massive structures were set up in the centre of Belfast churches erected during his episcopate—Christ Church (1833), the Magdalen Chapel (1839), and Holy Trinity (1843).

[6] Legg, *Eng. Ch. Life*, 148, where he cites a letter from a London Clergyman to the *Orthodox Churchman's Magazine and Review* of 1804. The writer makes it clear that

later thought to be that of the primitive ambo.[1] Archbishop Trench complained not only of "the huge wooden fortress rising up in the centre, blocking out all view of the Chancel", but the position of the Communion table "safely nestled under the pulpit".[2] Almost every known case of the pulpit set against the eastern wall with the altar in front, clearly at variance with the Irish Canon 95, belongs to the period following the Act of Union of 1800 when the English Canons were sometimes regarded as superseding the Irish. Such was the arrangement of the new churches of St Andrew (1807) and St George (1813) and the one introduced into the older Churches of St Mark and St Thomas, Dublin. Of St Thomas's it was said in 1818 that the recent removal of the pulpit and reading-desk "from their usual absurd position in front of the communion table to the rear of it, while it does not obstruct the preacher's voice, renders the communion service more audible".[3] There was no theological or party significance; and all four churches at the time had daily prayers, and two of them had fortnightly Communion.[4] In 1843 Mant claimed that instances of the pulpit set behind the altar were "by no means common", and one which he remembered in the diocese of Connor had been "corrected some years ago".[5]

In Irish Cathedrals where the traditional arrangements of the choir remained the pulpit usually stood on the north side opposite the throne, though a "moving pulpit" was provided at Cork in 1716, and John Jebb could remember movable pulpits at Kilkenny and at the two Dublin cathedrals.[6] Larger cathedrals sometimes had a nave pulpit as well. In 1691 there was "a stone Pulpit fix'd about the middle of the nave" in each of the Dublin cathedrals,[7] and in 1700 a plan to provide a pulpit in the nave

the central pulpit with desks have not been set up in "the 50 new Churches, in and about London", but in the older churches "which have lately been improved". It would be precarious, therefore, to claim English Caroline precedent for the central pulpit.

[1] So Richard Brown, *Sacred Architecture* (1845), 278.

[2] Primary Visitation Charge, 1865.

[3] J. Warburton, J. Whitelaw, R. Walsh, *History of the City of Dublin*, 503.

[4] St Andrew's and St Thomas's, and from 1825 St Mark's and from 1828 St George's. That there is no necessary connection between Orthodoxy and correct ecclesiology is readily seen from the action of that champion of Orthodoxy, Philip Skelton, who finding the pulpit at Fintona too small for him, broke it down "and in its place raised the reading-desk to such a height, as to serve both for reading-desk and pulpit. This gave him more room for action, with which...he always set off his sermons." (*Works*, I, ci.)

[5] Op. cit., 32.

[6] R. Cauldfield, op. cit., 187; *Eccles.*, Oct. 1862, 252; *Choral Service*, 196.

[7] Bishop Dopping, *A Form of Reconciliation of Lapsed Protestants*, 15 seq.

of Armagh.[1] In smaller cathedrals there was a tendency to place the pulpit and reading-desk each side of the altar.[2]

Two divergent views were expressed in 1843 as to the character of the "Reading-Pew" mentioned in the first rubric of the Commination Service. Mant identified it with the "fit Seat for the Minister to read Service in" of Canon 94.[3] Slightly modifying the reading-pew described by Sparrow and Wheatley, Mant recommended one with two shelves or desks at right angles to each other, one for the Prayer Book looking across the nave, the other for the Bible looking west.[4] Mant objected to "the substitution proposed by the Cambridge Camden Society of a 'Litany-stool and eagle-desk or lettern', instead of the 'reading-pew'; namely, because such a substitution is not agreeable to the orders of the Church." [5] Mant, however, overlooked the distinction made by the rubrics of the Commination Service between "the reading-pew" and "the place where they are accustomed to say the Litany".

John Jebb, on the other hand, identified the "reading-pew" with the Lectern and regarded the "reading-desk" as "a piece of furniture alto-gether unknown to our ancient Choirs". In cathedrals, he maintained, "the Lessons ought always to be read from an eagle or Lectern in the centre of the Choir, not from the Minor Canon's place, as at Canterbury, Westminster, and Wells".[6] By special statute of 1692 the vicars of St Patrick's Cathedral were ordered to make "a civil obeydance" to the Dean at their "going to read any lesson, litanies..." [7] There are ancient lecterns in Christ Church Cathedral, Dublin, and at Limerick Cathedral; and before 1651 there were two in Waterford, one a "great standing pelican to support the Bible", the other a "brazen eagle";[8] and in 1712 the Chapter of Cork ordered an eagle to be made of the branch in the chest of the Chapter House.[9] There was certainly Caroline precedent for lecterns in cathedrals, but little for their use in parish churches, though Bishop Cosin encouraged them in his diocese, and in the Form of Con-secration of Churches which he drew up at the request of the Convoca-tion of Canterbury in 1662 he provides prayers to be said at "the place where the Lessons are to be read in the midst of the Church" and at "the

---

[1] See above, p. 223, n. 4.

[2] Leighlin, Kilfenora, Killaloe, and others. T. M. Fallow, op. cit., 33, 54, 60, 78, 88. This position was adopted at Downpatrick c. 1844, when the large central pulpit with desks was removed. There was a central pulpit at Derry and one of stone at Waterford in the last century.

[3] Op. cit., 26.   [4] Ibid., 28.   [5] Ibid., 29.

[6] Choral Service, 194 & n., 201.

[7] W. Monck Mason, op. cit., 91 n.m. seq.

[8] R. H. Ryland, op. cit., 139.   [9] R. Cauldfield, op. cit., 56.

place where morning and evening prayer is made".[1] John Jebb approved of a lectern in Leeds Parish Church (1841)[2] and Primate Lord John George Beresford held up as a model for his diocese the new furnishing of Grange Church, near Armagh, which included "an oak lettern".[3]

(e) The Litany-Desk

The rubrics of the *Irish Form of Consecration of Churches* (1666) mention "a foot-step raised higher than the floor" and "a footstool raised above the floor".[4] This is to stand "in the body of the Church, before the Chancel door, at a convenient distance". It is difficult not to identify this with "a low desk before the Chancel door called the fald-stool", also "in the body of the Church", where Bishop Andrewes directs the Litany to be said.[5] In the Dublin diocesan *Office to be used in the Restauration of a Church* (1719) the Bishop, attended with his clergy, is directed to "kneel down in the body of the Church, with his face towards the Altar, on a foot stool, raised above the Floor".[6] Likewise the Instrument of Consecration of 1666, reproduced in 1719, distinguishes between *suggestus ad legendam* and *suggestus ad precandum*, just as the rubrics of the Commination Service (1662) distinguish between "the reading-pew" and "the place where they are accustomed to read the Litany". Although Litany-stools were thus officially required in Irish churches at the end of the second decade of the eighteenth century, they seem to have fallen out of use by the end of the century, though their use in some cathedrals continued into the nineteenth century.[7]

(f) The Chancel Screen

"Rood-lofts, in which wooden crosses stood", remained in some Irish churches in 1634 when the Irish Canon 97 directed churchwardens, "with the Approbation of the Ordinary of the Place", to have them removed with all other "Monuments of Superstition". Only those connected with superstition appear to have been taken down. The ancient rood-screen at Youghal was not taken down until 1726, and in 1733 its many well-carved panels were incorporated in different pews. Thomas

---

[1] J. W. Legg, op. cit., 245; cf. 230.
[2] Op cit., 209. Jebb regarded the furnishing of Leeds Parish Church as being "in every respect Catholic".
[3] *Eccles.* (N.S., 68), Oct. 1852, 360.   [4] Appendix 1, 73–4; 671–2.
[5] *Minor Works* (L.A.C.T.), 149; cp. earlier injunctions cited in *Choral Service*, 434.
[6] *Offices* agreed to at a Synod of the Diocese of Dublin, 1719, 20.
[7] There were Litany-desks in Christ Church Cathedral, Dublin, and Limerick early in the nineteenth century.

Dinely described it in 1681 as having been "very rich and well carved, as appears by its remains doubly gilt over which are painted ye arms of the twelve tribes of Israel".[1] In 1639 the Archbishop of Dublin directed the churchwardens of St Audoen's, Dublin, an ancient church with a rood-stairway, to remove the solid rood-screen "whereon the Organs of the Church were lately placed", for practical reasons. It had become "ruinous" and not only a danger to the people "that sit thereabouts every Lord's Day, but likewise depriveth the rest of the congregation of the sight of the east window and holy table, causing the Minister's voice performing the Second Service there to be less audible". At the same time the Archbishop directed the erection, with all convenient speed, "between the nave and chancel", of "a new and comlie partition, such as may not in any wise debar or hinder the congregation of or from beholding the minister officiating at the Altar".[2] A month later the churchwardens promised to erect at the charge of the parish "a comely partition between ye Church and Chancel".[3]

Restoration ecclesiology also required chancel screens. In England Sir Christopher Wren provided them for some of his earlier churches: in Ireland the *Form of Consecration of Churches* (1666) assumes the separation of the chancel from the nave by a screen with doors. The Bishop is directed to kneel "before the Chancel doors", and later, having dedicated the furniture in the nave, to go with his clergy "towards the Chancel, the doors of which being shut".[4] The accounts of Holy Trinity, Cork, c. 1664, mention "a hanging lock for the Chancel door", suggesting an open screen, the chain of the lock passing round the central pillars of the door. When the new chancel of Waringstown was built in 1888 it was separated from the nave "by a low oak screen, previously existing and but slightly adapted to suit the altered arrangements".[5] This low screen, which has every appearance of belonging to a much earlier period if not to the original church of 1681, is about the same height as the screen erected by George Herbert at Leighton Bromswold c. 1627. Possibly other examples of earlier screens in the north were known to Bishop Mant,

---

[1] *Observations in A Voyage through...Ireland...1681*, 64 and ed. n. in loc.
[2] Marsh Library MS. "Memorial of St Audoen's", vol. II.   [3] Ibid.
[4] On the verso of p. 39 of one of the copies of the printed forms of 1666 (T.C.D., P. hh. 7. 5.) is a list written in faint ink of "Things to be provided for the Consecration", and underneath, in darker ink, another list headed "Praeparanda dec 17. 85." The earlier list, obscured by marginal cropping, includes "/n doore 14": the list of 1685 "Chan doores 14", p. 14 of the 1666 edition containing the rubrical direction for the doors of the chancel to be shut (lines 335-7). At p. 14 of this copy occurs a marginal scribbling, "chancell".
[5] E. D. Atkinson, *An Ulster Parish...Donaghcloney (Waringstown) 1898*.

who in 1843 recommended that the pulpit and reading-desk should stand westward of "the Chancel and Chancel-screen".[1] Although chancel screens were required in Caroline times none of them with the possible exception of Waringstown have survived.

By the eighteenth century the traditional plan for a new church had become greatly modified and the chancel little more than a shallow recess, and even in larger cruciform churches there was a tendency to extend the pews into the eastern arm. No chancel screens of this period, if ever provided, have survived, though there are structural screens in St Iberius, Wexford (*c.* 1760) and Castleisland Church, Co. Kerry, of a later date.[2] Glenealy (1783), arranged as a college chapel, has a western screen with canopied stalls each side facing east.

In Cathedrals, however, choir screens with returned stalls beneath, remained in use until the middle of the last century when the traditional arrangements of the choir were given up. Such a screen was provided in the modern Cathedral of Waterford (*c.* 1773), in Downpatrick (1818), and in Armagh (*c.* 1837). That in Downpatrick is the sole remaining choir screen of the traditional type in Ireland. The modern screens of stone in Limerick and Christ Church, Dublin, however, would meet the requirements of the first Caroline Archbishop of Dublin because they in no wise "debar or hinder the congregation of or from beholding the minister officiating at the Altar".

(g) Septum Altaris

Although the Irish and English Canons as well as the rubrics of the Prayer Book are silent about the rails enclosing the Communion table, Bishop Mant believed that there was medieval, Elizabethan, and Jacobean precedent for them, as well as the English Convocational order of 1640 and the English Articles of Inquiry.[3] Few Irish Articles of Inquiry have survived from the seventeenth century, but Anthony Dopping, Bishop of Meath, in 1696 included *Septum Altaris* in his *Index Rerum Visitandarum*,[4] and the enclosure of the Communion table by rails is frequently mentioned in Visitation reports, and some Instruments of Consecration of Churches.

---

[1] See above, p. 228. "A visible distinction between the Chancel and the body of the Church" is frequently mentioned in the later seventeenth century.

[2] The chancel of Wexford is separated from the nave "by an open screen of two pilasters and two columns", of Castleisland by a wall pierced with three arches.

[3] For possible Elizabethan and Jacobean precedents see G. W. O. Addleshaw and F. Etchells, op. cit., 118 & n. 1.

[4] *Tractatus de Visitationis Episcopalis*, Dublinii, 1696, 26; cf. 11.

Information about rails before the Commonwealth is extremely meagre. Alexander Clogie, Bishop Bedell's biographer, however, regarded the Communion table in Kilmore Cathedral, where the throne stood against the eastern wall, as exceptional. It stood, he tells us, in the centre of the choir "without steps of gradual ascension or circumvallation by railes, though the custom had prevailed in most churches".[1]

From the Restoration onwards we find very frequent contemporary references to the rails enclosing, and the raising of the floor of, the Communion table. Sometimes the rails enclosed the Altar on three sides, forming a rectangular enclosure,[2] sometimes they formed a semicircular enclosure,[3] sometimes they separated in a straight line the recess in which the altar stood from the outer chancel, as at Hillsborough, or the body of the church. There were interesting variations in the middle of the eighteenth century. Richard Pococke in 1752 gives a rough sketch of Richard Cassels' plan for Sligo Church showing a large oval-shaped enclosure standing a few feet clear of the eastern apse.[4] The rails in the chapel of the Rotunda Hospital in Dublin (1750–55) enclose the altar on three sides and, with the step, curve gracefully outwards towards the central doors.

Rails of the seventeenth century had doors, but few examples survive.[5] Often they were thrown down during James II's occupation when the "Rabble" broke into churches.[6] At Trim, for example, a "Church-Rapparee" was interrupted in the act of breaking down "one of the folding doors leading to the Communion Table".[7] Doors were general until recent times. They were required by the Dublin diocesan Office of 1719 for consecrating a new church: they were provided in the new churches by Thomas Cooley (d. 1784) and by Francis Johnson (1761–1829). The greatest care was taken both in the design and workmanship of the rails in the eighteenth century. When, for example, Christ Church, Cork, was rebuilt in 1720 the vestry decided that the rails, as well as the altar, should be of "Danzig oach" and the carver have three English

---

[1] E. S. Shuckburgh, *Two Biographies of William Bedell*, 153. In 1635 the floor of the altar in St John's, Dublin, was raised by two steps as that of St Patrick's had been by three steps a few years before.

[2] As at Ballinderry (1668), St Olave's, Waterford (1734), Down (1735), and most of Thomas Cooley's plans.

[3] As in Moira, Co. Down, and St Catherine's, Dublin, and formerly in Inch, Co. Down, Swords, and Killala Cathedral.

[4] Op. cit., 75.

[5] At Waringstown the seventeenth-century rails (1681) have been adapted to a nineteenth-century chancel, and have lost their doors.

[6] W. King, *The State of Protestants in Ireland*, 209.

[7] Ibid., 397.

crowns for "ye doing of ye capital of each column suitable to ye model shown us".[1] The surviving rails of the eighteenth century are of fine craftsmanship, as, for example, the oak rails in St Olave's, Waterford, and St Ann's, Shandon, and the wrought iron rails in Moira (1724), the Rotunda Chapel and St Werburgh's in Dublin, or Hillsborough, where they have a hand-rail of satinwood, or Rathvilly, where they are gilded.

Not only was the altar "decently" or handsomely railed in, but it stood upon a raised floor, often "Boarded" [2] or "laid with marble".[3] In the old Cathedral of Waterford it stood at the east end of the choir with seven steps leading to it on three sides;[4] in St Olave's, Waterford, there were steps of black marble on three sides,[5] and the upper step at Hillsborough was observed by Arthur Young in 1776 to be "one stone out of his Lordship's quarry, 21 feet long and 2 broad".[6] The raised floor of the sanctuary at Ballinderry was covered with small red tiles; at Churchtown, Co. Cork, paved with black and white marble;[7] at St Olave's, Waterford, "handsomely inlaid with wood in several geometrical figures";[8] at Hillsborough, "laid with fine white tiles, set diagonally, the corners being taken off and filled with black marble discs".[9]

"The Place of the Altar" was often given structural distinction particularly where it was set in a shallow recess or inner chancel. Sometimes the walls were adorned with stucco work, as at St Peter's, Drogheda, and St Catherine's, Dublin; sometimes the walls and roof with rich mouldings as at Hillsborough and the chapels by Francis Johnson of Dublin Castle and Kirwan House; sometimes the roof was "painted of an azure colour and inlaid with stars of gold" as at St Patrick's Cathedral in the seventeenth century,[10] St Mary's, St Werburgh's, the Castle Chapel, Dublin, and Knockbreda at later dates; sometimes the tetragrammaton adorned the roof above the altar as in the Dublin churches of St Mary and St George. There was a canopy over the altar of St Finbar's Cathedral, Cork, which the Chapter ordered to be taken down in 1720,[11] and the

---

[1] "Christ Church Annals", by W. A. Copinger, in an annotated edition of Smith's *Ancient and Present State of...Cork* (1893).
[2] Moynalty and Stackallen in 1733. J. Healy, *Meath*, II, 38.
[3] J. B. Leslie, *Raphoe*, under Conwall, Clondevaddock, Kilmacrenan.
[4] Plan of 1739 given by Sir James Ware, reproduced in T. M. Fallow, op. cit., 70.
[5] C. Smith, *Waterford* (1746), 180.
[6] *Tour in Ireland*, I, 133. The church had recently been rebuilt at the charge of Lord Hillsborough.
[7] C. Smith, *Cork*, I, 316.　　　　　　[8] C. Smith, *Waterford*, 180.
[9] "Memoir of Hillsborough Church in 1844."
[10] W. Monck Mason, op. cit., 8.
[11] R. Cauldfield, *Annals of St Fin Barre's Cathedral, Cork*, 59.

eighteenth-century baldachino in Waterford Cathedral, "clearly designed to be σεμγόγ and altar-like", so Street thought, can still be seen.[1]

The Altarpiece

We have little evidence of the treatment of the eastern wall before the Commonwealth. The setting up of the Decalogue, though not required by the Irish Canons, was not unknown. The Commandments had been "fairly painted" upon the partition filling the eastern arch of St Patrick's choir in Dublin before 1633 and were to be "engraven" upon the screen designed to stand behind the altar and westward of "the glorious tomb". At St John's, Dublin, they "were gilt" in 1621,[2] and in 1635 Prebendary De Cressy had "the Chancel panelled by the Holy Table" and "placed something like a reredos behind the altar".[3]

From the Restoration we find the east end treated in a variety of ways. Sometimes, as at Ballinderry and Hollymount, the oak wainscot stood below the east window and behind the altar and was continued round the church rising above the level of the pews. Sometimes the panelling at the east end was elaborately carved: at Hillsborough it was richly executed in oak and cedar. Sometimes the eastern window was included in the scheme. Thus in St Olave's, Waterford (1734), "the Altar-piece consists of four fluted pillars of the corinthian order, two on each side of the east window, over which is a handsome frieze and cornice".[4] More often, particularly in large churches and cathedrals, there was what was generally called "a corinthian Altar-piece" of the solid type, sometimes rising to a considerable height and concealing from view much of the east window, like the massive structure in the Chapel of the Royal Hospital, Kilmainham (1686–7).

The panels of the corinthian altarpiece often bore the Decalogue, and sometimes the Lord's Prayer and Creed in gold letters. That of Holy Trinity, Cork, in 1664, bore the Decalogue "with the effigies of Moses and Aaron",[5] and the corinthian altarpiece in Waterford Cathedral, which Dr Smith saw c. 1746, bore a representation of the delivery of the

---

[1] *Eccles.* (N.S., 54), 174.

[2] C. S. Hughes, *Church of St John Dublin*, 17.   [3] Ibid., 22.

[4] C. Smith, *Waterford* (1746), 181. Likewise the striking altarpiece (c. 1757) in the Rotunda Chapel, Dublin, by Bartholomew Cramillion, consists of eight corinthian pillars dividing the eastern window into three lights, with fine frieze and cornice over the two outer lights, supporting adoring angels looking inwards towards the Lamb sitting upon the book of the seven seals over the arch of the central light, a stucco curtain in red and gold, upheld by cherubim, extending on either side from a canopy over the Agnus Dei.

[5] Richard Cauldfield, *The Register of Holy Trinity, Cork (1643–1668)*.

Law at Mount Sinai above the Decalogue with Moses and Aaron on either side.[1] Gilded cherubim sometimes adorned the altarpiece:[2] that in the little apse of Mourne Abbey Church (1717) consisted of "six fluted pilasters of the corinthian order, with carved Cherubims neatly gilded between them", and in the panels, "the Lord's Prayer, Creed, and Commandments in gold letters".[3]

The altarpiece was often adorned with a Glory and sometimes with a gilded dove. Formerly St Patrick's, Waterford, had a Glory by Wander-Egan "well performed"[4] and Kilkenny Cathedral one brought from Italy by Bishop Pococke. The Glory sometimes surrounded, or partly encircled, the tetragrammaton as on the altarpieces of St Olave's and the present Cathedral, Waterford, and of St Werburgh's and St Catherine's, Dublin. More often it surrounded the sacred monogram. Over the altar of old St Peter's, Cork, in 1750 "the oldest Church standing in the city", was "a dove painted, surrounded by a glory in a pediment".[5] There is also a large gilded dove projecting outwards over the altar of St Werburgh's, Dublin (1759), and another standing on a pediment above the east window of Kilscoran Church (1818).

There were other variations later in the century. In 1774 Dr Charles Smith tells us that the altarpiece in old Waterford Cathedral he had described in 1746 has been removed and "an elegant one erected, consisting of groups of Angels".[6] About the same time "an Altar-piece of stucco" was ordered for Cloyne Cathedral.[7] And in 1784 a painting of the Resurrection by Vincent Waldron was placed behind the altar of the King's Hospital Chapel in Dublin.[8]

Towards the end of the century it became more common for the east window to be filled with "painted glass" representing some scriptural scene, as, for example, the east window of the Palace Chapel at Armagh, of the old Cathedral of Tuam, now a Synod Hall, or a little later of Dublin Castle Chapel, which is adorned with figures of the Evangelists and scriptural scenes including the Crucifixion and Ascension. The upper lights

---

[1] C. Smith, op. cit. (1746), 176.
[2] Two cherubim in Killaloe Cathedral were gilded in 1708. P. Dwyer, op. cit., 455 seq.
[3] Charles Smith, *Cork* (1750), 182. This altarpiece is no longer to be seen.
[4] C. Smith, *Waterford* (1774 ed.), 179.
[5] C. Smith, *Cork*, I, 379.
[6] C. Smith, *Waterford* (1774 ed.), 173; cf. ibid. (1746 ed.), 181.
[7] R. Cauldfield, *Annals of Cloyne Cathedral*, 34.
[8] F. R. Falkiner, *Foundation of the Hospital of King Charles II*, 218. At a later date a large painting in oils of a scriptural scene was inserted in a heavily canopied reredos at Swords, Co. Dublin.

of east windows often had hovering doves surrounded by Glories or cherubim.[1]

From the third decade of the nineteenth century the gothic reredos tended to replace that of the post-Restoration type. About 1825 Bishop Jebb gave "a handsome screen in the gothic style" to replace the decayed corinthian altarpiece in Limerick Cathedral;[2] and the ideals of the Cambridge Camden Society, founded in 1839, were partly anticipated by the Primate, Lord John George Beresford, in his munificent restoration of Armagh Cathedral between 1834 and 1837. The reredos consists of a series of niches filled with statues of Christ and the Apostles, with two larger niches each side of the east window. This interesting reredos is now concealed from general view by a stone screen standing two bays westwards against which the present High Altar stands and forming an eastern Lady Chapel. About a decade later a gilded gothic reredos bearing a text was erected at Grange within the parish of Armagh. Bishop Mant, however, resisted the ecclesiology of the Cambridge Camden Society. He thought the Decalogue "a suitable decoration of an Irish Church", although without Irish canonical direction. He gives various instances in his diocese and quaintly adds that the Decalogue, Lord's Prayer, and Creed in St James' Chapel of Ease, near Hillsborough, "were not only the offering of female piety, but the handy-work of female ingenuity and industry".[3] We learn from the Fourth and Final Report of the Down and Connor Church Accommodation Society, adopted in 1843, that they were "executed in needlework, by Mrs Mant, wife of the Lord Bishop, and mother of the Incumbent".[4] By the middle of the nineteenth century the gothic reredos in wood or stone had become general. Two in the diocese of Dublin, in All Saints, Grangegorman, and St Mary's, Donnybrook, with sculptured crosses in the centre, were erected before the Victorian Canon 36 became law.

(h) "The Altar or Communion Table" and its Ornaments

A provincial Synod of Dublin in 1186 prohibited the celebration of the Eucharist "on a wooden Table according to the usage of Ireland", and enjoined the use of stone altars, or alternatively of altar stones either fixed in a wooden altar or placed upon it for the purpose. Many stone altars

---

[1] As at Hillsborough, Swords, Dublin Castle Chapel, Lismore Cathedral, and elsewhere.
[2] P. Fitzgerald and J. J. M'Gregor, *History...of Limerick* (1826), 545.
[3] *Church Architecture Considered*, 21.
[4] Op. cit. (Belfast, 1843), 22.

have remained undisturbed as in the Abbey Churches of Holy Cross and
Athassel in Co. Tipperary, and Bishop Pococke noticed many others in
his journey round Ireland in 1752.[1] According to local tradition the stone
altar of at least one parish church remained undisturbed until the Commonwealth; and when Dundalk Church was rebuilt in 1707 what is
believed to be the old stone *mensa* was placed upon an open oak frame,
but in 1923 set in the floor beneath the new wooden altar.[2]

No Irish Injunction or Canon before the Victorian code of the 1870s
prescribed that the altar should be "a moveable Table of wood". The
ninety-fourth Canon of 1634 fixed the "fair Table" at the east end of the
chancel or church leaving the material indefinite. Bishop Mant thought
that either wood or stone met the requirements of the law, "provided the
Table be in an appearance to its station and purpose".[3]

Most of the known stone altars date from the first half of the eighteenth
century. That at Stackallen, Co. Meath, was described *c.* 1733 as "a most
beautiful Table of polished marble".[4] Probably, like the one in St Olave's,
Waterford, it resembled many elaborate domestic tables of the period.
The latter was unnoticed by Dr Charles Smith in 1746 and Bishop
Pococke in 1752, who accurately describe the other furniture, no doubt
because it was then covered with a carpet as the Canon required. The
inscription on the long black marble *mensa*, set on a wooden frame with
cabriole legs, shows that it was already *in situ* when they visited the
Church.[5] The altar of Inch Church, Co. Down (1742), now standing at
the east end of a later chancel, was, like the font, of "a red species of
marble resembling Porphyry" and supported by four pillars of the same
material, only two feet high with bases eight inches wide and five deep.
The *mensa* is three feet four and a half inches by two feet five inches, and
three inches thick: it bears the inscription without date: "Ex Dono Ant.
Chichester".[6] The solid stone altar, erected in Armagh Cathedral at its
restoration of 1834–7, is divided by mouldings into panels with the
sacred monogram in the central. Stone altars, however, seem to have
been exceptional, and wooden altars, according to the ancient use of
Ireland, the general rule.

[1] *Tour in Ireland in 1752, passim.* He describes, for example, a stone altar in a
chapel of Ballintobber Abbey, Co. Mayo, adorned with "the figures of our Saviour
and the eleven Apostles in relief". Ibid., 100.

[2] J. B. Leslie, *Armagh Clergy and Parishes*, 287; *Supplement*, 107.

[3] *Church Architecture Considered*, 21.

[4] J. Healy, op. cit., II, 38. It has since been replaced by a table of wood.

[5] "Altare St Olivi Waterford Ao Dni 1733."

[6] "Some Account of the Parish Church of Inch, County and Diocese of Down,
1843" (Down and Conor Diocesan Library).

The few seventeenth-century altars of wood which remain in Ireland[1] suggest similar proportions to the many Caroline altars which can still be seen in England, where the High Altar in the wide choir of Lincoln Cathedral in 1668 was only seven feet long and three feet high, but it was three feet broad.[2] The Caroline altar was both shorter and wider than the Victorian, its dimensions being determined by practical considerations. It was sufficiently wide, often up to three feet, for the Celebrant standing at the north end, the normal Caroline position, to have within convenient reach the Service Book, often on a cushion, the paten, the chalice, and the flagon: it was at the same time sufficiently short, often little more than four feet, for him to be seen by the communicants on both sides of the chancel or church in the sacramental actions of breaking the Bread and of pouring the wine from the flagon into the chalice. Altar tables of the seventeenth and early eighteenth century were of oak and often carved.[3] Although hidden from the sight of man by a decent carpet the greatest care was taken of their construction as became the Table of the Lord.

The Caroline Canons of 1634 required the "fair Table" to "stand covered in time of Divine Service, with a carpet of silk, or other decent stuff, thought meet by the Ordinary of the place, (if any question be made of it;) and with a fair linnen cloath, at the time of the ministration, as becometh that Table." [4] They also distinguish between "a cup of Silver for the Celebration of the Holy Communion" [5] and what is undoubtedly the flagon, "a clean and sweet standing pot, or stoop of Pewter, if not of purer metal", in which "the wine for the Communion shall be brought to the Communion Table".[6] The *Irish Form of Consecration of Churches* (1666) contains a rubric[7] directing the solemn presentation and dedication of "the Carpet, the Communion cloth and Napkins, the Chalice, Paten,

---

[1] The original altar (1668) of Ballinderry was for a time in use in the modern church and a replica placed in the old. It now stands again in the old church together with its replica. Other seventeenth-century altars can be seen, for example, in Leighlin Cathedral and at Waringstown (1681). In 1634 Bramhall complained of Communion tables in the diocese of Down and Connor "ten yards long, where they sit and receive the Sacrament together like good fellows." *C.S.P. (Irel.) 1633–47*, 88.

[2] *Hierurgia Anglicana*, II, 250.

[3] Thomas Cooley's Specifications include "the fitting up of a Communion Table with Drawers, etc."

[4] Canon 94.

[5] Ibid. Not mentioned in the English code of 1603.

[6] Canon 95. About this time Bishop Richardson of Ardagh gave to Trinity College Chapel "a chalice, paten, and stoup of silver". The "stoup of silver" is a very beautiful flagon.

[7] Appendix I, 417–27.

and the other Vessels, Books, and Utensils for the Communion". The Deacon is directed to lay them orderly on the Communion table, excepting only the chalice and paten, "which two Priests shall (when the Table is covered) humbly on their knees lay upon it". As this rubric is reproduced in the Dublin diocesan Office of 1719 it may be taken to represent what Ornaments were required for the altar from the Restoration to at least the second decade of the eighteenth century. We shall examine them in the order in which they were presented.

First the Deacon receives from the Bishop the carpet which has been presented and places it over the altar so that it falls to the ground on three if not all four sides; for the Caroline frontal seldom covered the altar only on its western side. Sometimes the central part of the altarpiece was filled with the same material as the carpet. For example, William Fuller, who had been successively Dean of St Patrick's and Bishop of Limerick, a few months after his translation to Lincoln, asked Dean Sancroft to get him material for a new carpet to be made of alternate "panes" of cloth of gold and damask of sky blue, and to be extended two yards above the altar to "the cornish". The new carpet was for solemn days: the existing carpet of purple cloth "paned with crimson damask" at other times.[1] No doubt Bishop Fuller was influenced by what he had seen in Ireland. A similar arrangement survived at Christ Church Cathedral, Dublin, into the last century. In the central compartment of the post-Restoration reredos was "a panelling of crimson velvet, with the sacred monogram and a Glory in the midst", and a carpet of rich crimson velvet, with the same device, was placed on the altar "on all Sundays and festivals".[2] Before 1679 there was a carpet of "crimson taffety and purple mohair" in the Chapel of Dublin Castle,[3] and in the middle of the next century Bishop Pococke gave to Kilkenny Cathedral a carpet of purple velvet "richly embroidered with gold lace". There are many contemporary references to velvet, sometimes "Genoa velvet", or "velvet and gold", usually purple if the colour is mentioned.[4] Other material includes "sattin", "wool", "cloth", "broadcloth", "common Burge cloth", and "English shagg". The colour seems to have had no liturgical significance, though Bishop Fuller may have derived from Irish Restoration use his design for a richer carpet "for solemn days", and it would seem that a richer carpet was used at Christ Church in Dublin for "all Sundays and festivals". Likewise the

[1] *Hierurgia Anglicana*, II, 250.
[2] *Eccles.*, Oct. 1862, 252.
[3] Inventory of goods in Dublin Castle, March 1678/9. *H.M.C.*, *Ormonde* (N.S.), VII, 499.
[4] But green at Tipperary in 1788.

R

inventory of St Werburgh's, Dublin, of 1731 includes "one velvet Carpet for the Altar with gold lace and binding", "one green sattin Carpit", presumably for secondary use, and in a later hand, c. 1753, "one crimson sattin one".[1] John Jebb, in 1843, speaks of the custom of covering the altar "with stuff of a purple or grey colour" in Lent "and black during Passion Week" as continuing in some places.[2] At other times it would appear that purple and green were the more general colours before, and crimson or red after, 1800.[3] As only vegetable dyes were used in our period, the colours would be softer and more beautiful than the modern ecclesiastical colours. The carpet was regarded as a necessary provision as long as the Canons of 1634 remained law, the few exceptions being noticed with disapprobation in Visitation and rural deans' returns.[4]

Having covered the altar with the carpet, the Deacon receives from the Bishop "the Communion cloth" and lays it over the carpet "upon"[5] the Communion table. Though St Iberius, Wexford, had in 1669 "one linen cloth of Holland for covering the Communion table containing eight yards", the Communion cloth from the Restoration was usually equal in width to the table, but longer and extended over the edges at the north and south. Such is the beautifully made Communion cloth still in use, ninety-two inches by twenty-seven, inscribed in cross-stitch: "Tipperary Church 1786".

Having placed the carpet over the altar and the Communion cloth "upon it", the Deacon next places the napkins, which would at least include the smaller "fair linen cloth" for covering "what remaineth of the consecrated Elements". The cloth used for this purpose before the rubrical direction of 1662 was variously called: "the Corporall or nap-

---

[1] Vestry Book.   [2] *Choral Service*, 214.

[3] *Green* was used at St John's, Dublin, in 1621; St Audoen's, Dublin 1652; St Catherine's, Dublin 1657; St Werburgh's, Dublin 1731, Rosbercon 1731, St Kevin's, Dublin 1740, Killaloe Cathedral 1742, Drummully 1772, Tipperary 1788, Emly 1780, Bohoe 1824; *Purple* in Bishop Wilde's Chapel at Faughan in 1665, Cloyne Cathedral 1686, Kilkenny Cathedral c. 1755, Galoon 1775, Ballymoden 1849; *Blue* in Killala Cathedral 1724, Monea 1824; *Crimson or red*, St Werburgh's, Dublin (secondary use), between 1731 and 1753, Christ Church, Dublin c. 1800, Rathaspeck 1809, St Andrew's, Dublin c. 1850, Hillsborough 1844.

[4] The Victorian Canon 34 requires a "decent covering", but this can hardly mean the utility covering which extends only a few inches downwards from the top of the altar, for which there is much Roman, but no Caroline precedent.

[5] The fourth rubric before the Communion Office directs the fair linen cloth to be placed "upon" the table, that is, upon the top and not falling like the carpet to the ground in front. There is no suggestion that the Communion cloth should replace the carpet for the Communion Service.

kin" in the consecration of Abbey Dore in 1634–5, "a fair linen cloth or corporal" in the Scottish Rite of 1637, "I Diaper napkin for a Corporall" in the list of gifts provided by Jeremy Taylor at Uppingham in 1639. In Caroline usage the term "Corporal" seems to have been used exclusively for the cloth covering the consecrated Elements. No doubt the Anglican practice of consecrating the Eucharistic bread on the paten,[1] which became fixed in 1662, led to the disappearance until recent times of the "corporas", the square of cloth placed under the chalice, of the 1549 Rite, where by the wording of the rubric it might be taken as an alternative to the paten. "Napkins" are frequently mentioned in church accounts from the Restoration.

When the table is covered, two Priests receive from the Bishop the chalice and the paten which they then "humbly upon their knees lay upon it". The ninety-fourth Canon in prescribing "a Cup of Silver" without mentioning a paten no doubt intended "a Silver Cup with Cover" so often mentioned in church inventories, the cover acting as a paten from the Offertory onwards. Thus the paten at Birr is inscribed "the Cover of the Communion Cup of the Parishe of Parsontowne in the Kings Countie, Anno Domini 1636".[2] More often before the Commonwealth the cover bore no inscription, nor was it mentioned in the inscription on the cup to which it belonged.[3] Many fine examples of Communion plate given at the Restoration remain: the fine chalice and paten at Cashel Cathedral in memory of Thomas Fulwar, Archbishop (1661–7); the chalice and paten of beaten silver given to Tuam Cathedral by Samuel Pullein, Archbishop (1661–7); the massive chalice and salver given to Hillsborough Church at its consecration in 1663, engraved with the sacred monogram, surmounted with a cross, and with rails beneath the letters, surrounded by rays; or the chalice and paten of pure silver given to Dromore Cathedral by the widow of Jeremy Taylor. In 1682 the old Communion plate of Christ Church Cathedral, Dublin, was sold to Bishop Ottway of Ossory for £116 13s. 4d. and new plate bought in London to the value of £369 19s. 10d.[4] During the next century costly gifts of

[1] For the modern Irish use of "the north Napkin" for the chalice and paten to stand on at the Consecration, and "the central Napkin" for the rest of the Service, see Claude Chavasse, *Public Worship according to the Use of the Church of Ireland*, 48.

[2] R. Wyse Jackson, "Old Church Silver of East Killaloe" (*North Munster Antiquarian Journal*, 1940), 66.

[3] As, for example: "This Cvp was given to the Chvrch of St Mary Shandon without Corke the yeare 1627...", or "Calix Hic Ecclesiae Sti. Collemanni, Clon: dicat:" *c.* 1640. C. A. Webster, *The Church Plate of the Diocese of Cork, Cloyne and Ross*, 23, 79.

[4] Henry Cotton, *Fasti Ecclesiae Hibernicae*, II, 44n.

Communion silver continued to be made and inscribed with scriptural texts.[1]

The chalice and paten being placed upon the altar by two Priests, the Deacon receives from the Bishop in turn "the other Vessels, Books, and Utensils for the Communion" and lays them "orderly upon the Communion Table". The "other Vessels" would include the flagon, the "clean and sweet standing pot, or stoop of Pewter, if not of purer metal", required by Canon 95, and also "the decent bason" required by the rubric. The Books are clearly in addition to the Bible and two Books of Common Prayer required by the Canon. Although the term "Utensil" is fairly comprehensive, it cannot here include additional chalices and patens which were to be handled by two Priests, and not by the Deacon; and it can hardly include additional flagons and alms basons, which are better covered by "other Vessels for the Communion". Metal pomes for warming the celebrant's hands, like Bishop Ken's pome preserved at Frome-Selwood, were probably exceptional, and the modern metal book-stand unknown. The use of a silver knife for cutting the Sacramental Bread lingered on into the nineteenth century,[2] but this alone cannot exhaust the meaning of "other Utensils". Within a short time of the publication of the consecration form in 1666 we find the term "utensils" used to include candlesticks. Thus William Fuller, who had been Bishop of Limerick in 1666, told Dean Sancroft on his translation to Lincoln that he had found "in the Inventory of Church utensils, before they were imbezil'd, a paire of copper candlesticks gilt",[3] and John Parry, Bishop of Ossory, from 1672, mentions in his will of 1677 "a pair of large Silver Candlesticks gilt, and other Utensils for the Use of the Altar".[4] Of the Bishops in 1666 Primate Margetson and two others are known to have given candlesticks for the use of the altar: it is also known that candlesticks were in Caroline times sometimes presented and dedicated with the Communion plate. Thus in Bishop Andrewes' Order of Consecrating Plate for the Altar, used at Worcester Cathedral before the Commonwealth, first "the Presenter" gives the Bishop the paten, then the chalice,

---

[1] For example: "Calicem salutis accipiam, et Nomen Domini Invocabo. Ecclesiae cathedralis S. Finbarry, Corke. Ex Dono T.B. 1638." "Deo Sacratum et Ecclesiae Cathedrali Sancti Finbarry, Corcag, 1672. Hic est panis, qui de coelo descendit. Qui manducat hunc panem vivet in aeternam." Two patens given in 1700 to St Catherine's, Dublin, are inscribed with John 6. 50 and 51 respectively. A large chalice given to St Mary's, Shandon, in 1715 bears the inscription: "Quid retribuam Domino?"

[2] As at Athlone, Abington, and St Peter's, Dublin.

[3] *Hierurgia Anglicana*, II, 251.

[4] Sir James Ware (ed. Harris), *Irish Bishops*, 428.

then the flagons, then the candlesticks, and then the censer.[1] Likewise the intention of the 1666 form seems to be that the gifts should be presented in this order: first the carpet, the Communion cloth, and napkins, and when the table is covered, the chalice and paten, the flagons and alms bason, the books for the altar, and then the candlesticks. In any case, Irish Caroline Archbishops and Bishops gave candlesticks for the use of Irish altars, and they must be included in our picture of Irish Caroline churches.

The Irish and English Canons make it clear that the flagon should be "of Pewter, if not of purer metal".[2] Many country churches in Ireland had only pewter flagons, though in the course of time silver flagons were often given to them. Larger churches and cathedrals usually had massive flagons of silver, often belonging to a set of Communion plate, as the two large flagons (each 43 oz. 18 dwts.) given to St Fin Barre's Cathedral, Cork, in 1638. They were designed to stand on the altar with the Communion plate, and to be used for the Caroline Sacramental Actions of pouring the wine into the chalice. Inscriptions on two flagons at St Catherine's, Dublin, of 1715 and 1717 make it clear that they were "for ye use of ye Altar", on a flagon at Dromore Cathedral of 1703 that it was for use at the Consecration,[3] and on one at Loughilly of 1811 that Communion plate was still dedicated separately at the consecration of a church early in the nineteenth century.[4]

The alms bason varied in material, size, and design. Sometimes it was of pewter,[5] but more often it was of silver and richly engraven. Often it stood upright in the centre of the east side of the altar. "The frame for ye Bason", for example, is mentioned in the Vestry Book of St Catherine's, Dublin, in 1661. Sometimes it was designed to be part of the Communion set:[6] sometimes to match the candlesticks between which it stood out of "Communion-time".[7] In Anglican usage, until modern times the alms bason was connected with the Eucharist, and not with Morning and Evening Prayer, and for this reason it was sometimes

---

[1] Given in *Anglicanism*, ed. P. E. More and F. L. Cross, 546 seq.

[2] The cruet of glass is modern.

[3] "Poculum Benedictionis cui Benedicimus Nonne communio sanguinis Christi est?"

[4] "...dat dicat consecrat Reverendissimus Pater Gulielmus Archiepiscopis Armachensis A.D. MDCCCXI. Aedibus sacris nuper restauratis."

[5] St Michan's, Dublin, has a pewter alms basin of 1676, and a silver one of 1724.

[6] That of St Columba's Swords, has, like the paten, a richly embossed border with grapes and sheaves of wheat.

[7] Christ Church Cathedral, Dublin, 1778 in the same classical style as the candle-sticks of 1778.

engraven with a representation of the Breaking of Bread at Emmaus or of the Last Supper.[1]

In ordering "Books for the Communion", in addition to the books required by the Canon, the Irish consecration form of 1666 and the Dublin diocesan Office of 1719 give sanction to a well established Caroline provision. Before the Commonwealth a richly bound Prayer Book and Bible often stood upright at the back of the altar, as at Peterborough; and among the gifts of Jeremy Taylor provided for the altar of Uppingham Church and the Bishop of Peterborough dedicated in 1639 were "1 Bible. 1 Booke of common prayer". Later in the century Archbishop Lamplugh of York (1688–91) gave to the Minster "three large Common Prayer-books and a Bible for the use of the Altar".[2] Inserted on the blank page at the end of one of the extant copies of the 1666 form[3] are two lists of "Things to be prepared for the Consecration" with page references to the rubrics connected with them. The first list has been erased: the second in darker ink bears the date 17 December 1685. Both lists include "C.P.B." and "bible" with reference to the rubric in question. The Bible would be needed for the Communion which followed as the text of the Epistle and Gospel is not given in the printed form of 1666;[4] nor is the text of those appointed for 23 October given in the Irish Prayer Books of 1666 and 1680. Church accounts from the Restoration mention books for the altar, and rural deans' reports from the late eighteenth century notice their absence.[5] Sometimes they rest on cushions[6] at either end of the altar: sometimes they stood upright at the back. In 1731 St Werburgh's, Dublin, had "two long cushions for the Altar" as well as two large Prayer Books "for the Altar".[7] Books stood upright at the back of the western altar of Armagh Cathedral before 1834, and more recently of the altar in the Lady Chapel of St Patrick's Cathedral, Dublin.[8]

[1] Holy Trinity, Cork, 1741; Christ Church Cathedral, Dublin, 1698 and 1778.
[2] *Hierurgia Anglicana*, I, 109; cf. 74; 103 seqq.
[3] T.C.D., P. hh. 7.5.   [4] Appendix I, 650–2.
[5] Archdeacon Hewetson bequeathed a Prayer Book to Donegal Church "for the Service of the Altar". Before 1843 there were richly bound "Altar Books" in Waterford Cathedral which Bishop Daly, a Low Churchman, replaced with "Communion Books". *Memoir of Robert Daly*.
[6] There were cushions on the altar of Bishop Wilde's Chapel at Faughan in 1665, in Killala Cathedral in 1760, in Waringstown in 1828, and one was "required" (R.D. Report) for Clough Chapel-of-Ease in 1845.
[7] Vestry Book. The modern book-stand has Roman, but not Caroline precedent.
[8] Picture in Armagh vestry: plate in John Harvey's *Dublin* (Batsford) opp. p. 102. Books stood upright on the altar of St Andrew's, Dublin, before 1860 (Thomas Cunningham's drawing in the vestry), and the *Guardian* (11 April 1866) reported that the altar of St Bride's, Dublin, "had upon it three Books resting against the east

Candlesticks do not appear to have been general in Ireland before the Reformation. A monumental brass in St Patrick's Cathedral, Dublin, for example, shows Dean Fyche (d. 1537) kneeling near an altar covered with a carpet but without any Ornaments standing on it at all. Waterford Cathedral had up to 1577 two pairs of silver-gilt candlesticks, one pair weighing 105 ounces, and the other fourscore,[1] and up to 1651 "two great standing Candlesticks above a man's height".[2] After the Restoration Primate Margetson, who had been Archbishop of Dublin (1661–3), presented a pair of silver candlesticks to St Michan's, Dublin. Upon his translation from Limerick to Lincoln Bishop Fuller found in the Cathedral there "a pitiful paire of ordinary brasse candlesticks" which he was "asham'd to see" and could "indure no longer", and therefore had to give them "a paire of faire Candlesticks".[3] In 1677 Bishop John Parry of Ossory, formerly Dean of Christ Church, Dublin, "bequeathed to the Dean and Chapter thereof 200 l to buy a pair of large Silver Candlesticks gilt, and other Utensils for the Use of the Altar", and to Kilkenny Cathedral £100 to buy plate "as like as possible to the Plate of Christ Church, Dublin".[4] And John Parker, Archbishop of Dublin (1679–82) bequeathed £40 to Christ Church "to buy a pair of Silver Candlesticks for the Communion Table".[5] Not only were candlesticks presented by Irish Restoration Bishops, but they continued to be provided into the nineteenth century. In 1682 the Dean and Chapter of Christ Church bought two candlesticks costing £116 12s. 9d.;[6] in 1698 the same cathedral was further enriched by the magnificent plate presented by William III which included two silver-gilt candlesticks,[7] and further still in 1778 by another set of plate including two silver-gilt candlesticks of classical design, thirty inches in height, each bearing on the three sides of the base a Glory with cherubim above.[8] In 1693 Pierce Butler, fourth Viscount Ikerron, gave to Trinity College, Dublin, a large pair of silver candlesticks "for the use of the Altar",[9] and in 1745 Aland Mason Esq. presented two silver candlesticks to Waterford Cathedral.[10] In 1685 two candlesticks were bought "for the

wall, and having on their backs crosses, and crimson markers also ornamented with crosses".   [1] R. H. Ryland, op. cit., 135.   [2] Ibid., 139.
[3] *Hierurgia Anglicana*, II, 251.   [4] Sir James Ware, op. cit., 428.
[5] Ibid., 358.   [6] H. Cotton, op. cit., II, 44n.
[7] With tripod bases, 2 ft. 7½ in. high. E. H. Lewis-Crosby, *Christ Church Cathedral, Dublin*, 23.
[8] One of them was on view, with the alms basin of same design, at the exhibition of church silver in Lincoln, 1951.
[9] *The Book of Trinity College Dublin (1591–1891)*, 272.
[10] I am indebted to Dr J. Wyse Jackson for this information extracted from the Vigors MSS. on church silver (R.C.B.L.).

Altar" of St John's, Dublin; in 1731[1] "two large Candlesticks for the Altar" are mentioned in the inventory of St Werburgh's, Dublin;[2] and the two eighteenth-century candlesticks of gilded wood, now in the Lady Chapel of Christ Church, Dublin, were formerly in St Audoen's, Dublin. There were also candlesticks for the altar of Loughur Chapel, Co. Tipperary, in the later seventeenth century,[3] of Lord Mornington's Chapel at Dangan, Co. Meath, in the later eighteenth,[4] and of Dublin Castle Chapel (1814) for several decades of the nineteenth.

In 1865 John Jebb recollected "candlesticks with large tapers (though unlit) being always placed on the Altar of Christ Church, in Dublin, on days when the Holy Communion was administered and when light was required at evening service. But they were lit on winter afternoons at St Patrick's though now for many years removed. There have been always in the Chapel of Trinity College two silver candlesticks with unbleached tapers (lit at evening service only) placed upon the Altar from Christmas Day to Epiphany; but there were no candles at other times".[5] Here we see the survival of older Anglican practice: in one case the candlesticks with unlighted candles are placed upon the altar for the Eucharist as part of the Communion plate; in another they are placed there with lighted candles in them when Evening Prayer is performed by candlelight; in another candles are lighted to mark the Christmas festival. The removal of the candlesticks in St Patrick's, on the other hand, was in line with the prevailing reaction in Ireland to ceremonial developments in England. For in 1851 the candlesticks in Waterford Cathedral were exchanged by the Dean and Chapter for a flagon,[6] those given by Primate Margetson after the Restoration to St Michan's were sold to Lord Iveagh,[7] and on 20 January 1862 the Bishop of Limerick was formally thanked for removing the "Symbols of Puseyism" out of the Cathedral on the preceding Christmas Day.[8] The Victorian Canon 35 prohibits the use of lighted candles on the Communion table "except when they be necessary for the purpose of giving light". It does not prohibit the presence of candlesticks or of candles on the altar, but restricts the lighting of them according to older Anglican usage. They had probably been

---

[1] Vestry Book.   [2] Vestry Book.
[3] St J. D. Seymour, *Church Plate and Parish Records (Diocese of Cashel and Emly)*, 16.
[4] John Jebb, *Choral Service*, 153.
[5] *The Ritual Law and Custom of the Church Universal*, 41 n.H.; cf. *Eccles*. (CXLII), 252.
[6] Vigors MSS.; see above, p. 247.
[7] J. B. Leslie, *Armagh Clergy and Parishes*, 6.
[8] M. Lenihan, *Limerick* (1866), 523n. Possibly the candlesticks, typical of the post-Tractarian period, which I saw in the Chapter Room in 1949.

absolutely necessary in the 1730s when some Dublin churches had early Sacraments at 6 on winter mornings,[1] as necessary as candles in the reading desk for early Morning Prayer. In the inventory of St Werburgh's Dublin, of 1731 "candlesticks for the Altar" are not included with the Communion plate, but with the branches and candlesticks for the pews, pulpit, and desks as part of the necessary lighting system of the church. By 1807, however, the time of early Sacraments in Dublin had generally been changed to 8 in winter,[2] though it was at 7 in four city churches of Cork in 1824.[3] Modern methods of lighting would further restrict the necessity of candles. The silver candlesticks, for example, in the vestry of Killaloe Cathedral remained on the Altar until the installation of electricity in the present century.

Thus with the help of the elaborate rubric in the 1666 consecration form, which we must next examine more fully, have we been able to form a picture of an Irish altar in the late Caroline period. The Communion table stands against panelling or a reredos in the post-Restoration style. It is covered with a carpet of green or purple, perhaps paned with gold, falling loosely on three sides to the ground. On Sacrament days a Communion cloth is placed upon it as well. At other times two books for the Communion rest on cushions at either end or stand upright at the back between the alms bason on a frame in the centre and the candlesticks on the outside. A Communion table furnished in this way is perfectly consistent with the Irish Caroline and Victorian Canons, and has a marked dignity, simplicity, and symmetry. There is no Irish Caroline precedent for the altar cross,[4] the metal book-stand,[5] or flower vases,[6] and it does not come within the scope of this book to discuss them. Immediately

---

[1] In 1728 St James', St Audoen's, St Andrew's had a monthly, St Catherine's a twice-monthly, St Mary's, St Michael's, St Michan's a quarterly early Sacrament at 6 a.m., and St Ann's a twice-monthly Sacrament at 7 a.m. Watson's *Almanack*.

[2] Ibid.   [3] Cork *Almanack* for 1824.

[4] The altar Cross was forbidden by the Victorian Canon 36 before it had found its way to Ireland and at a time when it was only still finding its way in England. The Canon was designed to preserve the *status quo* and check innovation. It is extremely unjust, therefore, to suggest that it was intended to slight the scriptural truth of which the forbidden Ornament is a symbol. No more theological significance can be attached to the absence of the altar cross in Ireland than to its presence in some Unitarian chapels in England.

[5] The modern book-rest, borrowed from Rome, is often a memorial gift, which cannot be denied to have practical value. Unlike the cushion it cannot be left at the north end when not in use without detracting from the symmetry and simplicity of the Communion table.

[6] Although the use of flower vases on the Communion table is modern, the flowers in them may help to hide an ugly Victorian reredos, but the greatest care should be taken that the vases and the flowers in them be symmetrically arranged.

after the reproduction of the elaborate rubric of 1666 in the Dublin diocesan Office of 1719 is Archbishop King's prayer for the dedication of the gifts for the "Sanctuary", which gives liturgical expression to the spirit of the Anglican *via media*. In it petition is made "that nothing necessary or decent for the Celebration of thy publick Worship may ever be wanting, or misapplied to prophane or unlawful uses, or be made an Instrument of Superstition or Idolatry...that we thy Servants avoiding the Extreams of Sordidness and vain Pomp, may, without destroying the Beauty of Holiness, evermore worship thee in Spirit and in Truth."

5

A CAROLINE FORM AND ORDER OF CONSECRATION OF CHURCHES

I. THE 1666 IRISH CONSECRATION FORM

THE TENDENCY for the Church of Ireland to move on parallel, but not identical, lines with the Church of England is well illustrated by the steps taken in both Churches at the Restoration to provide a settled Form and Order of Consecration of Churches. In England the Upper House of the Convocation of Canterbury, according to an earlier design of 1640, commissioned Bishop Cosin on 22 March 1661/2 to prepare such a form, which was presented by him on 20 June 1662, referred to a sub-committee of four Bishops, described by Archbishop Sheldon in 1666 as containing "something amiss" and "for the present laid aside",[1] used by Bishop Cosin in his diocese in 1668, and left in manuscript for two centuries. In Ireland, on the other hand, we have complete silence about a similar design or commission, but in 1666 we have, not a disputed draft form, but what was undoubtedly the first Anglican consecration form to be printed for general use and with every appearance of high ecclesiastical sanction. It was:

A | Form | of | Consecration or Dedication | of | Churches | and | Chappels, | Together with | What may be used in the Restauration | of | Ruin ed Churches, | and | Expiation of Churches | Desecrated or Prophan'd | Dublin, Printed by John Crook, Printer to the Kings | Most Excellent Majesty, and are to be sold | by Sam. Dancer in Castle-street, 1666

On the back of the title-page is this licence:

Imprimatur
Haec formula Consecrationis &c.
Ja. Armachanus. Mich. Dublin. Can.[2]

The three offices have their separate headings at pp. 1, 27, and 33,[3] while the Instrumentum follows at p. 37. The last page is blank. Copies of this

---

[1] Letter, Archbishop Sheldon to the Bishop of Oxford, 15 March 1665–6 (B.L. MS. Add. C. 308). Sheldon expresses some hope of reviving the matter when the Bishops next meet at Parliament.
[2] James Margetson, Archbishop of Armagh and Primate of All Ireland (1663–78), and Michael Boyle, Archbishop of Dublin (1663–78) and Lord Chancellor of Ireland (from 1665).   [3] Text in Appendix 1, lines 1, 662, 731.

251

small quarto edition of 1666 (T.P.+40 pp.) are very scarce.[1] The printer seems to have corrected the heading to the first office in two stages after the first impression had been made and bound together. At first a corrected version of the leaf containing pp. 1 and 2 (without the conjugate) was inserted immediately after the first:[2] at a later stage the corrected version became the final replacement of the first and the conjugate of the leaf containing pp. 7 and 8.[3] In the first version the heading on p. 1 is *A | Form | of | Consecration, | or, | Dedication of Churches and Chappels*, The comma, instead of a full-stop, after "Chappels" may suggest the expectation of fuller instructions depending on fuller sanction; for in the corrected version on p. 1 (signature italic *A*) there is added: *ac- | cording to the use of the Church of Ireland*.

With the corrected heading as title, the form of 1666, with its two dependent offices, was annexed to some of the larger Prayer Books printed in Ireland from 1700 to 1757.[4] By the nineteenth century its Caroline origin had been lost sight of and it was regarded as appearing for the first time in the reign of William III until Dr William Reeves, then Dean of Armagh, investigated the history of this "admirable performance" and communicated the result in a letter to the *Irish Church Society's Journal*.[5]

Dr Reeves found "no entry upon the subject in the meagre records of the Irish Convocation" [6] of 1661–6; nor has there since appeared any con-

---

[1] In addition to copies referred to, Dr Reeves, in 1876, mentions one in Lough Fea Library; J. B. Garstin, in 1893, one in Derry Cathedral Library and one he bought for 10s.; and I am grateful to Canon J. Purser Shortt, of Dublin, for drawing my attention to a third, not catalogued with the other two, in the Library of Trinity College, Dublin, and to the Librarian of Magdalen College, Oxford, for giving me particulars of another.

[2] The reproduced leaf is contained in these copies: Trinity College, Dublin (P. hh. 7. 5); National Library of Ireland (P. 514. 7); Marsh Library, Dublin (T. 3. 4. 9); Magdalen College, Oxford. The following have only the first version, though the inserted leaf may have fallen out: Cashel Loan Collection at the R.C.B., Dublin (VII 28); T.C.D. (P. dd. 24).

[3] The copy at Cambridge University Library (Hib. 7. 666) contains only the corrected version (signature *A*) now the conjugate of pp. 7 and 8.

[4] Dr Reeves mentions reprints of the 1666 form in the quartos of 1700, 1716, 1736, 1742, and in Grierson's folios of 1721, 1739, and one of the two of 1750 (*Hierurgia Anglicana*, III, 189). Canon J. Purser Shortt has drawn my attention to this reprint in two quartos of 1757. I have since seen it in two other quartos of 1757 (C.U.L. and Derry Cathedral Library) and in two of 1751 (C.U.L. and Waringstown Church). *An Essay on Church Consecration* (1777) by "Z", attacking the form, refers the reader to Grierson's folio of 1760. The form was also reprinted from the Irish folio Prayer Book in four editions (1858–79) of the *Directorium Anglicanum*; again in 1893 by the S.P.C.K., together with a reprint of Dr Reeves' letter to the *Irish Church Society's Journal*; and, with this letter as Introduction, in the 1904 edition of *Hierurgia Anglicana*, III, 194–225.   [5] The letter, dated 20 Nov. 1876, was published in 1877.

[6] *Hierurgia Anglicana*, III, 188.

temporary evidence throwing light upon the original publication of 1666.[1] The silence of the records undoubtedly led the next Irish Convocation of 1703–11—it had not met in William III's reign—to believe that the form had been published in 1666 with as little authority as it had been annexed to the quarto Prayer Book of 1700.[2] The only survivors of the Caroline Convocation were Bishop Sheridan, the Non-juror who had been deprived, and Archbishop Vesey of Tuam, who at 71 may not have had a clear memory of 1661 to 1666. Archbishop King of Dublin had been a schoolboy in 1666, and he expressed the general opinion in a letter of 1715 to the Bishop of Carlisle: "We have a form in Ireland, but with no authority, and I altered it to my mind, which I reckoned myself as a bishop empowered to do, because the canon requiring bishops to consecrate churches, but prescribing no form, leaves the form to their discretion." [3] The views of the Irish Convocation of 1703–11 and of Archbishop King led Dr Reeves to believe at first that the form of 1666 wanted full synodical assent.

If, however, the forty-third Irish Canon of 1634 was sufficient authority for Archbishop King to use whatever form he liked in 1715, it may also be regarded as giving the Irish Bishops at the Restoration sufficient authority to design, agree upon, and publish a settled form for an exclusively episcopal function, without referring the matter to the Lower House, even if Archbishop King's copy, through which the records of the Convocation of 1661–6 are now known, was sufficiently complete to prove that the published form lacked full synodical assent. Archbishop

[1] In 1893, J. B. Garstin, in a tantalizing note inserted in the Archbishop Marsh Library copy of the form, claims to have "a large collection illustrative of this and other kindred forms". (T. 3. 4. 9. No. 3.) Although the MS. Carte in the Bodleian Library contain a wealth of material relating to the Church of Ireland at the Restoration, there is no entry in the MS. Calendar in many volumes to the form in question, only to the new office for 23 Oct. Nor is there any reference in the H.M.C. Reports on the Ormonde manuscripts in Kilkenny Castle. In 1949 the Garstin papers were still concealed in tin boxes both sides of the Border, and the present writer has failed to get any information about those preserved in Northern Ireland.

[2] By this time the Lower Houses of Anglican Convocations had become very constitutionally minded and expected a large hand in the drawing up of liturgical forms. In England the consecration form had been commissioned and presented in the Upper House only in 1662: the Lower House had much to say in the forms of 1712 and 1715. In Ireland the Lower House complained of the lack of an "unexceptionable authentick form for consecration of Churches", while the Upper House in 1709 assumed the want of "any Settled or approved form" for the purpose. The form of 1666 had been annexed to the 1700 Prayer Book by the King's Printer, while Primate Michael Boyle, who had given his Imprimatur to the form of 1666, was still alive.

[3] *Hierurgia Anglicana*, III, 191.

King's copy, however, shows many signs of being incomplete;[1] and the similar silence about other matters of importance, which independent contemporary evidence connects with this Convocation, confirms the impression that the original records, if complete in the first place, have been imperfectly copied.

For there is likewise no entry in "the meagre records of the Irish Convocation" about Bishop Taylor's *Discourse of Confirmation*, undertaken at the entreaty of those who had power to command him[2] and "Publish'd by Order of Convocation" in 1663.[3] Nor is there any entry about the long discussion in the Upper House which led to its commissioning Bishop Taylor to write his *Dissuasive from Popery*.[4] There is no record of the fact, stated in the preamble to the Irish Act of Uniformity of 1666, that the revised English Prayer Book had been recommended to the Irish Convocation. And although there is an entry, under 18 September 1662, of a petition of the Lower House for the compilation of a new office for 23 October, and another, under 11 November 1662, of a decision to have such an office in the "Transmiss", there is complete silence about the preparation, presentation, and agreement upon this office. It is from Primate Margetson's note, sent with an offprint of it to Lord Arlington in August 1666 for Royal Warrant, that we learn that the new office for 23 October "was agreed upon by the two houses of Convocation".[5] The

---

[1] T.C.D., MS. N. 2. 3. This manuscript is in several hands including one in which the records of the 1639–40 Convocation begin immediately after the abrupt adjournment of the later Convocation from 22 March 1665/6 to 29 March 1666 (at the foot of the preceding page). There are several gaps. For example, under 24 July 1661, a blank space, 3 in. deep, is left after "in haec verba sequitur"; another blank space, 3½ in. deep, occurs instead of an entry under 26 Feb. 1662/3, to which Convocation had been continued from 19 Feb. There are also several breaks in the forms of adjournment. This copy may have been made in connection with a committee of the Lower House appointed on 17 Feb. 1703/4 to inspect the Journals of the Convocations of 1661–6 and 1639–40, which from its observations was more interested in constitutional points, forms of adjournment etc. than in the real work of the Church. The later sessions particularly have every appearance of being hurried over, while the records of 1630–40 appear to be added almost as an afterthought.

[2] *Works*, v, 609.

[3] T.P. of Dublin edition of 1663, but not of London editions: cf. T.C.D., MS. 1062, p. 70.

[4] *Works*, VI, 171 seqq.

[5] P.R.O. (London): S.P. 63–321, 139. The Royal Licence on the verso of the last page of this office in the 1680 Prayer Book is dated 15 Aug. 1666. The existence of an offprint before the granting of the Royal Licence may suggest a parallel with the printing of the consecration form before the granting of sufficient sanction to add the words, "according to the use of the Church of *Ireland*". One of the two copies of the Prayer Book (Dublin, 1666) in the R.C.B. Library, Dublin (W. Cat., 44), contains no Royal Warrant: the other (W. Cat., 45) one covering only the English Services for 5 Nov., 30 Jan., and 29 May, but not the Irish Service for 23 Oct.

similar silence about the consecration form cannot, therefore, be taken to rule out the strong probability that it was prepared at the request of the House of Bishops by one of their Order, presented by him, considered, and finally, like the new office for 23 October, "agreed upon by the two houses of Convocation".

Dr Reeves, in 1890, gave his latest opinion that "the Forms in question were presented to and received some Convocational acceptance".[1] The following considerations would further strengthen this view:—the apparent harmony between the two Houses of 1661–6, Primate Marget-son, the President of the Upper House from 1665, having been Prolocutor of the Lower in 1639–40; and the readiness with which the Upper House heeded the petition of the Lower for an office for 23 October; the joint Imprimatur of the Primate of All Ireland and Dr Michael Boyle, Arch-bishop of Dublin and (from July 1665) Lord Chancellor of Ireland, the only two Archbishops present at the closing sessions of the Convocation in 1665–6; the publication of these forms by the King's Printer in con-junction with Samuel Dancer, who has been called "the recognized Publisher to the Irish Convocation",[2] which on 22 February 1665–6 had sent him to England to get the necessary Royal authority for the Prayer Book, which together with the King's Printer he brought out in 1666, as he had Bishop Taylor's *Discourse of Confirmation* "by Order of Convoca-tion" in 1663, the Canons of 1634 in 1664, and also many Proclamations and Government Orders;[3] the extreme improbability that the King's Printer and the recognized Publisher to the Irish Convocation would together bring out liturgical offices claiming to be "according to the use of the Church of *Ireland*" unless they had received the fullest measure of ecclesiastical sanction required by Caroline standards; the trouble taken by the King's Printer in adding this claim to the heading of the first office, by the insertion of a corrected leaf after the first impression had been made and bound, further suggesting that this publication was intended as a supplement to the Prayer Book of 1666 which bore on its title-page the very words added to the heading, "according to the use of the Church of *Ireland*".[4]

[1] *Hierurgia Anglicana*, III, 193.
[2] J. B. Garstin, *The Book of Common Prayer*, 16.
[3] As for example, P.R.O. S.P. 63–322, 49, 56, 152; 323, 41.
[4] There was no available space for these additional words on the T.P. of the three offices which are there given a comprehensive title.

II. STRUCTURE AND SOURCES

The English and Irish compilers who drew up forms of consecration of churches at the Restoration would naturally be influenced to some extent by the use of their churches before the Commonwealth. Although Irish Bishops are known to have consecrated churches long before the forty-third Canon of 1634 directed the practice,[1] no Anglican form of Irish origin before 1666 has yet come to light. We are told, however, by his chaplain that Primate Ussher used Bishop Andrewes' form "with little variation" in his consecration of a chapel near Drogheda, there being no form appointed for the purpose "in our Constitutions".[2] Bishop Andrewes' form of 1620 was also being increasingly adopted by English Bishops in preference to the simpler form used by Bishop Barlow in 1607. At the Restoration Bishop Andrewes' form was followed very closely by Bishop Cosin in the draft he presented to the English Upper House in 1662; but it was only used as one quarry among others by the Irish compiler of the 1666 form. A brief examination of Bishop Andrewes' form will throw considerable light upon the English and Irish Restoration rites.

Bishop Andrewes takes over most of Bishop Barlow's material and refashions it, so that it would be almost impossible to detect any independent following of the simpler form by the Restoration compilers The Bishop makes a solemn entry into the new church, which the Founder has surrendered, reciting Psalm 24 and part of 122. Kneeling down he says a long consecratory prayer beginning with 1 Chronicles 29. 10 seqq. The Bishop then goes in turn to the font, pulpit, reading-desk, Holy table, and the places of marriage and burial, saying a short prayer of dedication at each. He afterwards says a series of short prayers for the Church and worshippers. Then follow the services of the day, with special Psalms, Lessons, Epistle, Gospel, and with special prayers adapted from Barlow, after the third Collect, in the Litany, and at the Communion. The Bishop says a second long consecratory prayer, taken from 2 Chronicles 6 and 7, after the Nicene Creed. The most distinctive features

---

[1] George Downame, Bishop of Derry (1617–33), consecrated churches before the Regal Visitation of 1622 (J. B. Leslie, *Derry Clergy and Parishes*, 131, 281). Richard Boyle, Bishop of Cork (1620–38), is said to have consecrated more new churches "than any other Bishop of that age" (Sir James Ware, *Works*, I, 566). One of the earliest known cases of the consecration of a church by an Anglican Bishop was in the diocese of Bristol in 1606 during the episcopate of John Thornborough, who had been Bishop of Limerick from 1594 to 1603.

[2] Nicholas Bernard, *Clavi Trabalis*, 64.

of this form are the first consecratory prayer and the provision for the blessing of the furniture.

Bishop Cosin, in his third form,[1] which has been identified with the draft he presented in Convocation,[2] follows Bishop Andrewes closely, though with a number of minor variations. The furniture of the church is blessed in a slightly different order ending with the Table of the Lord together with the Communion plate which is first presented and placed upon it; and Andrewes' second long consecratory prayer is omitted altogether. Otherwise most of the earlier material is used and very little original matter added.

The Irish compiler, on the other hand, makes very limited use of Bishop Andrewes' form. The furniture of the Church is blessed not only in a different order but with far greater solemnity and with original prayers of great beauty. Andrewes' first consecratory prayer has also suggested the use of 1 Chronicles 29. 10 seqq. (lines 76-93 of the text)[3] and a similar narrative recalling scriptural and primitive examples of piety in providing holy places for the worship of God (ll. 101-48). Beyond this there is very little trace of Bishop Andrewes' or any other earlier Anglican form.[4] Other sources have been used extensively and much original matter introduced.

In his extensive use of other sources the Irish compiler breaks away from previous Anglican usage. Dr J. Wickham Legg, who made an exhaustive study of English consecratory forms of the seventeenth century, said that the Bishops who compiled them "seem to have made no use of the Roman or other Pontifical, as they might well have done, for the great consecratory preface *Adeste precibus* would have excellently served their ends".[5] The Irish compiler, however, has drawn from this source. The main line of thought of the preface *Adeste precibus* can clearly be seen in one prayer (ll. 171-9; 189-200) and less clearly in another (ll. 455-9), while slight traces of the *Prefatio super Altare* are to be found in

---

[1] The text is given in Legg's *Eng. Ch. Orders*, 237 seqq.

[2] Ibid., 365.

[3] Appendix 1, p. 300 seqq. Hereafter the references to the lines of the 1666 form are given in parentheses.

[4] There are slight points of contact between the Irish form and Bishop Barlow's second form of 1610, which appears only to have been followed on one occasion by Bishop Tilson of Elphin in Yorkshire in 1651. In some ways it is easier to believe that Tilson found this form in use in Ireland than that he found it for the first time in England during the Commonwealth. In both forms a preliminary circuit is made of the churchyard, the word "Dormitory" used, the baptismal water blessed with the font, and Luke 7. 1-11 selected for the Gospel.

[5] Op. cit., xxvi.

S

a third (ll. 488–94). The *Actiones nostras quaesumus Domine*, following medieval precedent, occurs at the beginning of the rite (ll. 27 seqq.). Likewise medieval precedent may have suggested the procession of the Bishop with his clergy "round about the Church within" (ll. 207 seq.; 739 seq.) or "round about the Church new built" (ll. 665 seq.).

There are also marks of Greek influence: the intercessions on the Greek model (ll. 180–4), the Prayer of St Clement (ll. 522 seqq.), the Anathematism (ll. 539 seqq.), and the Euphemismos ending with the Trisagion (ll. 577–636). None of these, however, are taken from the Greek Office for consecrating a church, though the Trisagion was said thrice in what was originally a separate Greek office for the bringing of relics from another church. The absence of psalmody at the entrance into the new church (ll. 16 seq., 70), the vesting of the Bishop and clergy within (ll. 16 seq.), and the saying of the solemn consecratory prayers kneeling "before the Chancel door" (ll. 71 seq.) has an interesting parallel in the Greek rite, where the Bishop with his clergy, having entered the new church in silence, vests, and says the solemn consecratory prayer "before the Holy Doors".[1]

There are also parallels with the Armenian Office for consecrating a church, where the Bishop and clergy gather "at the third hour" (cf. ll. 11 seq.), stand reciting Psalm 118. 19 before the closed door (cf. ll. 335 seqq.; 368 seq.), and where deacons prepare the altar (cf. ll. 422 seqq.).[2]

Yet another quarry is provided in the works of Jeremy Taylor. The Irish compiler takes over a private prayer at the end of the "Discourse of Holy Places" in the *Great Exemplar* and turns it into a public prayer (ll. 496 seqq.). He also uses Taylor's peculiar version of the Trisagion (ll. 629 seqq.).

A comparison of the structure and sources of the Irish and English Restoration forms may now be made:

---

[1] Goar, *Euchologion*, 835. In the Greek Office Psalm 51 (8–9) is sung after Psalm 84: in the Irish form Hymn I includes part of Psalm 84 and Hymn II Psalm 51 (15–19).

[2] The Armenian Rite is given in *Rituale Armenorum*, ed. F. C. Conybeare and A. J. Maclean. There are also common features in the Armenian and Irish Offices for reconciling a profaned church. (See also note to line 570.) In the Silas fragment of the now lost Mozarabic rite for consecrating churches Ps. 118. 19 seq. was used at the solemn entry of the relics into the new church. *Le Liber Mozarabicus Sacramentorum et les Manuscrits Mozarabes*, par D. Marius Ferotin, 890.

BISHOP COSIN'S DRAFT FORM OF 1662

"The Form and Order of Consecration or Dedication of Churches and Chappels...according to the use of the Church of England."

The Bishop is attended by his chaplains.

Surrender of the Building

Petition of the Founder.
Short prayer for the Founder.

Solemn Entrance

Psalm verses are recited.

Consecratory Prayer

(based upon Andrewes)
(a) 1 Chron. 29. 10 seqq.
(b) Narrative recalling scriptural and primitive precedents for holy places.
(c) Solemn blessing of the church.

THE IRISH PRINTED FORM OF 1666

"A Form of Consecration, or, Dedication of Churches and Chappels according to the use of the Church of *Ireland*."

The Bishop is attended by a convenient number of his clergy (of which the Dean or Archdeacon to be one).

The Bishop, clergy, and Patron walk round the cemetery in silence while the bell tolls.

The Bishop and clergy enter the empty church in silence, the Patron and people standing without, vest, kneel down in the body of the church, and say the Lord's Prayer and *Actiones nostras precibus Domine*.

Surrender of the Building

The Bishop questions the Patron (or his deputy) at the west door.

The Patron kneels and the Bishop blesses him laying his hand upon or over his head.

All enter the church.

Three Consecratory Prayers

(first group)
I. 1 Chron. 29. 10 seqq. with additions.
II. Based upon Andrewes (b), but with much original matter introduced.

III. Based upon the medieval preface *Adeste precibus*, but interwoven with Scripture and original matter.

The Procession

The Bishop and clergy "go in procession round about the Church within" saying Hymn I ex psalmis 127, 84 (1611 version).

ENGLISH DRAFT FORM	IRISH PRINTED FORM

The Blessing of the Furniture | *The Blessing of the Furniture*

I. *The Burial Place:*
The Archdeacon reads a Lesson, and the Bishop says a prayer (original).

II. *The Font*
The Bishop, with his clergy, goes to the font and pours pure water presented by the Verger or Clerk into it.

I. *The Font*
The Bishop says a short prayer at the font, (after Andrewes' prayer).

The "senior Priest" reads a Lesson and the Bishop blesses the font and the Baptismal water (original prayer).

III. *The Pulpit*
The Bishop, "attended as before", lays his hand upon the pulpit, and after the lesson read by "one of the Priests" blesses it (original prayer).

II. *The Pulpit*
The Bishop says a short prayer (original).

III. *The Pavement*
The Bishop says a short prayer (original).

Solemn Entrance through the Chancel Doors

IV. *Lectern*
The Bishop says a short prayer (after Andrewes).

V. *Reading-Desk*
The Bishop says a prayer (original).

The doors of the chancel being closed the Bishop and priests stand before them reciting alternately Psalm 118. 19 seqq. and other psalm verses (1611 version).

The doors being opened, the Bishop with his clergy enters and ascends to the Communion table.

IV. *"The Altar or Communion Table"*

VI. *"The Table of the Lord" and the Communion Plate*
The Bishop goes up to "the Table of the Lord" and places on it the Communion plate which the Founder presents to him.

He kneels "before the Table" and dedicates it together with the plate (original).

The Bishop sits on the south side of the altar while the Archdeacon reads a Lesson.
The Bishop kneels "before the Altar" and dedicates it.

V. *The Solemn Presentation and Dedication of the Communion Plate and other Gifts*
Some persons selected by the Patron bring the carpet, the Communion cloth,

the napkins, the chalice, paten, and other vessels, books and utensils for the Communion; and humbly presenting them to God, the Bishop receives them severally, and delivers them severally to the Deacon, to be laid orderly on the Communion table; excepting only the chalice and the paten, which two priests (when the table is covered) humbly on their knees lay upon it.

"Then the Bishop returning to the Altar, shall with reverence and solemnity (his face being Eastward) lay his hands upon the plate, and say this prayer standing." (The prayer is based upon I Chron. 14 seqq.)

Prayers for the Worshippers

The Bishop says these short prayers (Andrewes) in the body of the Church: in Andrewes' form they were said by the Bishop kneeling before the Holy Table.

Four Consecratory Prayers
(second group)

The Bishop goes to "the North end of the H. Table" and says the Salutation, followed by these prayers:
I and II incorporating parts of the *Adeste precibus* and of the *Prefatio super Altare*.
III. A personal prayer from Jeremy Taylor, converted into a public prayer.
IV. The Prayer of St Clement.

Reading of the Instrument

The Bishop reads the Instrument himself.

Reading of the Instrument

The Bishop sits "covered" while the Chancellor reads the Instrument.

The Anathematism

The Bishop and Clergy say alternately this Hymn ex Psalmis (1611 version) ending: "Glory be to God on high..."

The Euphemismos

The Bishop and clergy say alternately this Hymn ex Psalmis (1611 version) ending with the TRISAGION and Sanctus.

"So ends the Office of Consecration."

ENGLISH DRAFT FORM	IRISH PRINTED FORM
	The bell tolls "a little in the interval".

Morning Prayer

The chaplains read "the Morning Service".
Additional Sentence.
Psalms 15, 84, 122.
First Lesson: Gen. 28. 10 to end.

Second Lesson: John 2. 13–17.
Special Collect after that of the Day (Andrewes' adaptation of Barlow's consecratory prayer).

Morning Prayer

The Dean reads "the Morning prayer, or first Service".

Psalms 122, 125, 132.
First Lesson: Gen. 28. 10 to end; or 1 Kings 8. 10–61.
Second Lesson: Matt. 21. 1–17.
Special Collect after that of the Day (original).

Litany

Two additional suffrages. Barlow's prayer after that for the clergy and people is substituted for that of St Chrysostom.

The Rite of Confirmation
The Communion

The Communion

The Bishop kneels before the Table of the Lord and the chaplains place themselves at each end of the Table, where he that is at the north, begins the Communion Service.
Proper Collect (after Andrewes' adaptation of Barlow's).

"The Bishop shall read the Second Service, and administer the Communion."

The same original Collect is provided for the First and Second Service, and is to be said together with the Collect of the Day.
Epistle: Acts 3. 1–16.
Gospel: Luke 7. 1–10.

Epistle: 1 Cor. 3. 16; or Acts 7. 44.
Gospel: John 10. 22.

Offertory

Additional prayer.
Then the Bishop offers upon the Lord's Table (a) the Act of Consecration, (b) the Bread and Wine for the Communion, (c) his own alms and oblations. Then one of the priests receives the alms and oblations. The "chief Minister" says a short prayer.

Before the Blessing

The Bishop says a prayer (after Andrewes).

The main characteristics which distinguish the Irish form of 1666 from earlier Anglican rites or from the contemporary draft prepared by Bishop Cosin may be briefly summarized: the silent entry into the church; the blessing of the Patron; the procession round about the church within; the four hymns ex Psalmis—Hymn I, Hymn II, the Anathematism, and the Euphemismos ending with the Trisagion and Sanctus; the provision of Lessons before the dedication of the vault, font, pulpit, and Communion table; the pouring of pure water into the font; the solemn entrance through the chancel doors taking the place of the solemn entry into the church in other Anglican rites; the solemn presentation of the gifts; the covering of the altar by the Deacon and the laying thereon of the plate for the Communion by two priests kneeling; the tolling of the bell between the Office of Consecration and Morning Prayer; the Rite of Confirmation between the Litany and the Communion; the absence of long consecratory prayers within the framework of Morning Prayer, Litany, and the Communion; the extensive use made of ancient eastern and western material; the large number of persons employed in the rite, the Patron or his deputy, the Chancellor of the diocese and the Registrar, the Verger or Clerk, "some persons by the Patron's appointment", the Archdeacon, the Dean, "the senior Priest", "one of the Priests", "two Priests", and the Deacon, all of whom have a definite part to perform; the directions for the Bishop to perform all the solemn acts of dedication "with the Clergy attending" and to say the solemn hymns with "the Clergy answering alternately"; and the admirable clarity of the rubrical directions which are the best guide to the structure of the most elaborate and composite Anglican form of the seventeenth century.

The Irish form of 1666 was not without its influence upon subsequent rites. It provided the general structure and several rubrics of Archbishop King's Dublin diocesan office of 1719. It provided the main substance and much of the actual language of two prayers used by Bishop John Skinner of Aberdeen at the consecration of St Andrew's Chapel, Aberdeen, in 1795.[1] It provided Bishop John Wordsworth with Anglican precedent for following Greek sources and for the Lessons he placed in his form before the separate dedication of the font and other furniture of the

[1] Appended to *The Presence of Christ in Places of Christian Worship* (Aberdeen, 1795), 53 seqq. Also Hall's *Fragmenta liturgia*, v, 310 seqq.

church. Its direction for tolling the bell between the Office of Consecration and Morning Prayer survived in the Dublin provincial Office of 1760 and in another Irish rite of 1860.[1] At the same time, the Irish form of 1666, by reason of its composite character, has many points of contact with those modern Anglican rites which have drawn from the Roman Pontifical or from the Greek Euchologion. In this way it is an important landmark in the history of the development of Anglican rites for the consecration of churches.

III. THEORIES OF AUTHORSHIP

In 1947 the present writer worked out from internal evidence what he believed to be an original theory about the authorship of the Irish form of 1666 from its many close parallels with the works of Jeremy Taylor. For this purpose he used Bishop Heber's edition (1839) of Taylor's *Whole Works* and, at a later stage, C. P. Eden's revised and corrected edition of the same (1847–54). Early in 1949 he found in a later impression of Eden's edition (1850–6) the following editorial note in Volume VIII at p. 701, appearing there for the first time:[2]

There is in the Irish Book of Common Prayer a Service for the "Consecration of Churches" which in style closely resembles Taylor's compositions; but without any external evidence assigning it to him. It is found in the Irish Prayer-book put forth in Dublin in the reign of William the third; also in an edition of 1721, a copy of which is in the British Museum.

This editorial note has been completely overlooked by subsequent writers who have paid any attention to the Irish form of 1666; and the position has since been obscured by Dr Reeves' investigation into the history of "this admirable performance".[3]

"There is no entry upon the subject", writes Dr Reeves,

in the meagre records of the Irish Convocation, but we know that in 1640 there was a design in deliberation of the Convocation of Canterbury for the preparing an English Pontifical, one item in which was to be a form for consecrating churches, churchyards, and chapels; and in 1661,[4] on the 22nd of March, the Upper House

---

[1] *The Form to be used at the consecration of Churches* (Cavan, 1860).

[2] The editorial note is in Vol. VIII bearing the date 1854: it is not in my copy of Vol. VIII bearing the date 1850.

[3] Dr Reeves first developed his theory of authorship in a letter of Nov. 1876 to the *Irish Church Society's Journal* where it appeared in 1877. It reappeared as a Tract by the Royal Irish Academy, and in 1893 as an Introduction to a reprint of the 1666 form by the S.P.C.K. This Introduction and reprint are included in Vol. III of *Hierurgia Anglicana* to which reference is here made.

[4] 22 March 1661/2 (Cardwell, *Synodalia*, II, 668).

unanimously committed to Dr John Cosin, the Bishop of Durham, the preparation of such a form; which, on the 20th of June, was presented by him, and referred to a sub-committee of four prelates for consideration. (*Synodus Anglicana*, pp. 106, 107, 118; Cardwell's *Synodalia*, vol. ii, pp. 596, 668, 677.) What became of this draft form we are not told; probably local considerations, and especially the recollection of the outcry that was raised against Laud in the matter of the Consecration of St Catherine Creed Church, in 163½, caused the English Bishops to hesitate in adopting any elaborate form, though this was only a modification of Bishop Andrewes'; and thus the matter was allowed to become a dropped proposition; but the Irish Bishops, glad to obtain a composition which proceeded from so able a hand, were prepared, with the Prayer Book, to receive a collateral formula of great merit, though wanting the ratification of synodical assent. Such is my conjecture.[1]

Dr Reeves' theory depends entirely upon the absence of any known consecration form of Bishop Cosin's composition. Already there had appeared in the second volume of Cosin's correspondence by the Surtees Society in 1872 a consecration form, extracted from the Hunter MS. (lxxxiii) in Durham Chapter Library, with this general heading:

The Forme and Order of Dedication or Consecration of Churches and Chappels Together with the Church-yards or Places of Burialls According to the Use of the Church of England.[2]

According to an appended note in the hand of Archdeacon Basire, "this form was used at the consecration of Christ's Church neere Tinmouth" by Bishop Cosin on 5 July 1668.[3] The editor, G. Ormsby, suggested that this form was "probably identical" with that which Cosin prepared for general use and presented in Convocation.[4] This view, assumed by J. H. Overton before 1887,[5] was later expressed by two liturgical scholars, Bishop John Wordsworth in 1899[6] and Dr J. Wickham Legg in 1911. "Our President, the Bishop of Salisbury," writes Dr Wickham Legg, "considers that this form was discussed in Convocation, and the boldness with which it is declared to be 'according to the use of the Church of England' strengthens the suggestion." [7] With this form[8] Dr Wickham Legg prints Bishop Cosin's other forms: the one for the consecration of Sir Thomas Fanshaw's chapel before 2 September 1661[9] and, therefore, before the Upper House commissioned him on 22 March

[1] *Hierurgia Anglicana*, III, 188 seq.
[2] *The Correspondence of John Cosin, D.D.*, Part II, 175 seqq.
[3] Ibid., 175n. [4] Ibid., xix.
[5] Article in the *D.N.B.* on John Cosin.
[6] *On the Consecration of Churches* (C.H.S.), 28.
[7] *Eng. Ch. Orders*, 28. [8] Ibid., 237 seqq. [9] Ibid., 218 seqq.

1661/2 to prepare a form for general use: the other for the consecration of the restored chapel at Auckland Castle in 1665, which is almost identical with the general form, though punctuated with anthems requiring trained singers.[1] Dr Wickham Legg had also compared Bishop Cosin's three forms with the Irish form of 1666, and set against Dr Reeves' opinion "the little resemblance the three forms printed above have to the Irish form".[2] We have already noticed how different the Irish form is from Cosin's general form in structure and use of sources; and further considerations of style and theological emphasis make it impossible to suggest that the Irish form represents a fourth of Bishop Cosin's composition.

Dr Reeves had been misled partly by the complete silence of the Irish Convocational records, partly by believing the three entries in the English Convocational records exhausted our knowledge of Bishop Cosin's draft form, and partly by the work of the Irish Prayer Book Revision Committee of which he was secretary when he made his investigation. This Committee, for example, had reported to the General Synod in 1873 that the new Irish Form of Consecration of Churches was "taken, for the most part, from a form drawn up by the Convocation of Canterbury in 1715".[3] Likewise the new Form of Thanksgiving for the Blessings of Harvest was drawn largely from a form agreed upon by the Convocation of Canterbury in 1862. It would be extremely easy to read the present into the past and to imagine that the Church of Ireland, which was then drawing upon English Convocational forms of 1715 and 1862, would with the same readiness at the Restoration adopt a form presented to the English Convocation in 1662. Dr Reeves can also be excused for not having noticed the general form of Bishop Cosin which had appeared for the first time, not in a liturgical collection, but almost concealed, and without notice in the index, among his later letters. In spite of the appearance in 1911 of Bishop Cosin's three forms in Dr Wickham Legg's valuable collection of consecration forms, Dr Reeves' theory, which he himself abandoned in 1890, has been repeated. Not only has the Irish form been ascribed to Bishop Cosin as recently as 1948,[4] but Dr Reeves' theory attributed to Dr Wickham Legg in 1932.[5]

In 1890 Dr Reeves, now Bishop of Down, Connor and Dromore, gave his latest opinion in a letter to the Reverend T. P. Morgan, of Larne, who

---

[1] *Eng. Ch. Orders*, 224 seqq.   [2] Ibid., 332.

[3] *Revision Committee Report to the General Synod of 1873*, 103.

[4] G. W. O. Addeshaw and Frederick Etchells, op. cit., 201n.

[5] *Liturgy and Worship* (1933 corr. ed.), 710.

prepared the reprint of the 1666 form, and its two dependent offices, for the S.P.C.K. He now believed that these three offices reprinted from 1700 to 1757 "in the Irish folio Prayer Book were the compilation of Archbishop King of Dublin".[1] But Archbishop King, in *Quaedam Vitae Meae Insigniora*, tells us that he entered Trinity College, Dublin, in 1667 at the age of 17, a year after the form in question first appeared, and that before entering College he had heard nothing "concerning the public or private worship of God".[2] King's later correspondence makes it clear that his own practice, as a Bishop, was to alter the form of 1666 to his own mind,[3] and that he himself was drawing up offices for the consecration and restoration of churches.[4] These offices were agreed upon at a Synod of the diocese of Dublin in 1719, but never claimed to be "according to the use of the Church of Ireland", nor did they ever appear in the larger Irish Prayer Books between 1700 and 1757. Writing as a busy diocesan Bishop at the age of 75 Dr Reeves has obviously confused the Dublin diocesan form of 1719 with the Irish forms of 1666 which alone were printed in "the Irish folio Prayer Book".

We are now free to look for another author, but we must first decide in which country to look for him. The three offices, as they first appeared in 1666, show many signs of having been prepared for use in Ireland, and not in England. The Convocation of Canterbury neither planned in 1640 nor discussed in 1662 additional offices to be used in the restoration and reconciliation of churches. Annexed to the Irish form of 1666 are *An Office to be used in the Restauration of a Church*, "when the Fabric of a Church is ruined, and a new Church built upon the same foundation", and also *A Short Office for Expiation and Illustration of a Church Desecrated or Prophan'd*, to be used "if a Church hath been desecrated by murther or blood shed". The very provision of these offices strongly suggests Ireland as the place of their origin. The Irish Bishops at the Restoration found several cathedrals and many parish churches, six out of seven in the diocese of Ossory alone, in ruins. "Let not the churches lie waste in ruinous heaps", pleaded Bishop Jeremy Taylor preaching at the opening of the Irish Parliament in 1661.[5] Eight years later the Lord Deputy and Council observed that in most parts of Ireland the parish churches by the confusion of the late Rebellion of 1641 and the Cromwellian "usurpations" which followed "were utterly broken down, ruined, and

---

[1] *Hierurgia Anglicana*, III, 193.
[2] Given in C. S. King, *A Great Archbishop of Dublin*, 1 seq., 7, 9 seq.
[3] *Hier. Ang.*, 191. [4] Ibid.
[5] *Works*, VIII, 355; cf. V, 609, "Our churches are still demolished".

demolished".[1] Dean Swift maintained that in England churches were defaced during the Commonwealth, but in Ireland they were "not defaced, but totally destroyed".[2] During the Rebellion and Cromwellian occupation, moreover, churches had often been "desecrated by murther and blood shed". We read, for example, of "fifty murther'd at Black-water-Church", of "about 100 murther'd within the Church" at Loughall,[3] of the burning by Cromwell of the steeple of St Peter's, Drogheda, in which 100 people had taken refuge,[4] and of the storming of the Rock of Cashel by Lord Inchiquin and the massacre of many in the Cathedral which the rebels had fortified.[5]

The Irish Bishops at the Restoration would, therefore, realize the need for both these additional offices. They are very short and depend by rubrical direction entirely upon the framework of the "Office" or "Form of Consecration" (lines 723–7; 730–1; 799–800; 806–13). Internal evidence points to the same author of all three offices; and if the two appended offices were drawn up for use in Ireland, the *Form of Consecration*, to which their rubrical directions refer, most probably had its origin there.

In the *Form of Consecration*, moreover, the Patron humbly desires the Bishop to dedicate the new church by his "prayers and holy Ministeries, according to... the Laws and Customs of this Church". No English Canon of 1603 directed the consecration of churches, but the forty-third Irish Canon did.[6] The words, "according to the Laws of this Church", would far better fit a form drawn up for use in Ireland.

If these forms were drawn up to meet the peculiar needs of the Church of Ireland at the Restoration, there is no reason why the Irish Bishops should have had them prepared outside Ireland. In Caroline times, more-over, consecration forms were drawn up by individual Bishops, and not as fifty years later in Convocational committees. This may limit our search for an author to the Irish episcopate at the Restoration. Of the Irish Bishops between 1660 and 1666 only Primate Bramhall, Henry Leslie of Meath, George Wilde of Derry, Thomas Bayly of Killala,

---

[1] An Order of the Lord Deputy and Council 31 May 1669. Quoted from Report on the MSS. Carte by Russell and Prendergast (1871), 105.

[2] *A Sermon upon the Martyrdom of King Charles I.* Cf. William King, *State o, Protestants in Ireland*, 210.

[3] Edward, E. of Clarendon, *History of the Rebellion and Civil Wars in Ireland*, 306 seq.

[4] J. B. Leslie, *Armagh Clergy and Parishes*, 247.

[5] W. Alison Philips, op. cit., III, 83. Cf. Letter, Inchiquin to Lenthall, 12 Sept. 1647 (Tanner MSS.).

[6] "*Of the Consecration of Churches.* As often as Churches are newly built, where formerly they were not...they shall be dedicated and consecrated..."

Griffith Williams of Ossory, Edward Wolley of Clonfert, William Fuller of Limerick, and Jeremy Taylor of Down and Connor are known to have written anything at all. Of these Henry Leslie died before the opening session of Convocation, and Griffith Williams was severely censured by the Upper House in November 1665 for a book he had published in 1664. Of the rest only Bishop Wolley, consecrated in 1665, and Bishop Taylor can properly be called devotional writers, though Bishop Wilde compiled a curious form for the laying the first stone of his private chapel at Faughan in 1665,[1] and Primate Bramhall's directions for the consecration of the twelve Bishops in 1660-1 reveal the same clarity and care as the rubrics of the 1666 form. The compositions of Bramhall, Wilde, and Wolley, however, are so entirely different in style that no useful purpose could be served in attempting a comparison.

Bishop Taylor, on the other hand, was known as well for his liturgical knowledge as for his devotional writings. *The Worthy Communicant*, published as recently as 1660, contained many prayers after the manner of *The Great Exemplar*, *Holy Living*, *Holy Dying*, *Unum Necessarium*, and the *Golden Grove*. His *Collection of Offices* of 1658, as composite as the 1666 form, had been "collected out of the devotions of the Greek church, with some mixture of the Mozarabic and Ethiopic and other liturgies".[2] In any case, as we have seen, his works provided one prayer and the curious version of the Trisagion in the 1666 form. A century ago C. P. Eden thought that the form printed in the Irish Prayer Books from 1700 to 1757 "in style closely resembles Taylor's compositions", but believing it appeared for the first time in the reign of William III he could see "no external evidence assigning it to him". We must next consider whether there is any external evidence making it extremely improbable that the Irish Bishops would commission Bishop Taylor to prepare the form in question.

IV. AN IRISH RESTORATION BISHOP AND WRITER

The impression given by some biographers is that Jeremy Taylor was altogether a lonely and embittered diocesan Bishop, who pursued a fanatical policy entirely of his own, kept aloof from his brother Bishops, and died unnoticed and unlamented. It has been hinted that the Duke of Ormonde refused to allow his translation to Meath, and that there was a mental aspect to his illness of the winter of 1665-6. For our purpose it is important to see Taylor in relation to other Irish Restoration Bishops,

[1] Given in Legg, *Eng. Ch. Orders*, 294 seqq.   [2] See below, p. 291.

rather than as an isolated diocesan, and to discover to what extent, if any, they valued his gifts as a writer, and to notice his connection with the Convocation during its sessions between 10 May 1661 and 5 March 1662/3, and after the long prorogation of Parliament, between 4 November 1665 and the last recorded session on 22 February 1665/6.

Taylor, who had been given a refuge at Portmore in 1658, returned to Ireland in the early autumn of 1660 as Bishop of Down and Connor and as Vice-Chancellor of the University of Dublin. Having visited the College and made known the Chancellor's desires regarding conformity "to the laws of the Church and the particular statutes of the house",[1] he visited various centres of his future diocese taking up residence in "a little house" near Hillsborough Castle.[2] Although some Presbyterian ministers gave him "private notice that they would turn Nicodemus's"[3] it soon became clear that the Presbyterian opposition to his appointment as Bishop was steadily growing.[4] The newly appointed Primate, John Bramhall, kept Ormonde, or his secretary, Sir George Lane, informed of the Presbyterian designs against Taylor, and of a petition for no less than his removal from among them,[5] and later, of another, on the very eve of the long delayed consecration of the twelve Bishops, to accuse him to the King "for a Socinian and an Arminian".[6] Bramhall regarded these charges as groundless and most unjust to "an orthodox son of the Church of England, who is ready to subscribe to all the articles of the English Church with his pen and if need be with his blood".[7] On 27 January 1660/1 Taylor had the singular honour of preaching at his own and the consecration of eleven other Bishops, and his sermon was published at the request of the Lords Justices, Primate Bramhall, and the other Bishops.

Three days later Michael Boyle, Bishop of Cork, who later as Archbishop of Dublin and Lord Chancellor gave his Imprimatur with Primate Margetson to the form in question, recommended Taylor for the primary bishopric of Meath should Henry Leslie, the present Bishop, die in the near future. Its nearness to Dublin would "enable him to answer his engagements to the Church, to the Council Table, and to the University with a greater accommodation".[8] For Taylor was "a person of singular

---

[1] Letter, Taylor to Ormonde, 3 Oct. 1660, *Works*, I, xciv.
[2] Letter, Taylor to Lord Montgomery of the Ards, 27 Oct. 1660, B.L., MSS. Carte 31. 58.   [3] Ibid.
[4] See Robert Maxwell's letter to Taylor, 3 Dec. (1ober) 1660; *C.S.P.* (*Irel.*) 1660-2, 115 seq.
[5] MSS. Carte 221, 79.
[6] Ibid., 221, 150.   [7] Ibid.   [8] Ibid., 45, 129.

ability to do God and the King good Service".[1] When Leslie died on 7 April 1661, Primate Bramhall thought Taylor a most suitable candidate for the primary see. "He is fit for it, and it for him"; but his continuance in Down and Connor was more necessary "until the work be done in some measure for which he was sent thither".[2] Moreover, "all his friends in that country are very desirous to keep him where he is, and to encourage him to stay there, that Dromore may be united to Down for this turn."[3] Taylor's resolution on this choice was expected the next day.[4] On 13 April Bramhall sent Sir George Lane two letters from Taylor[5] showing "that he desireth to hold Down and Dromore united". Bramhall repeats his own judgement that Taylor's translation from Down and Connor "would hinder the reformation of that schismatical part of the country".[6] The union of Dromore with Down and Connor "pro hac vice tantum"[7] was sanctioned on 30 April, but owing to an unexpected change in the translations upon which this union depended did not take effect until 21 June, the day following Robert Leslie's translation from Dromore to Raphoe.

In the meanwhile Taylor preached at the opening of the Irish Parliament on 8 May 1661 and was introduced later in the day into the House of Lords, which the following day thanked him for his sermon and desired it to be printed. During the next three months he was diligent in his attendance in Convocation,[8] which assembled on 10 May, as well as in the House of Lords, where he was appointed to serve on various sub-committees. On 14 May, for example, he was one of the Lords to whom was entrusted the care of drawing up the important Declaration on Episcopal Government and the Liturgy; and when the House on 11 July resolved itself into a Grand Committee, "the Lord Bishop of Down taketh the Chair by Order of the Lords".[9] During the prorogation of Parliament from 31 July to 6 September Taylor preached at the metropolitical Visitation of his dioceses by Primate Bramhall the sermon, *Via Intelligentia*, which he had already preached in a slightly different shape before the University. On 7 November Taylor was appointed to serve with

---

[1] Ibid.   [2] Ibid., 221, 170.   [3] Ibid.   [4] Ibid.

[5] Now missing according to a note in the MS. Calendar of the MSS. Carte.

[6] MSS. Carte 221, 174.

[7] In spite of Sir Edmund Gosse's quibble, subsequently repeated that Taylor had no right to be called Bishop of Down, Connor and Dromore, he is so called in the Journals of the House of Lords under 14 June 1662, in records of the metropolitical Visitations of his dioceses, 1661 and 1664, and in the Journal of Convocation under 5 Feb. 1662/3.

[8] Journal of Convocation, under 10, 24, 29 May; 3, 10, 24 July.

[9] *Journal of the House of Lords, passim.*

three Bishops and his old friend, Dr Dudley Loftus, the Registrar, on a Committee of the Upper House of Convocation entrusted with the examination and revision of the Canons. Taylor was still connected with this work on 12 February 1662/3 when it was nearing completion and almost ready for publication.[1]

"I am so full of public concerns and troubles of business in my diocese", Taylor wrote to Sir John Evelyn on 16 November 1661, "that I cannot yet have leisure to think much of my old delightful employment. But I hope I have brought my affairs almost to a consistence, and then I may return again." [2] Taylor was not "so full of public concerns" in 1662. He attended the House of Lords less often and Convocation only on 3 June and 2 September, though he was in Dublin between 26 August and 2 September when Bramhall with the Bishops present in the city read through the revised Prayer Book lately published in London. He preached three sermons in Christ Church Cathedral, Dublin, on 4 May, 10 August, and 11 February 1662/3, which he published under the general title of *The Righteousness Evangelical*.

Between writing to Evelyn on 16 November 1661 and the prorogation of Convocation early in 1663 Taylor must have returned to his "old delightful employment"; for his *Discourse of Confirmation* was published in 1663 "by Order of Convocation". He had undertaken this work, he told Ormonde, not on his own, but was entreated to it by those who had the power to command him. At the end of the 1663 Dublin edition, in a list of "Books Printed at the King's Printing House", is this delightfully ambiguous notice of another of Taylor's works: "There will shortly be published his Treatise against Popery, of the necessity of which no man can be ignorant." The *Dissuasive from Popery*, undertaken at the earnest request of the Irish Bishops, was almost ready for publication, but apparently not in time for the final sanction of Convocation before its long prorogation. The list also includes "His Funeral Sermon at the Funeral of the Lord Primate", which Taylor preached on 16 July 1663.

Parliament opened on 25 October 1665, but Taylor was taken ill on the way[3] and did not reach Dublin until the last few days of January. It has been suggested recently that Taylor's illness "may not have been only physical",[4] on the ground that Lord Conway, in a letter of

---

[1] No doubt the work was shelved owing to the long prorogation of Parliament and Convocation, during which the Canons of 1634 were published without change. No draft of this work is extant.   [2] *Works*, I, cviii.

[3] Letter, Sir George Rawdon to Lord Conway, 25 Oct. 1665. (P.R.O., S.P. 63–319, 186).

[4] Hugh Ross Williamson, *Jeremy Taylor*, 162.

2 February 1665/6, expressed confidence that Valentine Greatrix, the Irish stroker, "would recover the Bishop of Down".[1] Lord Conway was replying to Sir George Rawdon's letter of 29 January 1665/6, telling him that Taylor had just reached Dublin hoping "to get amendment of the stiffness of his arms which he cannot lift up to his head".[2] Rawdon kept Conway informed of Taylor's gradual improvement; on 21 February that he was "something amended" but could not "get up his hands to his head yet";[3] in the following weeks he was "mending";[4] and finally, on 7 April, "The Bishop of Downe went home pretty well recovered ten days since."[5] In spite of illness Taylor attended Convocation on 27 January and 22 February, and the House of Lords on 13 February, when he was "added to the Committee of Privileges", on 8 March, when he was added to another committee, and again on 20 March. Although Taylor's signature to an official document on 20 February reveals great difficulty in writing,[6] his final extant letter of 26 December 1666,[7] is in his usual neat handwriting. Rawdon's subsequent letters to Conway show that Taylor was very active in his diocese and in unusually good spirit for the remainder of his life.

When Taylor died on 13 August 1667, Ormonde informed Archbishop Sheldon that he was "much lamented by his Brethren here and by all that love the Church",[8] and, in a letter to Primate Margetson, spoke of his death as "a great and unseasonable loss to the Church".[9] Margetson passed on to Ormonde Taylor's deathbed request that his son-in-law, Francis Marsh, should be his successor.[10] Margetson thought that Dean Marsh would be able, by his prudence, "to set in order and manage that disorderly and disaffected bishoprick, and, by his learning furnished with power, to vindicate the honour of the Church, and the memory of his diseased father-in-law from those calumnies of the Papists, which I forsee will be brought upon both in their rejoinder to a reply of the bishop's to their answer unto his Dissuasive from Popery."[11]

Thus we have seen that Taylor had the confidence of Ormonde, of Primate Bramhall, Primate Margetson, Archbishop Boyle, and of the other Irish Bishops.[12] Not only was he chosen to preach on such occasions

---

[1] Letter, Lord Conway to Sir G. Rawdon, in M. H. Nicholson, Conway Papers, 267 seq.

[2] P.R.O., S.P. 63–320, 29. [3] Ibid., 320, 49.

[4] Ibid., 320, 57, 59. [5] Ibid., 320, 86.

[6] P.R.O., S.P. 63–320, 48. [7] MSS. Carte, 45, 116.

[8] Ibid., 49, 429. [9] Ibid., 45, 218. [10] Ibid., 45, 220.

[11] Ibid.

[12] Bishop Worth, however, as a member of a Commonwealth Convention of ministers in May 1658 had spoken much against Taylor's first coming to Ireland.

T

of importance as the Consecration of the twelve Bishops, the opening of Parliament, the metropolitical Visitation of his own dioceses, and at the funeral of Primate Bramhall, but he was commissioned by the House of Bishops to write the *Discourse of Confirmation* and the *Dissuasive from Popery*; and the Convocational order to publish the former suggests that he had the confidence of the Lower House as well.[1] If the Irish Bishops, appreciating the ability of Taylor and his gifts as a writer, commissioned him to write these two works of importance, there is no reason why they should not have commissioned this well-known liturgical compiler to prepare forms of consecration, restoration, and reconciliation of churches.

V. INTERNAL EVIDENCE

We have already noticed among the sources used by the compiler of this consecration form a prayer in Jeremy Taylor's *Great Exemplar* and the *Trisagion* in the peculiar version used three times in his *Holy Living* though it had already appeared in the *Psalter of David* of 1644. These could have been used by any compiler between 1661 and 1666. In looking for further points of contact with Jeremy Taylor we shall notice common words and expressions, including quotations from Scripture, similarity of style of theological emphasis, and other evidence which may reveal the mind of the compiler.

(a) Common Material

The common words and expressions are set out in the order in which they occur in the text, as given in the Appendix, p. 298. In the left-hand column reference is given to the lines of the text: in the right-hand column to the volume and page of C. P. Eden's revised and corrected edition of Bishop Heber's *Whole Works of Jeremy Taylor*. Although the author believes that sufficient evidence is contained in this edition, he feels that the close parallels with the *Psalter of David*, given in Volume xv of Bishop Heber's edition but not in C. P. Eden's, should not be overlooked, and where they occur reference is given thus: *Ps. D.*, Heber xv.

A FORM OF CONSECRATION	WORKS OF JEREMY TAYLOR
A. *The Surrender of the Building and the Blessing of the Patron*	
....some *Lords day*, or other *great Festival* of the Church...*solemnity* (7–8)	Let the Sunday-*festival* be called the Lord's Day (1, 109); no man shall fast

---

[1] The Prolocutor, Dr Mossom, had like Taylor used the Prayer Book in Anglican Congregations in London during the Commonwealth.

upon the *Lord's Day*, nor upon the *great festivals* (x, 362); *solemnity* (II, 316; and frequently used for any religious rite including the consecration of Churches)

vest themselves *in* their respective *Ecclesiastick habits* (18)

vested in an *ecclesiastical habit* (VIII, 631: rubric in Baptism Office)

for the service of God (41)

for the service of God (II, 315)

Ministeries of Religion (41)

Ministeries of Religion (I, 9)

holy Ministeries (44–5)

holy...ministeries (I, 51)

The Lord bless you, *and prosper* you; *the Lord make his face to shine upon* you... *sanctifie* his heart, *purifie* his *intentions.* ... *Enrich* him and his family *with all blessings of thy Spirit, and thy Providence* for ever, *through Jesus Christ our Lord. Amen* (58–66)

The Lord bless thee and keep thee; *the Lord make his face to shine upon* thee... he keep thee from all evil.... *Spirit... Providence...prosper...through Jesus Christ our Lord* (VIII, 671);... *bless* them with *thy Providence, sanctify...enrich* them *with* thy wisdom (VIII, 666 seq.); pure *intentions* (II, 327); *enrich* us *with thy holy Spirit* (VIII, 664); *with all blessings...of thy Spirit and providence* (I, 65; cf. VIII, 670; IV, 272)

Ministry (66)

Ministry (frequently used for all solemn acts particularly in *Clerus Domini*, I, 5 seqq.)

Chancel door (72)

Chancel door (v, 328)

B. *Consecratory Prayers before the Chancel Door*

I

Father of our Lord Jesus Christ (76) *God of Mercy* and *Father of men and Angels* (90–1)

Father of our Lord Jesus Christ (VII, 639; VIII, 578, 583, 644, etc.); *God of Mercy* (VIII, 666, 696 seqq.); *Father of men and Angels* (IV, 40; VIII, 578, 589, 631, 638, 639, etc.; *Ps. D.*, Heber xv, 114)

imploy us in thy *service* (97) *duties* which we shall *perform*...by the *assistances of thy holy Spirit* (99–100)

his *service* thy *employment* (VIII, 671); *the assistances of* the *Holy* Ghost to help us in *performing* our *duty* (II, 556); *assistances...of thy Holy Spirit* (*Ps. D.*, Heber xv, 135); *assistances of* the *Spirit* (v, 271)

II

immensity (102)

immensity (II, 62; VIII, 46, 53, 615, etc., *Ps. D.*, Heber xv, 115)

weaknesses (112)	*weaknesses* (VII, 59 and frequently)
services (112)	*services* (III, 215 and frequently)
for *the invocation of* thy holy *Name. In Paradise* there was a *proper place...* called *The Presence of the Lord* (115–17)	to *the invocation* of his *Name* (II, 314); ...*in paradise*...a distinct *place* where He manifested himself present in a *proper* manner.... *The presence of the Lord* (II, 320)
And thou didst meet the Patriarch *Jacob* at *Bethel,* and he consecrated a *stone* for thy *memorial,* and it became *dreadful and venerable* (118–20)	...*at Bethel* where *Jacob* laid the first *stone* of a Church...God's *memorial* (II, 315) *dreadful and venerable* (VIII, 625); cf. *Venerable and dreadful* (*Ps. D.,* Heber xv, 163)
in all the *generations of the world* (136)	*in all generations of the world* (VIII, 678)
deplore our sins (146)	*deplore...sins* (III, 217)
Ministeries of Salvation (148)	*Ministeries of Salvation* (VIII, 623)
Admit (150)	*admit* (VIII, 629, 636, 691, etc.)
Graciousness (152)	*graciousness* (IV, 312; II, 722; VII, 82, 237, 240, etc.)
Depute thy holy *Angels* to abide *here...* and to drive away *all* the power *of the Enemy* (152–4)	Let *thy Holy Angels* dwell *here*...Repel far from us *all the* snare *of the Enemy* (*Ps. D.,* Heber xv, 223)
perfect their repentances (160–1) *rejoyce in thy mercies and loving kindnesses for ever and ever* (162)	*perfect...their repentance* (I, 67; VIII, 596) *rejoice in Thy mercies and lovingkindnesses for ever and ever* (VIII, 601)
Grant this for his sake...our blessed Lord and Saviour Jesus (163; 165–6)	*Grant this for his sake...our blessed Lord and Saviour Jesus* (VIII, 53)
who is the *King of the Saints,* and the *Head of the Church, the great lover of souls,* and our *High Priest,* who continually *makes intercession for us* (163–5)	*King of the Saints* (III, 244) O blessed *High Priest...King of the* world *and Head of the Church...* making intercession *for us* for ever (VIII, 613); *great lover of souls* (III, 233, 245; VII, 236; VIII, 614, 647, 658, etc., and *Ps. D.,* Heber xv, 225)

III

	Ministeries (VI, 267, and frequently) *Sacramentals* (V, 144, 631, 661; VI, 267; IX, 183, 631)
Be present with thy grace *in* all our *ministeries* of *Sacraments* and *Sacramentals* (172–3)	*Be present* with us *in* the dispensation of thy holy word and *Sacraments* (VIII, 595)

the dew of thy Divine blessing (175–6)

the dew of Divine blessings (Ps. D., Heber xv, 138)

Spare *all the penitents, relieve the distressed, comfort the comfortless, confirm the strong, and strengthen the weak: Ease the afflicted, heal the* wounded and the *sick:* provide for the widows, and *be a father to the fatherless* (180–3)

Pardon *all the penitents* (VIII, 629); *relieving the distresses of the afflicted* (Heber xv, 229), *comfort the comfortless* (ibid.). *Strengthen the weak and confirm the strong* (VIII, 584). *Ease* the pains of *the sick* (I, 67). *Heal the sick* (Heber xv, 227) *be thou...a Father of the fatherless* (VIII, 681)

Eternal peace (186–7)

Eternal peace (VIII, 671)

cords of vanity (194)

cords of vanity (II, 669)

with *the lanthorn of thy Word, and the light of thy Spirit* (195–6)

by *the lantern of thy Word, and the light of thy Spirit* (II, 546)

Preserve their *souls from* sin, their *eyes from tears, and* their *feet from falling* (202–3)
...*to whom with thee, O Father, and thy most Holy Spirit, be all honour and glory, praise and thanksgiving, love and obedience, for ever and ever. Amen* (203–6)

redeemed our *souls from* death our *eyes from tears,* and our *feet from falling* (VIII, 583, 690; Heber xv, 229, 232)
to whom with thee, O gracious Father, and the Holy Spirit, be all glory and honour, love and obedience, for ever and ever Amen (Heber xv, 233). *Be all honour and glory, praise and thanksgiving, love and obedience* (VIII, 644)

HYMN I Ex Psalmis 127, 1; 84, 5, 7, 1, 2, 3, 4, 10, 11, 12, 13 (authorized version) (210 seqq.)

In the authorized version Psalm 84. 4, 5, 12 occur in the Hymn Petitionary for the Church and Clergy, and verses 12, 13 in the Hymn after the second Lesson at Evening Prayer (*Collection of Offices*: VIII, 655, 590). Verses 1, 2, 4 occur in a prayer (III, 222)

C. The Dedication of the Furniture and Plate of the Church

I

Dedication of the Burial Place

(236 seqq.) The Lesson in the Coemetery: 1 Sam. 31. 11; 2 Sam. 2. 4; *Eccles.* 6. 3; 8. 10; 11. 8

The piety of the men of Jabesh-Gilead cited (III, 188, 450): *Ecclesiastes* is referred to over fifty times

For *the dust shall return to the earth as it was, and the Spirit shall return unto God that gave it.* Chap. 12. 7. (260–1)

Then *shall the dust return to the earth as it was, and the Spirit shall return unto God that gave it.* (Last verse of Lesson in Burial Office, VIII, 683)

O Almighty God, with whom do live the spirits (263)

O Almighty God, with whom do live the spirits (VIII, 684)

may lie down with *the righteous*, and their souls *may be gathered unto* their *Fathers in the bosom of Christ* (265-7)

may die the death of *the righteous* (VIII, 684) *may be gathered unto* our *fathers* (III, 442) *in the bosom of Christ* (IV, 635) [*may*] pass *into*... *the bosom of* Jesus,

they may hear *the sentence of the right hand* (269)

there to expect *the* merciful *sentence of the right hand* (VIII, 570; cf. VIII, 680)

II
Dedication of the Font

Fountain of all *Purity* (284)

Fountain of purities (IV, 215). *Fountain of* eternal *purity* (Heber XV, 137). *Fountain of purity* (ibid., 209)

bless and sanctifie the waters (284), *be presented unto thee*, and washed in this *Lavatory* (286-7)

bless and sanctify...this *water* (VIII, 632) that in this *water*...the soul *presented unto thee* may be cleansed (VIII, 632). Fount or...*Lavatory* of silver (VIII, 631: cf. II, 600, where *Lavatory* is used of Baptism)

that they may receive *the baptism of the Spirit*, and may have *a title* and portion in *repentance*, remission of sins, *and all the promises of the Gospel* (287-9)

we are... admitted into the Church by *the baptism of* water and *the Spirit* (II, 241) *title to the promises* evangelical (VIII, 637) *a title to the promises*, the covenant of *repentance*, and a right to pardon (VIII, 634) *and all the promises of the Gospel* (III, 91; VII, 638; VIII, 98)

an unreproveable faith (293)

an unreproveable faith (VII, 635; VIII, 320)

a perfect obedience (294)

a perfect obedience (VII, 21)

III
Dedication of the Pulpit

by thy Word, and by thy Spirit (316)

By thy Word, and by thy Spirit (VIII, 578, 588, 592; 621; cp. 637, etc.)

Grant that this place may be always filled *with wise and holy* persons, who may dispense thy *word* faithfully, *according to the ability* thou *givest*... *feed*-ing the *flock* of God... not for filthy lucres sake, but readily, and of a good mind (318-24)

O *grant* unto thy *flock* to be *fed with wise and holy* shepherds; men fearing God and hating covetousness: free from envy and full of charity (VIII, 237). Let every minister be diligent in preaching the *Word* of God, *according to the ability* God *gives* him (I, 107)

...let thy holy *Spirit* for ever *be the Preacher*, and *imprint* thy word in their minds, opening their *hearts*, convincing their *understandings*, overruling their

where the *Spirit* is *the preacher* (VIII, 255; cf. III, 436, and VIII, 376). The Spirit of God...is to be found...in pulpits. *Imprint* in our *hearts* (VIII, 608). The

wills, and governing their *affections, that they may not be hearers of the Word onely, but doers of good works*; that they by their holy *lives adorning the Gospel* of God, and seeking for *glory* and honour, and immortality, may attain *eternal* life (327–33)

Holy Spirit...enlightens our *understandings*, sanctifies our *wills*, and orders and commands our *affections* (VII, 606) *that they may not be only hearers of the word* of life, *but doers of good works*... living an unblameable *life* (VIII, 595) that we may *adorn the gospel of* thee our Lord...may receive the gift of *eternal glory* (II, 447)

IV

The Dedication of the Altar

The *Altar or Communion Table* (390–1)

Altar or Communion Table (x, 407)

O Eternal God (393)

O Eternal God (III, 37, 39, 44, 139, 140, 143; VII, 122, 297, 640; VIII, 614, 644, 658, 678)

who in an *infinite mercy* (393)

infinite mercy (III, 32, 221, 245; cf. VIII, 231)

didst send thy holy Son (393–4)

didst send thy holy son (VIII, 647)

to be a sacrifice for our sins (394) *and the food of our souls, the Author and finisher of our faith*, and the great *Minister of eternal glory*; who also now *sits* at thy *right hand*, and upon the *heavenly altar perpetually presents* to thee *the Eternal Sacrifice*, and a *never ceasing* prayer (394–8)

to become a sacrifice for our sins...the meat and the drink *of our souls* (VIII, 630) *the food of our souls* (VIII, 18, 53, 618). There He *sits*...and intercedes as our high priest...the *minister* of the sanctuary...*the author and finisher of our faith* (VII, 605) *eternal glory* (III, 43) in heaven...He *sits perpetually representing*...to the Father the...*Sacrifice* (III, 214) what is performed at the *right hand* of God (VIII, 73) at the celestial *altar* (II, 483) at the eternal *altar* in the *heavens* (VIII, 231) the celestial *altar* and *the eternal sacrifice* (VIII, 38) *the eternal sacrifice* which our blessed Lord *perpetually* offers (VIII, 618)

be present...in the dedication of a *Ministerial* altar...for the *performance* of this great *Ministry*, and in *imitation of* Christ's *Eternal Priesthood, according* to our duty, and *his Commandment*. (398–402)

a *ministerial* celebration of Christ's sacrifice (II, 644) *performance* (I, 41; cf. V, 329 seq. Liturgies were always *performed* at the *altar*) Christ was admitted to *the* celestial and *eternal priesthood* in heaven, where...He... represents an *eternal sacrifice* (VIII, 37). *This Ministry*...being *according to* Christ's *commandment*, and...an *imitation of Christ's* intercession (VIII, 39) *according to his commandment* (VIII, 38)

a savour of life unto life (404)

...may indeed *hunger* after *the bread of life, and thirst for the wine of elect souls* (405–6)

...*by faith*...*a holy hope*...*an eternal charity* (406–7)

Let no *hand* of any *that* shall *betray* thee be ever up*on this table* (408)

The holy body and blood (409)

...*Sacramentally represented and exhibited* (410)

...*come with prepar'd hearts*, and with penitent *souls*, and loving *desires* (411–12)

all the benefits of his passion (413–14)

Grant this for his sake...our most blessed Lord and Saviour Jesus (414; 416)

who is the Priest and the Sacrifice, the feeder and the food, the Physician and the physick of our souls (414–15)

---

a savour of life unto us (VIII, 228)

may *hunger and thirst for the bread of life and the wine of elect souls* (III, 249; cf. VIII, 53)

a strong *faith*, and *a holy hope*, and a never failing *charity* (II, 659) *eternal charity* (VIII, 593)

Let it never be said... "The *hand*... *that betrayeth* me is...*on the table*(III, 253). Let not the *hand* of Judas...(VIII, 232)

Thy holy body and blood (VIII, 617, 630)

represented and exhibited (VIII, 24 seqq., 73 etc.) *represent* in heaven...*exhibited* ...*sacramentally* (III, 252)

come with holy desires, and a longing soul ...and a prepared heart (V, 660)

all the benefits of his passion (VII, 638)

Grant this...for his sake...our most blessed Lord and Saviour Jesus (VIII, 53). Grant this...for his sake who is both Sacrifice and Priest (Ps. D., Heber xv, 212) thou art the Priest and the Sacrifice, the master of the feast and the feast itself, the physician of my soul (III, 250) the physician and the physic...of our souls (VIII, 630) food and physic (II, 698)

V

The Presentation and the Dedication of the Gifts

the Chalice, Paten, and other Vessels... and Utensils for the Communion; and humbly presenting them on their knees to God...to be laid orderly on the Communion Table (419–23)

with reverence and solemnity (425–6)

...enlarged heart...to serve thee with their souls and bodies, with all their time, and all their goods (434–6)

---

the Paten and Chalice (VIII, 627)* the utensils of the altar (I, cclxxi) Vessels are with more solemnities dedicated (ibid.) in an humble manner present it to God, laying it on the Communion Table (VIII, 622) presenting...to God on her knees (VIII, 641)

with reverent addresses...and solemnity (II, 325)

Give us enlarged and sanctified hearts (Ps. D., Heber xv, 194)...with our souls and with our bodies, with our time and with all our estate (VIII, 611) *the lot of thine inheritance* (439)

...and *by a Guard of Angels* they may be *preserved from all evil*, and by the perpetual presence of the *holy Spirit*, they may be *led into all good*, and *accepted to pardon*, and preserved in *peace*, and *promoted* in *holiness*, and conducted certainly to *Life Eternal* (442–6)

the portion *of Thine* own *inheritance* (VIII, 680)

the *guard of angels* to *preserve* them *from evil*, and the *conduct* of thy *holy Spirit* to *lead* them *into all good* (VII, 637; cf. 630) *from evils by the guard of angels*, and didst *lead me into all good* by the *conduct* of thy *holy Spirit* (VIII, 644) he keep thee *from all evil* by the *custody of angels*, and *lead* thee *into all good* by the *conduct* of his good Spirit...*bring thee* to the regions of *holiness* and *eternal peace* (VIII, 671) may be *accepted* by thy *mercies* (VIII, 691) *promoted* our eternal interest (VIII, 596) That it may become ...a blessed instrument...of *pardon* and *peace*...of *holiness* and *life eternal* (VIII, 624)

D. Consecratory Prayers at the Holy Table

H. Table (448)

Altar or *Holy Table* (for the difference is but nominal (V, 328)

The Lord be with you. Answer. And with thy Spirit. Let us pray (450–3)

The Lord be with you. Answer. And with thy Spirit. Let us pray (VIII, 606, 643; 657; cf. VIII, 582, 591, 600, where *people* is substituted for *answer*)

I

O *Most Glorious and Eternal God*...*we worship and adore thy glories* (455; 458)

Most glorious and Eternal God...*I worship and adore thee*, (III, 33). *We adore thee*, and *praise thy glories* (VIII, 600 seq.)

who *makest all* things by thy *power*, and *adornest all* things with thy *bounty*, and *fillest all* things with thy *goodness* (455–7)

That God is *eternal*...that he *made all* the world; that he is present in all places; that he is the foundation of *bounty* and *goodness* (VII, 593)

and *sanctifiest* the *hearts and gifts* of thy servants by thy *Spirit* (457–8)

send thy Holy Ghost...that...he may *sanctify*...our *hearts*...and *sanctify* these *gifts* (VIII, 624)

who *fillest all* the world *by thy presence* (458–9)

who *fillest all* things *with thy presence* (III, 43)

and *sustainest* it by thy *Almightiness* (459)

sustainest (VIII, 695) He shows himself to be the Lord of the sea, by *sustaining* there the creatures...and in the wilderness the bittern and the stork...feel the force of his *almightiness* (III, 23) *almightiness* (IV, 612)

We *humbly* pray thee by the *Death* and Passion, by the *Resurrection and Ascension*, and by the glorious *Intercession* of our Lord (462–4)

humbly represent the sacrifice of thy eternal Son...his life and *death*; his *resurrection and ascension*, his charity and intercession (VIII, 238) and beg of thee for his *death and passion's sake, by* his *resurrection and ascension* (III, 385)

effusion (466)

effusion (II, 675; VIII, 38, 53)

Let *the Sun of Righteousness* for ever shine here, and let the brightest *illumination of the holy Spirit* fill all our hearts for ever *with thy glorious presence* (466–9)

Sun of Righteousness (II, 410; VIII, 600 and frequently) O *Sun of Righteousness*, that camest to bring light unto the world by thy word, and example, and *illumination of thy Holy Spirit.* (Ps. D., Heber XV, 179) *thy glorious presence* (VIII, 606)

That which we have blessed, do thou bless; that which we offer, do thou *accept* (469–70)

Cf. Taylor's comment on 1 Kings 9. 3 ("I have hallowed this house...") that is,...what you have dedicated, I have *accepted*; what you have consecrated, I have hallowed (II, 315)

II

the *glory of thy Grace* (475–6)

glories of thy grace (VII, 388)

Drive from hence all *Sacrilegious* hands ...all *prophane persons*, all *proud* and unquiet *Schismaticks*, all *misbelieving Hereticks* (477–80)

there is a defiling of a temple...by *profanation*...and *sacrilege* (V, 321) *sacrilegious persons* (Ps. D., Heber XV, 149). From a *schismatical* and *heretical* spirit (VII, 633). Reduce every *misbeliever* to the fold...subdue the pride of men (VIII, 673)

powers of darkness...

no corrupt ayre (480–1)

powers of darkness (VIII, 644)

Avoid all pride, as you would flee from the most frightful apparition (I, 102) From phantasms, spectres, and illusions of the night (VII, 633)

Let the title of this Church abide until the *second coming* of Christ (488–9)

Preserve thy Church in peace...to thy *second coming* (VIII, 673) *celestial* food (VIII, 626)

Celestial Banquet (490)

Divine Banquet (VIII, 627)

participation (493)

participation (I, 66; II, 48, 213, 317, 484; VIII, 30, 36, 230, 618, etc.)

III

O *Eternal God, who art pleased to manifest thy presence amongst the sons of men by*

O *Eternal God...who art pleased to manifest thy presence amongst the sons of men* special issues of the favour and benediction, make our bodies and souls to be Temples pure and holy, apt for the entertainments of the Holy Jesus, and for the inhabitation of thy holy Spirit. Lord, be pleas'd, with the powers of thy grace, to cast out impure lusts, all worldly affections, all covetous desires from these Thy Temples, that they may be places of prayer and holy meditation, of godly desires and chaste thoughts, of pure intentions and great zeal to please thee, that we also may become Sacrifices as well as Temples, eaten up with the zeal of thy glory, and even consumed with the fires of thy love; that not one thought may be entertain'd by us, but such as may be like perfume exhaling from the Altar of Incense; and not a word may pass from us, but may have the accent of heaven in it, and sound pleasantly in thy ears.

O dearest God, fill every faculty of our souls with the impresses of Religion, that we loving thee above all things in the world, worshiping thee with frequent and humblest adorations, continually feeding upon the apprehensions of thy Divine sweetness, and living in a daily observation of thy Divine commandments, and delighted with the perpetual feast of a holy Conscience (495-515)

may by the Spirit be seal'd up to the day of Redemption, (515-16)

and the fruition of thy glories in thine everlasting kingdom (516-17)

through Jesus Christ our Lord, to whom with thee, O Father of mercies, Father of our Lord Jesus Christ, and with thee, O blessed and Eternal Spirit the Comforter, all honour and power be ascribed from generation to generation for ever and ever. Amen (517-21)

by special issues of thy favour and benediction, make my body and soul to be a Temple pure and holy, apt for the entertainments of the Holy Jesus, and for the habitation of the Holy Spirit. Lord, be pleased, with the rod of paternal discipline, to cast out all impure lusts, all worldly affections, all covetous desires from this thy temple, that it may be a place of prayer and meditation, of holy appitites and chaste thoughts, of pure intentions and zealous desires of pleasing thee, that I may become a sacrifice as well as a temple, eaten up with the zeal of thy glory and consumed with the fire of thy love; that not one thought may be entertained by me, but such as may be like breathing from the Altar of incense; and not a word pass from me, but may have the accent of heaven upon it, and sound pleasantly in thy ears.

O dearest God, fill every faculty of my soul with impresses...of Religion, that loving thee above all things in the world, worshipping thee with humblest adorations and frequent addresses, continually feeding upon the apprehensions of thy divine sweetness...and observations of thy righteous commandments, and the feast of a holy conscience as an antepast of eternity, and consignation to the joys in heaven... (II, 327-8)

Living by thy Spirit....may by him be sealed up to the day of our redemption (VIII, 614; cf. III, 35, and Taylor's frequent use of Eph. 4. 30) fruition of thy everlasting glories (Ps. D., Heber xv, 227) fruition of the joys of God in thy eternal kingdom (VIII, 613)

Father of mercies...Father of our Lord Jesus Christ...

and eternal Spirit...the Comforter...for ever and ever. Amen. (VIII, 578) from generation to generation for ever. Amen. (VII, 630)

The Prayer of S. Clement

...*our Lord Jesus* (524)

...*faith* and *fear, peace* and *patience,* long-suffering and *temperance,* with *purity* and wisdom (526–7)

...*our Lord Jesus* (VIII, 644)

...with *fear* and caution, with hope and *purity*...with *temperance* and *peace,* with *faith* and *patience*...(VIII, 608)

E. The Anathematism (539)

Ex Psalmis 79, 83, 129 (540–68)

The Bishop.

Glory be to God on high.

Answer.

And on earth peace to men of good will.

anathematisms (X, 256)

The Hymn for Christmas Day

Minister.

Glory be to God on high.

Answer.

And on earth peace, good-will towards men (VIII, 610; cf. Taylor's version of the Cherubikon in his Communion Office, ending *Glory be*... *good-will towards men.* Hallelujah, VIII, 624)...*to men of good will* (II, 88 seq.) Gloria Deo in excelsis In terris pax hominibus bonae voluntatis (VI, 168)

Bishop.

Amen.

Answer.

Amen. (570–6)

Minister.

Amen.

Answer.

Amen. (VIII, 610)

F. The Euphemismos or Acclamation

Ex Psalmis 150, 68, 87, 99, 100 (584–622)

Worship Jesus (624)

"*Worship Jesus*" IV, 638 (St Cyprian's reading of "Worship God" in Rev. 22. 9); quoted twice at VIII, 223, love and *worship Jesus* (VIII, 223, 624) Adora Jesum (VIII, 239)

We *worship and adore* the *great King of heaven and earth,* the *blessed Saviour of the world.* (626–7)

...*worship and adore* (III, 33)...*great King of heaven and earth* (VIII, 592) *the blessed Saviour*...*of the world* (VIII, 578, 589)

Holy is our God.

Holy is the Almighty.

Holy is the Immortal.

Holy, Holy, Holy Lord God of Sabbath

Holy is our God.

Holy is the Almighty.

Holy is the Immortal.

Holy, holy, holy Lord God of Sabaoth...

(III, 38, 41, 233; cf. another version in Ps. D.: *Holy, holy, holy, Lord God of Sabaoth; holy is our God, holy is the Immortal, holy is the Almighty*, Heber xv, 209)

blessed be thy *Name* in Heaven and Earth *for ever and ever. Amen. Amen.* (629-36)

Blessed be the *Name* of our God *for ever and ever. Amen* (VIII, 629). *Amen Amen* (III, 238; VIII, 85, 220)

So ends the Office of Consecration. (637)

So ends the Office of Baptism (VIII, 638)

G. An Office for the Restoration of a Church (662-731)

O Lord God of heaven and earth (707) *thou art righteous, and just,* and *true; thou art* also *good and gracious,* and *of great mercy and loving kindness* (707-9)

O Eternal God Lord of heaven and earth (VII, 58) *thou art just* and *merciful, righteous and true* (VIII, 651) *thou art righteous and...true...thou art just and righteous* (VII, 236) *thou art good and gracious* (VIII, 625) *mercies and loving-kindness* (VIII, 673)

that we may *no more provoke thee to anger, or to jealousy* (711-12)

may never *provoke thee to anger or to jealousy* (III, 31; cf. III, 566; etc.)

but give us thy *holy Spirit to lead us into the ways of righteousness* (714-15)

let thy *holy Spirit...lead us into the way everlasting* (VIII, 614) *in the ways of righteousness* (III, 144)

Defend thy Church, and *bless* thine *inheritance* (715-16)

Thine *own inheritance...defend, O God,* Thy *Church...* (VIII, 628)

...give thee thanks in the congregation of thy redeemed ones (717-18)

... give thee thanks in the congregation of Saints (*Ps. D.,* Heber xv, 128) *give thee praise in the congregation of thy redeemed ones* (ibid., 137) *glorify thee...the congregation of thy redeemed ones* (VIII, 670)

H. A Short Office for Expiation & Illustration of a Church Desecrated or Prophan'd (732 seqq.)

illustrations (II, 82); *illustrate* (IV, 18, 435, 436, etc.; VIII, 617)

O Almighty God, who art *of pure eyes,* and *canst not behold impurity, behold the Angels are not pure in* thy *sight,* and *thou hast found folly in* thy

O Almighty God...in whose *sight* heavens *are not pure,* and the *angels* tremble, *and the saints are charged with folly...in* thy *glorious presence* (VIII,

Saints (744-6) We acknowledge ourselves un*worthy* to appear *in thy glorious presence*, because we are *polluted in thy sight* (748-50)

it is just in thee to . . . (750)

where thy holy feet have trod (752) . . . Cast out all iniquity from *within us* (756-7)

and may be *accepted by* the gracious *interpellation* of our *High Priest*, the *most glorious Jesus* (760-2)

a *Royal Priesthood*, *a chosen Generation* (766-7)

O look upon thy most holy *Son*, and regard *the cry of* his *blood, and let it on our behalf speak better things than the blood of Abel* (769-71) . . .

Holy *Lamb*, who wast *slain from the beginning of the world* (772-3)

and *keep our bodies and souls and spirits unblameable to the coming of* our *Lord Jesus* (777-8)

. . . grant that we being *presented* unto thee without *spot* or wrinkle, or any such thing, may . . . *walk in white* with *the Lamb* in the Kingdom of our God for ever and ever (779-82)

Grant this, O Almighty God, our Most *gracious Father* (782-3)

Te decet Hymnus (814)

---

606) I am *in thy sight* . . . a *polluted* person . . . I am not *worthy* to come *into thy presence* (VIII, 207)

it is just in thee to . . . (VIII, 207)

where thy holy feet have trod (VII, 643; cf. II, 71) *Cast out all iniquity from us* (VIII, 577)

accepted by his *interpellation* (IV, 344) . . . in the way of prayer and *interpellation*, Christ . . . as *high-priest* (VIII, 40). Cf. by a ministry of *interpellation* of prayer (I, 50); the Spirit makes *interpellations* (III, 307) *most glorious* . . . *Jesus* (VIII, 86, 612)

a *chosen generation*, *a royal priesthood* (VIII, 659)

O *let the cry of thy Son's blood*, who offers an eternal Sacrifice to thee, *speak on* my *behalf*, and *speak better things than the blood of Abel* (VIII, 207)

Lamb slain from the beginning of the world (IV, 435, 665; VII, 36, 356; VIII, 38)

Sanctify them throughout in their *bodies, and souls, and spirits,* and *keep* them *unblameable to the coming of* the *Lord Jesus* (III, 33; VIII, 260, 289)

presented to God washed and cleansed, pure and *spotless* (VII, 643; cf. VIII, 236: *present* a Church *to thee* . . . *spot*less) . . . and *walk in white* whithersoever *the Lamb* shall go (VIII, 680)

Grant this, Almighty God and Father . . . *O Almighty God and gracious Father* (III, 111)

Te decet Hymnus appears below a print of David with his harp before the Psalter of the 1658 edition of the *Collection of Offices* as also on the frontispiece of early editions of *The Psalter of David*.

One prayer, however, requires closer examination. The second prayer before the chancel door (101 seqq.) provides three important links with Jeremy Taylor.

(1) The curious addition of "for ever" to our Lord's quotation from Isaiah 56. 7:

...and that amongst all Nations *for ever*, Thy house shall be called the house of Prayer. (126 seq.)

Taylor's own comment on our Lord's use of Isaiah 56. 7 is likewise:

For all nations, now and *for ever*...the time is unlimited as the nations were indefinite and universal.[1]

(2) The curious addition of "great" to "Lover of Souls" of Wisdom 11. 26 (164), which Taylor nearly always renders as "Great Lover of Souls".[2] This we may compare with the curious substitution in another prayer (773) of "beginning" for "foundation" of Revelation 13. 8, which Taylor also repeatedly renders as "the Lamb, slain from the *beginning* of the world".

(3) The marginal reference (139):

πάντες ἐπὶ, τὸ ἀυτὸ· πάντες ἐπὶ τον ναὸν τοῦ θεοῦ.
S. Ignat. Epist. ad Magnes.

This is an abbreviated reference to two short extracts from Chapter VII of the Epistle of Ignatius to the Magnesians, as given in the Long Recension, each beginning πάντες...[3] The first appeared in 1658 on the title-page of Taylor's *Collection of Offices*:

πάντες ἐπὶ τὸ ἀυτὸ ἐν τῇ προσευχῇ ἅμα συνέρχεσθε· μία δέησις ἔστω [κοινή], εἷς νοῦς.

Taylor had already used this passage to the same extent in his *Apology*[4] *for Authorized and Set Forms of Liturgy* of 1647,[5] and had quoted more extensively the same passage from a Latin version of the long recension in the *Great Exemplar*: "Omnes...Omnes...ad unum Jesum Christum, &c.—S. Ignat. ad Magnes"; and this may represent the full extent of the passage referred to in the marginal note.[6] The fact that Taylor used this

---

[1] II, 350; cf. v, 323, where Taylor says that Christ meant not the Jewish Temple, which would soon be destroyed, but Christian Churches.

[2] III, 233, 245; VII, 236; VIII, 614, 647, 658, etc.; Ps. D., Heber xv, 225.

[3] Bishop Lightfoot, *Apostolic Fathers*, II (Sect. II), 754 seq.

[4] VIII, 571.   [5] V, 301.

[6] "Omnes ad orandum in idem convenite: sit communis precatio, una mens, una spes in charitate et fide inculpata in Christum Jesum; quo nihil est praestantibus. Omnes velut unus quispiam ad templum Dei concurite, velut ad unum altar, ad unum Jesum Christum." II, 319n.

passage three times shows that it was one which was readily in his mind, and the fact that he quoted from the long recension in works of 1647, 1649, 1658, 1660,[1] and 1667,[2] long after the appearance of Ussher's reconstruction of the true Ignatius in 1644, would readily account for the marginal reference to the long recension in the consecration form of 1666.

Moreover, all the unusual words in the 1666 form are used by Taylor in a similar way:—*Immensity, Almightiness, Effusion, Illustration, Lavatory* for the Font or waters of Baptism, *Anathematism, Sacramentals,* and *Interpellation.* Of these *Sacramentals* are used in the 1666 form to include at least the Occasional Offices; in Taylor to include Confirmation, Ordination, Absolution, the Visitation of the Sick, Marriage, and "the blessing of single persons":[3] *Interpellation* is used in the 1666 form of the intercession of Christ; in Taylor exclusively of the intercession of the Second or Third Person of the Trinity.

Of simpler words used by Taylor frequently, *sanctify* occurs in the 1666 form three times, *holiness* (four), *glories* (four), *glorious* (five), *desires* (six), *ministeries* (six), *mercies* (seven), *honour* (eight), *grace* (nine), *Name* (ten), *accept* (fourteen), and *eternal* (seventeen). As in Taylor, moreover, *eternal* is used to qualify *God, life, Sacrifice, Priesthood, peace, charity,* and *goodness.* Again, the form speaks of "*Ministerial* Altar" just as Taylor speaks of "*Ministerial* Priesthood" and "*Ministerial* Offices".

From the close parallels set out above a number of expressions and phrases common to the Irish form and to Taylor will be noticed, the most frequent being "*the Lord Jesus*" (five times), "*by the Spirit*" (five), "*High Priest*" (four), and "*thy holy Spirit*" (four). There also occur in the Irish form "*Father of man and angels*", "*thy holy Son*", "*thy most holy Son*", "*the Holy Jesus*", "*thy holy Son Jesus*", "*the most glorious Jesus*", "*thy most holy Spirit*", "*by thy Word, and by thy Spirit*", "*all the promises of the Gospel*", "*Ministeries of Salvation*", "*Ministeries of Religion*", "*portion of thine inheritance*", "*lot of thine inheritance*", "*a Guard of Angels*", "*dreadful and venerable*", "*a holy hope*", "*eternal charity*", "*an unreproveable faith*", "*a perfect obedience*", "*assistances of the Holy Spirit*", "*with reverence and solemnity*", "*in the bosom of Christ*", "*the sentence of the right hand*", "*wise and holy*", "*sacramentally represented and exhibited*", "*hunger after the bread of life and thirst for the wine of elect souls*", "*enlightened with the lanthorn of thy*

---

[1] In the *Worthy Communicant* Taylor follows the long recension in a citation from the Epistle to the Ephesians. *Works,* VIII, 186.

[2] In the *Dissuasive* (Pt. II) Taylor by accepting the genuineness of the Epistle to the Philippians showed that at the end of his life he had not absorbed the work of Ussher. Ibid., VI, 438.

[3] Ibid., V, 631.

Word, and the light of thy Spirit". The close parallels, the common expressions and phrases, the prayer from the *Great Exemplar*, and Taylor's peculiar version of the Trisagion, strongly suggests that his hand was at least in this liturgical work published the year before his death.

(b) Style and Use of Ancient Material

C. P. Eden believed that the form of 1666 "in style closely resembles Taylor's compositions", though he thought it had first appeared in 1700. We have already noticed a common use of words, some of which are now obsolete. There are also a number of common words which seem to have been chosen for their musical value: *abide, abode, adorn, deplore, implore, imprint, magnify, grace, glory, gracious, glorious, graciousness*. There are also in this form, as in Taylor, the same plural forms: *issues, graces, glories, favours, mercies, promises, weaknesses, services, repentences, intentions, impresses, apprehensions, entertainments, inconveniences, adorations, understandings, loving-kindnesses*. Sir Edmund Gosse attributed the apparent length of Taylor's sentences to "the rhetoric 'and' with which he loves to link the independent sequents of them".[1] We find examples of this use in the form.[2] He also frequently uses "and" to arrange blessings, gifts, and virtues in pairs;[3] and thus we find it introduced into his beautiful translation of the Prayer of St Clement: "faith *and* fear, peace *and* patience, long-suffering *and* temperance, with purity *and* wisdom..."[4] We find, moreover, the same rhetorical use of "all" introduced into the last of a series of short clauses: "...and to drive away *all* the power of the Enemy"; "...and *all* the promises of the Gospel"; "...and to perform *all* the Ministeries of Salvation"; "...and receive *all* the benefits of his Passion".[5]

The opening of one prayer (455-9) deserves attention as revealing a similar construction to some of Taylor's prayers and a similar use of ancient material.

O most glorious and eternal God who makest all things by thy power,
    and adornest all things by thy bounty,
    and fillest all things with thy goodness,
    and sanctifiest the hearts and gifts of thy servants by thy Spirit,

[1] *Jeremy Taylor*, 226.
[2] Lines 404-7; 410-14; 432-47; 773-9.
[3] For example: "...with fear *and* caution, with hope *and* charity, with diligence *and* devotion...with love *and* obedience...with temperance *and* peace, with faith *and* patience, with health *and* holiness..." VIII, 608.
[4] Lines 526-7. Cf. Bishop Lightfoot's translation: "faith, fear, peace, patience, long-suffering, temperance, chastity and soberness."
[5] There are many examples in Taylor, particularly a remarkable passage on the gifts of the Magi, where "all" is used in this way four times. II, 96. ("These Magi presented...all His glories".)

U

we worship and adore thy glories,
  who fillest all the world by thy presence, and sustainest it by
  thy Almightiness.

Here we find, as in many of Taylor's prayers, an address to God, extended into several clauses, and followed by an act of adoration.[1] In this prayer, however, the clauses seem to have been influenced by a passage in the *Prefatio in medio ecclesiae* said by the Bishop in the Office for consecrating churches in the Pontifical:

...*quae omnis purificas, omnia mundas, omnis exornas...quae cuncta imples, cuncta contines, cunctaque disponis...quae omnia sanctificas, omnis benedicis, omnia locopletas...*

Here the compiler seems to have chosen material largely for its musical value, taken it out of its setting, and adapted it to his own inimitable style.

In another prayer (168–205), however, the compiler has followed more closely the main sequence of thought in the medieval *Prefatio*, but interwoven it with scriptural quotations and phrases of his own. Thus three petitions, though retained in their order, have been converted into scriptural phrases:

Pontifical	*Irish Form*
(1) Hic quoque sacerdotes sacrificium tibi laudis offerant:	Here let thy Priests be clothed with righteousness, and let thy Saints sing with joyfulness.
(2) hic fideles populi vota persolvant:	Here let thy people make their prayers, and perform their vows, and offer thee free-will offerings with a holy worship.
(3) hic peccatorum onera solvantur.	Here let the weight of their sins that so easily besets them, be laid aside.

A little further on we find *caeci illuminentur* changed into the language of Taylor, "let the blind eyes and hearts be inlightened with the lanthorn of thy Word and the light of the Spirit", and *vincula peccatorum* become "the chains of their corruption, and the cords of vanity". In a similar way the compiler has followed the main sequence of part of Bishop Andrewes' long consecratory prayer of 1620 (76–166), but interwoven many scriptural quotations and phrases of his own.

This use of ancient or earlier material is perfectly in line with Taylor's own method. Thus in *Holy Living* we find *Ex Liturgia S. Basilii magna ex*

---

[1] "O eternal and most blessed Jesus...we adore thee, and praise thy glories". VIII, 600 seq. "O most gracious and eternal God...I bless and glorify thy name, and adore thy goodness." III, 249.

parte where he introduces many scriptural quotations and phrases of his own. To the description of the Lord Jesus as "the true light", he adds, "that lighteneth every man that cometh into the world", and he gives many additional attributes to the Holy Spirit. He introduces the *Sanctus* with his curious version of the *Trisagion*; and the greater part of the *Post Sanctus* is divided into sections by Psalm 107. 8.[1] This method is still further developed in the *Collection of Offices* of 1658, which he claims to have been "collected out of the devotions of the Greek Church, with some mixture of Mozarabic and Æthopic, and other liturgies, and perfected out of the fountain of scripture".[2] The compiler of the Irish form has likewise collected his material from ancient and other sources "and perfected them out of the fountain of scripture".

(c) Theological Emphasis and other Points of Contact

The prayer for the dedication of the altar or Communion table contains the same emphasis which we find in Taylor on the eternal and celestial Sacrifice, Priesthood, and Intercession of Christ as High Priest, the earthly ministry at the "Ministerial Altar" being an imitation of the heavenly which is performed at the heavenly Altar, of which the Holy table is a copy. The presence of Eucharistic language in the consecration form (164–5; 316; 462–5; 760–2; 769–75) apart from the Eucharistic action is perfectly in line with Taylor's view that all forms of prayer are connected with Christ's eternal Priesthood and Intercession.[3] Thus in 1661 he laid down that in all towns of his diocese the daily offices "must be read in churches, that the daily sacrifice of prayer and thanksgiving may never cease". Likewise it would be natural for the author of the *Discourse of Confirmation* (1663) to provide for the administration of the Holy Rite of Confirmation between the Litany and the Communion (646–7), and of the *Ductor Dubitantium* to include prayers "for all them whose consciences being accused of sin come with confidence to the Throne of Grace" and who "in humility and contrition shall confess their sins" (158–61; 183–5). Nor need we be surprised to find so many petitions for the clergy and worshippers in the new church when we remember that Taylor believed "the best ornament and beauty of a church" to be "a holy priest and a sanctified people".[4]

There are also many minor ways in which we can detect the mind of

---

[1] *Works*, III, 232 seqq.

[2] Ibid., VIII, 537. The slight use of the Armenian Consecration Office was no doubt intended as a compliment to the Registrar of the Upper House, Dr Dudley Loftus, who was engaged at this time in translating Armenian and liturgical and other texts.

[3] See Chapter 2 above, 97 seq.   [4] Ibid., II, 326.

Taylor. The compiler has too much love for the Book of Common Prayer and is too much of an artist to intrude long prayers of his own, after the manner of Andrewes and Cosin, into the framework of Morning Prayer, the Litany, and the Communion. Apart from special Psalms and Lections a very short Collect is provided "at Morning Prayer, and the Communion, together with the Collect of the Day". Otherwise "the Office of Consecration" ends before the beginning of Morning Prayer, "the Bell tolling a little in the interval" (638 seq.). Taylor had a similar love of the Prayer Book and only published his *Collection of Offices* to meet a desperate situation when it was proscribed. He had a special veneration for the variety, energy, and power of the Prayer Book Collects, which "are cleared from a neighbourhood of tediousness by their so quick intercision and breakings off".[1] This is also true of the special Collect for Morning Prayer and the Communion (655 seqq.), which falls naturally into the five traditional divisions, and has been praised by Dr J. Wickham Legg as being "a true Gregorian Collect".[2]

Of all Taylor's works the Irish form of 1666 has the greatest number of parallels with *A Collection of Offices or Form of Prayer in Cases Ordinary and Extraordinary. Taken out of the Scriptures and the ancient Liturgies of Several Churches, especially the Greek. Together with the Psalter or Psalms of David, according to the Kings Translation; with Arguments to the same.* This original publication of 1658 has been obscured rather by its abridgement in the editions of Heber and C. P. Eden. The edition of 1658 shows not only many of the hymns ex Psalmis in the offices, but the actual Psalter, divided into the days of the month, to be "according to the King's Translation", and this is the version used for the hymns ex Psalmis in the 1666 consecration form. The title-page of the Psalter, moreover, bears the ascription, *Te decet Hymnus*, which also occurs in large type at the end of the three offices of 1666 (814), while the first title-page, as we have already noticed, bears part of the quotation from St Ignatius to which marginal reference is made in the form (139). There are also many parallels between the rubrics of the Irish form and Taylor's *Offices* of 1658,[3] and also between the form of dedication of the font in the one and

---

[1] *Works*, v, 245.   [2] *Eng. Ch. Orders*, 332.

[3] For example: *Then rising up; arising from their knees; great Festival of the Church; the —— shall read this lesson; verse — to — inclusively; The Psalms appointed for ——; immediately before; the Prayer of S. ——.* (In the Irish form, as in Taylor generally, S. is used instead of St.) In the Irish form we find two hymns called the *Anathematism* and the *Euphemismos* or *Acclamation*: in Taylor's Communion Office the General Warning is called the *Commination*, and the *Cherubikon* the *Exphonesis* or *Denounciation*.

the Baptism Office in the other. In the one the blessing of the Baptismal water is directed apart from the administration of the Sacrament of Baptism (272–4; 284) and the font called the *Lavatory* (287): in the other the Baptismal water may be kept "as is usual in the Churches both of East and West" [1] and "a *lavatory* of silver", presumably a portable font, may be used. [2] The Consecration Office of 1666 ends with the rubrical note, *So ends the Office of Consecration*: Taylor's Baptism Office, *So ends the Office of Baptism*.

The liturgical conclusion of the Office of Consecration, however, is the *Trisagion* in Taylor's peculiar version, together with the *Sanctus*, which he always uses with it. Taylor was fond of using the *Trisagion*, which he believed "was taught to the Greek Church by angels". [3] He had fallen back upon some part of it for an ascription of praise at the end of earlier works. Thus we find [῞Ο]῞ΑΓ ΙΟΣ ῾ΙΣΧΥ ΡΟΣ at the end of *Clerus Domini*, [4] the *Liberty of Prophesying*, [5] and the Second Part of the *Great Exemplar*, [6] and ῾ΑΓΙΟΣ ῾ΑΟΑΝΑΤΟΣ at the end of the Third Part. [7] It would therefore be quite natural for Taylor to make the *Trisagion* the conclusion of the *Acclamation* with which the Consecration Office ends.

Finally, we may detect the mind of Taylor as a diocesan Bishop from 1661. The rubrical reference to "some Lord's day, or other great Festival of the Church" (7 seq.) is in line with Taylor's advice to his clergy in 1661 only to "use primitive, known, and accustomed words" and "let the Sunday festival be called 'the Lord's day' ". [8] One prayer (474 seqq.) contains petitions in picturesque language which seem to reflect not only the persecution of the Church of Ireland from 1641 but the peculiar difficulties of his own diocese from 1661.

Drive from hence all sacrilegious hands, all superstitious Rites, all prophane persons, all proud and unquiet Schismaticks, all misbelieving Hereticks: Let not the powers of darkness come hither, nor the secret arrow ever smite any here: Let no corrupt ayre...no blood-shed...ever pollute this place dedicated to thy holiness.

During the Rebellion of 1641 Irish parish churches had often been taken over for "superstitious Rites" and polluted by bloodshed, secret arrows having smitten Anglican worshippers; and during the subsequent Cromwellian occupation "sacrilegious hands" had often seized, and "prophane persons" occupied, church buildings. On first coming to his diocese

[1] *Works*, VIII, 631. [2] Ibid. [3] Ibid., V, 240.
[4] Ibid., I, 61. [5] Ibid., V, 605. [6] Ibid., II, 499.
[7] Ibid., 730. [8] Ibid., I, 109.

Taylor had found a number of churches in his diocese occupied by Scots ministers whom he regarded as "proud and unquiet Schismatics" and as "misbelieving Heretics".[1]

(d) The Probable Authorship

Any theory of authorship must be based upon the printed form of 1666 and the circumstances in which it was published. The discovery in the future of any contemporary manuscript version of the form, either in the hand of Taylor or of another, would be of interest but of little consequence. Actually part of the Lesson (240–57) and the Prayer (263–71) at the Burial Place are to be found in a contemporary hand, but included in a manuscript "Form of Consecration of the New Burial Ground near St Patrick's Cathedral Close, Dublin, commonly called 'the Cabbage Garden'" in 1667 (Trinity College, Dublin: MS. 647, F. 1. 7.).[2] Although this form is "possibly by Dr Boyle, Archbishop of Dublin",[3] the manuscript copy of it is in the handwriting of Dr Dudley Loftus.[4] Likewise the manuscript of Bishop Cosin's first consecration form (British Museum: Add. MS. 29,586, fol. 26) "is thought by some to be in the handwriting of Christopher Hatton, who died in 1670".[5] So often seventeenth-century laymen copied out liturgical forms which were not printed, and there is no reason to suppose that either Dr Dudley Loftus or Christopher Hatton compiled the forms in question. The Irish consecration form, on the other hand, was published in 1666 with the highest ecclesiastical sanction, the King's Printer making more than one impression of it in that year. There would, therefore, be no need for any manuscript copy of it to be made, and the compiler's original version of it probably perished at the King's Printing House in Dublin soon after publication.

Thus far we have established that the consecration form printed in the Irish folio Prayer Books from 1700 to 1757, the only version known to

[1] Taylor said of Bramhall, at his funeral, that "at his coming to the primacy he knew he should at first espy little besides the ruins of discipline, a harvest of thorns, and heresies prevailing in the hearts of the people, and churches possessed by wolves and intruders...and therefore he set himself to weed the fields of the church..." VIII, 420. Picturesque language was of course used on both sides.

[2] Legg, *Eng. Ch. Orders*, 261 seqq. The parts taken from the 1666 form are at p. 262 seq. The beautiful prayer from the 1666 form is in such marked contrast to the other three prayers of 1667 that no useful purpose could be served in suggesting that the author of the 1667 form was the author of the 1666. Probably Taylor's death in 1667 accounts for the fact that the Office for a Burial Ground was completed by another compiler.

[3] Ibid., 261.

[4] G. T. Stokes, *Some Worthies of the Irish Church*, 52n.

[5] Legg, *Eng. Ch. Orders*, 218.

C. P. Eden, was first published in Dublin in 1666, the year before Taylor's death, and that it is entirely different in structure, style, and theological emphasis, from the draft form presented by Bishop Cosin in the English Convocation, and also from the Dublin diocesan consecration form of 1719, drawn up by Archbishop King, who was but a schoolboy in 1666. We have further seen reason to believe that the form of 1666 was drawn up in Ireland at the request of the Irish Bishops by one of their Order, and that Bishop Taylor, who at their request wrote the *Discourse of Confirmation* and the *Dissuasive from Popery* was the most likely Bishop to be entrusted by them with its preparation. The internal evidence makes it clear that the devotional works of Taylor were not simply one source among others, for earlier material, ancient and Anglican, is taken over and refashioned in the same inimitable style; and that there are so many parallels with the works of Taylor that it is difficult to believe that this liturgical composition is the work of any other author. The case for Taylor's authorship must rest upon the accumulated evidence set forth above; and the reader is asked to study the liturgical text in Appendix 1 and then decide for himself whether it should be included in the canon of Taylor's works, which in any case must now be reopened to receive his altogether forgotten, but perfectly genuine, Latin letter of 1662, which for the first time is reprinted here in Appendix 2. The form of 1666, moreover, is worth reading as a remarkable expression of the Caroline Churchmanship of the Church of Ireland.

APPENDED NOTE

THE IRISH FORM OF 1666
AND THE *PSALTER OF DAVID* OF 1644

Early in 1955 Mr Robert Gathorne-Hardy presented a case for Jeremy Taylor's authorship of the *Psalter of David* of 1644,[1] which seventeenth-century advertisements attributed first to Sir Christopher Hatton, and then to Taylor, pointing to several close parallels between this work and the works of Taylor, though without noticing many common expressions, as for example, "Prince of the Catholic Church", "the Master of the Feast and the Feast itself"; "testimony of a good conscience", and "sermons of the Gospel".

[1] "Jeremy Taylor and Hatton's 'Psalter of David' ", *The Times Literary Supplement*, 18 Feb. 1955, p. 112.

This case should be considerably strengthened if we remember the expressions in the *Psalter of David* which occur in the Irish form of 1666, which can hardly by any stretch of the imagination be attributed to Hatton, but which can probably be attributed to Taylor. These expressions include: "Father of men and Angels"; "assistances...of thy Holy Spirit"; "thy Immensity"; "*great* lover of souls"; "comfort the comfortless"; "the dew of Divine blessings"; "be all glory and honour... love and obedience for ever and ever"; "Fountain of purity"; "eternal charity"; "Grant this for his sake...who is both Sacrifice and Priest"; "enlarged hearts"; "guard of angels"; "Sun of Righteousness...illumination of thy Holy Spirit"; "fruition of thy...glories"; "Holy, holy, holy, Lord God of Sabaoth; holy is our God, holy is the Immortal, holy is the Almighty"; "...give thanks in the congregation of..."; "in the congregation of thy redeemed ones"; "Te decet Hymnus". Of these "*great* lover of souls" is Taylor's favourite rendering of "lover of souls" in Wisdom 11. 26; and "Holy is our God...", instead of "Holy God...", Taylor's peculiar translation of the Trisagion, which he always gives with Sanctus, though in *Holy Living* and the Irish form the Trisagion is placed first. Part of the Trisagion in Greek was used as an ascription at the end of some of Taylor's works, and the Trisagion in Latin at the end of the first seven editions of the *Psalter of David*. *Te decet Hymnus* appears above the frontispiece of some early editions of the *Psalter*, below a print of David with his harp in *A Collection of Offices* of 1658, preceding "the Psalter or Psalms of David, according to the Kings Translation; with Arguments to the same",[1] and in large type at the end of the third Irish Office of 1666. In all three works "the Kings translation" of the Psalms is used.[2] In the prayer following Psalm 110 in the *Psalter of David* thanksgiving is offered for "Christ's continual mediation and intercession, by which he doth officiate in his eternal Priesthood, which is after the order of Melchisedeck". This fits Taylor's emphasis on the celestial ministry of Christ as High Priest almost as closely as the prayer for the dedication of the altar in the Irish form. Among the plural forms common to the works of 1644 and 1666 are *apprehensions, impresses, assistances, recompences, glories, ministries, lovingkindnesses, adorations, understandings*.

The preface, which bears marks of Taylor's style, fits the little we know of his life between his ejection from Uppingham and his settlement in

[1] Not included in the editions of Heber and Eden. In that of 1658 the Psalms are divided, as in the *Psalter of David*, into the Prayer Book division of the days of the month.

[2] In the Consecration Office, but the Prayer Book version is used in the Restoration Office.

Wales. He had certainly been deprived of his books and his "retirements", and inasmuch as he had no settled ministry and little immediate prospect of any he could truthfully say: "I wait not at the Altar". Nor was it expedient for Taylor to publish any work in his own name in 1644. During that year the life of his former patron, Archbishop Laud, was in the balance. Prynne had combed Laud's private papers, including his book of private devotions, and made much capital out of an indiscreet letter written by another young protégé, James Croxton, to the Archbishop boasting that he had "sacramentally heard" the confessions of his parishioners at Gowran, near Kilkenny, at Easter 1638.[1] Articles had been brought against Laud in the autumn of 1643, and his trial lingered on from 12 March 1644 to 4 January 1645. Had the *Psalter* been published at that time under the name of one of Laud's chaplains it would have been combed for Popery and Arminianism and used in evidence against the aged Archbishop or even against his chaplain. It was, therefore, much safer for it to be published anonymously,[2] as indeed *A Collection of Offices* and the Irish form of 1666 were, though for different reasons, at a later date. Nor is there any need to believe that the plan of the work was suggested by Hatton; for the Preface makes it clear that it had been suggested by earlier Psalters, one by Cassander, another by an Anglo-Saxon cleric, and two later ones, and these are more likely to have received close attention from Taylor than from Hatton.

[1] See above, p. 16.
[2] All but the eighth edition (1672) by Royston with Taylor's name on the title and at the end of the Preface.

Appendix I

A FORM OF CONSECRATION, OR, DEDICATION OF CHURCHES AND CHAPPELS,[1] ACCORDING TO THE USE OF THE CHURCH OF IRELAND.[1]

¶ *The Patron, or the chief of the Parish where a new Church is erected,* 5
is to give timely notice to the Bishop of the Diocess, and humbly to
desire him to appoint a convenient time, some Lords day, or other great
Festival of the Church for performance of the solemnity.

¶ *At the day appointed, the Bishop, with a convenient number of his*
Clergy (of which the Dean or Archdeacon to be one) and the Chan- 10
cellor of the Diocess, and his Register shall come between the hours of
eight and ten in the morning; and when they are neer, the bell is
to ring till they be entred into the Church appointed to be consecrated.

¶ *First, the Bishop and his Clergy, together with the Patron or his*
Deputy, shall go round about the Coemitery, or Church-yards; which 15
done, the Bishop and his Clergy shall enter into the Church at the
West door, the Patron and people standing without, while the Bishop
and Priests do vest themselves in their respective Ecclesiastick habits.

¶ *When they are vested, they shall kneel down in the body of the Church,*
with their faces to the East, and say together, 20

Our Father which art in Heaven, Hallowed be thy Name, thy
Kingdom come, thy Will be done in earth, as it is in heaven:
Give us this day our daily bread, and forgive us our trespasses, as
we forgive them that trespass against us; and lead us not into temptation, but deliver us from evil. *Amen.* 25

¶ *Then the Bishop shall pray,*

Prevent us, O Lord, in all our doings with thy most gracious favour,
and further us with thy continual help, that in all our works begun,
continued, and ended in thee, we may glorifie thy holy Name, and
finally, by thy mercy obtain everlasting life, through Jesus Christ 30
our Lord. *Amen.*

¶ *Then rising up, they shall go together to the West door, and the Dean*

---

[1] For the addition of these words, see above, p. 252 & n.

or Archdeacon on one hand, and the Chancellour on the other, shall
bring the Patron to the threshold, of the West door, and present him to
the Bishop; who shall thus say to him, 35

Sir, I am come hither at your desire; I aske therefore for what intent
you have desir'd my coming?

¶ *The Patron shall answer; or some of the Clergy at his request and*
  appointment, shall answer for him,

He hath [or, *mutatis mutandis*] I have caused a house to be built for 40
the service of God, and the publick Ministeries of Religion, and
separated a burying place for my dead; and [his, or] my humble
desire is, that it may be set apart from all common and prophane
uses, and dedicated to the honour of God by your prayers, and holy
Ministeries, according to the Word of God, and the Laws and 45
Customs of this Church.

¶ *Then shall the Bishop say,*

Whiles it remained, was it not thine own? and before it is given to
God, was it not in thine own power? but when once you gave it to
God, it can never be recalled, but is in his propriety for ever. 50

¶ *The Patron or his Deputy shall answer,*

I humbly desire he will be graciously pleased to accept it, and that it
may remain his own for his service, and his honour for ever.

¶ *Then shall the Patron kneel down and receive the Bishops blessing in*
  the words following. 55
¶ *The Bishop laying his hand upon or lifting it over the Patrons head,*
  shall say,

The Lord bless you, and prosper you; the Lord make his face to
shine upon you, and be merciful unto you. Remember thy servant,
O God, concerning this also; accept his gift, sanctifie his heart, 60
purifie his intentions, reward his loving kindness, and spare him
according to the greatness of thy mercies. Enrich him and his family
with all blessings of thy Spirit, and thy Providence for ever, through
Jesus Christ our Lord. Amen.

And now in the Name of God, and to the honour of our Lord 65
Jesus Christ, let us perform this Ministry.

¶ *Then the Patron arising; the Bishop shall call for the instrument of*
  Donation; which the Bishop receiving from the hands of the Patron,
  shall deliver to the Register, to be read publickely in that place.

¶ Which being done, all may enter into the Church: Then shall the 70
Bishop, attended by his Clergy, kneel in the body of the Church;
before the Chancel door, at a convenient distance, upon a footstep
raised higher than the floor, and shall say,

Let us pray.

I   75

Chron.   Blessed be thou, O Lord God, Father of our Lord Jesus Christ for
29. 10. &c. ever and ever. Thine, O Lord, is the greatness, and the power, and
the glory, and the victory, and the Majestie: All that is in the heavens,
and in the earth is thine. Thine is the Kingdom, O Lord, and thou art
exalted as head above all. Both riches and honour come of thee, and   80
thou reignest over all; and in thine hand is power and might, and in
thine hand it is to make great, and to give strength unto all. Now
therefore, our God, we thank thee, and praise thy glorious Name,
that thou hast put it into the heart of thy servants to build a house
for the honour of thy Name, and the service of thy Majestie. O   85
Lord our God, What are we, and what is this people, that from thy
servants any thing should be given and offered unto thee by us?
All things come of thee, and of thy own we give unto thee. But we
know also, O God, that thou triest the heart, and hast pleasure in
uprightness. O Lord God of our Fathers, God of mercy, and Father   90
of men and Angels, keep this, and all thankfulness, and piety, and
devotion in the imagination of the thoughts of the heart of thy
servants for ever; and prosper thou the works of our hands unto us,
O prosper thou our handy-work. Confirm this thing which thou
hast wrought in us, from thy holy Temple which is in Jerusalem,   95
which is from above, and is the Mother of us all: And for ever be
pleased to imploy us in thy service, to strengthen us in all obedience,
to lead us in the way everlasting, and to accept us in those Religious
duties which we shall perform by thy Commandment and by the
assistances of thy holy Spirit, through Jesus Christ our Lord. Amen.   100

II

O Almighty and Eternal God, who by thy Immensity fillest all
places both in heaven and earth, and canst not be limited or circum-
scrib'd in any: Thou art the most High, and dwellest not, as we do,
in houses made with hands; for Heaven is thy Throne, and the earth   105
is thy foot-stool; And what house can we build for thee? And what is
the place of thy rest, that we can furnish out for thee? Surely every
place is too little, and too low for thee, who dwellest on high, and
thy glory is above the Heavens: And yet thou humblest thyself to

behold the things that are in heaven and earth, and thy delight is 110
to be with the sons of men. Thou speakest our words, thou com-
pliest with our weaknesses, thou acceptest our services, and wilt be
worshipped and ador'd according to what thou hast put into our
power. Thou therefore hast been pleas'd in all ages to meet with
thy servants in places separate for thy worship, and for the invoca- 115
tion of thy holy Name. In Paradise there was a proper place which
thy servant *Moses* called, *The presence of the Lord*; and thy servant
Abraham called on thy Name, in the *place of the Altar:* And thou
didst meet the Patriarch *Jacob* at *Bethel*, and he consecrated a stone
for thy memorial, and it became dreadful and venerable, the House 120
of God, and the Gate of Heaven; and *Rebekah* had a proper place
whither she went to inquire of the Lord. Thou also didst fill the
Tabernacle with thy presence, and the Temple with thy glory; and
when the fulness of time was come, thou by thy most holy Son didst
declare, that thou wilt be present in all places, where two or three 125
are gathered in thy Name; and that amongst all Nations for ever,
Thy house shall be called the house of prayer; and by thy Apostle
hast signified to us, that our dwelling houses are to eat and drink in,
but that we must not despise the Churches of God. For thou art a
jealous God, and wilt not endure that thy Temples should be 130
defiled. Our God is a consuming fire, and he that defiles a Temple,
him will God destroy.

Therefore in confidence of thy goodness, in expectation of thy
favours, in full assurance of thy promises, in obedience to the manifold declaration of thy pleasure, and in imitation of the piety of thy 135
servants, who in all the generations of the world have separated
places and houses for thy service, and left great monuments of their
piety for our comfort and example, that we may come together
into one place,* and by a joyn'd prayer, wrastle with thee for blessings, and not depart thence till thou hast blessed us: We thy servants 140
walking in the steps of their most holy faith, partakers of the same
hope, fellow Citizens with the Saints, and of the household of God,
are this day met together in thy fear and love, to dedicate a house
to thee, and to the glories of thy Name, that we may not neglect
the assembling of ourselves together, but meet here to implore thy 145
mercies, to deplore our sins, to deprecate thy anger, to magnifie
thy goodness, to celebrate thy praises, to receive thy Sacraments, to
bless thy people, and to perform all Ministeries of Salvation.

Be pleased therefore, most gracious Lord and Father, to accept
the devotion and oblation of thy servants: Admit this place and 150
house into the portion of thine own inheritance: Let it be a resting
place for thy feet, and the seat of thy Graciousness. Depute thy holy
Angels to abide here, to defend thy servants, and to drive away all

1.
4.

.
17.

ντες ἐπὶ
αὐτὸ.
ντες ἐπὶ
ν ναόν
ῦ θεοῦ.

Ignat.
ist. ad
gnes

the power of the Enemy. Place thy mercy-seat among us also: Let thine eyes and thine ears be open towards this house night and day, 155 and hear the prayers of thy people which they shall make unto thee in this place; granting to them all the graces which they shall need and ask: And whensoever in humility and contrition, they shall confess their sins unto thee, be thou more ready to hear, than they to pray: forgive them all their sins, encrease and perfect their 160 repentances, remove thy judgments far from them, and let them feel and rejoyce in thy mercies and loving kindnesses for ever and ever. Grant this for his sake who is the King of the Saints, and the Head of the Church, the great lover of souls, and our High Priest, who continually makes intercession for us, our blessed Lord and Saviour 165 Jesus. *Amen.*

III

O Almighty God, who art the Father of the faithful, and a gracious God to all that call upon thee in truth and love; thou hast taught us by thy holy Apostle, that every thing is sanctified by the word of 170 God and prayer: Attend this day and ever to the prayers of thy servants: be present with thy grace in all our ministeries of Sacraments, and Sacramentals; and bless all the labours, and accept all the religious duties, and satisfie all the holy desires of them who in this thy house shall make their supplications before thee. And let the 175 dew of thy Divine blessing descend and abide for ever upon this house, which by invocation of thy holy Name, and to the honour of the Lord Jesus, and the Ministeries of thy servants, we, though unworthy, consecrate and dedicate unto thee.

Spare all the penitents, relieve the distressed, comfort the com- 180 fortless, confirm the strong, and strengthen the weak: Ease the afflicted, heal the wounded and the sick; provide for the widows, and be a Father to the fatherless; and unto all them whose consciences being accus'd for sin, come with confidence to the Throne of Grace, Give help in all times of their need, that whensoever thy Name is 185 called upon, thy blessings may certainly descend. Let thy Eternal peace be to this house, and to them who in this house come to thee to be eased and refreshed.

Here let thy Priests be cloth'd with righteousness, and let thy Saints sing with joyfulness. Here let thy people make their prayers, 190 and perform their vows, and offer thee freewill offerings with a holy worship. Here let the weight of their sins that so easily besets them, be laid aside: here let the chains of their corruption, and the chords of vanity be broken. Let the lapsed be restored, let the sick be cured, let the blind eyes and hearts be inlightened with the 195

lanthorn of thy Word, and the light of thy Spirit. Here let the
power of Satan be lessened and destroyed; and let thy servants find
a cure for all their wounds, a comfort for all their sorrows, a
remedy to all their inconveniences: that all who shall enter this
house now dedicated to thy service, may obtain all their desires,   200
and triumph in the Name of the Lord our God who hath perform'd
all their petitions. Preserve their souls from sin, their eyes from tears,
and their feet from falling, for Jesus Christ his sake, to whom with
thee, O Father, and thy most Holy Spirit, be all honour and glory,
praise and thanksgiving, love and obedience, for ever and ever.   205
Amen.

¶ *Then the Bishop and Congregation arising from their knees, the
Bishop attended by his Clergy, shall go in Procession round about the
Church within, and say this Hymn alternately.*

HYMN I   210

1. Except the Lord build the house, they labour in vain to build it:
except the Lord keepeth the city, the watchman waketh but in vain.
2. Blessed is the man whose strength is in thee, in whose heart are
thy ways.
3. They go from strength to strength: every one of them in Sion   215
appeareth before God.
4. How amiable are thy Tabernacles: O Lord of Hosts.
5. My soul longeth, ye even fainteth for the courts of the Lord, my
heart and my flesh crieth out for the living God: when shall I come
and appear before the presence of God?   220
6. The sparrow hath found her an house, and the swallow a nest
for her self, where she may lay her young: even thy altars, O Lord
of Hosts, my King and my God.
7. Blessed are they that dwell in thy house; they will be always
praising thee.   225
8. For a day in thy courts is better than a thousand: I had rather be a
door-keeper in the house of my God, than to dwell in the tents of
wickedness.
9. For the Lord God is a Sun and a shield: the Lord will give grace
and glory, and no good thing will he withold from them that walk   230
uprightly.
10. O Lord of hosts: blessed is the man that trusteth in thee.
   Glory be to the Father, and to the Son, and to the Holy Ghost:
   As it was in the beginning, is now, and ever shall be world
    without end. *Amen.*   235

¶ *Then shall the Bishop go to the vault appointed in the Church for the*

almis
7. 84.

*burial place (in case there be any) or else standing in the most open
pavement of the Church, the Archdeacon shall read this lesson.*

℣ The Lesson in the Coemetery.

1 Sam.
31. 11.

And when the Inhabitants of Jabesh Gilead heard of that which the   240
Philistims had done to Saul: all the valiant men arose, and went all
night, and took the body of Saul, and the bodies of his sons from the
walls of Bethshan, and came to Jabesh and burnt them there. And
they took their bones, and buried them under a tree at Jabesh, and
fasted seven days.   245

2 Sam.
2. 4.

And they told David, saying, that the men of Jabesh Gilead were
they that buried Saul. And David sent messengers unto the men of
Jabesh Gilead, and said unto them, Blessed be ye of the Lord, that
ye have shewed this kindness unto your Lord, even unto Saul, and
have buried him.   250

Eccles.
6. 3.

And the son of David, King Solomon, said, If a man beget an
hundred children, and live many years, so that the days of his years
be many, and his soul be filled with good, and also that he have no
burial; I say that an untimely birth is better than he.

Eccles.
8. 10.

And so I saw the wicked buried, who had come and gone from   255
the place of the Holy, and they were forgotten in the city where
they had so done.

Chap.
11. 8.

But let a man remember the days of darkness, for they shall be
many.

Chap.
12. 7.

For the dust shall return to the earth as it was, and the Spirit   260
shall return unto God that gave it.

℣ *Then the Bishop standing in the same place shall pray,*

O Almighty God, with whom do live the spirits of them that die
in the Lord, grant unto all thy servants whose bodies shall be buried
in this dormitory, that they may lie down with the righteous, and   265
their souls may be gathered unto their Fathers in the bosom of
Christ, and their bodies may rest in peace unto the latter day; and
when thy holy Son shall come to judge both the quick and the dead,
they may hear the sentence of the right hand, and may have their
perfect consummation and bliss in thine eternal and everlasting   270
glory, through Jesus Christ our Lord. *Amen.*

℣ *Then the Bishop, with the Clergy attending, shall go to the Font, and
the Verger or Clerk presenting pure water to him, he shall pour the
water into the Font.*

℣ *Then shall the senior Priest read this Lesson.*   275

℞ The Lesson at the Font.

ιt.
18.

And Jesus came and spake unto them saying, All power is given
unto me in heaven and in earth. Go ye therefore and teach all
Nations, baptizing them in the Name of the Father, and of the Son,
and of the Holy Ghost: teaching them to observe all things which I 280
have commanded you; and lo I am with you alway even unto the
end of the world. *Amen.*

Then shall the Bishop pray,

O Eternal God, Fountain of all Purity, bless and sanctifie the waters
which thou hast ordained and constituted for the mystical washing 285
away of sin: and grant unto all those who shall come hither to be
presented unto thee, and be washed in this Lavatory, that they may
receive the baptism of the Spirit, and may have a title and portion
in repentance, remission of sins, and all the promises of the Gospel,
that they may not onely have the washing of the filth of the flesh, 290
but the answer of a good conscience towards God; that they dying
unto sin, and being buried with Christ in his death, may live unto
righteousness, and become thy Disciples in an unreproveable faith,
and a perfect obedience, and at last may partake of the Resurrection
of thy Son to life Eternal, through the same Jesus Christ our Lord. 295
Amen.

℞ *Then the Bishop shall go, attended as before, to the Pulpit, and laying
his hand upon it, shall appoint one of the Priests to read the following
Lesson.*

℞ The Lesson at the Pulpit.   300

'im.
·

I Charge thee therefore, before God and the Lord Jesus Christ,
who shall judge the quick and the dead at his appearing, and his
Kingdom, Preach the Word, be instant in season, and out of season,
reprove, rebuke, exhort with all long-suffering and doctrine: For
the time will come that they will not endure sound doctrine, but 305
after their own lusts shall they heap to themselves teachers having
itching ears.

3. 8.

This is a faithful saying, and these things I will that thou affirm
constantly, that they who have believed in God might be careful
to maintain good works: these things are good and profitable unto 310
men. But avoid foolish questions, and genealogies, and contentions,
and strivings about the Law, for they are unprofitable and vain.

im.
·

But let the man of God watch in all things, endure afflictions, do
the work of an Evangelist, and make full proof of his Ministery.

¶ *Then shall the Bishop pray,*   315

O Almighty God, who by thy Word, and by thy Spirit dost instruct thy servants, and teach them all truth, and lead them in the way of salvation, Grant that this place may be always filled with wise and holy persons, who may dispense thy word faithfully, according to the ability thou givest, and the charge which thou   320 imposest, and the duty thou requirest; giving to every one their portion in due season, and feeding the flock of God, not of constraint, or of necessity, but willingly and cheerfully; not for filthy lucres sake, but readily, and of a good mind. O send faithful labourers into thy harvest, and grant that all the people which from   325 this place shall hear thy word, may not receive it as the word of man, but as the good word of God, able to save their souls: and let thy holy Spirit for ever be the Preacher, and imprint thy word in their minds, opening their hearts, convincing their understandings, over-ruling their wills, and governing their affections, that they may   330 not be hearers of the Word onely, but doers of good works; that they by their holy lives adorning the Gospel of God, and seeking for glory and honour, and immortality, may attain eternal life through Jesus Christ our Lord. *Amen.*

¶ *Then the Bishop and Clergy shall go towards the Chancel, the doors*   335 *of which being shut, he shall stand there, and with the Priests recite this Hymn alternately.*

HYMN II

1. Open to me the gates of righteousness, I will go into them, and praise the Lord.   340
2. This is the gate of the Lord, into which the righteous shall enter.
3. The stone which the builders refused, is become the head stone of the corner.
4. This is the Lords doing, and it is marvellous in our eyes.
5. This is the day which the Lord hath made: we will rejoyce and   345 be glad in it.
6. Save now, I beseech thee, O Lord: O Lord I beseech send us now prosperity.
7. Blessed be he that cometh in the Name of the Lord: we have blessed you out of the house of the Lord.   350
8. God is the Lord which hath shewed us light: bind the sacrifice with chords, even to the horns of the altar.   [praise.
9. O Lord open thou my lips: and my lips shall shew forth thy

10. For thou desirest not sacrifice, else would I give it thee: but thou delightest not in burnt offerings.   355

11. The sacrifices of God are a broken spirit: a broken and a contrite heart, O God, thou wilt not despise.

12. Do good in thy good pleasure unto Sion: build thou the walls in Jerusalem.

13. Then shalt thou be pleased with the sacrifice of righteousness, with burnt offerings, and whole burnt offerings: then shall they offer bullocks upon thine altar.   360

14. Whoso offereth praise, glorifieth me, and to him that ordereth his conversation right, I will shew the salvation of God.

Glory be to the Father, and to the Son, and to the holy Ghost.   365
As it was in the beginning, is now, and ever shall be, world without end. *Amen.*

¶ *Then the doors being open'd, the Bishop with his Clergy shall enter, and ascend to the Communion Table, and sitting in a chair on the South side of it, shall appoint the Dean or Archdeacon to read this* 370 *Lesson.*

¶ The Lesson at the Communion Table.

_{Cor.}
_{15.}

I Speak as to wise men, judge what I say. The cup of blessing which we bless, is it not the communion of the bloud of Christ? The bread which we break, is it not the communion of the body of Christ? 375 For we being many, are one bread, and one body, for we are all partakers of that one bread. Ye cannot drink the cup of the Lord, and the cup of Devils: ye cannot be partakers of the Lord's table, and the table of Devils. Do we provoke the Lord to jealousie? Are we stronger than he? Whether therefore ye eat or drink, or what- 380 soever ye do, do all to the glory of God.

_.
_{10.}

We have an altar whereof they have no right to eat, which serve the Tabernacle. Wherefore Jesus also, that he might sanctifie the people with his own blood, suffered without the gate. Let us go forth therefore unto him, bearing his reproach. For here we have no 385 continuing city, but we seek one to come: By him therefore let us offer the sacrifice of praise to God continually, that is, the fruit of our lips, giving thanks to his Name. But to do good, and to communicate, forget not; for with such sacrifices God is well pleased.

¶ *Then the Bishop arising from his Chair, shall kneel before the Altar,* 390 *or Communion Table, and say,*

¶ Let us pray.

O Eternal God, who in an infinite mercy to mankind, didst send
thy holy Son, to be a sacrifice for our sins, and the food of our souls,
the Author and finisher of our faith, and the great Minister of   395
eternal glory; who also now sits at thy right hand, and upon the
heavenly altar perpetually presents to thee the Eternal Sacrifice, and
a never ceasing prayer, be present with thy servants, and accept us
in the dedication of a Ministerial altar, which we humbly have
provided for the performance of this great Ministery, and in   400
imitation of Christs Eternal Priesthood, according to our duty, and
his Commandment. Grant that all the gifts which shall be presented
on this table, may be acceptable unto thee, and become unto thy
servants a savour of life unto life. Grant that all who shall partake
of this table, may indeed hunger after the bread of life, and thirst   405
for the wine of elect souls, and may feed upon Christ by faith, and
be nourished by a holy hope, and grow up to an eternal charity.
Let no hand of any that shall betray thee, be ever upon this table:
let no impure tongue ever taste of the holy body and blood which
here shall be Sacramentally represented and exhibited. But let all   410
thy servants that come hither to receive these mysteries, come with
prepar'd hearts, and with penitent souls, and loving desires, and
indeed partake of the Lord Jesus, and receive all the benefits of his
passion. Grant this for his sake, who is the Priest and the Sacrifice,
the feeder and the food, the Physician and the physick of our souls,   415
our most blessed Lord and Saviour Jesus. *Amen.*

¶ *Then the Bishop arising shall return to his Chair, and sitting covered;*
some persons by the Patrons appointment shall bring the Carpet, the
Communion cloth and napkins, the Chalice, Paten, and other Vessels,
Books and Utensils for the Communion; and humbly presenting them   420
on their knees to God, the Bishop shall receive them severally, and
deliver them to the Deacon, to be laid orderly on the Communion
Table; excepting onely the Chalice, and the Paten, which two Priests
shall (when the Table is covered) humbly on their knees lay upon it.
Then the Bishop returning to the Altar, shall with reverence and   425
solemnity (his face being Eastward) lay his hands upon the plate, and
say this prayer, standing.

1 Chron.
29. 14.

What are we, O God, and what is this people, that we should be
able to offer so willingly after this sort? For all things come of thee,
and of thine own we have given thee. Accept the Oblation of thy   430
servants, who in the uprightness of their hearts have willingly
offered these things, and give unto them a perfect heart to keep thy

Commandments, thine Ordinances, and thy Sacraments: and be pleased to grant to them a greater ability, an enlarged heart, and an increasing love to serve thee with their souls and bodies, with all 435 their time, and all their goods, that thou maist be honoured with all their heart, and all their strength; and grant that these gifts may be received into the lot and right of God, and of Religion, and the Donours be continued for ever in the lot of thine inheritance: that by thy grace accepting these gifts, they may in all their other 440 possessions be blessed, and by the use of these gifts in the Ministeries of thy holy Religion, they may be sanctified, and by a Guard of Angels they may be preserved from all evil, and by the perpetual presence of thy holy Spirit, they may be led into all good, and accepted to pardon, and preserved in peace, and promoted in 445 holiness, and conducted certainly to life Eternal, through Jesus Christ our Lord. *Amen.*

¶ *Then the Bishop shall go to the North end of the H. Table, and turning to the people shall say,*

The Lord be with you.   450

Answer.

And with thy Spirit.

Let us pray.

I

That ause is be mitted hen the ishop ily dedites any lation: ld so are e other auses hich are closed in]

O Most Glorious and Eternal God, who makest all things by thy 455 power, and adornest all things with thy bounty, and fillest all things with thy goodness, and sanctifiest the hearts and gifts of thy servants by thy Spirit, we worship and adore thy glories, who fillest all the world by thy presence, and sustainest it by thy Almightiness: We love and magnifie thy mercies, that thou hast been pleased to enable 460 and admit thy servants [*to build an house to thee,* * *and*] out of thine own store to give gifts to thee, who givest all that we possess. We humbly pray thee by the Death and Passion, by the Resurrection and Ascension, and by the glorious Intercession of our Lord, that thou wouldst vouchsafe to sanctifie [*this house, and*] these gifts to 465 thy service, by the effusion of thy holiness from above. Let the Sun of Righteousness for ever shine here, and let the brightest illumination of the Holy Spirit, fill [*this place, and fill*] all our hearts for ever with thy glorious presence: That which we have blessed, do thou bless; that which we offer, do thou accept; that which we 470 place here, do thou visit graciously, and for ever, through Jesus Christ our Lord. *Amen.*

II

Let this house be for the Religious uses of thy servants; let it be the abode of Angels, let it be the place of thy Name, and for the glory 475 of thy Grace, and for the mention and honour, and the memorial of the Lord Jesus; Let no unclean thing ever enter here: Drive from hence all sacrilegious hands, all superstitious Rites, all prophane persons, all proud and unquiet Schismaticks, all misbelieving Hereticks: Let not the powers of darkness come hither, nor the secret 480 arrow ever smite any here: Let no corrupt ayre, and no corrupt communication, no blood-shed, and no unclean action ever pollute this place dedicated to thy holiness.

By the multitudes of thy mercies and propitiations, to the visitors of this place, coming with devotion and charity, let there be peace 485 and abundance of thy blessings. Hear them that shall call upon thee, sanctifie their Oblations, let the good word of God come upon them, and dispense thy good things unto them. Let the title of this Church abide until the second coming of Christ, and let thy Holy Table stand prepar'd with the blessings of a Celestial Banquet. Bless 490 the gifts and the givers, the dwellers and the dwelling, and grant unto us here present, and to all that shall come after us, that by the participation of thy heavenly graces, we may obtain Eternal life through Jesus Christ our Lord. *Amen.*

III   495

O Eternal God, who art pleas'd to manifest thy presence amongst the sons of men, by the special issues of thy favour and benediction, make our bodies and souls to be Temples pure and holy, apt for the entertainments of the Holy Jesus, and for the inhabitation of thy holy Spirit. Lord, be pleas'd, with the powers of thy grace, to cast 500 out impure lusts, all worldly affections, all covetous desires from these thy Temples, that they may be places of prayer and holy meditation, of godly desires, and chaste thoughts, of pure intentions, and great zeal to please thee, that we also may become Sacrifices, as well as Temples, eaten up with the zeal of thy glory, and even 505 consumed with the fires of thy love; that not one thought may be entertain'd by us, but such as may be like perfume exhaling from the Altar of Incense; and not a word may pass from us, but may have the accent of Heaven in it, and sound pleasantly in thy ears.

O dearest God, fill every faculty of our souls with the impresses of 510 Religion, that we loving thee above all things in the world, worshipping thee with frequent and humblest adorations, continually feeding upon the apprehensions of thy Divine sweetness, and living in a daily observation of thy Divine Commandments, and delighted with the perpetual feast of a holy Conscience, may by thy Spirit be seal'd up to the day of Redemption, and the fruition of thy glories in thine everlasting Kingdom, through Jesus Christ our Lord, to whom with thee, O Father of mercies, Father of our Lord Jesus Christ, and with thee, O blessed and Eternal Spirit the Comforter, all honour and power be ascribed from generation to generation for ever and ever. *Amen.*

¶ *Then adde the Prayer of S. Clement.*

God, the beholder and discerner of all things, the Lord of Spirits and all flesh, who hath chosen our Lord Jesus, and us through him, to be a peculiar people, grant unto every soul that calleth upon his glorious and holy Name, faith and fear, peace and patience, long-suffering and temperance, with purity and wisdom, to the well-pleasing of his Name, through our High Priest and Ruler, by whom unto him be glory and Majestie, both now and to all ages evermore. *Amen.*

¶ *Then the Bishop arising, shall sit in his Chair, at the South end of the H. Table, and being covered, shall cause the Chancellor to read the Instrument of Consecration, and give command that it be entred into the Registry, and an Act made of it* in perpetuam rei memoriam: *A Duplicate of which Instrument, attested under the Registers hand and seal of the Office, is to remain with the Patron or Founder, and the Original with the Bishop.*

¶ *After which, this Anathematism shall be read by him and his Clergy alternately, all standing up.*

¶ The Anathematism.

1. Keep not thou silence, O God: hold not thy peace, and be not still, O God.
2. Let not thine enemies make a tumult, and they that hate thee lift up their head.
3. Let them not come into thine inheritance to defile thy holy Temple, lest they lay waste thy dwelling places, and break down the carved work thereof with axes and hammers.
4. Make their Nobles like Oreb and Zeeb: yea, all their princes like Zeba and Zalmunna.
5. Who say, let us take to ourselves the houses of God in possession.
6. O my God, make them like unto a wheel, as the stubble before the wind.
7. As the fire burneth the wood, and as the flame setteth the mountains on fire.

[marginal notes:]
ement
pist. ad
rinth.
fine.

x Psalmis
. 83.
29.

8. So persecute them with thy tempest, and make them afraid with thy storm.   555

9. Fill their faces with shame, that they may seek thy Name, O Lord.

10. That men may know, that thou, whose Name is Jehovah, art the most High over all the earth.

11. For the Lord is righteous, he will cut asunder the chords of the   560
wicked.

12. Let them all be asham'd that hate Sion.

13. Let them be as the grass upon the house tops, which withereth before it groweth up.

14. Wherewith the mower filleth not his hand: nor he that bindeth   565
sheaves his bosom.

15. Neither do they which go by say, The blessing of the Lord be upon you: we bless you in the name of the Lord.

The Bishop.

Glory be to God on high.   570

Answer.

And on earth peace to men of good will.

Bishop.

Amen.

Answer.   575

Amen.

¶ *Then shall the Bishop conclude with this* εὐφημιζμὸς *or Acclamation, the Clergy answering alternately.*

¶ *The Bishop first saying.*

Seeing now, dearly beloved in the Lord, that by the blessing of God,   580
and his gracious favour, we have dedicated to God [this House of Prayer, and] these gifts for the Ministeries of Religion, let us give hearty thanks to Almighty God for these benefits, and say,

Ex Psalmis   1. Praise ye the Lord: praise God in his sanctuary, praise him in the
150. 68.   firmament of his power.   585
87. 99.
100.   2. Blessed be the Lord who daily loadeth us with benefits: even the God of our salvation.

3. He that is our God, is the God of salvation: and unto God the Lord belong the issues from death.

4. The chariots of God are twenty thousand, even thousands of Angels: the Lord is among them as in Sinai, in the holy place.

5. They have seen the goings of God, even the goings of my God, my King in the sanctuary.

6. The singers went before, the players on instruments followed after: amongst them were the damsels playing with the timbrels.

7. Bless ye God in the congregations: even the Lord from the fountains of Israel.

8. Thy God hath commanded thy strength: strengthen, O God, that which thou hast wrought in us.

9. O God, thou art terrible out of thy Holy places: the God of Israel is he that giveth strength and power unto his people. Blessed be God.

10. His foundation is in the holy mountains: The Lord loveth the gates of Sion more than all the dwellings of Jacob.

11. Glorious things are spoken of thee, O thou city of God: and of Sion it shall be said, This and that man was born in her, and the Highest himself shall establish her.

12. Exalt ye the Lord our God: and worship at his footstool, for he is holy.

13. Moses and Aaron among his Priests: and Samuel among them that call upon his name: they called upon his name, and he answered them.

14. Thou answeredst them, O Lord our God: thou wast a God that forgavest them, though thou didst take vengeance of their inventions.

15. Exalt the Lord our God, and worship at his holy hill: for the Lord our God is holy.

16. Enter into his gates with thanksgiving, and into his courts with praise: be thankful unto him, and bless his name.

¶ *Then shall all together say,*
For the Lord is good, his mercy is everlasting, and his truth endureth to all generations.

Bishop.

Worship Jesus.

Answer.

We worship and adore the great King of heaven and earth, the blessed Saviour of the world.

Bishop.

Holy is our God.

Answer.   630

Holy is the Almighty.

Bishop.

Holy is the Immortal.

All together.

Holy, Holy, Holy Lord God of Sabbath, blessed be thy Name in   635
Heaven and Earth for ever and ever. Amen. Amen.

So ends the Office of Consecration.

¶ *Then the Bell tolling a little in the interval, the Bishop shall appoint*
the Dean to read the Morning Prayer, or first Service, in the reading
Desk.   640

¶ *The Psalms appointed for the day.*
Psalm 122, 125, 132.

¶ *The first Lesson is* Gen. 28. *verse* 10. *unto the end. Or else* 1 Kings 8.
verse 10. *unto verse* 62. *exclusively.*

¶ *The second Lesson is* S. Matthew 21. *ver.* 1. *unto v.* 17. *inclusively.*   645

¶ *At the end of the Letany, the Bishop shall confirm such persons as can*
be conveniently brought to him, fitted to that purpose.

¶ *The Bishop shall read the second Service, and administer the Com-*
munion.

¶ *The Epistle is taken out of the third of the* Acts, *vers.* 1. *unto vers.* 16.   650
inclusively.

¶ *The Gospel is* Luke 7. *vers.* 1. *to the* 10. *inclusively.*

¶ *The Collect to be said at Morning prayer, and the Communion, to-*
gether with the Collect of the day.

O Almighty God, who dwellest amongst thy Saints, and hast   655
plac'd thy Tabernacle in the hearts of thy servants, give thy heavenly
blessings, and encrease to the place where thine honour dwelleth;
that what is founded by thy Providence, and built according to thy
Commandment, may be established for ever, and blessed in all
things by thy Eternal goodness, through Jesus Christ our Lord.   660
Amen.

AN OFFICE TO BE USED IN THE RESTAURATION OF A CHURCH.

¶ *When the Fabrick of a Church is ruined, and a new Church built* 665
upon the same foundation; the Bishop attended by his Clergy, shall
enter into the Church-yard, and go in procession round about the Church
new built; and recite alternately Psalm 74.

. . . . .

¶ *Then entring into the Church, the Bishop and Clergy shall vest*
themselves; which being done, and the people in their places, the Bishop 670
shall kneel down in the body of the Church, on a footstool rais'd above
the floor, and say,

Our Father which art in Heaven, hallowed be thy Name, thy
Kingdom come, thy will be done in earth, as it is in Heaven: Give
us this day our daily bread, and forgive us our trespasses, as we 675
forgive them that trespass against us; and lead us not into temptation,
but deliver us from evil.

¶ *The Clergy and people repeating after him every petition.*
¶ *Then shall the Bishop say,*

Prevent us, O Lord, in all our doings with thy most gracious favour, 680
and further us with thy continual help, that in all our works begun,
continued, and ended in thee, we may glorifie thy holy Name, and
finally by thy mercy obtain everlasting life, through Jesus Christ
our Lord. *Amen.*

¶ *Then the Bishop standing up with his face to the people, shall pray* 685
in the words of Ezra, *paucis mutatis, ut sequitur.*

Ezra 9.   O Lord our God, we are asham'd, and blush to lift up our faces unto
thee, O God; for our iniquities are increased over our heads, and
our trespasses grown up unto the heavens. Since the days of our
Fathers have we been in a great trespass unto this day; and for our 690
iniquities have we, our Kings and our Priests been delivered unto
the hands of our Enemies, to the sword, and to the spoil, and to
confusion of face, as it is this day. And now for a little space hath
grace been shewed to us from the Lord our God, to leave us a
remnant to escape, and to give us a nail in his holy place, that our 695
God may lighten our eyes, & give us a little reviving from our
afflictions. For our God hath not forsaken us, but hath extended

mercy to us in the sight of our enemies, to give us a reviving, to
set up the house of our God, and to repair the desolations thereof.
And now, O our God, what shall we say after this? For we have   700
forsaken thy Commandments which thou hast commanded us by
thy servants the Prophets. And after all that is come upon us for our
evil deeds, and for our great trespasses, seeing that thou our God hast
punished us less than our iniquities deserve, and hast given us such a
deliverance as this, should we again break thy Commandments?   705
Wouldst not thou be angry with us till thou hadst consumed us?

O Lord God of Heaven and earth, thou art righteous, and just,
and true; thou art also good and gracious, and of great mercy, and
loving kindness; and though thou hast punished us for our inventions, yet thou hast forgiven our misdeeds, and restor'd us to a   710
rejoycing this day. O give unto us abundance of thy grace, that we
may no more provoke thee to anger, or to jealousie; that we may
never force thee to severity, and to pour forth thy heavy judgments
upon us: but give us thy holy Spirit to lead us in the ways of
righteousness, and to prepare us for thy mercies for ever. Defend   715
thy Church, and bless thine inheritance; feed them, and set them up
for ever: So shall we thy people give thee thanks in the Congregation of thy redeemed ones, and rejoyce in giving thee praises for the
operations of thy hands, who hast mightily delivered thy sons and
servants through Jesus Christ our Lord. *Amen.*   720

℣ *Then shall be said or sung* Psalm 144. *alternately.*

.   .   .   .   .   .

℣ *After which, the Bishop attended with the Clergy, shall go to the Font,
and use the same Office as is appointed for the consecration, or dedication
of Churches; and so to the end: Omitting the word* [place, or places]   725
*because the place was consecrated before, and so was the Coemetery.
In other things proceed without change.*

℣ *The first Lesson at Morning Prayer shall be* Haggai 1.

℣ *The second Lesson* Luke 12. *beginning at verse* 32. *to the end.*

℣ *The Collect the same as is used at Morning-prayer in the Office of*   730
consecration.

A SHORT OFFICE FOR EXPIATION
& ILLUSTRATION OF A CHURCH
DESECRATED OR PROPHAN'D

¶ *If a Church hath been desecrated by murther and blood-shed, by un-* 735
cleanness, or any other sort of prophanation, the Bishop attended by
two Priests at least, and one Deacon, shall enter into the Church,
which shall be first prepared by cleansings and washings, &c.

¶ *The Bishop and his Clergy being vested, shall go in Procession about*
the Church on the inside, saying alternately the seventh Psalm, and 740
the ninth Psalm.

¶ *After which, the Bishop with his Clergy shall go to the Holy Table,*
and there kneeling down shall pray.

O Almighty God, who art of pure eyes, and canst not behold
impurity, behold the Angels are not pure in thy sight, and thou 745
hast found folly in thy Saints; have mercy upon thy servants, who
with repentance and contrition of heart, return unto thee humbling
our selves before thee in thy holy place. We acknowledge our
selves unworthy to appear in thy glorious presence, because we are
polluted in thy sight, and it is just in thee to reject our prayers, and 750
to answer us no more from the place of thy Sanctuary; for wickedness hath entred into the Courts where thy holy feet have trod, and
have defiled thy dwelling place, even unto the ground, and we by
our sins have deserved this calamity. But be thou graciously
pleased to return to us as in the days of old, and remember us accord- 755
ing to thy former loving kindnesses in the days of our Fathers. Cast
out all iniquity from within us, remove the guilt of that horrible
prophanation that hath been committed here, that abomination of
desolation in the holy place, standing where it ought not; and grant
that we may present unto thee pure Oblations, and may be accepted 760
by the gracious interpellation of our High Priest, the most glorious
Jesus. Let no prophane thing enter any more into the lot of thine
inheritance; and be pleased again to accept the prayers which thy
servants shall make unto thee in this place. And because holiness
becometh thine house for ever, grant to us thy grace to walk before 765
thee in all holiness of conversation; that we becoming a Royal
Priesthood, a chosen Generation, a people zealous of good works,
thou mayest accept us according to thy own loving kindness, and
the desires of our hearts. O look upon thy most holy Son, and
regard the cry of his blood, and let it on our behalf speak better 770
things than the blood of *Abel*.

O let that sprinkling of the blood of the Holy Lamb, who was slain from the beginning of the world, make this place holy and accepted, and purifie our hands and hearts, and sanctifie our prayers and praises, and hallow all our Oblations, and preserve this house,   775 and all the places where thy Name is invoked, from all impurity and prophanation for ever, and keep our bodies and souls, and spirits unblameable to the coming of our Lord Jesus. Then, O blessed Father, grant that we being presented unto thee without spot or wrinkle, or any such thing, may be clothed with the   780 righteousness of the Saints, and walk in white with the Lamb in the Kingdom of our God for ever and ever. Grant this, O Almighty God, our most gracious Father for Jesus Christ his sake, to whom with thee and the Holy Spirit, be all worship, and love, and honour, and glory from generation to generation for ever. *Amen.*   785

¶ *Then the Bishop and Clergy arising from their knees, shall say the Anathematism unto the* εὐφημιζμὸς, *or Acclamation, as in the form of Consecration: After which, kneeling down shall be said the* III. *prayer plac'd in that Office a little before the Anathematism. And next to that, the* II. *Prayer which is immediately before that; and then*   790 *the Prayer of S. Clement.*

¶ *After which arising from his knees, the Bishop shall say,*

Seing now, dearly beloved in the Lord, we have by humble prayer implor'd the mercy of God and his holy Spirit, to take from this place, and from our hearts, all impurity and prophanation, and that   795 we hope by the Mercies of God in our Lord Jesus Christ, he hath heard our prayers, and will grant our desires, let us give hearty thanks for these mercies, and say,

¶ *Then shall be said the* εὐφημιζμὸς, *or Acclamation, as at the end of the Office of Consecration of Churches,* &c.   800

¶ *And then shall the Priest whom the Bishop shall appoint, begin Morning-prayer.*

¶ *The Psalms for the day are Psalm* 18, *and Psalm* 30.

¶ *The first Lesson is Zechariah* 1.

¶ *The second Lesson Mark* 11. *unto verse* 26. *inclusively.*   805

¶ *The Collect the same with that at Morning-prayer in the Consecration of Churches.*

¶ *If any Chalice, Paten, Font, Pulpit, or any other Oblation or Utensil for the Church, be at any time newly to be presented; the Bishop is to use the forms of Dedication of those respective gifts, which are parti-*   810 *cularly used in the dedication; and this to be done immediately after the* Nicene *Creed, at the time of the Communion; ever adding the Anathematism and Acclamation.*

Te decet Hymnus.

NOTES TO THE TEXT

Line 27 seqq. The fourth Collect after the Communion Office in the B.C.P., which is based upon the *Actiones nostras, quaesumus Domine, asperando preveni,* which occurs in some Anglo-Saxon and later Pontificals at the beginning of the Rite for the consecration of a Church.

Line 76 seqq. 1 Chron. 29, 10b to 18, omitting verses 15, 16, 17b; but interpolating other matter. Andrewes' first consecratory prayer begins with part of the same passage, but not in the authorized version.

Line 102 seqq. This prayer also follows the main sequence of thought in Andrewes' first consecratory prayer, which has been refashioned and adapted to the style of the Irish compiler.

Line 168 seqq. This prayer seems in part to have been influenced by the medieval *Prefatio in media ecclesiae:* "Aeterne deus: adesto precibus nostris. adesto sacramentis: adesto etiam piis famulorum tuorum laboribus. nobisque misericordiam tuam poscentibus. Descendat quoque in hanc ecclesiam tuam quam sub invocatione sancti nominis tui in honore sancti N. indigni consecramus spiritus sanctus tuus septiformis gratiae ubertate redundans ut quotienscumque in hac domo tua sanctum tuum nomen fuerit invocatum eorum qui te invocaverint a te pio domine preces exaudiantur. (Cf. lines 171-9.) Hic quoque sacerdotes sacrificium tibi laudis offerant: hic fideles populi vota persolvant: hic peccatorum onera solvantur: fideliumque lapsa reparentur. In hac ergo quessumus domine domo tua spiritus sancti gratia egroti sanetur: infirmi restituantur: claudi curentur: leprosi mundentur: ceci illuminentur: demonia eitiantur. Cunctorum hic debilium egrotationes te domine annuente pellantur: omnium etiam vincula peccatorum absolvantur: ut omnes qui hoc templum beneficia iusta deprecaturi ingrediuntur. cuncta se impetresse letentur: ut concessa misericordia quam precantur. perpetuo misericordia tue munere glorientur. Per... (Cf. lines 189-99.)

Line 455 seqq. The verbs in the first six lines of this prayer seem to have been suggested by those in the middle section of the medieval Preface, *Adesto precibus:* "O beata et sancta trinitas que omnia purificas: omnia mundas. omnia exornas. O beata maiestas dei que cuncta imples: cuncta contines: cuncta disponis. O beata et sancta manus domini, que omnis sanctificas: omnia benedicis: omnia locupletas..."

Line 486 to 494. These petitions may be compared with those in the *Prefatio super altare* in the medieval rite: "...ut hic orantes exaudias. hic quoque benedicta distribuas. Sit ergo ecclesie tue titulus sempiternus: sit mensa celesti spiritualique convivio preparata. Tu ergo domine proprio ore tuo hostias super hoc impositas benedicito. et benedictas suscipito. atque nobis omnibus tribue: ut participatione earum. vitam adquiramus sempiternam. Per." The compiler, however, has misunderstood the traditional meaning of "titulus" in the Pontifical, where the plural forms indicated in the sentence support the Roman translation of "titulus" as "altar".

Line 489 *until the second coming*: Cf. "Preserve it firm and undisturbed from all trial until the manifestation of the second coming." (Armenian Canon for Dedicating a Profaned Church.)

Line 496 seqq. This prayer is an adaptation for public use of Jeremy Taylor's Prayer at the close of the "Discourse of Religious places" in *The Great Exemplar* (see above, p. 282 seq.).

Line 629 seqq. The Trisagion is given here in a version peculiar to Jeremy Taylor, who always uses the Sanctus with it.

Although Instruments drawn up in the seventeenth century differ from each other considerably, the Instrument appended to the 1666 Irish forms is verbally similar to that drawn up for the consecration of Peterhouse Chapel at Cambridge on 17 March 1632/3. Possibly the Instrument, which appears again at the end of the Dublin consecration form of 1719, was already in use in Ireland before the Commonwealth.

Spaces are left for the measurements of the new church "in longitudine ab Oriente ad Occidentem", and "in latitudine vero ab Aquilone ad Austrum". The church is furnished "sacra mensa decenter ornata, suggestis ad precandum, legendum, et poedicandum". Public worship is to be performed in the English language, "aut alio Idiomate ipsis communite intelecto recitandum". (Cf. Canons 8, 86, and 94 for the use of Irish in public worship.)

Appendix 2

JEREMY TAYLOR'S LONGER
LATIN LETTER[1]

Doctissimo viro Johanni Stearne, *Juris utriusq; simul & Medicinæ Professori;
amico meo undiquaq; colendissimo.*

A Nimam humanam nunquam quiescere sed semper aliquid meditari,
cernere, aut tractare non insipienter dixit Modernorum Philosophorum
facilè princeps *Cartesius*; atq; hujusce sententiæ veritatem qui non
agnoscunt, te videant, atq; ilicò Manus dabunt. Enimverò (vir Doctisime)
nullo tu die operas typographicas otiari sinis, sed ex gazophylacio tuo
semper promis aliquid aut vetus aut novum; semper cum bono publico,
nisi nolint homines qui tecum non sentiunt. In hâc autem diatribâ quam
tu (nisi fallor) paras ut legant omnes docti, certum est te omnem omnimo-
dò fortunam initurum fore; bonam, malam; optimam, pessinam, &
mediam; pro Captu scilicet lectoris, pro interesse hominum, pro præ-
judiciis litigantium, pro maximo & minimo Judicio mortalium; hoc
autem sine vaticinio tibi prædico facilè:

> *Nunquam placabis genus irritabile vatum.*

Incidis enim hodie in manus sectarum, dicam, an insectorum? hominum,
qui de Deo malè sentiunt, & loquuntur mala; de te autem bonum ut
eloquantur planè desperandum est; quorum scilicet Dianam depretiaris,
Hylam jugulas, Endymiona Confodis; istiusmodi enim sunt, quibuscum
dimicas, ut causa apud eos odii nulla major sit quàm te aliter sapere,
aliter sentire; atq; quod longè sit deterius, multis rationibus illorum in
Dordrectanâ, Alensi, Lambethanâ & Charentonensi Synodis sententias
juratas olim, & in æternum pertinaces averruncas. Omnia malè ominata
numina, *Væjoves*, & *Averruncos*, *Robigum* & *Robiginem*, quinimò *Murceam*
& *Febres* in caput tuum invocabunt. Tu autem Medice cura te ipsum,
& Macte esto in asserendâ Divinâ misericordiâ, excolendâ justitiâ, pro-
pagandis religiosis rationibus Divinorum attributorum. Verùm ut ingenuè
viro amicissimoenarrem quod sentio; tu nova quædam in hoc scripto
meditaris, quæ si probabiliter enarras, vix tamen persuadebis huic sæculo,
& certè quæ ego fortassis alitèr enunciari velim; saltem in modo loquendi.
Video enim ea quæ alicubi asperrimè & solus dicis, alibi cum virorum
doctorum populari magis sententiâ candidiùs explicas. In alieno autem
libro, nolo ego esse ingeniosus; multa dicis moderatè, præclarè plurima;

---

[1] For the first appearance of this letter, see above, p. 39 seq.

alia sunt sed pauca; de quorum novitate ego quidem respondebo, de veritate tu videris. In hâc autem quæstione quam tu de fato hominis, & consilio Dei adornas novis rationibus, metuo ne sient plurimi qui cum *Domitio Calderino* dicturi sint, *Eamus ad Communem errorem, & metuamus omnem sententiæ novitatem*. Cave autem tu, nè adversantium quem tu aggrederis Grex habeat quidem quod nimis rectè reprobent. Quam facili enim sententiâ omnes non suæ sectæ homines hi reprobaturi sint, tu & ego nimis experiendo novimus; quod si rectè quicquam accusent, nullo pessulo os illis obturatum dabis. Nosti poëtæ illud,

——vix ullo thure litabis
Hæreat in multis brevis ut semuncia recti.

Hoc autem, Erudite vir, si rectè capio quod tu solerter scribis & doctissime, illud est quò tu telum omne dirigis, nimirùm ut ingeniosum medium excorgites, ut planum sit, salutis οἰκονομίαν etiam humanæ rationi maximè consentaneam, néq; consilium, nec præscientiam Divinam ullam ponere necessitatem in rebus, ullam legem in consiliis hominum, ullum fatum in eventu animarum; atq; ut hoc clarius sit, omne omnino ante-cedens decretum Dei elevas vel absolutum vel respectivum; (condi-tionatum enim planè dejeras.) Antecedens enim necessitas nulla est, libertas omnino est, si nihil ante finem vitæ statuatur; si omnia permit-tantur ad messem; si decernatur nihil ante adventum Archangeli. Mirabilis quidem est evadendi techna; sed cave ne eâdem manu Dianæ restituas ædes, quâ nuperrimè supposuisti flammam. Quicquid enim futurum est ad finem mundi præsenti oculo æquè intuetur Deus πανταγνώστης atq; illud quod primâ creavit die; atq; ergo eandem dicet in eventibus certi-tudinem. Statuit Deus in generali omnes perseveraturos in fide & gratiâ Christi salvandos iri. Sic enim regnum præparavit Christus ab initio mundi; & novit idem summus Deus omnes suos, quos ab initio signavit, quibus statuit media subministrare quibus rectè usuri sunt electi; atq; ex his præmissis immediatè sequetur; etiam & hos in particulari electos Cœlo præmiandos & donandos, gratiosissimè quidem sed certissimè. Et quid ex novo dogmate lucri accedit veritati quam tu strenuè defendis, ego nondum planè exquisivi: sed suspicor delicias istas tuas ingenii maximi & singularis ponere voluisse fundamentum novum antiquo dogmati; quod si firmum & stabile in futurum explicatiùs enarrando dederis, totus liter-atorum orbis, gratias tibi æternas pendet.

Duo autem sunt quibus maximè incumbis, quæ certè veritatem maxime profuturam piis, acritèr & solertissimè demonstrant. Infinitam intelligo Dei φιλανθρωπίαν quam explicitè demonsratam exhibes; & *ampli-tudinem regni cœlestis*, quam sæpiusculè, sed præclarè, sed piè insinuas. De priori dixerunt multi ante te; quos quidem si non antecellis, certe æquas planissimè: neq; quidem facile est in hâc materiâ non rectè eloqui. Quis enim patiatur de Deo quicquam dici quod boni viri de se enarrari petienter non ferrent? *Achillis* pessimum erat ingenium, & execranda indoles, quam narravit Satyra,

Nescios fari pueros Achivûm
Horat.   *Ureret flammis etiam latentes*
Matris in alvo.

Nec mirum est qui hujusmodi dicteria in Deum jaculantur, si pessimos ipsi habeant mores, cùm sæviendo, fallendo, improperando, se Deum imitari falsi homines & iniqui sentiant. Dixit (ni malè memini) *Bertius* in Enchiridio suo Geographico, Calvinismum ubicunque introductum nullibi sine tumultu, aut Cæde, sine jurgiis, & perduellione diù perdurâsse; quippe quòd *nullum malum sine authoramento,* dixit *Seneca:* Et per picturam exemplo Jovis stuprantis, ad libidinem adolescens in Comœdiâ incendebatur; ad inhumanos mores aspirare illos homines qui Deum crudelem & tyrannum colunt; novum non est. Sed de tuis nolo amplius; nec de eorum libris: Ephesiæ sunt literæ (quod in proverbio dictum est) & incantamenta mera.

Ite mali versus, animam qui perditis, ite.

Nollem certè studiosam Dei & bonorum imorum juventutem istiusmodi hominum libris initiari qui fabulas meracissimas de optimo Deo conficiunt; & quorum non rarò scripta tam putida tam frigida ut

——*Illis incendi frigidus ævo*
Laomedontiades, vel Nestoris hernia possit.

Rectum illud erat quo *Alexander Severus Vetronium Turinum* multavit; ut scilicet fumo puniantur qui fumum vendunt: fumum quidem istiusmodi homines venalem propinant, sed cui sit perennis & inexorabilis flamma proxima: sed hasce & omnes finitimas αἱρέσεις καὶ ἑτεράσεις tu scriptis tuis doctissimis æternæ oblivioni damnabis & devovebis.

Placet autem vir doctissime, vel maximè te bona de bono Deo eloqui, & misericordiam æternam summi numinis prædicare, & amplitudinem regni cœlestis tam suaviter insinuare aut aperire. Nemo enim imò tu non potes reserarc quæ Deus signaculo tenebrarum & æternæ nubis consignavit; atqui ergò libentissimè velim, ut omnes de Divinis decretis parciùs philosophentur: sed legem Dei, conditionem salutis, inclyta promissa, verendas comminationes, viam vitæ planam, omnibus eleganter & lubenti animo enarrare; atque ad augendam spem, adeoq; hominum industriam omne momentum argumentorum accumulare. Huic quidem operi ego sæpiùs uti tu scis (Erudite vir) chartulas quasdam designaveram ut quibus mediis optimus Deus viam vitæ struxerit & muniverit enarrarem in honorem Dei, & cum iis quæ tu præclarè meditatus es exirent in bonum publicum; sed infinitis objectionibus & privatis & publicis præpeditus curis nondùm à meis rebus licentiam hisce perficiendis obtinui; sed non possum abstinere quin *εὐκαίρως, ἀκαίρως* enarrem gloriam Dei, & magnalia Regni Cœlestis, certè non claudendi infra angustissimos opinionum novarum & immitium limites, & decretorum quæ nullibi nisi in somniis malè opinantium existunt.

Præterquàm enim quòd Deus Pater est, & paucis contentus, modò adsit probus animus, & mandatis Dei rectè intentus; *paululum enim supplicii satis est patri*, Dixit Comicus; nec exactissimas semper strictè mensuras exquirit in finalibus judiciis benignus omnium parens; Deus etiam Judex est totius mundi; nequè amat, nequè creavit mortem, sed unicuique secundùm bonæ mentis & probabilis vitæ mensuras metiens; incorrigibiles quidem æternæ permittens morti: sed infirmos nunquam ultra propriam rationem, ultra quod rectè & clementer possit & debet à terrâ & cineribus expectari. Novit autem Deus neminem posse in æterno vivi-comburio incolatum suum prolongare; novit quàm intolerabilis & tremendus ille status sit quem *planè impiis* est interminatus; atquè ergò nè quisquam in illum incidat, omne frænum Diabolo injicit; omnes omninò candoris, & gratiæ exercet artes; mille argumentorum genera; acceptat infirmorum conatus, & vires auget; prævenit nos gratiâ suâ, comitatur, sequitur: Omni modo urget, movet, suadet; publicè invitat, clam hortatur; operatur in nobis velle & perficere; frequenti allicit benedictione; infrequentibus Judiciis reprimit & metum injicit. Hæc sunt infiniti amoris testimonia, & quàm illibenter quemquam perire sinit pater optimus. Imò majus adhuc est quod suadere possit hujus argumenti propria materia. Hostis humani generis neminem potest cogere, neminem in perniciem nolentem trahere. At aliter nobiscum Deus. Neminem perire velit; & major est Divina gratia omni nostrâ resistentiâ; operatur velle & perficere; est voluntatis dominus; pellit suaviter, compellit, trahit: multò aliter & imperiosè magis in animis hominum potest Divinus spiritus quàm impius *ὁ κοσμοκράτωρ* & *ἀπολλύων*. Spiritus mundi fallere potest; at Spiritus Dei demonstrat: tentat Satanas; at paternum Dominium exercet Deus; nemo potest Deo resistere; at si resistas Diabolo, fugiet impotens. Odit quidem animas, sed hamum habet in naribus & frænum in maxillis, & quàm maximè velit, minùs potest; quia Deus summus est amator animarum & potest omnia quæcunq; velit, & nihil magis vult quàm salutem hominum: atqui ergò paucissimos mortalium salvandos iri, suadere satagit Diabolus, ut desperare faciat meticulosos & superstitiosos homines, & alios ad improperium Dei adigat, & malè de summo Bono suspicari, & ut omnium pertinacem interrumpat laborem, & spem instigatricem minuat, ut quod falsò suadere in principiis velit, verum fiat in eventu infœlicissimo. Sic enim qui Astrologos consulunt & credunt futurum illud quod enarrant; ipsi patrant suis manibus, & credulitate suâ efficiunt quod timuerunt fatum, & mendacium vertunt in oraculum.

Recordari autem potest humana mens neminem esse qui non tenetur resistere Satanæ tentanti ad desperationem: atqui ergò nemo est qui salutem æternam sperare non potest & debet; nemo inquam qui Deo promittenti unquam credidit, & Deum loquentem audiverit, qui patrem sentit, qui Dominum agnoscit, qui Creatorem veneratur, qui facit quod est præ manibus, qui Christum non abnegat. Quinimò & sanctum est illud quod dixit Apostolus; *conclusit omnes sub peccato Deus*, (non inquam ut omnes aut plurimos perderet) sed *ut omnium misereretur. Misericordia enim Dei prævalitura est super omnem malitiam hominis*, dixit Propheta. Imò misericors Deus qui nobis hanc gratiam imponit ut remittamus fratri sua debita septuagies septies quolibet die, hoc est, (explicante Sancto Hieronymo) sæpiùs quàm quisquam peccare poterit, certè cereus ipse est ad veniam; facilis ad misericordiam, lætatur enim si vivet peccator, non lætatur ut pereat.

Hæc paucula possunt quidem sufficere ad demonstrandum quàm certò quàm seriò velit Deus omnes salvari: quàm facilè, quàm sine omni dubio possint si velint homines. Sed quid futurum est in eventu? nolunt enim qui possunt; & inexcusabiles facti sumus, sed adhuc nimis verum est valdè paucissimos in parte Dei numerandos fore. At aliter certè Divina pagina, aliter analogia fidei & Divinarum revelationum, & Cœlestis misericordiæ œconomia.

Misericordiâ Dei plenus est terrarum orbis, dixit Divinus Psaltes; omnes ubiq; gentium sentiunt & ultrà sentire possint. Deus enim pater est omnium quos fecit; & neminem odio habet, & προσωπολήπτης non est. & omnem omninò hominem ad Deum posse *accedere qui credit Deum esse & esse ἀγτενεργέτω*. D[i]xit Sanctus Paulus. Nolo quidem ego extra oleas philosophari, nequè conjecturam facere quo modo Gentes, gratiam quæ est per Jesum Christum participare possint. Hoc scio; *præter Jesum nullum nomen salutis est*. Hoc autem edixit sanctus Spiritus, *in omni gente timens Deum & operans justitiam acceptus est*. Est autem & justitia naturalis, & *Lex Naturæ* & Gentium Symbolum, & communis Pater, & *Lex Dei in cordibus*, & promissa communia, & Jesus pro omni gente mortuus, & pro omnibus omninò mortalibus intercedens, & semper *pro reverentia sua exauditus*; quis ergò dicere poterit, Deum æternis sine remedio destinare flammis illos de quibus nihil novimus nisi quòd Deus eorum pater est, & Jesus Redemptor omnium, & Spiritus spirat ubi vult, & operatur modis omni humano ingenio incognitis? sed hæc permittenda Deo; secreta Dei Deo nostro; ego tantùm quæ revelavit Deus edixi, atquè indè si sperare quisquam possit bonum ab infinito bono progressurum ultra limites & inclementes sententias aliorum; Ego Deum adorabo, & misericordiam ejus venerabor tacitus, sed spem miserorum mortalium minuere mihi religo est. Sperent qui possint. Neminem certè desperare velit Deus, neque Dei homines: Quid futurum est Ethnicis ego nescio; *Dies revelabit*.

Hæc autem ego paulò confidentiùs de his qui in gremio Ecclesiæ nutriuntur. Edixit scriptura ut *neminem Judicaremus*; quis ergò audet pronunciare sententiam mortis contra creaturam Dei? Etenim *Regnum Dei intus est*; & quis potest certò dicere Spiritum sanctum in aliquo singulari homine nullatenùs inesse? non vigilare, non vocare, non restringere, non consulere? Certè judicium charitatis ad omnes debet extendere & extendi; & si totus mundus in maligno positus pauculos verè bonos ostentet; hoc tamen novimus, quòd vix videantur grana cùm area trituratur; & Electos Dei, *Dei Secretos* vocat sancta pagina; atquè ergò quantus sit salvandorum numerus, nullam aliam rectè possimus conjecturam facere quàm per analogiam ad universalem in Ecclesiis hortationem, communia promissa, & infinitam misericordiam.

Nisi etiam & hoc aliquid momenti apud cordatos habiturum sit Deum esse Regem maximum, & *in multitudine populorum honorem Regis esse*, dixit *Solomon*; atquè ergò regnum cœlorum fore provinciam paucorum admodùm incolarum non adeò credibile est. Certè charitas Dei operiet multitudinem peccatorum, & salvabit innumerabiles populorum multitudines. Bonum enim quod dissunditur majus est: atqui ergò infinita bonitas in arctis lineis non clauditur. Invidia est bonum restringere; gloria Dei est dilatare & extendere. Atquè ergò non usquequaquè certum est, in eventu rerum, malum fore bono majus; regnum tenebrarum tot parasangis extendi ultra regnum Christi, ut justitia super-exaltetur, & triumphet super misericordiam. *Multi autem venient ex oriente & occidente*, dixit Christus: *Ex omni linguà multitudinem, quam nemo potest numerare*, vidit Sanctus Johannes in Spiritu. *Tanta massa processura est de hâc areâ ut impleat horreum cœli*, dixit Sanctus *Augustinus* (*Serm. 32. de verbis Domini*.) Ex his si exaltari possit misericordia divina, satis est: nollem certè ut contingenter & incuriosè viventibus accreseat confidentia: Deus enim neminem salvat, si nolit: quos autem volentes facit, & religiosos & fideles, hos salvare gloriatur. Chistus olim *gregem suum pusillum* dixit; & certè erat: sed plures oves posteà vocavit & annumeravit in Ovili suo, & in dies numerabit. Erit enim *plenitudo Gentium*, & Christus toti orbi tandem prædicabitur. Atq; ergò etiamsi verum foret, minorem hodiè esse Christi partem quam mundi, attamen cùm ubertas & plenitudo gratiæ è fontibus Salvatoris effluxerit, Christi Regnum erit ex omnium Gentium plebe confertum. Erit & revocatio Judæorum; de quorum obstinatâ à Messiâ aversione olim loquens dixit Christus, *multi vocati & pauci electi*: cùm autem dies ille maturabitur in quo revelabitur Spiritus Christi Judæis redeuntibus, nova extruetur Jerusalem, & iterum propriis indigenis ad implebitur. Interim *porta angusta est*, quia nos coangustamus: *via stricta est*, quia nos ambulando in præceptis Domini eam non terimus & ampliamus. Its autem *perditio nostra à nobis est*, ut nobis imputandum planè sit si ullus omninò mortalium tandem pereat. At tandem regnabit Dominus Jesus in cordibus mortalium, & nova consarcinabitur multitudo, & novas inibit Deus rationes, & regnum Diaboli paulatim destruetur, & ampliabitur thronus Christi, ut in multitudine populorum glorificetur Rex Regum & Dominus Dominantium.

Huc usq; Erudite vir, gratulor tibi sententiam rectam omninò & bonam de bono Deo; reliqua sunt nodosa satis, & quibus ego facilè immergi nolo. Ego enim decretorum Dei rationem non satis calleo: imò cùm Deum aliquid prædeterminare, præscire, desiderare & consulere dictum sit: *vox hominem sonat*, & ad nostrum captum Sermo instituitur, sicut loquuntur ii qui Deo oculos, manus, & lacertos imputant; imò & ipsum *velle Dei* aliud esse à nostrâ volitione necesse est; aut tu non rectè loqueris, cùm generalem volitionem salutis hominum à Deo tollis; Ait enim ipse de se Deus, *nollem mortem peccatoris: sed ut convertatur & vivat.* Et de Hierosolymâ dixit Dominus, *quàm volui te colligere, & tu noluisti;* & nisi Deus voluisset ut omnes salvarentur, certè nunquam voluit in vitâ hominum, quod noluit in morte: id est, prophetas non misisset renuentibus, & media salutis omnibus sufficientia non contulisset: ergò, Dei volitionem, efficacem, & humani moris voluntatem, quâ facit quis quod potest, ad optatum eventum consequendum, intelligere necesse est. Sic enim intellectam generalem salutis hominum volitionem non habere Deum, verum est, quia omnes non salvantur & Deo resistere nemo potest, quin faciat quod velit; sed cui bono hæc! Atqui ergò disputare de rebus arduis, quæ nec intelligimus nec eloqui possumus, nisi per figuras, & sententiarum convulsiones, infirmitatis nostræ potiùs quàm ipsius rei testis est, & instituere quæstiones philosophicas de Metaphoris; Tam doctè autem possunt pueruli de formatione & nomenclaturâ literarum rixas & jurgia movere. Miror certè istiusmodi hominum αὐθάδειαν qui methodum Divinorum decretorum & ordinem fingunt. *Quis enim Deum edocuit, aut quis illi consiliarius?* Ille enim solus hæc secreta edocebit. Tu in his non immoraris, sed in modo docendi apud veterem Ecclesiam usitatissimo salvare φαινόμενα ingeniosè contendis; si fieri res posset; tuum hoc ingenium nobis perfectum exhiberet; sed metuo ego in hisce rebus nè minor sit humana mens quàm quæ possit capere quæ capienda non sunt.

Rectum igitur iniisti consilium Cl. vir: acumen ostendisti priùs; prudentiam & pietatem in appendice. Adversarios in diatribâ refellis, in Enchiridio peccatum destruis; rectè philosophari in quibusdam alios doces, alios autem rectiùs vivere: & qui sic philosophatur vanus esse non potest. Multa sunt in scripto hoc, de quibus in æternum possint disputare otiosè negotiosi homines: Laudo ergò ingenium tuum qui ab intricatissimis quæstionibus; ilicò ad theoremata, bonos mores instruentia transilis. Consilium quidem placet; ut scilicet si quis acumine tuo pungatur in prioribus, in sequentibus liniatur oleo & quiescat in charitate. Vale. Omnia tibi prospera vovet & precatur

Tui amantissimus
JEREM. DUNENSIS.

BIBLIOGRAPHY

I. UNPUBLISHED SOURCES

Library of Trinity College, Dublin
Regal Visitation Report of 1615 (MS. 1066); of 1622 (MS. F. 1. 22); Records of the Irish Convocation of 1661-6, followed by that of 1639, being Archbishop King's copy (MS. N. 2. 3); Records of the Convocation of 1703-11 (MS. F. 1. 10, F. 3. 14., F. 3. 24); Bishop Reeves' Collection relating to the Irish Convocation (MS. 1062); Transcript of Archbishop King's Correspondence (N. 1. 7-9); Various volumes of King's Correspondence (N. 3. 5 and others); Papers by Edward Wolley, Bishop of Clonfert (1675-84) (MS. N. 2. 10.); Sermons by Bishop Anthony Dopping (MS. P. 3. 6-9); Interleaved Notes in Harris' revised edition of Sir James Ware's *Bishops* (MS. 1120).

Bodleian Library, Oxford
Carte MSS., Vols. 30, 31, 32, 33, 34, 35, 41, 42, 44, 45; 64; 67, 213, 214, 219, 220, 221, 222; Tanner MSS., Vol. 52; MS. Add. C. 308 (Bishop Sheldon's Letter Book).

Public Record Office, London
S.P. 83-286, 287, 303, 317, 319, 320, 321, 322, 323, 324.

Public Library, Armagh
Armagh Registry 1678 to 1713; Bishop Reeves' Copy of the Visitation of Armagh 1693; Procedure at Visitations of 1679, 1694, 1701-2, made by Bishop William King for the Primate with King's Letters relating to the same; Twelve Specifications for new Churches with sketches and plans by Thomas Cooley.

Marsh Library, Dublin.
"Memorials of St Audoen's, Dublin." Vol. II, containing extracts from a lost Vestry Book of the seventeenth century.

National Library of Ireland
"Abstract of Information in answer to Queries concerning the Parishes in the Dioceses of Killaloe and Kilfenora, 1820"; Clogher Visitation Returns and Rural Deans Reports from *c.* 1825.

Library of the Church Representative Body, Dublin
Transcript of the Vestry Book of St Catherine and St James, Dublin (1657-92). "Biographical succession list of the Clergy of Connor Diocese", by Canon J. B. Leslie.

Down and Connor National Library
Metropolitical Visitation Reports of Down, Connor, and Dromore, of 1661 and 1664; Various Papers connected with the Down, Connor, and

Dromore Church Architecture Society, including accounts of Inch, Downpatrick Cathedral, and Hillsborough, given in 1843–4.

Public Record Office, Northern Ireland
Clogher Visitation Books 1666–1829 (D.O.D. 242); Typescripts of Visitation Reports of dioceses of Armagh and Derry in 1693, and of Raphoe, Derry, and Dromore in 1733.

Tuam Diocesan Registry
Memoriale Tuamens Rerum Extra Judicaliter Gestanim Inchoatim (from 1666); Instruments for the Consecration of the Churches of St John the Baptist, Headford (1674), of St Charles late King of England and Martyr, Hollymount (1714), and of others; Various documents relating to the Board of the Commissioners of First Fruits.

Christ Church Cathedral, Dublin
Chapter Books of the early seventeenth century.

Cashel Cathedral
MS. Music belonging to the late eighteenth century, including a full setting for the Holy Communion Service by Robert Shenton (d. 1798).

Vestry Books of St Werburgh's, Dublin; St Peter's, Dublin; St Michan's, Dublin; St Iberius, Wexford. "Memorial of St Michan's," "The Poore Book For the Parish of St John Evangelist in Dublin Begun March 31st, 1700."

II. PRINTED SOURCES

Most of the printed sources have been given in the notes to the text. Copies of the Irish Canons of 1634 as printed in 1635, 1664, and 1667 are very scarce. These important Canons may be found in Vol. IV of Wilkins's *Concilia Magnae Britannicae et Hiberniae* (496–516), together with the Irish Articles of 1615 (447–54), and the Canons of Kilmore of 1638 (537–8). The Irish Canons of 1634, with those of 1711, are given in the larger Irish Prayer Books of the eighteenth and some of the early nineteenth century. The Irish Victorian Canons are given in Irish Prayer Books from 1878.

Y*

INDEX

Absolution, forms of, 58, 130, 137f.

Achonry, Cathedral, 222.

Adair, Archibald, Bp of Killala, tr. to Ferns, 19 & n.

Adair, Patrick, *True Narrative*, 34n, 35n, 38n.

Advertisements of Abp Parker (1568), 15, 199.

Alms: gathering of, 161, 163f; additional giving of, 104, 169; Bason, 163, 244; Chest, 212f.

"Altar or Communion Table": position of, 9f, 15, 212, 225, 229; material of, 238ff; Dedication of, 256f, 260, 308; furniture of, 240–50.

Altarpiece, 236ff.

Andrewes, Bp Lancelot, 37, 95, 135, 159f, 165, 169, 198; *see also* Consecration of Churches.

Andrews, George, D of Limerick, 11, 15.

Anthems, 148f, 153.

Ardagh: Diocese, 6; Cathedral, 204.

Ardfert: Diocese, 174n; Cathedral, 188.

Armagh: Province, 6, 33ff, 38, 142, 144, 173f; Diocese, 33f, 194, 206, 208; Cathedral, 34n, 175n, 188, 223, 238, 246.

Articles: Irish (1566), 3; (1615), 3f, 8, 11–14, 59, 63; English Thirty-Nine, 3, 8, 11–14, 33, 59, 63; Lambeth, 3f.

Ascription of Praise, 163 & n.

Baker, George, Bp of Waterford, 30n, 181, 185.

Bale, John, Bp of Ossory, 8, 198.

Banns, reading of, 162.

Baptism: doctrine of, 82–9; Ministration of, 155f.

Bayly, Lewis, Bp of Bangor, 94, 102.

Bayly, Thomas, Bp of Killala, 268.

Bedell, William, Bp of Kilmore, 5f, 134, 185; holds Diocesan Synod, 19; on Sacraments, 80f, 83, Eucharistic Sacrifice, 93.

Beresford, Lord John George, Abp of Armagh, 186, 188, 231, 238.

Berkeley, George, D of Derry, Later Bp of Cloyne, 50, 52 & n, 53f, 184f, 197n; admonishes adults at Long Island to be baptized, 87f; on Catholicity, 57, Episcopacy, 67, Internal Communion, 77f, private Confession, 136.

Bernard, Nicholas, 63, 256.

Bidding Prayer, 162.

Bolton, Sir Richard, Lord Chancellor, 22n.

Bolton, Theophilus, Chan. of St Patrick's, Bp of Clonfert, tr. to Elphin, then to Cashel, 48f, 208n.

Bonnell, James, exemplary Churchman, 41, 51ff, 114, 142, 145, 175, 178, 191ff, 196.

Book of Common Prayer: English (1549), 8, 198–203, (1552), 8, 139, 198, 203; (1604 version of 1559), 123, 139–70 *passim*, (1662), 139–90 *passim*; Scottish (1637), 16, 19, 94f, 101, 119, 139; Irish additions to 1662, xiii, 47, 140, 154, 254; Irish revision of 1662 (1871–8), xiii, 138, 266; standard of worship required by 1604 and 1662, 141; Dublin editions of 1662, 47f, 140, 252 & n.

Books "for the Communion", 160, 246, 308.

Boulter, Hugh, Abp of Armagh, tr. from Bristol, 49f, 53.

Bowing: towards the East, 145 & n, 147, 159 & n; at the Name of Jesus, 147.

Boyle, Michael, Bp of Cork, recommends Jeremy Taylor for Meath, 270; Abp of Dublin, 155, 167f, 173, 251, 294; Abp of Armagh, 43, 253n.

Boyle, Richard, Earl of Cork, 9.

Boyle, Richard, Bp of Cork, tr. to Tuam, 256n.

Boyle, Roger, Bp of Down, tr. to Clogher, 38n, 40f, 89n; on Ministry, 70f, Sacramental Grace, 80, Eucharist, 101, 113, Confirmation, 123, Church customs, 147f.

Brady, Nicholas, 121, 128n, 149, 157.

Bramhall, John, Bp of Derry, 8–12, 19f; in Convocation controversy, 12–16; defends Anglican Church in exile, 24; on Catholicity, 55f, Grecians, 58, Apostolic regiment and succession, 61f, non-episcopal orders, 73, Internal Communion, 76f, number of Sacraments, 78f, Baptism, 86f, Eucharistic Offering, 95, Eucharistic Presence, 104, 108f, Confirmation, 121, 123f, Confession and Absolution, 131f; Abp of Armagh, 30–7, 201f, 270–4; Letters of Orders, 33f; policy towards Ministers lacking Episcopal Ordination, 34f; directions for the Consecration of 12 Bishops in Dublin, 144, 151, 153, 169, 201, 264.

Branches, 214 & n, 249.

Brereton, Sir William, 17, 143, 217.

Broderick, Charles, Abp of Cashel, 186.

Browne, Jemmet, Bp of Dromore, tr. to Cork, then to Elphin, then to Tuam, 157, 181n.

Browne, Peter, Bp of Cork, 48, 154, 156f, 185, 209; Eucharistic devotions, 100, 115.